SUETONIUS · THE LIVES OF THE TWELVE CAESARS

THE TRANSLATION BY PHILEMON HOLLAND
REVISED FOR THE PRESENT EDITION, WITH AN
INTRODUCTION, BY MOSES HADAS AND
ILLUSTRATED WITH PAINTINGS
BY SALVATORE FIUME

THE HERITAGE PRESS
NEW YORK

INTRODUCTION

MOST of our reading, most of our conversation, most of our speculation, is about people. We want to know what people do and think, and if our neighbors are inarticulate or secretive or dull we turn to novelists, who can tell us all about the people they have themselves created. The most insatiable and the most widely shared curiosity is about the giants, genuine or spurious, whose names everyone knows. Whether our motive is to understand the inwardness of some significant historical conjuncture, or to study the morphology and pathology of greatness, or to savor vicariously the experience of power and prestige, or to be titillated by gossip made spicier by eminence, it is not to made-up stories but to the lives of real persons that we turn.

The trouble is that the lives of eminent people are themselves apt to be made-up, at least in the cosmetic sense. The biographies of the great, like their portraits, tend to show them swathed in official robes and wearing the mask their public relations counselors or their partisans have designed for them, or else, by a periodic reaction, stripped of even their business suits and exhibited to the world as puny and ludicrous frauds. To be just to the whole man, even when data are available, is not easy, for even if the biographer is untouched by imposing stature or an appetite for bawdry, it is still difficult for him to free himself from his own, often unacknowledged, political or moral or artistic predispositions. No record of any man is so complete that the interstices cannot, indeed must not, be filled out from the personal resources of the biographer. The great merit of Suetonius is that he leaves the interstices unfilled. We can surmise from his book what his scholarly ideals and techniques must have been, but we know nothing of his private reactions. His gallery includes a succession of men fascinating alike for their tremendous power and their extraordinary personalities; Suetonius never loses sight of their public images or of their private intimacies, and never adds the edifying *haec fabula docet*. He recovers as much of the significant record as he can, arranges it systematically, and leaves speculative moralizing to his readers.

It may seem odd, in view of men's consuming interest in other men, that the world had to wait so long for biography, that the classical Greeks, who were notoriously anthropocentric and who pioneered most of our literary forms, were so slow in developing biography as a literary genre. Personages in classical literature, like portraits in classical sculpture, tend to be idealized and stylized and shown frontally rather than in the round. This is because all classical art is formal and monumental, not literal reportage of man and his crises but their conscious distillation through the mind of the poet and received as such by his audience. It is only in the Hellenistic Age that haggard and tormented figures, with bulbous noses and flapping ears, appear in plastic art, and only then that biography came to be written.

Perceptive authors did of course observe telling details of an individual's personality and character as well as his public career, as Thucydides' thumbnail sketches of Themistocles and Pausanias at the end of his first book demonstrate. But Thucydides was interested in individuals only as they affected the course of history. Of Alcibiades, for example, whom he surely knew as well as any contemporary could, he tells us only so much as is relevant to political and military history; for Alcibiades' lisp and relations with his wife we must go to Plutarch, who comes half a millennium later. Even when Isocrates, in the generation following, devotes his *Evagoras* to a single career, his object is eulogy and edification, not properly biography. Xenophon's *Agesilaus* follows Isocrates' techniques and objectives, and so, ultimately, does Tacitus' *Agricola*, which approaches the date of Suetonius.

The systematic study of lives for their own sake, like the systematic study of poetry or political institutions or fish, seems to have been introduced by Aristotle and pursued by the Peripatetic school. We know of a treatise *On Physiognomies*, and we possess the *Characters* of Theophrastus, who was Aristotle's successor. These *Characters* were not intended as humorous sketches but as systematic studies of the characteristic behavior of such types as the Newsmonger, the Flatterer, and the Timorous Man. It is absurd to believe, as certain ancients did, that Theophrastus wrote his descriptions for Menander to use in his dramatis personae. If Menander's persons do follow Theophrastus' specifications the explanation is that the age had become interested in realistic individualization. It was natural for men to turn in upon themselves, when they found themselves diminished to insignificance in an enormously expanded world, and to cherish their idiosyncrasies. Stoic philosophy and Hellenistic portraiture are both expressions of the same impulse. A literary form characteristic of the age is the Mime, which presented ordinary people in the ordinary encounters of life; it is significant that writers of mimes were called "biologists," or students of life.

Mimes, like comedies, are species of belles-lettres; the moving impulse for biography was scholarship. The Alexandrians inherited the scientific outlooks of the Peripatetic school. Friedrich Leo, the pioneer modern student of ancient biography, drew a distinction between biography of literary personalities, which he assigned to the Peripatetic school, and that of statesmen, which he assigned to the Alexandrian. Actually the distinction has no validity; and if it had, the roles of the Peripatetics and Alexandria should be reversed. Most of what we know of the classical authors is a precipitate from Alexandrian biographical studies.

A surer and more meaningful distinction should be drawn between "historical" biography and aretalogy. Aretalogies are accounts of the careers of spiritually gifted teachers, usually containing elements of the miraculous, written to serve as a kind of scripture to propagate esteem of the teacher and his doctrines. The most familiar specimens of the form are of course the Synoptic Gospels, but there are traces of many pagan examples also, and at least two that are complete – Porphyry's *Life of Pythagoras*, and Philostratus' *Apollonius of Tyana*. The latter was the model for Athanasius' *Life of St. Anthony*, which is in turn the ancestor of a host of lives of the saints. Such works cannot properly be subsumed under the class of biography, but they did leave their traces in actual biography and frequently in the characterization of national heroes in patriotic historiography.

Speculations concerning origins and hypotheses concerning categories have their own specialist interest. For the literate world generally ancient biography evokes two names, the Greek Plutarch and the Roman Suetonius. Other surviving collections – Cornelius Nepos' generals, Philostratus' and Eunapius' sophists, Diogenes Laertius' philosophers, the later Roman emperors and usurpers attributed to the *Scriptores Historiae Augustae* – deserve their oblivion. Plutarch and Suetonius owe their survival to merits of different kinds, as a comparison of their premises and objectives will show.

Plutarch's aims were ethical, in the several senses of that word. He insists that he is writing not history but biography, in which a gesture or grimace may be more significant than a battle or oration. Even the public careers of his worthies are seen from a domestic angle; he is always ready, for example, to show the influence of his subject's wife or mother. Without reducing his lives to moral exempla he makes it plain that good traits are admirable and bad deplorable. The arrangement of the lives in parallel pairs has one obvious ethical aim and one less obvious: The Greeks had been under Roman domination for two centuries, and it would bolster their pride in their own tradition if it could be shown that distinguished Romans could be matched and often surpassed by distinguished Greeks. This may be the reason why Plutarch has not given us lives of poets and philosophers and artists – even the Romans were ready to acknowledge Greek superiority in fields other than military and political. As becomes a moralizer, Plutarch's stance is personal, and he is personal too in arrangement of materials and distribution of emphasis. He is quite conscientious in presenting factual backgrounds, but it remains true that his work is literary rather than historical, and that its aim is to communicate edification rather than information.

Suetonius' prime objective is information, and the information he communicates is not ethical or psychological, except by indirection, but historical. The transformation in Roman public life had made it natural for history to be presented through biographies of the Caesars. A sense of the new direction emerges from a comparison between Livy's books on the Republic and Tacitus' on the beginning of the Empire. Livy reflects the vitality of the Roman people. Generals and statesmen do perhaps receive more than their proper share of attention – how could it be otherwise when history was still political and military, not yet social and economic? – but the great figures are republican, with soldiers and voters always in the background. In Tacitus, by contrast, the Romans are a dim mass, and attention is centered on the Palatine hill, with family intrigues and rivalries and corruption raised to almost cosmic importance. Historiography has reverted almost to the dynastic records of the ancient Near East, and this may be construed as an index of the direction in which history itself was moving. The next logical step was frankly to ignore the voiceless mass and limit history to the occupants of the Palatine. The step is taken in Suetonius'

Lives of the Caesars, and after him carried on in the much inferior and more scandalous but still indispensable *Scriptores Historiae Augustae*.

Whatever his artistic merits may be, therefore, it is as a historian that we must first assess Suetonius. On conscientious use of sources he must rate high. As secretary to the Emperor Hadrian he had access to official archives, and his work shows that he made use of them. Whereas other Roman writers on historical subjects regularly grow fuller as they approach their own time (a year towards the end of Livy's work occupies more space than a century near its beginnings), the reverse is true of Suetonius. He is the typical closet scholar, more at ease with documents than with inquiry, and more attracted by earlier sources than by later. His inclusions and omissions and his distribution of attention reflect the nature of his sources rather than his own taste. Such scabrous gossip as disfigures the pages of the *Tiberius*, for example, had been written down, and Suetonius therefore included it in the section where his formula called for details of private life. He was himself neither malicious nor prurient, but merely unwilling to discount bias in his sources.

On such matters as official acts of the senate and people and imperial edicts he is a trustworthy source, and sometimes (as at *Caligula* 8) we see that he examined conflicting statements with care and intelligence and that he strove for impartiality. His own opinions he intrudes very rarely; examples are the eulogy at the opening of the *Titus* and a passage like *Tiberius* 23, where he refuses to believe that a prudent emperor could act inconsiderately in an important matter. His pattern is quite regular: ancestry, birth; years before accession to power, public life and private life, including reports of praise and blame; portents presaging death; death. His program like his pattern is that of the chronicler, and it is not for the chroniclers to censor his materials in accordance with preconceived standards of propriety or utility.

It is unfair to demand that the chronicler should also be philosopher, psychologist, or artist, but Suetonius' shortcomings in these respects must nevertheless be noticed. He is not concerned with the larger directions or movements of the imperial structure, with the calcification of authoritarianism, with development or change in character, with the psychological effects of absolute power upon those who wield it. For dealing with such questions a career like that of Augustus, who is surely one of the most influential figures in history, would offer ample scope; but what is apt to stick in the reader's mind is Augustus' partiality to long underwear. Are the neuroses of a Caligula or Nero or Domitian unconnected with their absolutism, are Vespasian's personality and politics not related to his peasant origin? Stripped of their purple the Julio-Claudians are indistinguishable from wastrel gentry in their own or other ages. So stripped, what claim can they have on our attention?

The point is that they are not stripped, and as rulers of the world at an important conjuncture of history they merit a legitimate curiosity, on the undress as well as the public level. Alone among ancient writers Suetonius provides the intimate details which enable us to see them in the round. His writing is direct and efficient, never ornate. His portraits stand to Plutarch's as the portrait busts of his subjects — bull-necked or scrawny, chinless or prognathous, bloated or haggard — stand to the idealized portraits of classical Greece. The latter we can only call serene; the ugly Roman busts supply matter for detailed analysis. So Suetonius gives us a systematic arrangement of what the record shows, and leaves the analysis to us. Whatever drama incidents in the *Lives* possess is due to the incidents themselves, not to Suetonius' manipulation of them, and modern playwrights and novelists have elaborated such incidents for their own artistic ends. By contrast, Plutarch himself provides an artistic end, which the modern need only adapt. Where both biographers have dealt with the same subject, as is the case with Julius Caesar, it is significant that Shakespeare follows Plutarch rather than Suetonius.

It remains to say a few words about the life of Suetonius himself and about his most attractive translator. Gaius Suetonius Tranquillus, to give him his full name, was born about A.D. 69 and died about 140. The best thing we know about him, aside from his writings, is that the Younger Pliny valued him highly. He procured for Suetonius the coveted *ius trium liberorum* and an offer of a military tribunate; he helped him purchase a piece of property, offered to procure the postponement of a lawsuit for him, encouraged him to finish and publish his books. Suetonius practiced law for a time, but his chief interest was scholarship. The tenth-century lexicon called *Suda* credits him with a long list of works (perhaps parts of a smaller number of works) which are lost: *On Famous Courtesans, On the Kings, On Public Offices, Roma, The Games of the Greeks, On Cicero's De Republica, Pratum, On Terms of Abuse in Greek, On Various Matters, On Critical Marks in Books, Historia*. But Suetonius' chief interest was in biography, and from 106 to 113 he published *Famous Men*, on various categories of literary men, of which parts are preserved. *Grammarians and Rhetoricians* is extant, as are a few *Lives* of Roman writers, all more or less abridged and interpolated. Jerome has thirty-three from *Poets*; most scholars accept *Terence, Horace,* and *Lucan* as genuine, and some also accept *Vergil, Tibullus,* and *Persius*. Jerome lists fifteen lives from *Orators* and six from *Historians*; of the former a brief abstract of the *Life of Passienus Crispus* is extant, and of the latter the *Life of Pliny the Elder*. The work of Suetonius which is extant in its entirety (except for a few chapters at the beginning of the *Julius*), and upon which Suetonius' reputation is based, is the *De vita Caesarum, On the Life of the Caesars*, published A.D. 121.

Philemon Holland (1552-1637) was a doctor of medicine and for most of his long life a grammar school teacher in Coventry. He was aptly called (by Thomas Fuller) "the Translator Generall in his age," for whereas others of the great Elizabethan translators – North, for example, or Adlington – were men of one book, Holland, who was the most scholarly and the best linguist of the group, produced versions of many authors – Livy, Pliny, and Ammianus Marcellinus, Xenophon's *Cyropaedia* and Plutarch's *Moralia*. The most appealing of his versions, by common consent, is his Suetonius.

For richness and vitality of language and style, Holland's English version is a more distinguished piece of writing than Suetonius' Latin. In the fashion of the great Elizabethan translators he is magisterial and exuberant; but he has good right to be, for he was an accomplished scholar and needed no French or other intermediary. If his version is sometimes prolix and sometimes freer than a more pedantic age would approve, the reason is never faulty understanding of the original but a desire to make it more intelligible, more idiomatic, more lively. For bookish readers, who find archaic speech quaint rather than antiquated, his version of Suetonius is surely the most attractive in any language.

The aim of the present edition is to leave Holland's verve and quaintness untouched, while removing unnecessary obstacles from the path of those to whom the Elizabethans are alien. A sober modern spelling has been substituted for Elizabethan exuberance, punctuation has been regularized to conform to current usage, an occasional unwieldy sentence has been broken up to clarify syntax. Because Holland is a monument of English his archaic diction has been retained even where his words have gone out of general use; only where a word has continued in use with a new and different meaning (as when *obnoxious* shifts from "liable" to "repulsive") has a different word been substituted, and only where the sense was truly obscure have his phrases been reworded. An exception has been made in Holland's preface "To the Reader," which is printed *verbatim et literatim* as it appeared in the 1606 edition.

MOSES HADAS

TABLE OF CONTENTS

TO THE READERS

That yee may with better contentment reade these Historicall reports of the twelve first Ceasars, which Suetonius hath delivered most truely, compiled as compendiously, and digested right methodically, I have thought it good with some few advertisments præmised, to commend the same unto you.

First therefore, whereas by the judgement of the best learned, and the Analogie of other Histories, hee seemeth to affect nothing so much as uncorrupt and plaine trueth, (the principall vertue of an Historiographer) forbearing to meddle with those Emperours[1] in whose daies he flourished; because he would not thrust himselfe into danger by revealing, nor betray the libertie of a writer in concealing the faults, much lesse incurre the note of Flatterie, extolling above measure the good parts of Princes then living; and to that purpose penned their lives, who were lately deceased, as one said very well, eadem libertate qua ipsi vixerunt: *if happlie in prosecuting of this point, he hath recorded ought that may be offensive to chast and modest mindes, yee shall do well to glaunce over with your eye such places lightly, as I with my pen touched unwillingly.*

Secondly, forasmuch as he continueth in generall the Narrations of the said Princes, from before their Nativitie unto their Death and Funerals: and in the severall discourses, of their ages, affaires, vertues, vices, feature and lineaments of bodie, first, after an uniform maner, proposeth throughout certain heads summarily, and then exemplyfieth the same in due order by perticulers (a most lightsome method and way of teaching) keeping him selfe still to the Subject matter, without any digressions at all: my advise is, that for your more expedite course in reading the whole, yee direct your minde thereunto. Now, for that his Julius Ceasar sorteth not with the rest, but appeareth ἀκέφαλος, *as whose auncestours, birth, childhoode, etc.*

1. Nerva, Trajanus, and Hadrianus, whose secretarie he was.

be not set downe, (which maime I impute rather to the injurie of time, than unto the purpose or oversight of the Authour) I have in some sort supplyed that defect, with the labours of Lewis Vives, Torrentius and others, which I finde præfixed in the last and best Editions.

Thirdly, considering that brevitie is many times the mother of Obscuritie, may it please those among you, who are not so conversant in such concise writings, as admit not one word superfluous, to have recourse, for the clearing of some doubts unto the margin, as also to those briefe Annotations, which for their sakes, out of mine owne readings, together with the select observations of Beroaldus, Sabellicus, Torrentius and Casaubonus I have collected. Which also will ease them of many difficulties that his succinct style and termes, not elswhere obvious, interlaced, may otherwise breed.

Finally, if there happen to occur some Errata, that might escape either my pen in writing, or the ordinarie diligence of meane Correctors in the printing, ye will of your judicious candour, I hope, either passe them over with connivency, if they be literall, or else taxe with some easie censure in case they bee materiall: so long as for your full satisfaction, ye may with small paines before yee begin either to read or judge, correct what is amisse, according to the Examen and Review annexed to the end of all. Farewell.

THE HISTORY OF
GAIUS JULIUS CAESAR

*The opening paragraphs of this Life are
wanting in the manuscripts.*

CAESAR

CAESAR IN THE SIXTEENTH YEAR OF HIS age lost his father. In the year following, being elected Flamen Dialis, he cast off Cossutia (of equestrian rank but very wealthy) affianced to him during his childhood, and espoused Cornelia, the daughter of Cinna, who had been four times consul. She bore unto him soon after his daughter Julia; neither could he by any means be forced by Sulla the dictator to put her away. Thereupon, deprived of his sacerdotal dignity, losing the dowry in the right of his wife, and forfeiting all his heritage descended unto him from his lineage and name, he was reputed one of the contrary faction. Hence he was constrained to hide his head, and (albeit the quartan ague hung sore upon him) to change almost every night the hiding places wherein he lurked, yea, and to redeem himself with a piece of money out of the inquisitors' hands that made search for him. At last, by the mediation of the Vestal Virgins, by the means also of Mamercus Aemilius and Aurelius Cotta, his near kinsfolk, he obtained pardon. Certain it is that Sulla, when he had denied a good while the request of those right worshipful persons and his singular good friends entreating in his behalf, and they persisted earnest suitors still, being thus importuned and at length overcome, broke forth aloud into these words, either in a divine prescience or some pregnant conjecture, "Go to," he said, "my masters; take him to you, since ye will needs have it so. But know this withal, that he whose life and safety ye so much desire will one day be the overthrow of the

3

nobles whose side ye have maintained with me; for in this Caesar there be many Mariuses."

2. The first time that Caesar served in the wars was in Asia, and that in the domestic retinue of Marcus Thermus, the praetor. Being sent by him into Bithynia for to levy a fleet, he made his abode with King Nicomedes, not without a foul rumor raised that he prostituted his body to be abused by the king. This rumor he augmented himself by coming again into Bithynia within a few days, under color of calling for certain money due to a freedman and client of his. The rest of his service he carried with better reputation, and at the winning of Mitylene, Thermus honored him with a civic garland.

3. He served also under Servilius Isauricus in Cilicia, but not for long, for upon intelligence of Sulla's death and hope of the dissensions set on foot by Marcus Lepidus he returned in all haste to Rome. And notwithstanding he was mightily solicited by many large offers and fair promises, yet forbore he to join in society with Lepidus, partly distrusting his nature and in part doubting the present opportunity, which he found nothing answerable to his expectation.

4. Howbeit when that civil discord and sedition was appeased, he judicially accused of extortion Cornelius Dolabella, a man who had been consul and triumphed. But seeing that the defendant was found unguilty and acquitted, he determined to retire himself unto the city of Rhodes, as well to decline the hatred of the world, as by occasion of that leisure and repose to learn the art of oratory under Apollonius Molon, a most renowned rhetorician in those days. As he crossed the seas thitherward (it being now wintertime) his fortune was about the isle Pharmacusa to be taken by pirates, and with them he remained in custody (not without exceeding indignation) for the space well near of forty days, accompanied by one physician and two grooms of his chamber. For his companions and

the rest of his servants belonging to his train he had sent away immediately at the very first, to procure him money with all speed for his ransom. After this, upon the payment unto them of fifty talents being set ashore, he delayed no time, but presently put his fleet to sea again, embarked, and never gave over pursuing the said pirates, until he had overtaken them; and no sooner were they within his power, but as he oftentimes had threatened in mirth, he put them all to death. Now while Mithridates wasted the countries next adjoining, because he would not be thought to sit still and do nothing in this dangerous and doubtful state of confederate nations and allies to the Romans, he left Rhodes whither he had directly bent his course, gathered a power of auxiliary soldiers, expelled the governor under the king out of the province, and so kept the cities and states in their allegiance, which were wavering and at the point to revolt.

5. In his military tribuneship, which was the first dignity after his return to Rome that befell unto him by the voice and election of the people, he assisted with all his might those patrons of the commons, who stood out for the restitution of their tribunes' authority, the force and strength whereof Sulla had abated. He effected moreover thus much, by virtue of an act proposed by Plotius, that Lucius Cinna his wife's brother, and they who together with him in the time of the civil discord above-said took part with Lepidus and after the consul's death fled unto Sertorius, might return safely into the city and enjoy their freedom. As touching which matter, himself made an oration before the body of the people.

6. Being quaestor he made, as the ancient manner was, funeral orations out of the public pulpit called rostra, in the praise of Julia his aunt by the father's side, and of his wife Cornelia, both late deceased. And in the commendation verily of his said aunt, speaking of the pedigree and descent by both sides,

namely of herself, and also of her father, he made report in these terms: "Mine aunt Julia," he said, "by her mother is lineally descended from kings, and by her father united with the race of the immortal gods; for from Ancus Marcius are derived the Marcii surnamed *Reges* (Kings), which name my mother was styled with; and from Venus the Julii draw their origin, of which house and name is our family. So then, in this stock there concur and meet together, as well the sanctity and sacred majesty of kings, who among men are most powerful, as the reverence of the gods, in whose power kings themselves are."

In the place of Cornelia departed he wedded Pompeia, daughter of Quintus Pompeius, and niece of Lucius Sulla. But her afterwards he divorced, suspecting that she had been naughty with Publius Clodius, of whom there went so constant a report abroad that at the celebration of certain religious ceremonies he had access, disguised in woman's apparel, that the senate decreed a judicial inquiry upon the pollution of those sacred rites.

7. As quaestor it fell to his lot to serve in Farther Spain. When he rode his circuit to keep the assizes there, by the command of the praetor, he came to Gades and there beheld an image of Alexander the Great in the temple of Hercules. At the sight thereof he fetched a deep sigh, and as one irked with his own slothfulness, in that he had performed yet no memorable act at an age when Alexander had conquered the whole world, he presently made suit for his discharge, in order to take the first opportunity to compass greater enterprises in Rome. Being moreover much dismayed with a dream the night before (for he imagined in his sleep that he had carnal company with his own mother) the diviners incited him to the hopes of most glorious achievements, making the exposition of the dream that it portended the sovereignty of the whole world, for his mother whom he saw under him betokened naught

else but the subjection of the earth, which is counted the mother of all things.

8. Departing therefore before his time was fully expired, he went to the Latin colonies, which were devising to sue for citizenship, and would no doubt have solicited and excited them to attempt some tumult and trouble in the state, but that the consuls for the avoiding of this very danger, kept back the legions for a while which were enrolled for to be sent into Cilicia.

9. And yet for all that, soon after he projected greater designs within the city. For, not many days before he entered upon his aedileship, suspected he was to have conspired with Marcus Crassus (a man of consular degree), with Publius Sulla likwise and Publius Autronius (who after they were consuls elect stood condemned for suing indirectly and by corruption for that place) to set upon the body of the senate in the beginning of their year; and that after they had massacred whom it pleased them, Marcus Crassus should usurp the dictatorship; himself be chosen by him master of the horsemen; and so when they had settled the state at their pleasure, Sulla and Autronius should be restored again unto their consulship. Of this conspiracy, Tanusius Geminus makes mention in his history, Marcus Bibulus in his edicts, and Gaius Curio the father in his orations. Cicero likewise seems to signify as much in a certain epistle unto Axius, wherein he reports that Caesar established in his consulship that kingdom and royal government which he plotted and thought upon when he was aedile. Tanusius writes farther, that Crassus, either repenting or else upon fear, was not present nor kept the day appointed for the said massacre, and therefore Caesar neither gave that signal which by agreement he should have given. Now agreed it was as Curio says, that he should let his gown fall from his shoulders. The same Curio and Marcus Actorius Naso do write

that Caesar conspired also with Gnaius Piso, a noble young gentleman, who, being in suspicion for a conspiracy within the city, had the province of Spain extraordinarily and without his own suit bestowed upon him; and complotted it was, that both he in foreign parts abroad and himself also at Rome, should at once make an insurrection for to alter the state; and that by the occasion and means of the Lambranes and inhabitants beyond the Po. But the design both of the one and the other was defeated and frustrated by reason of the death of Piso.

10. When he was aedile, besides the *Comitium*, the Forum, and stately halls of justice, he beautified the Capitol also with fair open galleries built for temporary use during the public shows and plays; wherein if the number of images, statues, and painted tables fell out to be greater than was needful, part of that furniture and provision might be set forth to the view of all men. As for the chasing and baiting of wild beasts, the stage-plays and solemn sights, he exhibited them both jointly with his companion in office, and also severally by himself. Whereby it came to pass, that howsoever the charges of these solemnities were borne in common by them both, yet Caesar alone went away with all the honor and thanks thereof; neither did Marcus Bibulus his colleague dissemble the matter, but utter as much, when he said that the same befell unto him which befell unto Pollux, "For like as," he quoth, "the temple erected in the common Forum of Rome unto both the twin brethren [Castor and Pollux] bears the name of Castor alone, even so my munificence in expense and Caesar's together in setting out these games and plays goes under the name of Caesar only." Caesar, over and above, did exhibit another show of sword-fight, but he brought into the place fewer couples of champions by a good many than he purposed; for, buying up (as he did) such a sort of fencers from all parts out of every school, and putting his adversaries of the other faction in great

affright thereby, he gave occasion unto the state to provide by a special act in that behalf, for a certain set number of sword-players, above which no man might retain any at Rome.

11. Thus when he had gained the hearts and favor of the people he attempted, through some of the tribunes, to have the province of Egypt by an act of the commons conferred upon him, taking occasion to sue for this extraordinary appointment because the Alexandrians had driven their king out of his realm, whom the senate had styled ally and friend, and their act was generally misliked. Howbeit he could not carry it, by reason that the faction of the nobles crossed him. Because he would by way of quittance impair their authority by all means possible, he erected the trophies of Gaius Marius, for subduing Jugurtha and the Cimbrians and Teutons, which Sulla had cast down. Also in sitting upon a prosecution of murderers, he reckoned in their number those who in the time of the proscriptions had received money out of the public treasury for bringing in the heads of Roman citizens, notwithstanding they were excepted by the Cornelian laws.

12. Moreover he suborned someone to indict Gaius Rabirius of high treason, by whose help especially some years before the senate had restrained the seditious tribuneship of Lucius Saturninus. And when he was chosen by lot to pass sentence on the accused, so willing was he to condemn him that when Rabirius appealed to the people nothing did him so much good as the rigor of the judge.

13. Having laid aside all hope of the foresaid province, he stood to be high priest, not without excessive and most lavish largess. Wherein, considering how deeply he engaged himself in debt, the same morning that he was to go unto the assembly for the election, when his mother kissed him he told her (by report) aforehand, that he would never return home but pontifex [high priest]. And so far overweighed he two most

mighty competitors, who otherwise for age and dignity much outwent him, that in their own tribes he alone carried more voices, than both of them in all throughout.

14. Being created praetor, when as the conspiracy of Catiline was detected, and all the senate generally awarded no lighter punishment than death for as many as were parties and accessory in that action, he only gave his sentence, that their goods should be confiscated, and themselves put into several free cities and boroughs under the people of Rome, there to be kept in ward; and furthermore he put those that gave sharper censure in such a fright (intimating eftsoons and setting before their eyes the exceeding great hatred of the Roman commons, which in time to come they should incur) that Decimus Silanus, consul elect, was not abashed nor unwilling to mollify his own sentence, with a gentle exposition (because it had been a shame to alter it and eat his own words) as if it had been taken and construed in an harder sense than he meant it (for there were already many drawn to Caesar's side, and among the rest, Cicero, the consul's brother) but that a speech made by Marcus Cato emboldened the whole house, and confirmed all the senators in their former sentence, who now were at the point to yield unto him. And yet for all this, he ceased not to hinder their proceedings, until such time as a troop of Roman knights, who stood round about the place in arms for guard and defense, threatened to dispatch him out of the way, in case he continued still in his obstinate contumacy, holding and shaking their drawn swords so near unto him, as that his next fellows forsook him as he sat with them, and very few taking him in their arms and putting their gowns between, hardly and with much ado saved him from violence. Then was he scared indeed, insomuch as he not only condescended unto them, but also for the rest of that year forbore to come into the senate house.

15. The very first day of his praetorship, he called Quintus

Catulus before the people to receive their order as touching re-edification of the Capitol, having withal promulgated a law by virtue whereof he transferred the charge of that work unto another. But he was not able to match the nobles and better sort, nor to make his part good with them, drawing in one line as they did. When he saw them run by heaps together, so fully bent to make resistance, that presently they left their attendance upon the new consuls, he gave over this action.

16. But, whereas Cecilius Metullus [surnamed Nepos for his riotous life and behavior], a tribune of the commons, proposed most turbulent and seditious laws, in spite of his colleagues' opposition, he showed himself a stout abetter and maintainer of him, most stiffly bearing him out in the cause, so long until both of them were by an injunction and decree of the senators removed from the administration of the commonwealth. Howbeit presuming nevertheless to continue in his magistracy, and to execute his jurisdiction, when he understood once that some were ready to prohibit him by force and arms, he sent away his sergeants, cast off his embroidered purple robe, and retired privily to his own house, minding there to keep himself quiet in regard of the troublesome times. And when two days after, the multitude flocked unto him willingly and of their own accord, promising after a very tumultuous manner their help and assistance in the recovery of his former place and dignity, he repressed them. Which thing happening thus beyond all expectation, the senate gave him hearty thanks; and that by the principal and noblest personages among them, sent for him into the Curia, and after they had in most honorable terms commended him, they restored him fully to his office, and reversed their former decree.

17. He fell again into another new trouble and danger, being called into question as one of Catiline's conspiracy, both before the quaestor Novius Niger in his house, and that by Lucius

Vettius who accused him; and also in the senate, by Publius Curius, unto whom for that he detected first the plots and designs of the conspirators, were rewards appointed by the state. Curius deposed that he knew much from Catiline, and Vettius promised to bring forth even his own handwriting which he gave unto Catiline. But this was such an indignity as Caesar in no wise thought tolerable; whereupon, craving the testimony of Cicero, by which he proved that he himself merely of his own accord had given some information unto him of the said conspiracy, he prevailed so much that Curius went without those rewards. As for Vettius, after his goods were arrested and stresses taken, his household stuff rifled, himself evilly treated, beaten, and in the open assembly of the multitude even before the rostra well near pulled in pieces, him he clapped up in prison. After the same sort he served Novius the quaestor, because he suffered him, a superior magistrate of state, to be accused and defamed in his house.

18. After this praetorship of his, having the government of the farther province in Spain allotted unto him, he dealt with his creditors (that were in hand to stay him) by the means of certain sureties who came in and undertook for him; and before the governors of the provinces were disposed of by the state, he, contrary to all right and custom, put himself in his journey; were it for fear of some judicial proceeding intended against him while he was a private person, or because he might more speedily succor the allies of the Romans, who craved help, it is uncertain. Well, when he had settled the province in peace, he made as great haste to be gone; and not awaiting a successor he departed, as well to ride in triumph as to take upon him the consulship. But after the proclamations were out for the election of consuls, when he might not be a candidate unless he entered the city in quality of a private citizen, and many withstood him laboring as he did to be exempt from

the laws, forced he was for fear of losing the consulship to forgo his triumph.

19. Of the two competitors with him for the consulship,
to wit, Lucius Luceius and Marcus Bibulus, he made choice
of Luceius to be his fellow candidate; upon this compact and
condition, that since he was a man not so gracious but better
moneyed than himself, he should of his own purse pronounce
in the name of both, and promise to deal monies among the
centuries. Which device being known, the nobles were afraid
that, being once a sovereign magistrate, and having a colleague
ready at his beck to agree and consent with him, he would
both dare and do anything; so they persuaded Bibulus to make
promise of as great a donation as the other did; and the most
part of them contributed their monies thereunto. Yea, Cato
himself verily was not against it, but said, this largess stood
with the good of the republic. Hereupon created consul he
was with Bibulus. For the same cause, the said nobles gave
order that the consuls for the year following should have the
provinces and commissions of least importance, to wit, the
looking unto forests and woods, unto lanes and paths. Caesar,
taking all this wrong and disgrace most to the heart, made
court all that he ever could, unto Gnaius Pompey, who had
taken offense against the senators, for that having vanquished
Mithridates, his [Pompey's] acts and decrees were not sooner
ratified and confirmed. He reconciled also unto Pompey,
Marcus Crassus, an old enemy ever since that consulship which
they bore together with exceeding much jarring and disagreement; he entered likewise into a society with them both, upon
this contract, that nothing should be done or passed in the
administration of the commonwealth, that displeased any of
them three.

20. When he was entered into this honorable place of consulship, he (first of all that ever were) ordained that all acts,

as well of senate as people, should day by day as they were concluded, be recorded also and published. He brought in likewise the ancient custom again, that in what month he had not the fasces borne before him, a public officer called *accensus* should usher him before, and the sergeants or lictors follow after behind. Having promulgated the Law *Agraria*, as touching the division of lands among the commons, when his fellow consul resisted his proceedings, he drove him out of the Forum by violence and force of arms. The morrow after, when the said Bibulus had made his complaint in the senate of this outrage, and there would not one be found that dared to move the house about so great a garboil and hurliburly as that was, nor give his censure thereof (as oftentimes in lighter tumults and stirs there had passed many decrees), Caesar drove him to such a desperate fear, that until he went quite out of his magistracy, he kept close within house and never prohibited any proceedings else but by way of edict. From that time forward, Caesar alone managed all the affairs of state, even as he would himself; insomuch as divers citizens pleasantly conceited, whensoever they signed, subscribed, or dated any writings to stand upon record, would merrily put it down thus, such a thing was done, not when Caesar and Bibulus, but when Julius and Caesar were consuls, setting down one and the same man twice, by his name and surname. Yea, and soon after, these verses were commonly current abroad,

> *Non Bibulo, quidquam nuper, sed Caesare, factum est;*
> *Nam Bibulo fieri consule, nil memini.*

> Caesar of late did many things, but Bibulus not one;
> For nought by consul Bibulus, can I remember done.

The Stellate fields, held consecrated and religious by our ancestors, together with the Campanian territory, reserved to yield rent and pay tribute for a subsidy to the commonwealth, he divided, without casting lots, among twenty thousand citizens who could show three children or more. The publicans making request for some easement he relieved by striking of a third part of their rents, and warned them openly that in the setting and letting of the new commodities and revenues of the city, they should not bid and offer too much. All other things likewise he gave and granted, according as every man's mind and desire stood thereto, and no man gainsaid him; but, went any about to thwart him, he was soon frightened away. Marcus Cato, when he seemed to interrupt and stop his proceedings, he caused to be haled violently out of the senate house by an officer, and committed to prison. As Lucius Lucullus stoutly withstood his doings, he put him into so great a fear of sundry actions and criminations, that he was glad to come and fall down before him at his knees. When Cicero pleading upon a time in court, had lamented the woeful state of those times, the very same day, at the ninth hour, Caesar brought Publius Clodius, Cicero's enemy, to be adoped into the house and name of a commoner; one who had long before labored in vain to go from the nobles, and be incorporated among the commons. Last of all, it is credibly reported, that he induced by rewards, against all those in general of the contrary faction, an informer to profess that he was solicited by some for to murder Pompey; who being produced forth by him before the body of the people, named (as he had instructions, and as it was agreed between them afore) those that set him a-work. But when one or two of them were named to no purpose, nor without pregnant suspicion of some fraudulent practice, he despairing the success of so rash and inconsiderate a project, poisoned the party whom he had suborned, and made him away for telling any more tales.

21. About the same time, Caesar took to wife Calpurnia the daughter of Lucius Piso, who was to succeed him in the con-

sulate; and affianced his own daughter Julia unto Gnaius Pompey, rejecting and casting off her former spouse Servilius Caepio, by whose help especially a little before he had impugned Bibulus. After this new contracted affinity, he began (in counsel) to ask Pompey's opinion first; whereas before he was wont to begin with Crassus; notwithstanding also the custom was that the consul should observe that order all the year following, in asking the senators' sentences, which he began with the first day of January.

22. Being backed therefore by the favor and assistance of his wife's father and son-in-law, out of all that choice of provinces he chose especially the Gauls, the wealth and commodity whereof might fit his hand, and minister matter sufficient of triumphs. And verily at the first by virtue of the Law Vatinia he took upon him the government of Gallia Cisalpina together with Illyricum. Soon after by the means of the senate, that also which was called Comata, for the nobility feared, if they had denied him it, the people would have bestowed the same upon him. With joy whereof he grew so haughty and proud, that he could not hold and temper himself, but some few days after made his boast in a frequent senate house, that he had gotten now what he desired in despite of his adversaries and full sore against their wills; and therefore from that time forward, would mount insult upon all their heads. Whereupon, when one by way of reproach denied that and said, that it was no easy matter for a woman so to do, he answered again, as it were alluding merrily to another sense, that, even in Assyria there some time reigned Queen Semiramis; and that the women named Amazons held in time past a great part of Asia in subjection.

23. When he had borne his consulship, Gaius Memmius and Lucius Domitius, praetors for the time being, put to question his acts passed the former year; whereupon he referred the

examination and censure thereof unto the body of the senate. But seeing they would not undertake the thing, after three days spent to no purpose in vain brabbles and altercations, he departed into his province. And immediately his quaestor [when he was consul], for to raise prejudice against him, was drawn into trouble and indicted upon certain crimes. Within a while himself also was brought judicially to his trial, and accused by Lucius Antistius, a tribune of the commons; but by appealing unto the college of the tribunes, he prevailed through their favor thus much (in regard of his absence about the affairs of commonwealth) that he should not be liable to the accusation. For his better security therefore against future times, he travailed much to oblige and make beholden unto him the magistrates every year; and of those competitors who sued for any honorable office, to help or suffer none other to be elected but such as covenanted with him, and undertook to defend and maintain him in his absence. For assurance of which, he stuck not to require of some an oath, yea, and a bill of their own hands.

24. But when Lucius Domitius, a candidate for the consulship, threatened openly that were he once consul, he would effect that which he could not while he was praetor, yea, and take from Caesar his armies, he made means to draw Crassus and Pompey unto Luca, a city within his province. Upon them he prevailed that for to give Domitius the repulse, they should both sue for themselves to be consuls the second time, and also labor that his government might be prorogued for five years longer; and he effected both. Upon this confidence he presumed to assume unto those legions which he had received from the state, others besides, maintained partly at the city's charges and in part with his own private purse. And one legion above the rest, enrolled from out of the countries beyond the Alps, he termed by a French word, for named it was *Alauda* [the

17

bird *galerita* or *cassita*, so called of a crest, upon the head]. This legion it should seem wore plumes of feathers in their crests of helmets, whereupon it took that name. Which, being trained in military discipline, armed also and set out after the Roman fashion, he afterwards enfranchised throughout and made Roman citizens. Neither from this time forward forbore he any occasion of war, were it never so unjust or dangerous, picking quarrels as well with confederate nations, as those that were enemies, savage and barbarous, whom he provoked to take arms. Insomuch as the senate one time decreed to send certain ambassadors for to survey and visit the state of the Gauls; yea, and some were of opinion that he should be delivered unto the enemies' hands. But by reason that his affairs sped well and had good success, he obtained in regard thereof solemn thanksgivings both oftener and for more days than ever any man did before him.

25. During the time of his provincial government, which continued nine years' space, these, in manner, were the acts which he performed. All that part of Gaul which from the Pyrenees, the Alps, and the hill Gebena is enclosed within the rivers Rhine and Rhone, containing in circuit 3200 miles, not accounting the associate cities and states who had deserved well of the people of Rome, he reduced into the form of a province, and imposed upon them a payment of tribute yearly. The Germans inhabiting beyond the Rhine, he of all the Romans first assailed by means of a bridge which he built over the said river, and those he grievously plagued and gave them many great overthrows. He set upon the Britains also, a people before time unknown, whom he vanquished and compelled both to pay money, and also to deliver hostages. In so many prosperous battles and fortunate exploits, he tasted of adverse fortune thrice only and no more; once in Britain, when his fleet had like to have been lost and cast away in a

violent tempest; a second time in Gaul, where a legion of his was discomfited and put to flight, near unto Gergovia; and last of all, in the marches of Germany, when Titutius and Aurunculeius his lieutenants were waylaid by an ambush and put to the sword.

26. Within the compass of which very same time he lost by death, first his mother, then his daughter Julia, and not long after his grandson. And in this meanwhile, the commonwealth being much troubled and astonished at the murder of Clodius, when the senate thought good there should be but one consul created, namely Gnaius Pompey, he dealt with the tribunes of the commons (who intended that he should be the colleague in office with Pompey) to propose this rather unto the people, that they would grant leave unto him in his absence, whensoever the term of his government drew toward an end, to sue for his second consulship, so that he might not be constrained upon that occasion, and while the war was yet unfinished, to depart out of his province. Which when he had once obtained at their hands, reaching now at higher matters and full of hopes, there was no kind of largess, no manner of dutiful office either in public to the whole city, or privately unto any person that he omitted and left undone. His forum he began to build with the money raised of the spoils gotten in war; the very plot of ground whereon it should stand cost him a hundred million sesterces and above. He announced also a solemn sword-fight and feast unto the people, in the honor and memorial of his daughter, a thing that never any man did before him. And to cause an expectation of these solemnities in the highest degree, the viands and whatsoever pertained unto the feast, albeit he had agreed with butchers and victualers for the same at a certain price, he provided nevertheless by his household servants. All the notable and well-known sword-players, when they fought so as upon the

mislike and displeasure of the beholders they were in danger to be killed, he charged they should be had away by force and reserved for himself. As for beginners, he trained them neither in any public school, nor under professed masters of that faculty, but at home in private houses, by knights of Rome, yea, and senators also, such as were skillful in their weapon and in feats of arms, praying and beseeching them earnestly (as appears in his epistles unto them) to take the charge of every one severally, and to have a special care to instruct each one, and give them rules in their exercises. The legionary soldiers' pay in money he doubled forever. And so often as there was plenty of corn, he gave them their allowance of it without stint and measure, and otherwhile he bestowed upon everyone a slave from among his captives.

27. Moreover, to retain still the bond of acquaintance, affinity, and good will of Pompey, he affianced and made sure unto him Octavia, his sister's granddaughter, wedded unto Gaius Marcellus; but withal he craved Pompey's daughter to wife, promised in marriage before unto Faustus Sulla. Having thus obliged and brought to his devotion all those about him, yea, and the greater number of senators, by crediting out his money unto them, either gratis, or upon a slight consideration; those also of other sorts and degrees, either invited kindly by himself, or resorting unto him of their own accord, he gratified with most magnificent bounty. The freedmen besides, yea, and the servants and pages belonging to everyone, according as any of them were in favor with their lord and master, tasted of his liberality. Moreover, there was not a man sued in court judicially and in danger of the law; there was not any deeply engaged and indebted unto their creditors; there were no prodigal young spendthrifts, but he was their only supporter and most ready to help them. (Unless they were those that either had committed such grievous crimes, or were so low brought,

or had been so excessive in riot as that they could not possibly be relieved by him. For such as these, he would say in plain terms and openly, that there was no other remedy but civil war.)

28. No less careful and studious was he to allure unto him the hearts of kings, yea, and whole provinces throughout the world; unto some, offering in free gift the delivery of captives and prisoners by thousands at a time; unto others, sending aid secretly and underhand without authority or commission of the senate and people, whither and as often as they would; and more than this, adorning with goodly building and excellent pieces of work the mightiest cities in Italy, Gaul, Spain, yea, and of Asia and Greece. This he did so long, until all men now were astonished thereat; and when they cast with themselves whereto this might tend, at last Marcus Claudius Marcellus the consul, after a preface and preamble made to his edict, namely, that he would speak as touching the main point of the commonwealth, proposed unto the senate, that forasmuch as the war was now ended, and peace abroad established, there might be one sent to succeed Caesar before his time was fully expired; also, that the victorious army ought of right to be dismissed and have their discharge from warfare. Also, that in the high court and assembly for the consuls' election his name should not be propounded, considering Pompey afterward had annulled that act of the people (by virtue whereof it was granted that he might be chosen consul in his absence). Now it had fallen out so, that he making a law as touching the right of magistrates, in that chapter and branch thereof wherein he disabled those who were absent for being capable of honors and dignities, forgot to except Caesar; and soon after, when the said law was once engrossed and engraven in brass and so laid up in the treasury, corrected his error and oversight. Neither was Marcellus content to deprive Caesar of his provinces and the privilege of a former act passed in especial favor of him,

but he made a motion moreover, that those inhabitants, whom by the Law *Vatinia* Caesar had planted in the colony of Novo-comum, should lose their Roman citizenship, for that this prerogative had been granted by ambitious means, and beyond the authority of law.

29. Caesar, highly displeased and troubled at these pro-ceedings, and judging it (as he was heard by report many times to give out) a harder matter for him, a principal man of the city, to be deposed and thrust down from the highest and first place of degree into the second, than from the second into the lowest and last of all, withstood him with all his might and power, partly by the opposition and negative voice of the tribunes, and in part by Servius Sulpitius the other consul. Also in the year following when Gaius Marcellus who succeeded his cousin Marcus in the consulship, essayed to bring the same about, he bribed with a mighty sum of money Aemilius Pau-lus, companion with him in office, and Gaius Curio, a most violent tribune, to stick unto him, and defend his honor. But seeing all things carried still against him more obstinately than before, and the new consuls elect took the contrary side and bent another way, he wrote unto the senate and humbly besought them not to suffer the benefit granted unto him by the people to be taken from him; or if they did, yet to give order that other generals likewise as well as he, might leave their armies; presuming confidently, as men think, upon this, him-self should be able whensoever he pleased to assemble together his soldiers more easily than Pompey to levy new. But with his adversaries he would have treated by way of capitulation in these terms, that after he had discharged and sent away eight legions, and given over the province of Gaul beyond the Alps, he might be allowed two legions with the province on this side of the Alps; or if not so, yet at leastwise one, together with Illyricum, until such time as he were created consul.

30. But perceiving that the senate came not between nor interposed their authority to stop the course intended against him, and his adversaries denied flatly to admit all manner of capitulating and composition concerning the commonwealth, he passed into the hither part of Gaul, and having kept the assizes there and executed his provincial jurisdiction, stayed at Ravenna, with full resolution to be revenged by open war, in case there had passed from the senate any sharp and cruel decree, touching the tribunes of the commons opposing themselves in his behalf, and quarrel. And verily this was the color and occasion which he pretended of civil war; yet men think there were some other causes and motives thereto. Gnaius Pompey was wont to give out that forasmuch as Caesar was not able of himself and with his own private wealth, either to consummate and finish those stately works and edifices which he had begun, or to satisfy the expectation of the people which he had raised and wrought of his coming, therefore he intended to trouble the state and set all on a garboil. Others say, that he feared lest he should be compelled to give an account of those things which in his first consulship he had done against the sacred auspices, the laws, and prohibitions of the tribunes (in the name of the people) considering that Marcus Cato had threatened and professed eftsoons, and not without an oath, that no sooner should he and his army be parted, but he would judicially call his name in question and bring him to answer; also for that it was commonly spoken abroad that if he returned once in quality of a private person, he should after the example of Milo plead before the judges, with a guard of armed men about the court and tribunal. And this seems to be more probable by that which Asinius Pollio writes, who reports that, in the battle of Pharsalia, when he beheld his adversaries before his face slain and put to flight, he uttered this speech word for word. "Lo, this was their own doing; this would

they needs have, and I Gaius Caesar after so many worthy exploits achieved should have been a condemned man, had I not craved help of mine army." Some are of opinion, that being so long inured and acquainted with sovereign command, and weighing his own power and the strength of the enemy in balance one against the other, took the occasion and opportunity to usurp that absolute dominion, which in the very prime of his years he aspired unto; and of his mind it seems Cicero was, who in his third book Of Duties writes that Caesar had always in his mouth, these verses of Euripides which Cicero himself translated thus,

> *Nam si violandum est ius, imperii gratia*
> *Violandum est, aliis rebus pietatem colas.*

> For if thou must do wrong by breach,
> Of laws, of right and equity,
> 'Tis best thereby a crown to reach,
> In all thing else keep piety.

31. When word therefore was brought unto him, that the tribunes' inhibition and negative voice was put down, and themselves departed out of the city, having immediately sent before certain cohorts privily, so that no suspicion might arise, he dissembled the matter and was present in person to behold a public game, and considered the plan according to which he was about to build a school of sword-fencers, and according to his usual manner gave himself to feast and banquet often. After the setting of the sun, he took up certain mules from a nearby bakery, harnessed them to his wagon, and as closely as possibly he could with a small retinue put himself in his journey. And when by reason that the lights were gone out, he had lost his way, after he had wandered a long time, at length meeting with a guide by that time it was day, he passed on foot throught most narrow cross-lanes and by-

paths until he recovered the right way again. Now when he had once overtaken his cohorts at the river Rubicon, which was the utmost bound of his province, he rested and stood still a little while; then casting in his mind, how great an enterprise he went in hand with, he turned unto them that were next unto him and said, "As yet, my masters, we may well return back; but pass we once over this little bridge, there will be no dealing but by force of arms and dint of sword."

32. As he thus stood doubtful what to do, a strange sight he chanced to see in this manner. All of a sudden there appeared unto him a certain man of an extraordinary stature and shape withal, sitting nearby and piping with a reed. Now when besides the shepherds and herdsmen many soldiers also ran for to hear him, and among them the trumpeters likewise, he caught from one of them a trumpet, leapt forth to the river, and beginning with a mighty blast to sound the battle, kept on his pace to the very bank on the other side. Then Caesar said, "Let us march on and go whither the tokens of the gods and the injurious dealings of our enemies call us. The die is cast."

33. And having thus conveyed his army over the river, he joined with the tribunes of the commons, who upon their expulsion out of the city were come unto him, and in a full and frequent assembly, with shedding tears and rending his garment down the breast, besought the faithful help and assistance of his soldiers. It is supposed also that he promised unto every one of them a knight's living; which happened upon a misunderstanding, for when in his speech and exhortation unto them he showed ever and anon the ring finger of his left hand, and therewith avouched and promised, for the satisfaction and contentment of all those by whose means he should maintain his honor and dignity, that he would willingly pluck the ring from off his own finger, those that stood hindmost in the assembly, who might better see than hear him

speak, took that for spoken which they imagined by bare sight, and so the speech went for current, that he promised them the dignity of wearing the ring together with 400,000 sesterces.

34. The order of those acts which from thence he achieved, summarily goes in this manner. He seized into his hands and held Picenum, Umbria, and Etruria. Lucius Comitius, who in a factious tumult was nominated to be his successor, and kept Corfinium with a garrison, he subdued and forced to yield; and when he had dismissed him, he marched along the coast of the Adriatic sea to Brundisium whither the consuls and Pompey were fled, intending with all speed to cross the narrow seas. Whose passage after he had essayed by all manner of lets to hinder and stop (but in vain) he turned his journey and took the way directly to Rome. And when he had called a meeting of the senators to consult as touching the state of the commonwealth, he marched upon the most powerful forces of Pompey, which were in Spain under the conduct of three lieutenants, Marcus Petreius, Lucius Affranius, and Marcus Varro; having given out before among his friends and openly professed, that he was going to an army without a captain, and would return from thence to a captain without an army. And albeit the besieging of Massilia, which city in his journey forward had shut the gates against him, and exceeding scarcity of corn and victuals was some impediment and stay unto him, yet within a short time he overcame and subdued all.

35. From thence having returned to Rome again, and passed over into Macedonia, after he had held Pompey besieged for the space well near of four months, and that within most mighty trenches and strong ramparts, he discomfited at the last in the Pharsalian battle and put him to flight. And following him hotly in chase as he fled to Alexandria, so soon as he understood that he was slain, and perceived likewise that King Ptolomaeus laid wait for his own person also, he warred upon

him; which, to say in truth, was a most difficult and dangerous piece of work, by reason that he managed it, neither in place indifferent, nor time convenient, but in the very winter season, and within the walls of a most wealthy and crafty enemy, being himself in distress and want of all things, and unprovided besides to fight. Having achieved the victory, he granted the kingdom unto Cleopatra and her younger brother, fearing to reduce it into the form of a province, lest at any time, being governed under some president of a stirring spirit and violent nature, it might give occasion of rebellion. From Alexandria, he went over into Syria, and so from thence into Pontus, upon the urgent news as touching Pharnaces, son of that great Mithridates, who, taking the opportunity of the troubles and civil war among the Romans, made war, yea, and now bore himself presumptuous and overbold for his manifold victories and great success. Yet within five days after Caesar's arrival there, and four hours after he came into sight of the enemy, he vanquished and subdued Mithridates in only one battle; eftsoons and oftentimes recounting the felicity of Pompey, whose hap it was to win his principal name for warfare of so cowardly a kind of enemies. After this, he defeated Scipio and Juba, repairing the relics of their party in Africa, and the children of Pompey in Spain.

36. In all the civil wars, he sustained no loss or overthrow but by his own lieutenants; of whom, Gaius Curio was slain in Africa; Gaius Antonius yielded himself into the hands of his enemies in Illyricum; Publius Dolabella in the same Illyricum lost his fleet; and Gnaius Domitius his army in Pontus. Himself fought his battles always most fortunately, and never was so much as in any hazard, save only twice; once before Dyrrhachium, where being discomfited and put to flight, when he saw that Pompey followed not on in chase, he said of him, that he knew not how to use a victory. A second time, in

Spain, at the last battle that ever he fought, what time being in great despair, he was of mind even to have killed himself.

37. Having finished all his wars, he rode in five triumphs, to wit, when he had vanquished Scipio, four times in one and the same month, but certain days between, and once again, after he had overcome the children of Pompey. The first and most excellent triumph that he solemnized, was that over Gaul; then followed the Alexandrine; after it the Pontic; next thereunto the African; and last of all the Spanish – every one set out diversely, with variety of ordinance, provision and furniture. On the day of his Gallic triumph, as he rode along the Velabrum [a street in Rome], he had like to have been shaken out of his chariot, by reason that the axle broke. He mounted up into the Capitol by torch-light, having forty elephants on his right hand and left, bearing branches and candlesticks. In his Pontic triumph, among the pageants and shows of that pomp, he caused to be carried before him the title and superscription of these three words, "*Veni, vidi, vici*" [I came, I saw, I conquered]; signifying not the acts achieved by war, as other conquerors, but noting his expedition in dispatching the war.

38. Throughout the legions of old soldiers, he gave in the name of pillage, unto every footman (over and above the 2000 sesterces which he had paid at the beginning of the civil tumult) 4000 sesterces; and to the horsemen 24,000 apiece. He assigned lands also unto them, but not lying all together, so that none of the owners should be thrust out of their livings. Among the people of Rome besides ten *modii* of corn, and as many pints of oil, he distributed and dealt 300 sesterces also, which he had in times past promised, with an overdeal of 100 apiece to boot, for the delay. He remitted moreover one year's house rent unto all tenants in Rome, if it amounted to 2000 sesterces and not above; but to those in Italy, if the said rent exceeded not 500. Furthermore, he made them a general

great feast, and distributed a dole of raw flesh; yea, and after his victory in Spain he gave them two dinners; for, deeming the former of them to have been made niggardly and not be-seeming his liberality, he bestowed upon them five days after, another, and in most large and plenteous manner.

39. He exhibited shows of sundry sorts, as namely a sword-fight of fencers at sharp. He set forth stage plays likewise in several quarters of the city, and those verily acted by players in all languages. Similarly, the solemn games *Circenses* he showed, and brought forth champions also to perform their devoir, and represented a naval fight. At the said solemnity of sword-players, there fought to the finish in the Forum of Rome, Furius Leptinus, descended from praetors, and Aulus Calpenus, one who had been sometime a senator, and a pleader of causes at the bar. There danced the Pyrrhic war dances the children of the princes and potentates of Asia and Bithynia. During the stage-plays aforesaid Decimus Laberius, a knight of Rome, acted his own poem or interlude; for which, being rewarded with 500,000 sesterces and a ring of gold, he passed directly from the stage by the orchestra to take up his place among the knights in the fourteen foremost rows. At the games *Circenses*, against which the circus was enlarged on both sides and moated around, there drove the steeds drawing chariots four and two together, yea and mounted the vaunting horses from one to another, the greatest gallants and bravest young gentlemen of the nobility. The warlike Trojan games were performed by a twofold troupe of greater boys and lesser. The hunting or baiting of wild beasts was presented five days together. And the last day of all, there was a fight between two armies of 500 footmen, twenty elephants, and thirty horsemen on a side, put to skirmish one against the other. For, to the end that they might have more scope to bicker together, the goals were taken up and removed; but instead

of them were pitched two camps confronting one another. As for the champions above-said, they having a place to exercise their feats of activity set out and built for the time being, strove for the prize together for three days in the region of Mars field. To set out the *Naumachia* or naval battle, there was a place dug for a great pool, in the lesser *Codeta*, wherein certain galleys as well with two ranks of oars as with three; the ships of Tyre also and of Egypt encountered, being manned with a great number of fighting men. To behold these sights and shows, such a number of people resorted from all parts, as most of the strangers were fain to abide within booths pitched to purpose; yea, and oftentimes very many were in the press crowded and crushed to death, among whom were two senators.

40. Turning after this to set the state of the commonwealth in good order, he reformed the calendar, which long since through the prelates' default, by their liberty of interlacing months and days at their pleasure, was so confused, that neither the festival holidays of harvest fell out in summer, nor those of the vintage in autumn. And he framed the whole year just unto the course of the sun, that it should contain 365 days; and abolishing the leap month, he inserted one day every fourth year. Now to the end that the computation of the times to come might from the new Kalends of January agree the better, between November and December he put two other months. So as, that year wherein all this was ordained had fifteen months, reckoning the ordinary interlaced month, which by course and custom fell just upon the said year.

41. He made up the full number of the senators, and chose unto that place new patricians. The number of praetors, aediles, quaestors, and of other inferior magistrates he augmented. Such as were displaced and put down by virtue of the censor's office, or otherwise by sentence of the judges condemned for unlawful bribery, and suing indirectly for any office, he re-

stored to their former rooms. In the election of magistrates he parted with the people thus far forth; as (excepting the competitors of the consulship) for all the number besides of candidates, the one half should be declared those whom the people were disposed to propound, the other half, such as himself would nominate. Which nomination passed by certain bills sent about unto the tribes, in a brief kind of writ, after this manner: "Caesar dictator, unto this or that tribe, Greeting. I commend unto you, such a one, that by virtue of your voices and suffrages they may have and hold the dignity they sue for." He admitted unto honorable places the children of those who had been proscribed and outlawed. He reduced all judgements unto two sorts of judges, namely of the knights' degree and the senators'; as for the tribunes of the treasury, which had been the third, he utterly abolished. The general survey and numbering of the people he held, neither after the accustomed manner, nor in the usual place, but street by street, and that by the landlords and owners of tenements standing together; and whereas 320,000 citizens received allowance of corn from the state, he brought and reduced them to the number of 150,000. And to the end that no new conventicles and riots at any time might arise about this review, he ordained, that every year, in the place of those that were deceased, the praetor should make a new supply and choice by casting lots, out of such as had not been reckoned and enrolled in the former survey.

42. Moreover, when as to the number of 80,000 citizens were bestowed in sundry colonies beyond the sea, he made a law for the more frequent inhabiting of the city of Rome, thus exhausted and depopulated; namely, that no citizen above twenty years of age, and under forty (unless he were a sworn soldier to the state, and so bound by his oath) should remain out of Italy above three years together. Also, that no senator's

son, except he belonged to the familiar train of a chief magistrate, should travel forth of Italy. Also, that no graziers should keep and retain fewer than a third part of freeborn young men among the keepers of their cattle. All professors of physic at Rome and teachers of the liberal arts he enfranchised citizens, that both they themselves might more willingly dwell in the city, and others besides desire there to inhabit. As touching money lent out, when he had quite put down the expectation of cancelling debts (a thing that was often moved), he decreed at length, that all debtors should satisfy their creditors in this manner, namely by an estimate made of their possessions, according to the worth and value as they purchased them before the civil war, deducting out of the principal whatsoever had been paid or set down in interest; by which condition the third part well near of the money credited forth was lost. All the societies and colleges, saving those that were of ancient foundation, he dissolved. The penalties of heinous crimes he augmented; and whereas the rich and wealthier sort fell to wickedness so much the sooner, because they merely went into banishment, and saved their whole patrimonies and estates; parricides therefore and willful murderers (as Cicero writes) he deprived of all their goods; other manslayers besides he fined with the loss of one half.

43. He ministered justice and decided matters in law, most painfully and with passing great severity. Such as were attainted and convicted of extortion he removed even from their senator's place and degree. He broke the marriage of a man that had been praetor, marrying a wife presently after two days that she was divorced and went from a former husband, albeit there was no suspicion at all of adultery and naughtiness. He ordained customs and imposts of foreign merchandise. The use of litters, likewise the wearing of purple clothes and of pearls he took away, saving only in certain persons and ages,

and upon special days. The Law *Sumptuaria*, to repress excessive cost in fare, he executed most of any other; and for this purpose, he set certain warders in sundry places about the shambles and markets where victuals were sold, to lay hold upon all cates and viands contrary to the prescribed rule of the law in that behalf, and to bring the same unto him. Otherwhiles also, he sent secretly his own officers and soldiers, to fetch away such meats out of the very dining parlors and banqueting rooms, even when they were set upon the board, if haply they had any way escaped the hands of the foresaid warders.

44. For, as concerning his purpose to adorn and beautify the city of Rome with gallant works, as also to maintain and amplify the empire, he had more matters in his head and greater every day than other. Principally, his intent and meaning was, to build so stately a temple in the honor of Mars, as the like was nowhere to be seen, having filled up and laid level that huge pit, wherein he had exhibited the show of a naval battle; and also to erect an exceeding great theater, fast adjoining to the Mount Tarpeius. Also, to reduce the whole corps of the civil law to a certain mean and mediocrity; and out of that huge and diffused number of laws, to choose out the best and necessary points, and those to bring into as few volumes as possibly might be. Also, to erect publicly the greatest libraries that he could, as well of Greek and Latin authors, committing unto Marcus Varro the charge, both to provide the said books, and also to digest and place them in order. Also, to drain the Pomptine marshes; to draw and let forth the lake Fucinus; to make a causeway from the Adriatic Sea by the side of the Apennines, as far as to the river Tiber; and to dig through the Isthmus. Moreover to bridle the Dacians who had invaded Pontus and Thrace; and soon after, to make war upon the Parthians by the way of Armenia the Lesser, but not to give them battle before he had made trial of them. Amid

these purposes and designs, death prevented him. Concerning which, before I enter into speech, it shall not be impertinent to deliver summarily those points which concern the shape, feature, and proportion of his body; his habit and apparel; his fashions and behavior; and withal, what may touch both his civil and also his martial affairs.

45. Of stature he is reported to have been tall; of complexion white and clear; with limbs well trussed and in good plight; somewhat full faced; his eyes black, lively, and quick; also very healthful, saving that in his latter days he was given to faint and swoon suddenly; yea and to start and be affrighted as he dreamed. Twice also in the midst of his martial affairs, he was surprised with the falling sickness. About the trimming of his body, he was over-curious: so as he would not only be shorn and shaven very precisely, but also have his hair plucked, insomuch as some cast it in his teeth and twitted him therewith. Moreover, finding by experience, that the deformity of his bald head was oftentimes subject to the scoffs and scorns of back-biters and slanderers, he took the same exceedingly to heart; and therefore he both had usually drawn down his hair that grew but thin, from the crown toward his forehead; and also of all honors decreed unto him from the senate and people, he neither received nor used any more willingly, than the privilege to wear continually the triumphant laurel garland. Men say also, that in his apparel he was noted for singularity, as who used to go in his senator's purple studded robe, trimmed with a jag or fringe at the sleeve hand; and he also always wore a girdle over it, and that very slack and loose; whereupon arose for certain that saying of Sulla, who admonished the nobles oftentimes, to beware of the boy that went girded so dissolutely.

46. He dwelt first in the Subura; but after he was high priest, in the street Sacra, in an official edifice. Many have written that he was exceedingly addicted to neatness in his house, and

sumptuous fare at his table. The manor house which he founded and with great charges finished at Nemi, because it was not wholly answerable to his mind, he demolished and pulled quite down, although as yet he was but of mean estate and deeply indebted. Finally, this speech goes of him, that in his expeditions he carried about with him pavements, of checkerwork made of quarrels square cut, so as they might be taken asunder, and set again together.

47. He made a voyage (as they say) into Britain, in hope of pearls, and otherwhiles, in comparing their bigness, would with his own hand balance them to find their weight. For to get and buy up precious stones, engraved and chased pieces, images, and antique pictures, he was ever most eager and sharp set. Slaves likewise, if they were anything fresh and new come, trimly set out withal and fine, he procured at an exceeding price, such as himself also was ashamed of; so as he forbade expressly the same should be brought in any of his reckoning and accounts.

48. It is reported of him, that in all the provinces which he governed, he feasted continually, and furnished two halls or dining chambers ordinarily; the one, wherein either Gauls in their warlike habit, or Greeks in their cloaks; the other, in which the gowned Romans, together with the more noble and honorable personages of the provinces sat. The domestic discipline of his house he kept so duly, so precisely, and with such severity, in small matters as well as greater, that he bound with fetters and irons his baker for serving up secretly unto his guests other bread than to himself; and a freedman of his own (whom otherwise he did set very great store by) he put to death for dishonoring by adultery a Roman knight's wife, albeit no man made complaint thereof.

49. His good name for continency and clean life nothing verily blemished, save only the abode and inward familiarity

with Nicomedes; but a foul stain that was, which followed him with shame forever; yea, and ministered taunting and reproachful matter unto every man. I omit the notorious verses of Calvus Licinius.

> *Bithynia quicquid,*
> *Et paedicator Caesaris, umquam habuit.*

> Look what it was that Bithyne land had ever more or less;
> And he that Caesar did abuse, in filthy wantonness.

I let pass the invectives and accusatory actions of Dolabella and Curio the Elder; in which Dolabella for his part terms him the king's concubine in the queen's bedroom; and Curio names him Nicomedes' filth and harlot, yea and the Bithynian brothel house. I overpass likewise those edicts of Bibulus, wherein he published his colleague, and made him known, by the name of the Bithynian queen; saying moreover, that before, he had loved the king, and now cast a fancy to the kingdom. At which very time, as Marcus Brutus makes report, there was one Octavius also, a man upon distemperature of his brain given to jest and scoff over broadly, who in a most frequent assembly, after he had called Pompey king, saluted Caesar by the name of queen; Gaius Memmius likewise laid it in Caesar's dish that he stood with the rest of the stale catamites as cup-bearer, to serve Nicomedes with wine at a full feast, where sat at the table divers merchants and citizens of Rome, whose names he puts down. But Cicero, not contented herewith, that in certain epistles he had written, how by the pensioners of the said king being conveyed into the king's bedchamber, Caesar lay down upon a bed of gold, arrayed in purple; and so the maidenhead of him who was descended from Venus, became defiled in Bithynia. One time also, as Caesar in the senate house pleaded to the cause and in the behalf of Nysa, Nicomedes' daughter, and therewith rehearsed up the gracious favors that the king had done unto him, Cicero said, "Let be these matters I pray you, and away with them, since it is well known, both what he bestowed upon you, and also what you gave to him." Finally, in the triumph over Gaul, his soldiers, among other sonnets (such as they used to chant merrily when they followed the triumphant chariot) pronounced also these verses so commonly divulged:

Gallias Caesar subegit, Nicomedes Caesarem,
Ecce Caesar nunc triumphat, qui subegit Gallias;
Nicomedes non triumphat, qui subegit Caesarem.

Caesar did subdue the Gauls, and him hath Nicomedes.
Behold, now Caesar doth triumph, who did the Gauls subdue;
But Nicomedes triumpheth not who Caesar had subdued.

50. An opinion there is constantly received, that he was given to carnal pleasures, and that way spent much; also, that he dishonored many dames, and those of nobles house, by name among others, Postumia the wife of Servius Sulpitius; Lollia, wife to Aulus Gabinius; Tertulla, Marcus Crassus' wife, and Mucia, the wife of Gnaius Pompey. For, certain it is, that not only the Elder and Younger Curios, but many others also reproached Pompey, that for Caesar's cause he had put away his own wife after she had borne him three children, and whom he was wont with a deep sigh and groan to call Aegisthus [who had committed adultery with Clytemnestra, the wife of Agamennon]. And Caesar's daughter Pompey espoused upon a desire of power and greatness by that marriage. But above the rest, Caesar cast affection to Servilia the mother of Marcus Brutus; for whom both in his last consulship he had bought a pearl that cost him six million sesterces, and also unto whom during the civil war, over and above other free gift, he sold in the open auction fair lands and most goodly manors at a very low price. What time verily, when most men marveled that

they went so cheap, Cicero most pleasantly and conceitedly remarked, "That you may know that she does well in the purchase, for the price is downed by a third (*tertia deducta est*)." [A clever pun on both meanings of *tertia*, a third part, and the name of Servilia's daughter (as explained below); as also on both senses of the word *deducta* (= lit., to bring down).] For it was thought that Servilia was bawd also to her own daughter Tertia, and brought her to Caesar's bed.

51. Neither forbore he so much as men's wives in the provinces where he was governor, as appears even by this distich, taken up likewise by his soldiers at the Gallic triumph.

> *Urbani, servate uxores; moechum calvum adducimus,*
> *Auro in Gallia stuprum emistis, hic sumpsisti mutuum.*

Guard your wives, ye city folk, the adulterer bring we home;
In Gaul he wantoned at a price, gratis he wantons in Rome.

52. He was enamored also upon queens, and among them he loved Eunoe the Moor, wife of Bogudes, king of Mauretania, upon whom, as also upon her husband, he bestowed very many gifts and of infinite value, as Naso has left in writing. But most especially he fancied Cleopatra; for, with her, he both sat up many times and feasted all night long even until the break of day; and also in the same barge had passed into Egypt, almost as far as to Ethiopia, but that his army refused to follow. And in the end having summoned her to Rome, he sent her back again, not without exceeding great honors, and enriched with many rewards; yea, and suffered her to call the son she bore after his own name. Whom verily, some Greek writers have recorded to have been very like unto Caesar both in shape and also in gait. And Marcus Antonius avouched unto the senate that by the same resemblance he knew him to be Caesar's son, averring withal, that Gaius Matius, Gaius Oppius, and the rest of Caesar's friends knew as much. Of

whom Gaius Oppius (as if the thing were so pregnant, that it required some apology and defense) put forth a book entitled thus, *That he was not Caesar's Son, Whom Cleopatra Fathered upon Him.* Helvius Cinna, a tribune of the commons, confessed unto many persons, that he had a law drawn out in writing and in readiness, which Caesar being absent himself, commanded him to propose, to this effect, that it might be lawful for him to marry what wives and as many as he would, for to get children upon. And that no man need at all to doubt how infamous he was, both for uncleanness and adulteries, Curio the Elder, in a certain oration, calls him a woman for all men, and a man for all women.

53. That he was a most spare drinker of wine, his very enemies would never deny. Whereupon arose this apophthegm of Marcus Cato, that of all that ever were, Caesar alone came sober to the overthrow of the state. For, about his food and diet Gaius Oppius shows he was so indifferent and without curiosity, that when upon a time his host set before him upon the board old rank oil instead of green, sweet and fresh, so that the other guests refused it, he only (by his saying) fell to it and ate thereof the more liberally; because he would not be thought to blame his host either for negligence or rusticity.

54. From other men's goods he held not his hands, neither when he had the command of armies abroad, nor when he was in place of magistracy at home; for in Spain (as some have recorded) he took money of the proconsul, and the allies there, and that by way of begging, to help him out of debt; and certain towns of the Lusitanes he sacked in hostile manner, albeit they denied not to do whatsoever he commanded them; and besides, did set open their gates for him against his coming. In Gaul he robbed and spoiled the chapels and temples of the gods, full of rich gifts and oblations. As for cities, he put them to the sack, more often for booty's

sake and pillage, than for any trespass committed. Whereupon it came to pass, that he got abundance of gold, so as of it which he had to spare and did set to sale, he sold throughout Italy and in the provinces for 3000 sesterces of silver the pound. In his first consulship, when he had stolen out of the Capitol three thousand pound weight of gold, he bestowed in the place thereof as much brass gilt. The privileges of society and alliance with the Romans, as also kings' titles he gave for sums of money; as who (for example) from Ptolomeus that was but one, took away well near 6000 talents, in the name of himself and Pompey. But afterwards by most open pilling, polling, and sacrileges, he maintained the charges both of civil wars, and also of his triumphs and solemn shows exhibited to the people.

55. In eloquence and warlike feats together, he either equalled or excelled the glory of the very best. After his accusation of Dolabella, he was no doubt ranged in the rank of the principal advocates at law. Certes, Cicero, in his catalogue of orators to Brutus, says, "He cannot see anyone unto whom Caesar might give place. For he holds an elegant and gay, a stately also, and in same sort a generous and gentlemanlike kind of pleading." And unto Cornelius Nepos, thus wrote he of the same Caesar, "What should a man say more? which of all the orators that practiced nothing else but oratory will you prefer before this Caesar? who is there in sentences either quicker or coming thicker? who for words, yielded more gallant or more elegant?" He seems while he was yet but young, to have followed that form of eloquence only, which Strabo Caesar professed; out of whose oration also intitled *Pro Sardis*, he transferred some sentences, word for word, into his own, called *Divinatio*. It is said that in this pronunciation he used a high and shrill voice; an ardent motion, and earnest gesture, not without a lovely grace. Some orations he left behind him in writing. Among which certain go under his name, but un-

truly, as namely that *pro Q. Metello*, which Augustus deems (and not without good cause) to have been written rather by notaries, who either took not his words aright, or wrote not so fast as he delivered them, than he penned by himself. For in certain copies I find that it had not so much as this inscription, *Pro Metello*, but *quam scripsit Metello*, being (as it is indeed) a speech coming from the person of Caesar, clearing Metullus and himself against the criminations and slanders of common backbiters to them both. The oration likewise, *Ad Milites* in Spain, the same Augustus hardly thinks to be his; and yet there be two of them extant; the one was pronounced at the former battle; the other, at the latter, when, by the report of Asinius Pollio, he had not so much as any time to make a speech, the enemies ran upon him and charged so suddenly.

56. He left commentaries also of his own acts, to wit, as touching the Gallic war and the civil war with Pompey. For, of the Alexandrian, African and Spanish wars, who was the writer it is uncertain. Some think it was Oppius, others, Hirtius, who also made up and finished the last of the Gallic war, which was unfinished. As concerning those commentaries aforesaid of Caesar, Cicero in the same book [*Ad Brutum*] writes thus, "He wrote commentaries exceeding well, I assure you, to be liked (naked they be, straight and upright, yea and lovely too, being divested, as it were, of all ornaments and trim attire of style). But while his mind was that others disposed to write a complete history should furnish and serve themselves with matter there ready to their hands, happily, to some foolish folk he did some pleasure, who are willing to curl and frizzle the same with their crisping pins, but surely the wiser sort he scared altogether from writing." Of the same commentaries, Hirtius gives this report, "They are in the judgement of all men so approved, that it seems he has prevented writers, and not given them any help. And yet, our

admiration of this matter is more than all men's beside. For, whereas others do know only how well and purely they were penned, we note also with what facility and expedition he wrote them." Asinius Pollio thinks they were compiled with small care and with as little regard also of sound truth, seeing that Caesar received and believed most things lightly, namely such as were by others achieved; and even those acts which himself exploited either of purpose or for default of memory he put down wrong. He supposes also that he meant to have written the same anew and corrected them. He left moreover two books, *de Analogia,* and as many *Anticationes,* besides a poem, entitled *Iter*; of which books the first he made in his passage over the Alps, what time as having ridden his circuits and finished the assizes, he returned out of the hither province of Gaul to his army; those next following, about the time of the battle at Munda. And the last of all, while he traveled from the city of Rome into the farther province of Spain, and performed that journey within twenty-four days. Extant, there be also epistles of his written unto the senate; which (as it seems) he was the first that turned into pages and leaves, even to a form of a book of remembrance; whereas before, the consuls and generals never sent any letters but written overthwart the paper. Missives likewise there be of his written to Cicero, and to familiar friends as touching home affairs. In which, if any matters of secrecy were to be carried, he wrote them by privy marks; that is to say, placing the letters in such order as there could not one word be made of them. Which if a man would decipher and find out, he must of necessity exchange every fourth letter of the alphabet, to wit, d for a and the rest likewise. Furthermore there be certain works of his abroad written when he was a boy and a very youth, as namely, *The Praises of Hercules, The Tragedy of Oedipus,* and *Collects of Sayings and Apophthegms*; all which pamphlets, Augustus forbade to be published, in a certain brief epistle sent to Pompeius Macer, whom he had appointed for the disposing and ordering of his libraries.

57. In handling his weapon most skillful he was, and in horsemanship as cunning; but what pains he would take, it is incredible. In the marching of his army, his manner was to be foremost; sometimes on horseback, more often on foot, bareheaded, whether the sun shone or the clouds poured rain. He made exceeding long journeys with incredible speed – even a hundred miles a day riding in some hired wagon if he were lightly equipped. Were rivers in his way to hinder his passage? cross over them he would, either swimming or else bearing himself upon blowed leather bottles; so that, very often he prevented the letter-carriers and messengers of his coming.

58. In performing his expeditions and martial exploits doubtful it is, whether he were more wary or adventurous. He neither led his army at any time through ways dangerous for ambushments, before he had thoroughly viewed and descried the situation of the quarter; nor put over his fleet in Britain, until he had beforehand in proper person sounded the havens and tried the manner of sailing and arrival to the island. Howbeit, the same man (as circumspect as he was) upon news brought unto him, that his camp was beleaguered in Germany, passed through his enemies' *corps de garde* in French habit, and so came unto his own men. From Brindisi to Dyrrhachium, he sailed over sea in winter, between two fleets of the enemy's riding opposite one to the other; and while his own forces which he had commanded to follow straight after him lingered still behind, having sent messengers oftentimes to call them away but all in vain, at last himself secretly in the night went aboard into a very small bottom, with his head hooded; and neither discovered who he was, nor suffered the pilot to give way unto the tempest that came full

affront the vessel before he was well near overwhelmed with the waves.

59. No religious fear of divine prodigies could ever fray him from any enterprise, or stay him if it were once in hand. As he sacrificed upon a time, the beast made an escape and ran away; yet for all that deferred not he his journey against Scipio and Juba. He fortuned also to take a fall then, even as he went forth of the ship to land; but turning this foretoken to the better presage, "I take possession," he quoth, "of thee, O Africa." Moreover, in very scorn, and to make but a mockery of those prophecies whereby the name of Scipio was fatal to that province and held lucky and invincible there, he had with him in his camp the most base and abject fellow of all the Cornelian family, and who in reproach of his life was surnamed Saluito.

60. He fought not often set fields appointed before hand, but upon the present occasion offered; many times he struck a battle immediately after his journey, otherwhiles in most foul and stormy weather, when no man ever thought he would once stir. Neither held he off, and detracted fight, but in his latter days; being then of this opinion that the oftener he had gotten victory, the less he was to venture and make trial of fortune; also, that a victory could gain him nothing so much as some disastrous calamity might take from him. No enemy put he ever to flight, but he discamped him and drove him out of the field. By this means he gave them whom he had once discomfited no time to bethink themselves. In any doubtful and dangerous service, his manner was to send away the horses, and his own with the first; to the end that when all means of flight were gone, they might of necessity be forced the rather to stand to it and abide to the last.

61. The horse he used to ride upon was strangely marked, with feet resembling very near a man's, and the hooves cloven like toes, which horse was foaled about home; and when the

soothsayers of their learning had pronounced that he presaged unto his owner the empire of the whole world, very careful he was to rear him and nourish him. Now when as the beast would abide no man else to ride him, himself was he that backed him first. The full portrait and proportion of which horse he dedicated also afterwards before the temple of Venus Genetrix.

62. Many a time himself alone renewed the battle when it was discomfited, standing in their way that fled and holding them one by one back; yea and by twisting their throats he turned them again upon the enemies. Thus dealt he I say with his own soldiers, when they were many times verily so fearfully scared that a standard-bearer threatened as he stayed him to smite him with the footpoint of the spear that carried the eagle; and another left behind him the ensign in Caesar's hand as he detained it.

63. Of his constant resolution these be no less tokens, if not greater (which I shall now rehearse). After the battle of Pharsalia, when he had sent his forces before into Africa, and himself crossed the seas through the Hellespont in a small passenger bark, where he met with Lucius Cassius one of the adverse part, with ten strong war-ships armed with brazen beakheads, he avoided him not, nor gave way; but affronting him, began to exhort him for to yield, and so upon his humble supplication received him aboard.

64. At Alexandria, being busy about the assault and winning of a bridge where by a sudden sally of the enemy he was driven to take a boat, and many besides made haste to get into the same, he leapt into the sea, and by swimming almost a quarter of a mile recovered clear the next ship; bearing up his left hand all the while, for fear the writings which he held therein should take wet, and drawing his rich coat armor after him by the teeth, so that the enemy should not have it as a spoil.

65. His soldiers he approved in regard neither of manner and behavior, nor of wealth and outward estate, but only of bodily strength; and he used them all with his severity, with like indulgence also and sufferance. For he awed and chastised them not in all places nor at all times, but only when the enemy was very near at hand; and then especially was he most severe and precise in exacting and executing of discipline. Insomuch as he would not give them warning of the time, either of journey or of battle, but kept them ready, intentive and pressed to be led forth upon a sudden every minute of an hour, whithersoever he would; this did he also many times without any cause, especially upon rainy days and festivals. And admonishing his soldiers ever and anon to observe and have an eye unto him, he would suddenly in the daytime or by night withdraw himself out of the way, yea and stretch out his journey more than ordinary, to tire them out who were late in following after.

66. As for his soldiers that were terrified with the rumor of their enemies, his manner was to animate and encourage them, not by denying or diminishing, but by augmenting the same to the highest degree, even above the truth. And thus upon a time, when the expectation of Juba's coming was terrible, he called his soldiers together and in a public speech unto them said, "Be it known unto you all, that within these very few days the king will be here with a power of ten legions, 300,000 horse, 1000,000 light armors, and three hundred elephants. Forbear therefore some of you to inquire or imagine further of the matter, but credit unto me, that know this for a truth; or else verily I will embark you in the oldest ship I can get and cause you to be carried away with any wind into what lands and countries it shall be your fortunes to fall upon."

67. As touching his soldiers' trespasses and delinquencies, he neither observed and took knowledge of them all, nor yet

punished them fully to the proportion. But as he made straight inquisition after those who traitorously forsook their colors, and were mutinous, and proceeded against them with rigor, so, at others he would wink. Sometimes also, after a great battle and victory obtained, he released them all of military duties; permitting them in all licentiousness to riot and roist wantonly here and there; being wont to give it out, that his soldiers, perfumed though they were with odors and besmeared with sweet oils, could fight valiantly. Neither called he them, in his public oration, plain soldiers, but by a more pleasing name, fellow-soldiers. Furthermore he maintained them so trim and brave that he stuck not to set them out in polished armor, damasked with silver and gold; as well for goodly show, as because they should in battle take better hold and keep the same more surely for fear of damage and loss. Moreover he loved them so affectionately, that when he heard of Titurius' overthrow, he suffered the hair of his head and beard to grow long, and would not cut the same before he had revenged their death [Titurius' and the legions' with him]. By which means, he both had his soldiers most devoted unto him, and also made them right valorous.

68. When he was entered into the civil war, the centurions of every legion presented unto him one horseman apiece, provided out of their own private stock; and generally all his soldiers offered their service freely, without allowance of corn or wages out of his purse; the wealthier sort taking upon them the finding and maintenance of the poorer. Neither all that long time of soldiery, was there any of them that once revolted from him; and very many being taken prisoners by the enemy, and having life granted unto them upon condition they would serve against him, refused it. Hunger and other extremities which necessarily follow war, not only while they were be-sieged, but also when themselves beleaguered others, they en-

dured so resolutely, that during their strong siege and fortification against Dyrrhachium, Pompey, when he saw what kind of bread made of a certain herb they lived upon, said, he had to deal with wild beasts; commanding withal the same quickly to be had away and not showed to anyone, for fear lest his own soldiers' hearts should be utterly daunted, seeing once the patience and constancy of their enemies. And how valiantly they bore themselves in fight, this one thing may testify, that having taken one foil in a battle before Dyrrhachium, they voluntarily offered to be executed therefor; insomuch as their general was more troubled about comforting them than punishing them. In all other battles they, fewer in number by many parts, easily vanquished infinite forces of their enemies. To conclude, one cohort and no more of the sixth legion, which had the keeping of a fort, made good the place and held out for certain hours against four of Pompey's legions; and were all of them shot into their bodies with a multitude of arrows, of which were found one hundred and thirty thousand within their trench and ramparts. And no marvel, if a man consider their several deeds singly by themselves, either of Cassius Scaeva, a centurion, or of Gaius Acilius a common soldier, to say nothing of many more. Scaeva, when his eye was smitten out, his thigh and shoulder shot through, and his buckler pierced likewise with the shot of 120 arrows, yet defended the guard of the fort committed to his charge, and kept it still. Acilius in a fight at sea before Massilia, after his right hand was quite cut off, wherewith he had caught the poop of his enemy's ship, following herein that memorable example of Cynegirus among the Greeks, leapt notwithstanding into the said ship, shoving and driving before him with the boss and pike of his buckler those that he met in his way.

69. In ten years' space during the Gallic war, they never so much as once mutinied. In the civil wars sometimes they

did, yet so as they were soon reclaimed and came again into order, not so much by the remiss indulgence as the authority of their captain. For never would he yield one jot unto them in these their seditious tumults; nay, he always withstood and crossed them. And verily the ninth legion at Placentia, notwithstanding Pompey yet was in arms with his power in the field, he discharged full and wholly, and sent away with shame; yea and after many humble prayers and supplications with much ado restored he them to their places again, and not before execution done upon the offenders.

70. As for the soldiers of the tenth legion, when as in Rome they earnestly called for their discharge from warfare, and required their rewards even with mighty threats, and that to the exceeding danger of the whole city, at what time also the war was very hot in Africa, he neither would admit them into his presence, nor yet dismiss them albeit his friends seemed to scare him from taking that course; but with only one word, whereby he named them *Quirites* [citizens], instead of *Milites* [soldiers], he did so gently turn and wind, yea and bring them to his bent, that forthwith they made answer, they would be his soldiers still; and so of their own accord followed him into Africa, notwithstanding he refused their service. And yet for all this, he amerced and fined the most mutinous sort of them with the loss of a third part, both of the pillage and also of the lands appointed for them.

71. In affectionate love and faithful protection of his dependants, he was not wanting in his very youth. Upon a time he defended Masintha, a noble young gentleman, against king Hiempsal, so earnestly that in the debate between them he flew upon Juba the king's son and caught him by the beard. After that the said Masintha was pronounced definitively the king's tributary, he forthwith both rescued him out of their hands that would have haled him away, and also kept

him close a long time in his own lodging. And soon after his praetorship there expired, when he went into Spain, he took the young gentleman away with him in his own litter among other followers and favorites and lictors that attended upon him with their fasces.

72. His friends he used at all times with so great courtesy and tender respect, that when Gaius Oppius who accompanied him in his journey through a wild forest fell suddenly sick, he gave him room in the only inn that was, while himself lay all night upon the ground. Moreover, being now become emperor of all, some of them he advanced even from the lowest degree unto the highest place of honor. And when he was blamed and reproved therefor, he professed openly, that if he had used the help of robbers by the highway side, of cutters and swashbucklers in maintaining of his own dignity, he would not fail but requite them and be thankful even to such.

73. He never entertained malice and hatred against any man so deeply but willing he was to lay down the same upon occasion offered. Although Gaius Memmius had made most bitter invectives against him, and again written unto him as bitterly, yet soon after, when the said Memmius stood for the consulship, he friended him all that he could with his good word and procured him voices. When Gaius Calvus after certain libels and defamatory epigrams against him, dealt by the mediation of friends for a reconciliation, he of his own accord wrote first unto him. As for Valerius Catullus (by whose verses concerning Mamurra he could not choose but take knowledge that he was noted and branded with perpetual infamy) when he excused himself unto him and was ready to make satisfaction, he bade him to supper that very day; and as he used before time, so he continued still to make his father's house his lodging.

74. Moreover, in his revengements he was by nature most mild. Those rovers by whom he was taken prisoner, after

he had forced to yield, because he had sworn before that he would hang them upon a cross, he commanded that their throats be first cut, and then to be crucified. Cornelius Phagita, whose waylaying him by night, he lying sick and latitant hardly had escaped (although he gave him a good reward), but had like to have been brought unto Sulla, he could never find in his heart to hate. Philemon, a servant and secretary of his, who had promised his enemies to take Caesar's life away by poison, he punished only by simple death, without any torment. Being cited and called much upon to bear witness against Publius Clodius, for being naughty with his wife Pompeia, who was accused besides for the same cause to have polluted the sacred ceremonies, he denied that he ever knew anything of the matter or was able to bring in evidence, albeit both his mother Aurelia and his sister Julia had simply related all upon their credits even before the same jury and judges. And being demanded thereupon, wherefore then he had put away his wife? "Because I deem," he said, "that those of my house ought to be clear as well of suspicion as of crime."

75. The moderation and clemency which he showed as well in the managing of the civil war as in his victory, was admirable. When Pompey denounced in minatory terms that he would reckon him for an enemy, whosoever he was, that failed to maintain the commonwealth, Caesar for his part pronounced openly, that he would make sure account of them to be his who stood indifferent between and were neuters. And so many, as upon the commendation of Pompey before time, he had given any charge or place of command unto in his army under him, he granted them all free leave and liberty to depart unto him. Upon articles and conditions of yielding moved and propounded to Pompey at Ilerda, while between both parts there passed reciprocal dealing and commerce continually, when Afranius and Petrius had taken within their

camp certain of Caesar's soldiers, and (which they repented
soon after) put them to the sword, he would in no wise imitate
the same perfidious treachery of theirs practiced against him.
At the battle of Pharsalia he cried out, "Spare all citizens!"
And afterwards he granted unto every one of his own soldiers
(none excepted) this favor to save each of them one of the
adverse part, whom he would. Neither were any found or
known slain, but in the very medley, except Afranius, Faustus,
and Lucius Caesar the Younger; and even those verily men
think, were not with his good will put to death. Of whom
notwithstanding both the former, to wit, Afranius and Faustus,
after pardon obtained had rebelled and entered into arms again,
and Lucius Caesar for his part, when in cruel manner by fire
and sword he had made havoc of his freedmen and bond-
servants, spitefully slew the very wild beasts also which Caesar
had provided against the solemnity of a public show to be
exhibited before the people. To conclude, in his very latter
days he permitted all those also whom beforetime he had not
pardoned to return into Italy, to govern as magistrates in the
city, and to command as generals in the field. Yea the very
statues of Lucius Sulla and Pompey which the commons had
overthrown and cast up and down, he erected again in their
due places. And if after this there was any plot intended or
word spoken against him by his adversaries to his hurt, he
chose rather to repress than to revenge the same. And so, diverse conspiracies detected and night conventicles he found
fault with no farther than by giving notice in some edict and
proclamation that he had intelligence thereof. And as for such
as gave out bitter speeches of him he thought it sufficient in
an open assembly to give them an admonition, not to persist
therein. Finally, when in a most slanderous book written by
Aulus Caecina, and certain verses as railing and reproachful as
if devised by Pitholaus, his credit and reputation was much

cracked and impaired, he took the matter no more to the heart, than one citizen would have done at another's hand.

76. Howbeit, the rest of his deeds and words overweigh and depress his good parts down, so as he might be thought both to have abused his sovereignty, and worthily to have been murdered. For, he not only took upon him excessive honors, to wit, continued consulship, perpetual dictatorship, and presidency of manners [censorship in deed though not in name]. And more than so, the forename of Emperor, the surname Father of his Country; his statue among the kings', an eminent seat of estate raised above the rest in the orchestra among the senators. But he suffered also more stately dignities than beseeming the condition of a mortal wight to be decreed and ordained for him, namely, a golden throne in the Curia, and before the tribunal a sacred chariot, and therein a frame carrying an image of himself as a god at the solemn pomp of his games *Circenses*; temples, altars, his own images placed near unto the gods; a sacred bed-loft for such images to be bestowed upon; a *flamen* [a special priest], certain *Luperci* [a college of priests]; and the denomination of one month after his own name. Besides, no honorable offices there were but he took and gave at his own pleasure. His third and fourth consulships in name only and title he bore, contenting himself with the absolute power of dictatorship decreed unto him with his consulships all at one time. And in both years he substituted two consuls under him for the last three months, so as, in the meantime, he held no election but of tribunes and aediles of the commons. Instead of praetors he ordained provosts, who should administer the affairs of the city even while he was present. And upon the very last day of the year, to wit next before the Kalends of January, the place of a consulship being vacant by the sudden death of a consul he conferred upon one that made suit to enjoy the same but a few hours. With the

same licentiousness despising the custom of his country, he ordained magistrates to continue in office many years together. To ten men of praetor's degree he granted the consular ornaments. Such as were but enfranchised citizens, and divers mongrel Gauls no better than half barbarians, he admitted to senatorial degree. Furthermore, over the mint and receipt of the city revenues, he set certain peculiar servants of his own to be rulers. The charge and command of three legions which he left in Alexandria, he committed wholly to a son of Rufinus his freedman, a stale youth and catamite.

77. Neither did some words of his which he openly delivered, betray less presumptuous lordliness, as Titus Ampius writes. For example, that the commonwealth was now no more any real thing, but a name only, without form and shape; that Sulla was altogether unlettered in giving over his dictatorship. That men ought now to speak with him more considerately, and to hold every word that he said for a law. Nay he proceeded to this point of arrogance, that when upon a time in a certain sacrifice, the soothsayer brought him word of unlucky innards in the beast, and such as had no heart at all, he made answer and said, that those which were to follow afterwards should prove more joyful and fortunate if it pleased him [i. e., should signify better fortune]. Neither was it taken for a prodigious and strange token, if a beast wanted a heart.

78. But the greatest envy and inexpiable hatred he drew upon himself by this occasion most of all. What time as all the senators in general came unto him with many and those most honorable decrees, he received them sitting still before the temple of Venus Genetrix. Some think that when he was about to rise, Cornelius Balbus stayed and held him back; others are of the mind, that he never went about it. But when Gaius Trebatius advertised him to arise unto them, he looked back upon him with a strange kind of look; which deed of

his was thought so much the more intolerable, for that himself, when Pontius Aquila, one of the college of tribunes, stood not up nor did reverence to him as he rode in triumph and passed by the tribunes' pews, took such snuff and indignation thereat that he broke out aloud into these words, "Well done, tribune Aquila, recover thou then, the commonwealth out of my hands." And for certain days together, never promised ought unto any man without this proviso and exception, "If Pontius Aquila will give me leave."

79. To this contumelious and notorious behavior of his toward the senate thus despised, he adjoined a deed much more arrogant; for when as in his return from the solemn sacrifice of the Latin holidays, among other immoderate and new acclamations of the people, one out of the multitude had set upon his statue a coronet of laurel tied about with a white band; and when Epidius Marullus, a tribune of the commons, together with his colleague Caesetius Flavus commanded the said band to be plucked off, and the man to be had away to prison, Caesar, taking it to heart, either that this overture to a kingdom sped no better, or (as he made semblance and pretended himself) that he was put by the glory of refusing it, sharply rebuked the tribunes, and deprived them both of their authority. Neither for all this, was he willing afterwards to put away the infamous note of affecting and seeking after the title of a king; albeit he both made answer unto a commoner, saluting him by the name of a king, that he was Caesar and no king; and also at the *Lupercalia*, when Antonius the consul imposed the diadem oftentimes upon his head before the rostra, did put it back again, and send it into the Capitol to Jupiter Optimus Maximus. Moreover, sundry rumors ran rife abroad, that he would depart forever to Alexandria or to Ilium, having at once translated and removed thither the power and wealth of the empire, dispeopled Italy with mustering of soldiers,

55

and withal betaken the administration of Rome unto his friends; as also, that in the next session of the senate, Lucius Cotta, one of the Quindecimvirs, would move the house to this effect, that forasmuch as it was contained in the fatal books of Sybil, that the Parthians could not possibly be vanquished but by a king, therefore Caesar should be styled king.

80. This gave occasion to the conspirators for to hasten the execution of their design, lest of necessity they should be driven to assent thereto. Their counsels therefore and conferences about this matter, which before time they held dispersed here and there and projected oftentimes by two and three in a company, they now complotted altogether, for that by this time the very people joyed not in the present state, seeing how things went; but both in secret and openly also distasted such sovereignty, and called earnestly for protectors and maintainers of their liberties. Upon the admission of aliens into the order of senators, there was a bill proposed in this form *Bonum Factum* etc., that no man would show the senate-house to any new senators. And these verses were commonly chanted:

> *Gallos Caesar in triumphum ducit, idem in curia*
> *Galli bracas deposuerunt, latum clavum sumpserunt.*

The French in triumph Caesar leads, in senate they anon
No sooner laid their breeches off, but purpled robes put on.

As Quintus Maximus substituted by Caesar to be a consul for three months entered the theater, and the sergeant commanded (as the manner was) that the people should observe and regard him according to his place, they all with one accord cried out, that he was no consul. After Caesetius and Marullus, the tribunes aforesaid, were removed out of their office, at the next solemn assembly held for election very many voices were found declaring them two consuls. Some there were who subscribed under the statue of Lucius Brutus these words, "Would God thou were alive." Likewise under the statue of Caesar himself,

Brutus for expelling the kings, was created consul the first.
This man for expelling the consuls is become king, the last.

There conspired against him more than three score, the heads of which conspiracy were Gaius Cassius, Marcus Brutus and Decimus Brutus; who having made doubt at first whether by dividing themselves into parts they should cast him down the bridge as he called the tribes to give their voices at the election in Mars field, and so take him when he was down and kill him right out; or set upon him in the high street called *Via Sacra*; or else in the very entrance to the theater. After that the senate had summons to meet in counsel within the Court of Pompey upon the Ides of March, they soon agreed of this time and place before all others.

81. But Caesar surely had fair warning of his death before it came, by many evident prodigies and strange foretokens. Some few months before, when certain new inhabitants brought by virtue of the Law *Julia* to dwell in the colony Capua, overthrew most ancient sepulchers for to build them houses to their lands; and did the same so much the more diligently and with better will, for that in searching they lit upon manufactures and vessels – a good store of antique work; there was found in that very monument, wherein by report, Capys the founder of Capua lay buried, a brazen tablet with a writing upon it in Greek words and Greek letters to this effect: "When the bones and relics of Capys happen to be discovered, it shall come to pass, that one descended from Julus shall be murdered by the hands of his near kinsfolk, and his death soon after revenged with the great calamities and miseries of all Italy." And lest any man should think this to be a fabulous tale and forged matter, know he that Cornelius

Balbus, a very inward and familiar friend of Caesar, is the author thereof.

And the very day next preceding his death, those troops of horses which in his passage over the river Rubicon he had consecrated and let go loose ranging here and there without a keeper (as he understood for certain) forbore their meat and would not to die for it touch any, yea, and shed tears abundantly. Also, as he offered sacrifice, the soothsayer Spurina warned him to take heed of danger toward him, and which would not be deferred after the Ides of March. Now, the very day before the said Ides, it fortuned that as the bird called kingbird was flying with a little branch of laurel into the Court of Pompey, a sort of other birds of diverse kinds from out of the grove hard by pursued after and there pulled it in pieces. But that night next before the day of his murder, both himself dreamed as he lay asleep, one while, that he was flying above the clouds, another while, that Jupiter and he shook hands; and also his wife Calpurnia imagined that the finial of his house fell down, and that her husband was stabbed in her very bosom, and suddenly withal the chamber door of itself flew open.

Hereupon, as also by reason of sickliness, he doubted a good while whether he should keep at home and put off those matters which he had purposed to debate before the senate, or no? At the last, being counselled and persuaded by Decimus Brutus not to disappoint the senators who were now in full assembly and stayed for his coming long since, he went forth when it was well near eleven of the clock. And when one met him by the way, and offered him a written pamphlet which laid open the conspiracy, and who they were that sought his life, he shuffled the same among other scrolls and writings which he held in his left hand as if he would have read it anon. After this when he had killed many beasts for sacrifices and could speed of the gods' favor in none, he entered the Curia [of Pompey] in contempt of all religion; and therewith laughed Spurina to scorn, charging him to be a false prophet, for that the Ides of March were come and yet no harm befell unto him; albeit he answered, that come indeed they were, but not yet passed.

82. When they saw once that he had taken his place and was set, they stood round about him as serviceable attendants ready to do him honor; and then immediately Cimber Tullus, who had undertaken to begin first, stepped nearer unto him, as though he would have made some request. When Caesar seemed to mislike and put him back, yea and by his gesture to post him off unto another time, he caught hold of his gown at both shoulders; whereupon as he cried out, "This is violence," Cassius came in full a-front, and wounded him a little beneath the throat. Then Caesar catching Cassius by the arm thrust it through with his stylus or writing punches; and with that being about to leap forward, he was met with another wound and stayed. Now when he perceived himself beset on every side and assailed with drawn daggers he wrapped and covered his head with his gown; but withal he let down the large lap with his left hand to his legs beneath, hiding thereby the inferior part also of his body, that he might fall more decently. And so, with three and twenty wounds he was stabbed; during which time he gave but one groan, without any word uttered, and that was at the first thrust; although some have written, that as Marcus Brutus came running upon him he quoth (in Greek) "Thou too, my son?" When all others fled sundry ways, there lay he a good while dead, until three of his own pages bestowed him in a litter; and so with one arm hanging down, carried him home. Neither in so many wounds was there, as Antistius his physician deemed, any one found mortal but that which he received second, in his breast. The conspirators were minded to have dragged his

corpse after he was thus slain into the river Tiber, confiscate his goods, and repeal all his acts; but for fear of Marcus Antonius the consul and Lepidus, master of the horsemen, they held their hands and gave over those courses.

83. At the demand therefore of Lucius Piso, whose daughter Caesar married, his last will and testament was opened and read in the house of Antonius; which will, upon the Ides of September next before, he had made in his own house at Lavicium and committed to the keeping of the chief Vestal Virgin. Quintus Tubero writes, that from his first consulship unto the beginning of the civil war he was ever wont to write down as his heir Gnaius Pompey, and to read the said will unto his soldiers in their public assembly. But in this last testament of his, he ordained three coheirs, the nephews all of his sisters. To wit, Gaius Octavius, of three fourth parts, Lucius Pinarius, and Quintus Pedius of one fourth part remaining. In the latter end and bottom of this testamentary instrument, he adopted also Gaius Octavius into his house and name; and many of those that afterwards murdered him he nominated for guardians to his son, if it fortuned he had any born [i. e. posthumously, after his death]. Yea and Decimus Brutus to be one of his second heirs in remainder. He bequeathed in his legacies unto the people his gardens about the Tiber to lie common; and three hundred sesterces to each man.

84. The solemnity of his burial being proclaimed, there was a pile of wood for his funeral fire reared in Mars field, near unto the tomb of Julia, his daughter. Before the rostra was placed a chapel all gilt resembling the temple of Venus Genetrix, and within it a bedstead of ivory, richly spread with cloth of gold and purple, and at the head thereof a trophy supporting the robe wherein he was slain. Now because it was thought, that those should not have day enough who came to his offerings and brought their oblations, commandment was

*When all others fled sundry ways, there
lay he a good while dead . . .*

given that without observing the strict order, every man might bring which way and by what street of the city he would, his gift into Mars field above said. During the games and plays then exhibited there were chanted certain verses fitly applied as well to move pity as hatred withal of his death, and namely out of the tragedy of Pacuvius, entitled, *The Judgement of Armor*:

Men' Men' servasse, ut essent qui me perderent?

Alas the while, that I these men should save;
By bloody death, to bring me to my grave?

as also another out of that of Accius to the same sense. Instead of a laudatory oration, Antonius the consul pronounced by the public crier, the act of the senate wherein they decreed for him all honor, both divine and human; likewise the solemn oath wherewith they all obliged themselves to defend the life and person of him and none but him; whereunto he added some few words of his own. The foresaid bed, the magistrates for the time being and such as had borne office of state already, had conveyed into the forum before the rostra; which when some intended to burn within the cell of Jupiter Capitolinus, others in the Court of Pompey, all of a sudden there were two fellows with swords girt to their sides and carrying two javelins, who with burning tapers set it on fire. With that immediately the multitude that stood round about got dry sticks together and heaped them thereupon, with the tribunal seats and other pews, of inferior magistrates, and whatsoever beside was ready and next at hand. After them, the minstrels and stage players disrobed themselves of those vestments which out of the furniture of his triumphs they had put on for the present use and occasion, rent the same in pieces, and flung all into the flaming fire. The old legionary soldiers also did the like by their armor, wherein they bravely went to solemnize his funeral. Yea and most of the city dames did no less by their jewels and ornaments which they had about them; their children's pendant brooches also and rich coats embroidered and bordered with purple also. In this exceeding sorrow and public mourning, a number there were besides from foreign nations, who every one after their country's manner, lamented round one after another, by companies in their turns; but above all other the Jews, who also for many nights together frequented the place of his sepulture and where his body was burnt.

85. The common people straight after his funeral obsequies went with burning fire-brands and torches to the dwelling houses of Brutus and Cassius. From whence being hardly repelled, they meeting with Helvius Cinna by the way, and mistaking his name, as if he had been Cornelius Cinna (one who the day before had made a bitter invective as touching Caesar and whom they sought for) him they slew, set his head upon a spear, and so carried it about with them. After this they erected in the forum a solid column almost twenty feet high, of Numidian marble, with this title graven thereupon, *Parenti Patriae* [TO THE FATHER OF HIS COUNTRY]. At which pillar for a long time they used still to sacrifice, to make vows and prayers, to determine and end certain controversies interposing always their oath by the name of Caesar.

86. Caesar left behind him in the minds of certain friends about him a suspicion, that he was neither willing to have lived any longer, nor cared at all for life; because he stood not well to health, and therefore neglected as well all religious warnings from the gods, as also what reports soever his friends presented unto him. There be that think how trusting upon that last act of the senate, and their oath aforesaid, he discharged the guard of Spaniards from about him, who armed with swords, gave attendance upon his person. Others contrariwise are of opinion, that seeing as he did how he was forelaid on every side, and confessing it were better once for all to undergo

those imminent dangers than always to stand in fear thereof, he was wont to say, it concerned not himself so much as it did the state that he should live and be safe; as for him, he had gotten long since power and glory enough; marry the commonwealth (if ought but well came to him) should not be at quiet, but incur the troubles of civil war, the issue whereof would be far worse than ever it had been.

87. This one thing verily all men well near are agreed upon, that such a death befell unto him as himself in manner wished. For not only upon a time when he had read in Xenophon, how Cyrus being at the point of death gave some order for his funeral, he setting light by so lingering and slow a kind of death, had wished to die quickly and of a sudden; but also the very day before he was killed, in a certain discourse moved at supper in Marcus Lepidus' house upon this point, what was the best end of a man's life? preferred that which was sudden and unlooked for.

88. He died in the fifty-sixth year of his age and was canonized among the gods, not only by their voice who decreed such honor unto him, but also by the persuasion of the common people. For at those games and plays which were the first that Augustus his heir exhibited for him thus deified, there shone a blazing star for seven days together, arising about the eleventh hour of the day; and believed it was to be the soul of Caesar received up into heaven. For this cause also upon his image there is a star set to the very crown of his head. Thought good it was to dam up the court wherein he was murdered; to name the Ides of March *Parricidium*, and that the senate should never meet in counsel upon that day.

89. Of those murderers, there was not one in manner that either survived him above three years, or died of his natural death. All stood condemned; and by one mishap or other perished, some by shipwreck, others in battle; and some again,

shortened their own days with the very same dagger wherewith they had wounded Caesar. [The latter being, namely,
Cassius, Brutus, and the two Cascas. A notable judgement of
Almighty God upon the unnatural murderers of their sovereign. – *Translator*.]

THE HISTORY OF
OCTAVIUS CAESAR AUGUSTUS

AUGUSTUS

T HAT THE PRINCIPAL NAME AND LINEAGE of the Octavii dwelt in times past at Velitrae, there be many evidences to show; for, both a street in the most frequented place of the said town long since carried the name Octavius, and also there was to be seen an altar there consecrated by one Octavius, who being general of the field in a war against the borderers, when he happened to be sacrificing to Mars, upon news brought that the enemy gave a sudden charge, caught the innards of the beast sacrificed half-raw as they were, out of the fire, cut and offered them accordingly, and so entered into battle and returned with victory. There is besides, a public act extant upon record, wherein decreed and provided it was, that every year after the innards in like manner should be presented unto Mars, and the rest of the sacrifice remaining, be carried back unto the Octavii.

2. These Octavii, being by king Tarquinius Priscus naturalized Romans, soon after translated and admitted by Servius Tullus into the senate among the patricians and nobles, in process of time ranged themselves with the commons, and with much ado at length, by the means of Julius of sacred memory returned to the patrician degree again. The first of these that by the people's election bore any magistracy was Gaius Rufus, who having been quaestor, begot Gnaius and Gaius. From them descended two families of the Octavii, and those for their estate of life far different. For Gnaius and all the rest from him one after another, attained to places of high-

est honor; but Gaius and his posterity everyone even unto the father of Augustus (such was either their fortune or their will) stayed in the order and degree of equestrians and rose no higher. The great grandfather of Augustus in the second Punic war served in quality of a military tribune in Sicily under Aemilius Papus. His father contenting himself with bearing office like another burgess in his own borough, being left wealthy by his father, grew to a good estate, and lived to be an old man, in much peace and tranquillity. But of these matters let others make report. Augustus himself writes no more but thus. That the house from whence he came was of Roman equestrians, wealthy and ancient withal, wherein the first that ever came to be senator was his father. Marcus Antonius hits him in the teeth with his great grandfather, saying he was but a libertine born, and by occupation a roper, and come out of a village of the Thurines; also that his grandfather was no better than a money-changer. Neither have I found any more, as touching the ancestors of Augustus by the father's side.

3. Octavius' father, from the very beginning of his age, was of great wealth and reputation; so that I cannot but marvel, that he also hath been reported by some a money-changer, yea and one of the dealers of money and servitors employed in Campus Martius by those that stand for offices; for having been from his very cradle brought up in wealth highly and plentifully, he both attained unto honorable dignities with facility, and administered the same with credit and reputation. Presently upon his praetorship, the province of Macedonia fell unto his lot. And in his journey thither, the fugitives, to wit the relics of Spartacus' and Catiline's forces, who then held the Thurine territory he defeated; having commission extraordinarily given unto him in the senate to do so; this province he governed with no less justice than fortitude. For having discomfited in a great battle the Bessi and the Thracians, he

dealt so well with the allies and confederates of that kingdom
that there be certain letters of Marcus Tullius Cicero extant,
wherein he exhorts and admonishes his brother Quintus (who at
the same time, little to his credit and good name, administered
the proconsulship of Asia) for to imitate his neighbor Octavius
in doing well by the allies, and winning their love thereby.

4. As he departed out of Macedonia before that he could
profess himself to be a suitor for the consulship, he died a
sudden death, leaving these children behind him alive, namely
two daughters, Octavia the elder, which he had by Ancharia,
Octavia the younger and Augustus likewise by Atia. This Atia
was the daughter of Marcus Atius Balbus and Julia, the sister
of Gaius Caesar. Balbus by his father's side was an Aricine, a
man that showed senators' images and arms in his house; by
his mother linked to Pompey the Great in the nearest degree
of consanguinity. And having borne the office of praetorship
he among the twenty commissioners divided by virtue of the
Law Julia the lands in the territory of Capua among the commons. But Marcus Antonius, despising the parentage and
pedigree of Augustus by the mother's side also, twits him and
lays in his dish, that his great grandsire was an African born;
saying one while that he kept a shop of sweet oils, ointments
and perfumes; another while, that he was a baker in Aricia.
Cassius verily of Parma, in a certain epistle taxes Augustus
as being the nephew not of a baker only, but also of a money-
changer, in these terms. "Thou hast meal for thy mother. And
then comes a money-changer of Nerulone, who out of a most
painful bakehouse in Aricia kneads and molds it with his hands
sullied by telling and exchanging money."

5. Augustus was born when Marcus Tullius Cicero and
Antony were consuls, the ninth day before the Kalends of
October, a little before the sun rising, in the palatine quarter
of the city, at a place called Capita Bubula, where now it hath

a sacred chapel, built and erected a little after he departed out of this world. For, as it is found in the records of the senate, when Gaius Lectorius, a young gentleman of the patrician order, pleaded to have some easier punishment for adultery, and alleged, over and besides his young years and parentage this also in his plea before the senators, that he was the possessor and as it were the warden and sexton of that ground which Augustus of happy memory touched first, and requested that it might be given and granted unto the said Augustus as to his domestic and peculiar god; decreed it was that the same part of the house should be consecrated to that holy use.

6. There is yet to be seen the place of his nursery, within a suburban house belonging to his ancestors, near unto Velitrae; a very little cabin, about the bigness of a larder or pantry. The neighbors are possessed with a certain conceit, as if he had been also there born. To enter into this room unless it be of necessity and with devout chastity, men make it scrupulous and are afraid, upon an old conceived opinion, as if unto as many as came thither rashly and inconsiderately, a certain horror and fearfulness were presented. And verily, this was soon after confirmed by this occasion: for when the new landlord and possessor of that farmhouse, either by chance and unawares, or else to try some experiment, went into it, there to take up his lodging, it happened that in the night within very few hours after, being driven out from thence by some sudden violence (he knows not how), he was found in manner half-dead, together with bed and all, before the door.

7. Being yet an infant, surnamed he was Thurinus, in memorial of the beginning of his ancestors; or else because in the country about Thurii, when he was newly born, his father Octavius fought a battle against the fugitives. That he was surnamed Thurinus, myself am able to report by a good and sufficient evidence, as having gotten an old little bust in brass,

representing him being a child, which had in iron letters and those almost worn out, this name engraven. This said bust, being given by me unto the prince [the emperor Hadrian], is now devoutly kept and worshipped among his other bed-chamber images. Moreover called he is oftentimes in taunting wise by Marcus Antonius in his epistles, Thurinus; and himself writes unto him back again as touching that point, nothing but this, that he marvels why that former name of his should be objected unto him as a reproach. Afterwards, he assumed the surname of Gaius Caesar, and after it of Augustus, the one by the last will of his great uncle by the mother's side, the other by the virtue of Munatius Plancus' sentence. For when some gave their opinion that he ought to be styled Romulus, as if he also had been a founder of the city, Plancus prevailed, that he should be called rather Augustus; not only for that it was a new surname, but also greater and more honorable, because religious and holy places, wherein also anything is consecrated by augury, is called Augusta, *ab auctu*, of growing, or else *ab avium gestu gustuve*, of birds' gesture and feeding. Like as Ennius also teaches writing in this manner:

Augusto augurio postquam incluta condita Roma est.

After that noble Rome was built by sacred flight of birds.

8. He was four years old when his father died; and in the twelfth year of his age he praised in a public assembly his grandmother Julia deceased. Four years after having put on his virile robe, he had military gifts bestowed upon him at the African triumph of Caesar, albeit by reason of his young years he had not once served in the wars. Soon after, when his uncle Caesar was gone into Spain against Gnaius Pompey's children, he followed within a while (being as yet not well recovered out of a grievous sickness), even through ways infested by enemies, with very few in his train to accompany him, and

having suffered shipwreck besides; whereby he mightily won his uncle's love, who quickly approved his towardly behavior and disposition, over and above his diligence in travel. When Caesar, after he had recovered Spain and brought it to his subjection, intended a voyage against the Daci, and from thence against the Parthians, he being sent afore to Apollonia, became a student there and followed his book. And so soon as he had certain intelligence that Caesar was slain, and himself made his heir, standing in doubt and suspense a long time, whether he should implore the help of the legions or no, at length he gave over that course verily, as too hasty and untimely, but when he was returned again to Rome, he entered upon his inheritance, notwithstanding his mother made some doubt thereof and his father-in-law Martius Philippus, a man of consular degree, much dissuaded him therefrom. And from that time having levied and assembled his forces, he governed the commonwealth first jointly with Marcus Antonius and Marcus Lepidus for the space almost of twelve years, and at the last for forty-four years by himself alone.

9. Having thus laid open the very sum as it were, of his life, I will go through the parts thereof in particular; not by the times but by the several kinds thereof, to the end the same may be showed and known more distinctly. Five civil wars he made, to wit, at Mutina, Philippi, Perusium, in Sicily, and at Actium. Of which the first and last were against Marcus Antonius; the second against Brutus and Cassius; the third against Lucius Antonius brother to the triumvir; the fourth against Sextus Pompeius, Gnaius Pompey's son. Of all these wars he took the occasion and quarrel from hence, namely, reputing and judging in his mind nothing more meet and convenient than the revenge of his uncle's death and the maintenance of his acts and proceedings.

10. No sooner was he returned from Apollonia but he pur-

posed to march upon Brutus and Cassius unawares; and (because upon foresight of danger they were fled secretly out of the way) to take the course of law, and in their absence to indict them of murder. As for the plays and games for Caesar's victory, because they durst not exhibit them whose lot and office it was so to do, himself set them forth. And to the end that he might go through all other matters also more resolutely, he professed himself to labor for the tribuneship in the room of one who fortuned to die, albeit he was one of the nobility, though not of the senate. But seeing that Marcus Antonius the consul withstood his attempts, whereas he hoped he would have been his principal friend in that suit, and vouchsafed not unto him so much as the assistance of his own public authority, or help procured from others in anything without he agreed and covenanted to yield unto him some exceeding consideration, he betook himself unto the protection of those nobles and chief senators unto whom he perceived that Antony was odious; in this regard especially, that Antony endeavored all that he could by force of arms to expel Decimus Brutus besieged at Mutina, out of that province which by Caesar was granted and by the senate confirmed unto him. And thereupon by the advice and persuasion of some he set certain persons privily in hand to murder Antony; which perilous practice of his being detected and fearing still the like danger to himself, he mustered the old soldiers with as bountiful a largess as possibly he could, for the defense as well of his own person as of the state. And being appointed to lead this army thus levied, in quality of propraetor, and together with Hirtius and Pansa, who had entered upon the consulship, to aid Decimus Brutus, he made an end of this war committed unto him within three months, in two fought fields. In the former of which, Antony writes that he fled, and without coat armor or horse appeared at length after two days and showed himself. But in the battle next following, well known it is that he performed the part not only of a captain but also of a soldier; and in the very heat and midst of the medley, by occasion that the standard-bearer of his own legion was grievously hurt, he supported the eagle with his own shoulders and so carried it a good while.

11. During this war, when Hirtius had lost his life in the conflict, and Pansa soon after of his wound, it was bruited rifely about that both of them were by his means slain; to the end that having defeated Antony, and the commonwealth being bereft of both consuls, he alone might seize upon the victorious armies. And verily the death of Pansa was so deeply suspected that Glyco the physician was committed to ward and durance, as if he had put poison into his wound. Aquilius Niger adds moreover that the one of the consuls, to wit, Hirtius, was in the very confused medley of the battle killed by Augustus himself.

12. But so soon as he understood that Antony after his flight was taken in by Marcus Lepidus, that other captains also and armies consented to take part with that side, he forsook without all delay the cause of the nobles and principal senators. And for the better pretense of this change and alteration of his mind, craftily and unjustly alleged the words and deeds of certain of them; as if some had given it out of him that he was a boy; others that he was to be adorned and got rid of, that neither himself nor the old beaten soldiers might be rewarded according to their deserts. And the better to approve his repentance of the former side and faction that he took, he fined the Nursines in a great sum of money and more than they were able to pay, for that upon the monuments or tombs of those citizens that were slain in the battle at Mutina (which at their common charges was reared) they wrote this title, that they died for the liberty and freedom of their city.

13. Being entered into society with Antony and Lepidus, he

finished the Philippian war also (although he was but weak
and sickly), and that with two battles; in the former being
discamped and driven out of the field, hardly he escaped by
flight and recovered the regiment or wing of Antony. Neither
used he moderately the success of his victory, but when he had
sent the head of Brutus to Rome for to be bestowed under the
statue of Caesar, he dealt cruelly with the noblest and most
honorable prisoners, and not without reproachful words. So
far forth verily, that to one of them, making humble suit and
prayer for his sepulture, he answered (by report) in this wise:
That it would be anon, at the dispose of the fowls of the air.
And when others, to wit, the father and son together entreated for their lives, he commanded them either to cast lots
or try by combat whether of them should have life granted;
and so beheld them both as they died, while the father who
offered himself to die was slain, and the son voluntarily took
his death. Whereupon the rest, and amongst them Marcus
Favonius, that worthy follower of Cato, when they were
brought forth with their irons and chains to execution, after
they had in honorable terms saluted Antony by the name
of emperor, openly reviled and let fly at him most foul and
railing words. Having parted between them their charges
and offices after this victory, when Antony undertook to
settle the East in good order, and himself to bring the old
soldiers back into Italy and to place them there, in the lands
and territories belonging to the free towns and boroughs, he
kept himself in favor neither with the said old soldiers, nor
the former possessors of those lands; while the one sort complained that they were disseized; and the other that they were
not well treated according to their hopes for so good deserts.

14. At which very time, he forced Lucius Antonius (who
confidently presuming upon the consulship which he then
bore, and his brother's power withal, went about to make an

insurrection and alteration in the state) to fly unto Perusia, and there for very hunger compelled him to yield. But yet not without great jeopardy of his own person, both before and after the war; for when at certain stage plays, he had commanded an ordinary soldier who was set within the fourteen ranks, to be removed by an officer, and thereupon a rumor was carried and spread by his malicious ill-willers as if presently after torture he had put the same soldier to death. There lacked very little, but that in the concourse and indignation of the military multitude, he had come to a mischief and been murdered. This only saved his life: that the man for a while missed suddenly was to be seen again alive and safe without any harm done unto him. About the walls of Perusia, as he sacrificed, he had like to have been intercepted by a strong company of sword-fencers that sallied out of the town.

15. After he had forced Perusia, he proceeded to the execution of very many, and ever as any went about either to crave pardon or to excuse themselves, with this one word he stopped their mouths, "Die you must." Some write that three hundred of both degrees, chosen out of them who had yielded, were killed as sacrifices upon the Ides of March, at the altar built in the honor of Julius Caesar of famous memory. There have been others who wrote, that of very purpose he took arms and made this war to the end that his close adversaries and those who rather for fear than of good will held in, upon occasion given and opportunity by Lucius Antonius their leader, might be detected; that having once vanquished them and confiscated their goods, the rewards promised unto the old soldiers he might the better perform.

16. The war in Sicily he began betimes, but drew it out for a long time; as being often interrupted; one while, for the repairing and rigging of his fleet which by two shipwrecks in tempest (and that in summertime) he had lost; another while

by occasion of peace made at the earnest cry of the people, for
the provision of their victuals cut off and kept from them,
and the famine thereby daily growing, until such time as
having built new ships, set free twenty thousand slaves, and
those put to the oar for to learn to row galleys, he made the
haven Julius at Baiae by letting the sea into the lakes Lucrinus
and Avernus. In which when he had trained and exercised
his sea forces whole winters, he overcame Pompey between
Milae and Naulochus. At the very hour and instant time of
which naval battle, he was suddenly surprised with such a
sound sleep, that his friends were fain to waken him and raise
him out of bed for to give the signal. Whereupon occasion
and matter was ministered (as I think) to Antony, for to cast
this in his teeth, that he could not so much as with his eyes
open see directly before him the battle set in array, but lay like
a senseless block on his back, looking only into the sky aloft;
nor once arose and came in sight of his soldiers, before that
Marcus Agrippa had put his enemy's twelve ships to flight.
Others blame and charge him both for a speech and deed also
of his; as if he should cry out and say, that seeing his own
regiment of ships were cast away by tempests, he would even
against the will of Neptune obtain victory. And verily the
next day of the Circensian games, he took out of the solemn
pomp there showed the image of the said god; neither in any
other war lightly was he in more and greater dangers. For
having transported one army into Sicily, when he sailed back
again for to waft over the rest of his forces from the continent
of Italy, he was unawares overtaken and surprised by Demo-
chares and Apollophanes, the lieutenants and admirals of Pompey, but at length with very much ado he escaped with one
only bark. In like manner as he traveled by land unto Re-
gium near Locria, kenning afar of Pompey's galleys sailing
along the coasts, and weening them to be his own, he went

down to the shore, and had like to have been caught and taken by them. And even then as he made shift to fly and escape through byways and blind lanes, a bond-servant of Aemilius Paulus, a companion of his, taking it to heart that his master's father Paulus was in times past proscribed and outlawed, and embracing, as it were, the good occasion and opportunity of revenge now offered, gave the attempt to kill him. After the flight of Pompey, when Marcus Lepidus, one of his colleagues whom he had called forth of Africa to his aid, bearing himself proud upon the confidence of twenty legions, challenged a sovereignty over the rest, and that, with terror and menaces, he stripped him of all his army, and upon his humble sub-mission and supplication, pardoned his life, but confined him forever to Circeii. The society of Marcus Antonius wavering always in doubtful terms and uncertain, and notwithstanding many and sundry reconciliations, not well knit and confirmed, he broke off quite in the end; and the better to prove and make good that he had degenerated from the civil behavior and modesty of a Roman citizen, he caused the last will and testa-ment of the said Antony, which he had left at Rome, and therein nominated even the children of Cleopatra among his heirs, to be opened, and read in a public assembly. Howbeit when he was judged by the state an enemy, he sent back unto him those of his nearest acquaintance and inward friends and among other Gaius Sosius and Titus Domitius, being consuls at that time still. The Bononians also, for that of old they were dependents of the Antonii and in their retinue and protection, he by a public act acquitted and pardoned for not entering into a confederacy with all Italy, on his side. Not long after, he vanquished him [Antony] in a naval battle before Actium, what time by reason that the fight continued until it was late in the evening he was forced to lodge all night, conqueror as he was, on shipboard.

17. When he had retired himself from Actium into the island Samos for his winter harbor, being disquieted with the news of his soldiers' mutiny demanding rewards and discharge from service, those I mean, whom after the victory achieved he had from out of the whole number sent before to Brundisium, he went again into Italy. But in crossing the seas thither, twice he was tossed and troubled with tempests; first between the promontories of Peloponnesus and Aetolia, again, about the cliffs Ceraunii. In both which places, part of his pinnaces were cast away and drowned; and withal, the very tackling of that ship wherein he embarked was rent and torn asunder; yea, and the rudder thereof quite broken. Neither stayed he at Brundisium above twenty-seven days, that is to say until he had settled his soldiers and contented them in their desires and requests; but fetching a compass about Asia, and Syria, sailed into Egypt. Where after he had laid siege unto Alexandria, whither Antony and Cleopatra were together fled, he soon became master of that city. And as for Antony, who now (all too late) made means for conditions of peace, he enforced to make himself away, and saw him dead. And to Cleopatra whom most gladly he would have saved alive for to beautify his triumph he set the Psylli to suck out the venom and poison within her body; for that supposed it was she died with the sting of the asp. This honor he did unto them both, namely to bury them in one sepulchre; and the tomb by them begun, he commanded to be finished. Young Antony, the elder of those twain whom he had by Fulvia, he caused to be violently haled from the statue of Julius Caesar of famous memory, unto which, after many prayers but all in vain, he was fled as to sanctuary, and so killed him. Likewise Caesarion, whom Cleopatra gave out openly that she had conceived by his father Caesar, he fetched back again from the place whither he was fled, and put him to death. The rest of the children of Antony

and the queen together, he both saved (no less than if they had been linked in near alliance unto himself), and also according to the state of every one of them, he maintained and cherished respectively.

18. About the same time, when he beheld the tomb together with the corpse of Alexander the Great, taken newly forth of the secret chapel where it was bestowed, he set upon it a coronet of gold, and strewing flowers thereupon worshipped it. And being asked the question, whether he would look upon the Ptolemies [i. e. their bodies] also? he answered that he was desirous indeed to see a king but not the dead. When he had reduced Egypt in the form of a province, to the end that he might make it more fruitful and fit to yield corn and victuals for the city of Rome, he scoured and cleansed by help of soldiers all those ditches whereinto the Nile overflows, which by long time had been choked with mud. And that the memory of his victory at Actium might be more renowned among posterity, he built the city Nicopolis over against Actium, and ordained certain games and plays there every five years. And having enlarged the old temple of Apollo which stood upon the promontory of Actium, and the place wherein he had encamped, he beautified with naval spoils and then consecrated it to Neptune and Mars.

19. After this, sundry tumults and the very beginnings of commotions and insurrections, many conspiracies also detected before they grew to any head, he suppressed, and those, some one time, and some at another; first one of Lepidus the younger; then, another of Varro Muraena and Fannius Capio; soon after that, of Marcus Genatius; and so forward of Plautius Rufus and Lucius Paulus, his niece's husband; and besides all these, that of Lucius Audasius accused of forgery and counterfeit seals, a man neither for years able nor body sound; likewise of Asinius Epicadus, descended from the Parthians, a mongrel;

and last of all, of Telephus, a base page, servant to a woman; for free was not Augustus from the conspiracy and danger, no not of the most abject sort of people. As for Audasius and Epicadus, they had intended to carry away Julia his daughter and Agrippa his nephew (out of those lands wherein they abode confined) unto the armies; and Telephus purposed upon a deep conceit that the sovereignty of dominion was by the destinies and will of God due unto him, even to lay upon him and the senate violent hands. And more than that, one time there was taken near unto his bed-chamber by night a camp-slave belonging to the Illyrian army, who had deceived the porters and gotten thither with a hunting knife at his side, but whether he were out of his wits, or feigned himself mad, it was uncertain; for nothing could be wrung out of him by examination upon the rack and torture.

20. Foreign wars he made in his own person two in all and no more; that is to say, the Dalmatian, when he was yet a very youth; and the Cantabrian, after he had defeated Antony. In the Dalmatian war, he was wounded also; for in one battle he got a blow upon his right knee with a stone; and in another, not his leg only, but also both his arms were hurt with the fall from a bridge. The rest of his wars he managed by his lieu-tenants; yet so as that in some of them, namely the Pannonian and the German, he would either come between times, or else remain not far off, making his progress from Rome as far as to Ravenna, or Milan or to Aquileia.

21. He subdued partly by his own conduct in proper person, and in part by his lieutenants having commission immediately from him and directed by his auspices, Cantabria, Aquitaine, Pannonia, and Dalmatia together with all Illyricum, Rhoetia likewise, the Vindelici, the Salassians and the nations inhabiting the Alps. He repressed also the incursions of the Dacians, having slain three of their generals with a great number of them

besides. And the Germans he removed and set further off; even beyond the river Albis. Howbeit, of these the Suevians and the Sicambrians, because they yielded themselves, he brought over into Gaul, and placed them in the lands next unto the Rhine. Other nations being malcontent, he reduced unto his obedience. Neither made he war upon any people without just and necessary causes; and so far was he from desire of enlarging his empire, or advancing his martial glory, that he compelled certain princes and potentates of the barbarians to take an oath in the temple of Mars the Revenger for to continue in their allegiance, and in the protection and peace which they sued for. Yea and from some of them he essayed to exact a new kind of hostages, even women [unusual in those days], for he perceived that they neglected the pledges of the males. And yet he gave them liberty, as often as they would, to receive their hostages again. Neither proceeded he at any time against those, who either usually or treacherously above the rest took arms and rebelled, to any punishment more grievous than this, even to sell them as captives; with this condition, that they should not serve in any neighbor country, nor be manumitted within the space of thirty years. By which fame of virtue and moderation that went of him, he induced and drew the very Indians and Scythians, nations known by report and hearsay only, to make suit of their own accord by ambassadors for amity of him and the people of Rome. The Parthians also, when as he layed claim unto Armenia, yielded soon unto him; and those military ensigns which they had taken from Marcus Crassus and Marcus Antonius they delivered unto him again at his demand, and moreover, offered hostages unto him. And finally when there were many competitors together at one time claiming a title to the kingdom, they would not allow of any, but one by him elected.

22. The temple of Janus Quirinus, which from the foundation

of the city before his days had once and twice been shut, he in a far shorter space of time (having peace both by sea and land) shut a third time. Twice he rode on horseback in an ovation into the city; once presently upon the Philippian war, and again, after the Sicilian. He kept three triumphs riding in his chariot; to wit, the Dalmatian, the Actian, and the Alexandrian, and these continued all for three days together.

23. Of shameful foils and grievous overthrows, he received but two in all; and those in no place else but in Germany; namely when Lollius and Varus were defeated. That of Lollius was a matter of dishonor more than loss and damage; but the other of Varus drew with it in manner utter destruction; as wherein three legions with their general, the lieutenants and auxiliaries, all were slain. Upon the news of this infortunity, he proclaimed a set watch both day and night through the city of Rome; for fear of some tumult and uproar. And the commissions of presidents and deputies over provinces, he renewed and enlarged their time of government, to the end, that the allies of the people of Rome might be kept in allegiance by governors, such as were both skillful and also acquainted with them. He vowed also the great Roman games and plays to the honor of Jupiter Optimus Maximus if the commonwealth turned to better state. This happened, during the time of the Cimbrian and Marsian war. For, therewith (by report) he was so troubled and astonished, that for certain months together he let the hair of beard and head grow still and wore it long, yea and other while would run his head against the doors, crying out, "Quintilius Varus, deliver up thy legions again." And the very day of this unfortunate calamity he kept every year mournful, with sorrow and lamentation.

24. In warfare and feats of arms, he both altered and also instituted many points; yea and some he reduced to the ancient manner. Military discipline he exercised most severely. He

permitted not so much as any of his lieutenants, but with much ado and discontentment, to visit otherwhiles their wives; and never but in the winter months. A Roman knight, for cutting off the thumbs of two young men his sons, to avoid the military oath and war service, he set in open auction, himself (I say) and all his goods. Whom notwithstanding, because he saw the publicans about to buy, and bid very well for him, he appointed and delivered to his own freedman, that being confined and sent away unto his living and lands in the country, he might permit him to live as free. The tenth legion, for being stubborn and unwilling to obey, he dismissed all and whole with ignominy; other legions likewise, requiring malapertly their discharge, he disbanded without allowance of rewards due for their service. Whole bands or cohorts, if any of them gave ground and recoiled, he tithed, that is to say, executed every tenth man of them; and the rest, he allowed barley instead of wheat to feed upon. Those centurions who forsook their stations, he punished with death, even as well as the common soldiers of their bands. And for other kinds of delinquency he put them to shame sundry ways, as commanding them to stand all the day long before the praetorium sometimes in their single coats and ungirt; otherwhiles with ten foot poles in their hands [in token of degradation or putting down to a lower place]; or else carrying turfs of earth.

25. After the civil wars, he called none of his soldiers either in any public speech, or by way of edict or proclamation, by the name of fellow-soldiers, but plain soldiers. Nay he would not suffer them otherwise to be termed so much as by his sons, or his wife's sons; thinking it was a more affected manner of appellation than stood either with martial law, or the quietness of those times, or the majesty of himself and his house. Libertines he employed in soldiery unless it were at Rome about fires by night (notwithstanding there was feared some

tumult and uproar by occasion of great dearth and scarcity)
but twice only; once in garrison for defense of those colonies
which bounded fast upon Illyricum; a second time, for keeping
the banks of the river Rhine. And those, being as yet bond,
levied upon men and women of the wealthier sort, but without delay manumitted, he kept with him to serve under one
of the foremost banners in the advance guard; neither intermingled with such as were freeborn, nor in the same manner
armed. As for military gifts he gave unto his soldiers trappers,
collars, and whatsoever stood upon gold or silver, much sooner
than mural coronets, which were more honorable. These he
bestowed most sparely; and when he did, it was without suit
made therefore, and many times upon the common and base
soldiers. He gave unto Marcus Agrippa after a naval victory
in Sicily a blue streamer. Those captains only who had triumphed, albeit they were both companions with him in his
expeditions and also partakers of his victories, he thought not
meet to be rewarded with any gifts at all; because they also
had power to bestow the same upon whom they would. Moreover he deemed nothing less beseeming a perfect and accomplished captain, than haste-making and rashness. And
therefore, these mots and sentences were rife in his mouth:
"Make haste slowly." "A safe commander is better than a bold."
"What is done well enough is done quickly enough." His
saying was, that neither battle nor war was once to be undertaken, unless there might be evidently seen more hope of gain
than fear of damage. Such as sought after the smallest commodities, not with as little danger, he likened unto those that
angle or fish with a golden hook, for the loss whereof, if it
happened to be broken off, no draught of fish whatsoever was
able to make amends.

26. He managed magistracies and honorable places of government before due time; some of them also of a new kind;

and others in perpetuity. The consulship he usurped and entered upon in the twentieth year of his age, presenting forcibly and in hostile manner his legions before the city, sending some of purpose to demand it in the name of the army for him. What time verily, when the senate made some doubt and stay of the matter, Cornelius, a centurion and the chief man of that message, casting off his soldier's jacket and showing his sword's haft, stuck not to say thus openly in the senate house, "This here shall do the deed, if you will not." His second consulship he bore nine years after; the third, but one year between; the rest ensuing he continued one after another unto the eleventh. Afterwards having refused many consulships when they were offered unto him, his twelfth consulship a greater while after, even seventeen years, himself made suit for; so did he again, two years after it, for his thirteenth; to the end that being himself the highest magistrate, he might bring honorably into the forum his adopted sons Gaius and Lucius to initiate their public careers. The five middle consulships between, to wit from the sixth to the eleventh, he held the whole year through; the other, for the space of six, or nine, four, or three months; but the second, very few hours; for upon the very Kalends of January, when he had sat a while upon his curule chair before the temple of Jupiter Capitolinus, he resigned up the office, and substituted another in his place. Neither entered he upon all his consulships at Rome, but the fourth in Asia, the fifth, in the island Samos, the eighth and ninth at Tarracon.

27. The triumvirate for settling of the commonwealth, he administered for the space of ten years; wherein verily, he stood against his colleagues' proceedings for a good while, that there might be no proscription; but when it was once on foot, he executed it more sharply than they both. For, whereas they were exorable and would be oftentimes entreated by favor and prayer to respect the persons of many, he alone was

very earnest, that none might be spared. Among the rest he proscribed Gaius Toranius also, his own tutor and guardian, yea and the companion in the office of aedileship with his father Octavius. Junius Saturninus writes moreover, that after the proscription was ended, when Marcus Lepidus had in the senate house excused all that was past, and given good hope of clemency for the time to come, because there had been execution enough done already, he on the contrary side professed openly, that he had determined no other end of the said proscription, but that he might have liberty still to proceed in all things as he would. Howbeit, in testimony of repentance for this rigor and obstinacy of his, he honored afterward with the dignity of knighthood Titus Junius Philopoemen, for that he was reputed to have in times past hid his own patron, that was proscribed. In the same triumvirate, he incurred many ways the ill will and heart-burning of the people; for he commanded that Pinarius, a knight of Rome (what time as he himself made a speech in an assembly whereunto he had admitted a multitude of country folk, and espied him there to take notes of what he said, supposing him to be over busy and a spy), should be stabbed to death even in his sight. Yea, and he terrified Tedius Afer, consul elect (because he had maliciously in some spiteful terms railed at something that he had done) with so great menaces, that in a melancholy he cast himself headlong and broke his own neck. Likewise, as Quintus Gallius, the praetor, held under his robe a pair of writing tablets, when he came to do his duty and salute him, he suspecting that he had a sword hidden underneath, and not daring straightways to search him farther for fear something else than a sword should be found about him, within a little while after caused him to be haled out of the tribunal seat by the hands of certain centurions, and put to torture like a bondslave; yea and seeing he would confess nothing, commanded him to be killed, having first with his own hands plucked his eyes out of his head. Howbeit Augustus writes that the said Gallius by pretending to confer secretly with him, laid wait for his life; whereupon he committed him to prison, and afterwards dismissed and enlarged him only to dwell in Rome; and that in the end he perished either by shipwreck, or else by the hands of thieves who waylaid him. He received and held the tribunate in perpetuity. Therein, once or twice, he chose and assumed unto him a colleague, for several *lustra* [the space of five years]. He took upon him likewise the government of manners and laws as a perpetual censor; in full right whereof, although he had not the honorable title of censorhip, yet he held a survey and numbering of the people thrice, the first and third with a companion in office, the middle by himself alone.

28. Twice he was in mind to have resigned up his absolute government; first, immediately upon the suppressing of Antony, mindful of that which oftentimes he had objected against him [Antony], namely, as if it had been long of him [Augustus] that it was not resigned and the commonwealth brought to a free state again; and secondly, by reason that he was weary of a long and lingering sickliness; what time he sent also for all the magistrates and the senate home to his house, and delivered up an account-book or register of the whole empire. But considering better with himself, that were he once a private person, he could not live without danger; and withal, that it would greatly hazard the commonwealth, to be put into the hands and dispose of many, he continued in the holding thereof still. And whether the event ensuing, or his will herein were better, it is hard to say. Which will of his, as he pretended oftentimes when he sat in place, so he testified also by a certain edict in these words: "O that I might establish the commonwealth safe and sound in her own proper seat, and thereof reap that fruit which I desire; even that I might be reported the

author of an excellent estate, and carry with me when I die this hope, that the groundwork and the foundations of the commonwealth which I shall lay, may continue and abide steadfast in their place." And verily what he wished, himself effected and brought to pass, having endeavored and done his best every way, that no man might repent of this new estate. For the city being not adorned according to the majesty of such an empire and subject to the casualties of deluges and fires, he beautified and set it out so, as justly he made his boast, that where he found it built of brick, he left it all of marble. And for the safety thereof, he performed as much for future posterity as could be foreseen and provided for by man's wit and reason.

29. Public works he built very many whereof the chief and principal was his Forum, together with the temple of Mars the Revenger; the temple of Apollo in Palatium; the temple likewise of Jupiter the Thunderer, in the Capitol. The reason why he built the said forum, was the multitude of men and their suits which because two would not suffice, seemed to have need of a third also. And therefore with great speed erected it was for that public use, even before the temple of Mars was finished. And expressly provided it was by law, that in it public causes should be determined apart, and choosing judges or juries by itself. The temple of Mars he had vowed unto the god in the Philippian war which he took in hand for the revenge of his father's death. He ordained therefore by an act, that here the senate should be consulted with as touching wars and triumphs; that from hence those praetors or governors who were to go into their provinces should be honorably attended, and brought onward on their way; and that hither they should bring the ensigns and ornaments of triumph, who returned with victory. The temple of Apollo he reared in that part of the Palatine which, being smitten with lightning, was by that god required, as the soothsayers out of their learning had

pronounced; hereto was adjoined a gallery, with a library of Latin and Greek books. In which temple he was wont in his old age both to sit oftentimes in counsel with the senate, and also to oversee and review the decuries of the judges. He consecrated the temple unto Jupiter the Thunderer upon occasion that he escaped a danger, what time in his Cantabrian expedition, as he traveled by night, a flash of lightning glanced upon his litter and struck his servant stone dead, that went with a light before. Some works also he made under other folks' names, to wit his nephew, his wife and sister; as the gallery and basilica of Lucius and Gaius; likewise the portico of Livia and Octavia; the theater also of Marcellus. Moreover divers other principal persons he oftentimes exhorted to adorn and beautify the city, every man according to his ability, either by erecting new monuments, or else by repairing and furnishing the old. By which means many an edifice was by many a man built; as namely the temple of Hercules and the Muses by Marcus Philippus; the temple of Diana by Lucius Cornificius; the Court of Liberty by Asinius Pollio; a temple of Saturn by Munatius Plancus; a theater by Cornelius Balbus; and an amphitheater by Statilius Taurus; but many and those very goodly monuments by Marcus Agrippa.

30. The whole space of the city he divided into wards and streets. He ordained that, as magistrates or aldermen yearly by lot should keep and govern the former, so there should be masters elected out of the commons of every street, to look unto the other. Against fires he devised night-watches and watchmen. To keep down inundations he enlarged and cleaned the channel of the river Tiber, which in times past was full of rammel and the ruins of houses, and so by that means narrow and choked. And that the avenues on every side to the city might be more passable, he took in hand himself to repair the highway Flaminia, so far as to Ariminum; the rest he

committed to sundry men who had triumphed for to pave, and the charges thereof to be defrayed out of the money raised of spoils and sackage. The sacred edifices decayed by continuance of time or consumed by fire he re-edified. Those together with the rest he adorned with most rich oblations brought into the tabernacle of Jupiter Capitolinus at one donation, 16,000 pound weight of gold, besides precious stones valued at 50 million sesterces.

31. But after that he entered now at length upon the high priesthood when Lepidus was once dead, which he never could find in his heart to take from him while he lived, what books soever of prophecies and destinies went commonly abroad in Greek and Latin, either without authors or such as were not authentical and of credit, he caused to be called in from all places, to the number of 2000 and above; and when he had burnt them, he retained those only of Sibyl's prophecies. And even of those also he made some special choice, and bestowed them close in two little coffers under the pedestal of Apollo Palatinus. The year's revolution reduced as it was into order by Julius of sacred memory but afterwards through negligence troubled and confused, he brought again to the former calculation. In the dispose whereof, he called the month Sextilis (rather than September wherein he was born), by his own name, because in it there befell unto him both his first consulship and also notable victories. Of all the priests, but especially of the Vestal Virgins, he augmented the number, the dignity and the commodities also. And whereas in the place of any Vestal Virgin deceased, there must another of necessity be chosen, he, perceiving many to make suit that they might not put their daughters to the lottery, protested with an oath, that if any one of his own daughters' daughters were of competent age he would present her to the place. Divers ancient ceremonies also which by little and little were disused he

restored again, as namely the augury of safety, the Flamenship of Jupiter, the sacred Lupercal, the secular plays and the *Compitalitii*. At the Lupercal solemnities, he commanded that no beardless boys should run. Likewise, at the secular plays, he forbade young folk of both sexes, to frequent any show exhibited by night; unless it were in the company of some ancient person of their kindred. The Tutelary images of crossways called *Lares Compitales* he was the first that ordained to adorn twice in the year with flowers of the spring and summer seasons. The principal honor next unto the immortal gods, he performed to the memorial of those worthy captains who had raised the Roman empire from a small thing to so high and glorious a state. And therefore both the works and monuments of every of them he repaired and made again, reserving their titles and inscriptions still; and all their statues also in triumphant form and shape he dedicated in the porches of his Hall of Justice. And in a public edict he professed thus much, that he devised it to this end, that both himself while he lived, and the princes or emperors his successors for the ages to come, might be called upon and urged by their subjects and citizens to conform themselves as it were to their patron and example. The statue likewise of Pompey, translated out of the court wherein Gaius Caesar was murdered, he placed over against the princely palace of his theater under an arch of marble.

32. Many most dangerous enormities and offensive abuses, which either had continued by custom and licentious liberty during the civil war, or else crept in and began in the time of peace to the utter ruin of the commonwealth, he reformed. For a number of bold roisters and professed robbers jetted openly with shortswords by their sides, under color of their own defense. Wayfaring men, as they traveled through the country, were caught up by them as well freeborn as slaves without respect, and kept hard to work in the prisons of landed men;

many factious crews also, under the title of a guild had their meetings and joined in fellowship to the perpetrating of mischief whatsoever. Whereupon he disposed strong guards and set watches in convenient places; he repressed those robbers; he surveyed the foresaid prisons; and all guilds save only those of ancient foundation and by law erected, he dissolved and put down. The bills of old debts due to the treasury he burnt, as being the chief occasion of malicious accusations. The places in the city whereof the tenure and hold was doubtful he adjudged unto those who were in present possession. The actions commenced against such as had been sued a long time, by whose distressed estate their adversaries sought for nothing but pleasure, he annulled, and denounced this condition withal, that if anyone would bring them into new trouble again, he should be liable to the like danger of punishment as the molested party was. And to the end that no lewd act might escape with impunity, nor business in court be shuffled over by delays, he added unto the term time thirty days; which days the honorary games and plays took up before. To three decuries of judges he added a fourth out of a lower and meaner degree, which went under the name of *Ducenarii* and were to judge of smaller sums. As for those judges he enrolled and elected them into the decuries after they were once thirty years of age; that is to say, five years sooner than they were wont. But seeing that most of them refused and were loath to execute this burdensome office of judging, he hardly granted that each decury should have their year's vacation by turns; and that the matters which were wont to be tried in the months of November and December should be omitted quite.

33. Himself sat daily in judgement, yea and otherwhiles until it was dark night, lying if he had not his health, in a litter which was of purpose set before the tribunal seat, or else in his own house; and he ministered justice not only with exceeding

93

severity, but also with as great leniency. For when upon a time there was one accused for a manifest parricide, so that he should not be sewed up in a leather bag (a punishment that none suffered but such as had confessed the fact), he examined by report in this manner, Certes thou never murderedst thy father, diddest thou? Again, in a matter as touching a forged will, when all the witnesses that set their hands and seals thereto were attaint by the Law Cornelia, he delivered unto the jurors who had the hearing of the cause, not only the two ordinary tablets of condemnation and acquittal, but a third also, whereby they might have their pardon who were certainly known to have been seduced to be witnesses either by fraud or error. As for the appeals in court, he yearly assigned those which were for the city-suiters unto praetors of the city; but if they were for provincial persons unto certain men of the consul's degree, such as he had ordained, in every province one, for to be in commission and to determine provincial affairs.

34. The laws made before time he revised and some also he ordained anew; as mainly on extravagance, on adultery, on sexual abuses, on political bribery, on intermarriage between classes. This act last named, when he had amended it with greater severity than the rest, he could not carry through, for the tumult of those that refused so to do, but that part of the penalties at length was quite taken away or else mitigated; an immunity also and toleration of widowhood, granted for three years, and the rewards besides augmented. And notwithstanding all that, when the order of knights stood out stiffly, calling publicly for the repealing of the said statute, he sent for Germanicus' children, and taking some of them himself, and bestowing the others in their father's arms, showed them unto their view, signifying by the gesture of his hand and by his countenance, that they should not be loath to imitate the example of that young gentleman. Moreover perceiving that

the force of that law was dallied with and avoided by the immaturity of young espoused wives, as also by often changing of marriages, he brought into a narrower compass the time of betrothal, and also limited divorces.

35. The number of senators growing still to a shameful and confused company (for there were not so few as one thousand, and some most unworthy; as who after Caesar's death were taken into the house for favor or bribes; whom the common people termed abortive, as it were untimely births), he reduced to the ancient stint [three hundred] and honorable reputation; and that in two elections; the former at their own choice whereby one man chooses his fellow; the second, according to his own and Agrippa's mind, at which time he is thought to have sat as president, armed with a shirt of mail under his gown and a short sword by his side, having a guard also standing about his chair, to wit, ten of the stoutest and tallest men that were of senator's degree, and all his friends. Cordus Cremutius writes that there was not so much as admitted then into the senate house any senator but singly one alone by himself, and not before his clothes were well searched and felt, for having any weapon under them. Some of them he brought to this modesty, as to excuse themselves; and yet for such as thus made excuse he reserved still the liberty to wear a senator's habit, the honor also to sit and behold the plays in the *orchestra*, together with privilege to keep their place at the solemn public feasts. Now, to the end that being chosen thus and allowed they might with more reverence and less trouble execute the functions belonging to senators, he ordained, that before anyone sat him down in his chair, he should make supplication and sacrifice with frankincense and wine at the altar of that god, in whose temple they assembled for the time; and that ordinarily the senate should not be held oftener than twice in a month, to wit upon the Kalends and Ides; and that in the

months of September and October none else should be bound
to give attendance, save those that were drawn by lot, by whose
number decrees might pass. Furthermore, he devised to in-
stitute for himself, and that by casting lots, a privy council for
six months, with whom he might treat beforehand of businesses and affairs to be moved unto a full senate. As touching
matters of greater importance put to question, he demanded
the opinion of the senators, not after the usual manner and in
order, but as it pleased himself; to the end that every man
should bend his mind so intentively thereto, as if he were to
deliver his own advice, rather than give assent unto another.

36. Other things there were besides, whereof he was the
author and beginner; and among the rest, that the acts of the
senate should not be published; and that no magistrates after
they had left their honorable places should immediately be
sent as governors into any provinces; that for proconsuls
there should be a certain rate in money set down and allowed
for their sumpter-mules and tents, which were wont before
time to be set out and allowed for them at the public cost of the
city; that the charge of the city's treasury should be translated
from the quaestors unto those that had been praetors, or to the
praetors for the time being; lastly, that certain decemvirs
should summon the centumviral court, which they only were
wont to do that had borne the office of quaestorship.

37. And to the end that more men might bear their part
in administration of the commonwealth, he devised new offices, to wit, the overseeing of the public works, the surveying
of the ways of the water courses of the channel of the Tiber,
and distributing corn among the people. Also the prefecture
of the city; one board of three men for choosing senators; and
another for reviewing the troops, so often as need required.
The censors, whose creation was discontinued, after a long
time between, he created again. The number of praetors he

augmented. He required also that so often as the consulship was conferred upon him, he might have one, instead of two colleagues in office; but he could not obtain it, for all men with one voice cried out, that his majesty was abridged enough already, in that he bore not that honorable office by himself, but with another.

38. Neither was he more sparing in honorably rewarding martial prowess, as who gave order that to thirty captains and above, there should be granted by public decree full triumphs, and to a good many more, triumphal ornaments. Senators' children, to the end that they might be sooner acquainted with the affairs of state, he permitted to put on even at the first their virile gown, to wear likewise the senator's robe with broad purple stripes, and to have their places in the senate house. Also at their first entrance into warfare, he allowed them to be, not only military tribunes in the legions, but also captains over the horsemen in the wings. And, that none of them might be unexpert of the camp affairs, he ordained for the most part over every wing two such senators' sons to be provosts. The troops and companies of Roman knights he often reviewed; and after a long space of time between, brought into use again the manner of their riding solemnly on horseback, to show themselves. Neither would he suffer any one of them during this solemnity to be unhorsed and arrested by his adversary, that pretended any matter in law against him, a thing that was usually done. And to as many as were known to be aged or to have any defect of body he gave leave to send their horses before, and to come on foot to answer whensoever they were cited. And soon after he did those this favor, to deliver up their public horses, who being above thirty-five years of age, were unwilling to keep them still.

39. Having obtained also by the senate ten coadjutors, he compelled every knight to render an account of his life. And

of such as were blameable and could not approve their living, some he punished, others he noted with shame and ignominy, the most part of them with admonition, but after sundry sorts. The lightest kind of admonition was the tendering unto them in open place a pair of writing tablets to read unto themselves in the place where they stood. Some also he put to rebuke for taking up of money on small interest for the use, and putting it forth again for greater gain and usury.

40. At the election of tribunes, if there wanted senators to stand for that office, he created them out of the degree of Roman knights; so as, after they had borne that magistracy, they might remain ranged in whatever degree they would themselves. Now, when as many of the Roman knights, having wasted their patrimony in the civil wars, durst not out of the fourteen foremost seats behold the public plays, for fear of the penalty by the law, called *Theatralis*, he pronounced openly that such knights were not liable thereto if either themselves or their fathers before them, were ever at any time valued to the worth of Roman knights. He made a review of the people of Rome, street by street; and to prevent that the common people should not be often called away from their affairs by occasion of the distribution of corn, he purposed to give out thrice a year, tickets for to serve four months; but when the people were desirous of the old custom he granted them again to receive the same upon the Nones of every month. The ancient liberty also, in elections he brought in again; and having restrained bribery for dignities by manifold penalties, upon the day of such elections he distributed out of his own purse among the Fabians and Scaptians, who were of the same tribes wherein himself was incorporated, a thousand sesterces apiece, so that they should not look for ought at any of their hands who stood for offices. Moreover supposing it a matter of great consequence to keep the people incorrupt and clear from all

base mixture of servile blood, he both granted the freedom of the city of Rome most sparingly, and also set a certain gauge and limitation of manumitting and enfranchising slaves. When Tiberius made request unto him for a Grecian client of his to be made a citizen, he wrote back unto him, that he would not grant it unless he came personally and could persuade him what just causes he had of his suit. And what time as Livia entreated the like for a certain Frenchman, tributary to the Romans, he flatly denied the citizenship, but offered in lieu thereof immunity and remission of tribute, avowing, that he would more easily abide that somewhat went from the public treasury, than have the honor of the Roman city to be made vulgar and common. Nor content that he had by divers straight edicts and provisos kept many slaves from all manner of freedom, but a great deal more from full freedom, as having precisely put in caveats both for the number and also for the condition of those that were to be made free. He added thus much moreover, that no slave who had ever been bound and imprisoned, or examined by torture, should obtain any kind of enfranchisement whatsoever. The old manner of dress also he endeavored to bring into use again. And having seen upon a time assembled to hear a public speech a number of citizens clad all in black cloaks [black, meaning sullied], taking great indignation thereat cried out withal, "Behold,

Romanos rerum dominos gentemque togatam.

The Romans, lords of all the world, and long-robed nation.

He gave the aediles in charge not to suffer any person from thence forward to abide or stay, either in the forum or thereabouts, but in a gown, laying aside all cloaks.

41. His liberality unto all degrees of citizens he showed oftentimes as occasions and opportunities were offered; for both by bringing into the city in the Alexandrian triumph the

treasures of the Egyptian kings he caused so great plenty of money that usury fell, but the price of lands arose to a very high reckoning. And also afterwards, so often as out of the goods of condemned persons there was any surplus of money remaining above their fines, he granted for a certain time the free loan and use thereof to as many as were able to put in security for the principal by an obligation in double the sum. The property qualification of senators he augmented, and whereas before it amounted to 800,000 sesterces, he fixed it at 1,200,000; and for those who had not so much, he supplied and made it up to the full. He gave congiaries oftentimes to the people, but of divers sums, one while 400, another while 300, and sometimes 250 sesterces; and he did not exclude boys under age, whereas they had not wont to receive such congiaries unless they were above eleven years old. He measured out also to the people by the poll, corn in times of scarcity oftentimes at a very low price, and otherwhiles without paying therefor; and as for the tickets of money, he doubled the sum in them contained.

42. And that you may know that he was a prince more respective of thrift and wholesomeness than desirous of popularity, when the people complained of the dearth of wine, he checked them with this most severe speech, that his son-in-law Agrippa had taken order good enough that men should not be athirst, by conveying so many waters into the city. Unto the same people demanding the congiary which indeed was by him promised, he answered, that his credit was good, and he able to perform his word. But when they earnestly called for one which he had never promised, he hit them in the teeth by a proclamation of their impudence, assuring them that give it he would not, although he had intended it.

And with no less gravity and resolution, when upon his proposing and publishing of a congiary, he found that many in the meantime were manumitted and inserted into the number of citizens, he rejected such, and said they should not receive any unto whom he had made no promise; and to all the rest he gave less than he promised, that the sum which he had appointed might hold out and be sufficient. When upon a time there was great scarcity of corn, being put to seek a difficult remedy, insomuch as he was driven to expel out of the city, all the slaves trimmed up for sale, as whole schools of gladiators, and foreigners, except physicians and schoolmasters; yea and some of the ordinary household servants. So soon as the market began to mend and victuals grew plentiful, he writes, that it took him in the head to abolish those public doles of corn forever, because upon the confidence of them tillage was clean laid down. Howbeit he continued not in that mind long, as being assured that the same doles might be set up again one time or other by the ambitious humor of princes his successors. And therefore after this he ordered the matter, so that he had no less regard of the city's farmers and purveyors of the public corn, than of the people of the city.

43. In number, variety, and magnificence of solemn shows exhibited unto the people he went beyond all men. He reports of himself that he set forth plays and games in his own name four times; and for other magistrates who either were absent or not sufficient to bear the charges, three and twenty times. Divers times, he exhibited plays by every street, and those upon many stages, and acted by players skillful in all languages not in the common forum only, nor in the ordinary amphitheater, but also in the circus. In the enclosure called Septa, he never represented any sports but the baiting and coursing of wild beasts. For the shows of athletes he built wooden scaffolds and seats for the nonce in Mars field. In like manner, he made the show of a naval battle about the river Tiber, having dug of purpose a spacious hollow pit within the ground, where

now is to be seen the grove of the Caesars. On which days he bestowed warders in divers places of the city, for fear it might be endangered by sturdy thieves and robbers, taking their vantage, that so few remained at home in their houses. In the circus he brought forth to perform charioteers, runners, and killers of savage beasts; otherwhiles out of the noblest young gentlemen of all the city. As for the warlike riding called Troy, he exhibited it oftenest of all other, making choice of boys to perform it, as well bigger as smaller; supposing it a matter of antiquity and honorable besides that the towardly disposition and proof of noble blood should thus be seen and known. In this solemnity and sport, he rewarded Gaius Nonius Asprenas, weakened [or lamed] by a fall from his horse, with a chain of gold, and permitted both himself and also his posterity to bear the surname of Torquatus. But afterwards he gave over the representation of such pastimes, by occasion that Asinius Pollio the orator made a grievous complaint in the senate of the fall that Aeserninus his nephew took, who likewise had thereby broken his leg. To the performance of his stage-plays also and shows of sword-fight, he employed sometimes even the knights of Rome; but it was before he was inhibited by virtue of an act of the senate. For after it verily, he exhibited no more, save only a youth called Lucius Itius, born of worshipful parentage, only for a show; that being a dwarf not two feet high, and weighing seventeen pounds, yet had an exceeding great voice. One day of the sword-fight that he set forth, he brought in through the midst of the showplace, the Parthian hostages who then were newly sent to Rome, and placed them in the second row of seats above himself. His manner was moreover, before the usual spectacles, if any strange and new thing were brought and worthy to be known, to bring it abroad for to be seen, and in any place whatsoever. As for example, a rhinoceros within the Septa; a tiger upon the stage;

and a serpent fifty cubits long, within the Comitium. It fortuned that during the great Circeian games which he had vowed before, he fell sick; whereby he lay in his litter and so devoutly attended upon the sacred chariots called Thensae. Again, it happened at the beginning of those plays which he set out when he dedicated the temple of Marcellus, that his curule chair became unjointed, and thereby he fell upon his back. Also at the games of his grandsons when the people there assembled were mightily troubled for fear that the theater would fall, seeing that by no means he could cause them to take heart again, he removed out of his own place, and sat down in that part thereof which was most suspected. The most confused and licentious manner of beholding such spectacles he reformed and brought into order, moved thereto by the wrong done to a senator, whom at Puteoli in a frequent assembly sitting at their games, no man had vouchsafed a seat.

44. Hereupon when a decree of the senate was passed, that so often as in any place there was ought exhibited publicly, the first course of seats should be kept clear for senators. He forbade the ambassador of free nations and confederates to sit at Rome within the *orchestra* because he had found that some of their libertine's kind were sent in embassage. The soldiers he severed from the other people. To married men that were commoners, he assigned several rows by themselves. To noblemen's children under age their own quarter, and to their teachers and governors the next thereto. He made an act also, that not one of the commons wearing black and sullied gowns should sit in the midst of the theater. As for women, he would not allow them to behold so much as the sword-fencers (who customarily in the time past were to be seen of all indifferently) but from some higher loft above the rest. To the Vestal Virgins he granted a place apart from the rest within the theater, just over against the praetor's tribunal. Howbeit from the

boxing show he banished all the female sex; so far forth, as
that during the pontifical games, he put off a match until the
morrow morning, and made proclamation, that his will was
that no woman should come into the theater before the fifth
hour of the day.

45. Himself beheld the circus games for the most part from
the upper lofts of his friends and freedmen, sometimes out
of the imperial box, sitting there with his wife and children.
From these shows and sights he would be absent many hours
together, and otherwhiles whole days, but first having craved
leave of the people, and recommended those unto them, who
should sit as presidents of those games in his turn. But so often
as he was at them, he did nothing else but intend the same;
either to avoid the rumor of men, whereby his father Caesar
(as he said himself) was commonly taxed, namely for that in
beholding those solemnities he used between whiles to give his
mind to read letters and petitions, yea and to write back again;
or else upon an earnest desire and delight he had in seeing such
pastimes, his pleasure and contentment wherein he never
dissembled, but oftentimes frankly professed. And therefore
he proposed and gave of his own, at the games of prize and
plays even of other men, coronets and rewards, both many in
number and also of great worth; neither was he present at any
of those Greek games, but he honored every one of the actors
and provers of masteries therein according to their deserts.
But most affectionately of all other he loved to see boxing,
and the Latins especially; not those only who by lawful calling
were professed (and even those he was wont to match with
Greeks), but such also as out of the common sort of townsmen,
fell together by the ears pell mell in the narrow streets, and
though they had no skill at all of fight, yet could lay on. In
sum, all those in general who had any hand in those public
games he deigned good rewards and had a special respect of

them. The privileges of athletes he both maintained entire, and also amplified. As for the sword-fencers he would not suffer them to enter into the lists, unless they might be given quarter. The power to chastise actors and players at all times and in every place (granted unto the magistrates by ancient law) he took from them, save only during the plays and upon the stage. Howbeit he examined straightly nevertheless at all times either the matches of champion wrestlers or the fights of sword-fencers. For the licentiousness of stage players he so repressed that when he had for certain found out that Stephanio, an actor of Roman plays, had a man's wife waiting upon him shorn and rounded in manner of a boy, he confined and sent him away as banished, but well beaten first with rods through all the three theaters. And Hylas the pantomime at the complaint made of him by the praetor he scourged openly in the courtyard before his house, and excluded no man from the sight thereof. Yea and he banished Pylades out of the city of Rome and Italy because he had pointed with his finger at a spectator who hissed him out of the stage, and so made him to be known.

46. Having in this manner ordered the city and administered the civil affairs therein, he made Italy populous and much frequented with colonies to the number of twenty-eight, brought thither and planted by him; yea he furnished the same with public works and revenues in many places. He equaled it also after a sort and in some part with the very city of Rome in privileges and estimation by devising a new kind of suffrages which the decurions or elders of colonies gave every one in their own township as touching magistrates to be created in Rome, and sent under their hands and seals to the city against the day of the solemn election. And to the end that there should not want in any place either honest and worshipful inhabitants, or issue of the multitude, those who made suit to serve as

men of arms on horseback upon the public commendation of any township whatsoever he enrolled and advanced unto the degree of knights. But to as many of the commoners as could by good evidence prove unto him as he visited the countries and regions of Italy that they had sons and daughters he distributed a thousand sesterces apiece for every child they had.

47. As for those provinces which were more mighty than others, and the government whereof by yearly magistrates was neither easy nor safe, he undertook himself to rule. The rest he committed to proconsuls by lot; and yet otherwhiles he made exchange of such provinces; and of both sorts he oftentimes visited many in person. Certain cities, confederate and in league with Rome, howbeit by overmuch liberty running headlong to mischief and destruction, he deprived of their liberties. Others again either deeply in debt he eased, or subverted by earthquake he re-edified, or able to allege their merits and good turns done to the people of Rome he endowed with the franchises of Latium; or else with the freedom of Rome. There is not, I suppose, a province (except Africa only and Sardinia) but he went unto it. Into these provinces, after he had chased Sextus Pompeius thither, he prepared to sail out of Sicily and to cross the seas, but continual storms and extreme tempests checked him; neither had he good occasion or sufficient cause afterwards to pass over unto them.

48. All those kingdoms which he won by conquest and force of arms, unless some few, he either restored unto those princes from whom he had taken them, or else made them over to other foreign nations. Kings which were in alliance with him he conjoined also together among themselves by mutual bonds of alliance, as being a most ready procurer and maintainer of affinity and amity of every one; neither had he other regard of them all in general than of the very natural members and parts of his own empire. Moreover, he was wont to set guardians

and governors over the said princes when they were either young and under age, or lunatic and not well in their wits, until such time as they were grown to ripe years or began to come again to themselves. The children of very many of them he both brought up and also trained and instructed together with his own.

49. Out of his military forces he distributed both legions and auxiliaries in the provinces. He placed one fleet at Misenum and another at Ravenna for the defenses of the upper and nether seas. A certain number of soldiers he selected for a guard, partly of the city, and in part of his own person, having discharged the regiment of the Calagurritans whch he had retained about him, until he vanquished Antony, and likewise of the Germans which he had enrolled among the squires of his body, until the disastrous overthrow of Varus. And yet he suffered not at any time to remain within the city more than three cohorts, and those without a permanent camp. The rest his manner was to send away to wintering places and summer harbors about the neighboring towns. Moreover, all the soldiers that were in any place whatsoever, he tied to a certain prescript form and proportion of wages and rewards, setting down according to the degree and place of every one, both their times of warfare, and also the commodities they should receive after the term of their service expired and their lawful discharge: lest that by occasion of old age or for want they should, after they were freed from warfare, be solicited to sedition and rebellion. And to the end that for ever, and without any difficulty, there might be defrayed sufficient to maintain and reward them accordingly, he appointed a peculiar treasury for soldiers with new revenues devised for their maintenance. And that with more speed and out of hand word might be brought and notice taken what was doing in every province, he disposed along the highways, within small dis-

tance one from another, first, certain young men as posts, and afterwards swift wagons to give intelligence. This he thought more commodious and better to the purpose, that they who from a place brought him letters might be asked questions also, if the matters required ought.

50. In charters, patents, writs, bills and letters he used for his seal, at first, the image of the Sphinx; soon after, that of Alexander the Great; and last of all, his own, engraven by the hand of Dioscurides. Therewith the princes and emperors, his successors, continued to sign their writings. To all his missives his manner was to put precisely the very minutes of hours, not of day only but of night also, wherein it might be known they were dated.

51. Of his clemency and civil courtesy there be many, and those right great, proofs and experiments. Not to reckon up how many and who they were of the adverse faction that he vouchsafed pardon and life, yea, and suffered to hold still a principal place in the city: he was content and thought it sufficient to punish Junius Novatus and Cassius Patavinus, two commoners, the one with a fine of money and the other with a slight banishment; notwithstanding that Junius Novatus in the name of young Agrippa had divulged a most biting and stinging letter touching him, and Cassius Patavinus at an open and full feast, gave out in broad terms that he wanted neither hearty wishes nor good will to stab him. Moreover in a certain judicial trial, when among other crimes this article was principally objected against Aemilius Aelianus of Corduba that he was wont to have a bad opinion and to speak but basely of Caesar, himself turned to the accuser, and as if he had been sore offended, "I would," quoth he, "thou wert able to prove this unto me: in faith Aelianus should well know that I also have a tongue; for I will not stick to say more by him." And farther than this he neither for the present nor afterwards in-

quired into the matter. Likewise, when Tiberius grieved and
complained unto him of the same indignity in a letter, and
that incessantly and after a violent manner, he wrote back
again: "Do not, my good Tiberius, in this point feed the humor
of your age; neither set it too near your heart that there is any
man who speaks evil of me; for it is enough for us if no man
be able to do us harm."

52. Albeit he wist well enough that temples were usually
granted by decree even unto proconsuls, yet in no province
accepted he of that honor, but jointly in the name and behalf
of himself and of Rome. For in Rome verily he forbore this
honor most resolutely: yea and those silver statues which in
times past had been set up for him he melted every one. With
the money realized from these he caused golden tablets to be
purchased, and those he dedicated to Apollo Patavinus. When
the people offered and instantly forced upon him the dictatorship, he fell upon his knees, cast his gown from off his shoulder,
bared his breast, and with detestation of the thing, besought
them not to urge him further.

53. The name and title of lord he always abhorred as a
contumelious and reproachful term. When upon a time, as
he beheld the plays, these words were pronounced out of a
comedy:

O dominum aequum et bonum

O good and gracious lord

whereupon the whole assembly with great joy and applause
accorded thereto, as if they had been spoken of him. Imme-
diatcly both with gesture of hand and show of countenance,
he repressed such indecent flatteries, and the next day he reproved them most sharply by an edict: neither would he ever
after suffer himself to be called *Dominus* [Lord], no not of his
own children and grandchildren either in earnest or jest. And

that which more is, such fair and flattering words he forbade them to use among themselves. By day he would not depart forth of the city or any town, nor enter into any place, but in the evening or by night, lest he disquiet any person in doing him honor by way of dutiful attendance. In his consulship he went commonly in the streets on foot; out of his consulship oftentimes in a closed chair or litter. In general salutations and duties done unto him he admitted the very commons, entertaining the suits and desires of all comers with so great humanity as that he rebuked one of them merrily, because in reaching unto him a supplication he did it so timorously as if he had brought a small piece of coin to an elephant. On a senate-day he saluted his nobles in the Curia, verily as they sat, every one by name without any prompter; and at his departure out of the house he used to bid them farewell one by one as they were seated, in the same manner. With many men he performed mutual offices yielding one kindness for another interchangeably. Neither gave he over frequenting their solemnities (as birthdays and anniversaries) until he was far stepped in years and because once upon a day of espousals he was in the press and throng of people sore crowded. Gallus Terrinius, a senator, and none of his familiar acquaintance, howbeit fallen blind and purposing resolutely to starve himself to death, he visited in proper person, and by his consolatory and comfortable words persuaded him to live still.

54. As he delivered a speech in the senate, one said to him, "I conceive you not," and another, "I would gainsay you if any place were left for me to speak." Divers times when upon occasion of excessive altercation and brabbling among the senators in debating matters, he was about to whip out of the senate apace in a great chafe, some of them would choke him with these words, "Senators ought to have liberty to speak their minds concerning the commonwealth." Antistius Labeo,

at a certain election of senators when one man choses another, made choice of Marcus Lepidus who sometime was Augustus' mortal enemy, and then in exile. Now when he demanded of the said Antistius if there were not others more worthy to be chosen, he returned this answer, that every man had his own liking and judgement by himself. Yet for all this, did no man's free speech or froward self-will turn him to displeasure or danger.

55. Moreover the defamatory libels of him cast abroad and dispersed in the Curia he neither was affrighted at, nor took great care to refute, making not so much as search after the authors. Only this he opined, that from thenceforth there should be inquisition made, and examination had of those that either in their own name or under other men's did put forth libels, rhymes or verses to the infamy of any person. Furthermore, to meet with the spiteful taunts and scurrilous scoffs of some, wherewith he was provoked, he made an edict against such. And yet, to the end that the senate should pass no act, for the inhibition of their licentious liberty in their last wills and testaments [wherein the manner was to use broad jests of any person], he interposed his negative voice.

56. Whensoever he was present himself at the election of magistrates, he went with his own candidates round about to the tribes, and humbly craved their voices according to the usual custom. Himself also gave a voice in his own tribe as one of the ordinary people. When he appeared as witness in judicial courts, he suffered himself right willingly to be examined upon interrogative, and also to be impleaded against and confuted. His forum he made less, and of narrower compass, as not daring to encroach upon the next houses and dispossess the owners. He never recommended his sons unto the people, but with this clause added thereto, if they shall deserve. When, being yet under age, and in their purple child's habit, all the

people generally that sat in the theater rose up unto them, and the standers below clapped their hands, he took it very ill and complained grievously thereof. His minions and inward friends he would have to be great and mighty men in the city; yet so, as they should have no more liberty than other citizens, but be subject to laws and judgements as well as the rest. When Asprenas Nonius, a man of near alliance and acquaintance with him was accused by Cassius Severus, for practicing poison, and pleaded for himself at the bar, he asked counsel of the senate, what they thought in duty he was to do? "For I stand in doubt," he said, "lest being here present as an advocate, I should acquit the defendant and so hinder the course of the law; again, if I be absent and fail him, lest I might be thought to forsake and prejudice my friend." Whereupon, by all their consents, he sat there in the pews certain hours, but spoke never a word nor afforded so much as a commendatory speech in the defendant's behalf, as the manner of friends was to do in the trial of such cases. He pleaded the causes even of his very clients, and by name, of a certain Scutarius, whom in times past he had called forth to serve him in the wars; he spoke I say in his defense, when he was sued in an action of the case. Of all those that were thus in trouble, he delivered one and no more from making his appearance in court, and him verily no otherwise, but by earnest prayers and entreating the accuser before the judges; and him he persuaded at length to let fall his action. And Castritius it was, a man by whose means he came to the knowledge of Murena's conspiracy.

57. How much, and for what merits of his, he was beloved, an easy matter it is to make an estimate. The acts and decrees of the senate concerning his honors I pass over, as which may be thought wrested from them either upon mere necessity or bashful modesty. The knights of Rome of their own accord and by a uniform consent celebrated his birth-feast always,

for two days together. All states and degrees of the city, yearly upon a solemn vow that they made, threw small pieces of brass coin into Curtius lake for the preservation of his life and health. Also, at the Kalends of January every year they offered a New Year's gift in the Capitol unto him, although he were absent. Out of which mass and gross sum he disbursed as much money as wherewith he bought the most precious images of the gods, and dedicated them in divers streets; as namely Apollo Sandaliarius, and Jupiter Tragedus, and others besides. For the re-edification of his house in Palatine consumed by fire, the old soldiers, the decuries of the judges, the tribes, and many several persons by themselves of all sorts, willingly and according to each one's ability, brought in their monies together. Howbeit, he did no more but slightly touch the heaps of such money as they lay, and took not away out of any one above one single denier. As he returned out of any province, they accompanied him honorably, not only with good words, but also with songs set in musical measures. This also was duly observed, that how often so ever he entered Rome, no punishment that day was inflicted upon any person.

58. The surname of *Pater Patriae*, they all presented unto him with exceeding great and unexpected accord. The commons, first, by a deputation which they sent unto Antium; then, because he accepted not thereof, at Rome as he entered the theater to behold the plays, they tendered it a second time themselves in great frequency, dight with laurel branches and coronets. Soon after, the senate did the like, not by way of decree nor acclamation, but by Valerius Messalla, who had commission from them all to relate their minds in this manner. "That," he said, "which may be to the good and happiness of thee and thy house O Caesar Augustus (for in this wise we think that we pray for perpetual felicity and prosperity to this commonwealth). The senate according with the people of

Rome, do jointly salute thee by the name of *Pater Patriae*."
Unto whom, Augustus with tears standing in his eyes, made
answer in these words (for I have set the very same down,
like as I did those of Messalla), "Now that I have, mine honorable lords, attained to the height of all my vows and wishes,
what remains else for me to crave of the immortal gods, but
that I may carry with me this universal consent of yours unto
my life's end?"

59. Unto Antonius Musa, his physician, by whose means he
was recovered out of a dangerous disease, they erected a statue,
by a general contribution of brass, just by the image of Aesculapius. Some householders there were who in their last wills
and testaments provided, that their heirs should lead beasts for
sacrifice into the Capitol and pay their vows, with this title
carried before them containing the reason of so doing, because
they had left Augustus living after them. Certain cities of
Italy began their year that very day on which he first came to
them. Most of the provinces, over and above temples and
altars, ordained almost in every good town, solemn games and
plays every fifth year in his honor.

60. Kings, his friends and confederates both, severally every
one in his own kingdom built cities calling them Caesareae, and
jointly altogether intended at their common charges fully to
finish the temple of Jupiter Olympicus at Athens which long
time before was begun, and to dedicate it unto his Genius.
And oftentimes, the said princes leaving their realms, going in
Roman gowns, without diadems and regal ornaments, in habit
and manner of devoted clients, performed their dutiful attendance upon him day by day; not at Rome only, but also when
he visited and traveled over the provinces.

61. Forasmuch as I have showed already what his public
carriage was in places of command and magistracies, in the
managing also and administration of the commonwealth

throughout the world both in war and peace, now will I relate his more private and domestical life, as also what behavior he showed and what fortune he had at home, and among his own, even from his youth unto his dying day. His mother he buried during the time of his first consulship, and his sister Octavia in the fifty-fourth year of his age. And as he performed unto them both, while they lived, the offices of piety and love in the best manner; so when they were dead, he did them the greatest honors he possibly could.

62. He had espoused, being a very youth, the daughter of Publius Servilius Isauricus; but upon his reconciliation unto Antony after their first discord at the earnest demand of both their soldiers, that they might be conjoined and united by some near affinity, he took to wife Antonius' stepdaughter Claudia, the daughter of Dame Fulvia by Publius Clodius, a young damosel, scarce marriageable. And upon some displeasure, falling out with Fulvia his wife's mother, he put her away, as yet untouched and a virgin. Soon after he wedded Scribonia, the wife before of two husbands, both men of consular dignity, and by one of them a mother. This wife also he divorced, not able to endure, as he writes himself, her shrewd and perverse conditions. And forthwith, took perforce from Tiberius Nero, Livia Drusilla his lawful wife and great with child. Her he loved entirely, her he liked only, and to the very end.

63. Upon Scribonia he begat Julia; by Livia he had no issue, although full fain he would. Conceive once she did by him; but she miscarried, and the infant was born before time. As for Julia, he gave her in marriage first to Marcellus the son of his sister Octavia, even when he was but newly crept out of his child's age. Afterwards, when Marcellus was departed this life, he bestowed her upon Marcus Agrippa, having by entreaty obtained of his sister, to yield up unto him her right and interest in her son-in-law. For at the same time Agrippa

had to wife one of the Marcellae (her daughters) and of her body begotten children. When this Agrippa was likewise dead, he cast about and sought for divers matches a long time, even out of the ranks of Roman knights, and chose for her his wife's son Tiberius; whom he forced to put away a former wife then with child, and by whom he had been a father already. Marcus Antonius writes that he had affianced the said Julia first to Antony his son and afterwards to Cotiso, king of the Getes, what time Antony himself asked to have a king's daughter likewise to wife.

64. By Agrippa and Julia he had three grandsons, Gaius, Lucius and Agrippa; granddaughters likewise twain, Julia and Agrippina. Julia he bestowed in marriage upon Lucius Paulus, the censor's son; and Agrippina upon Germanicus, his sister's grandson. As for Gaius and Lucius he adopted them for his own children at home in his house having symbolically bought them of their father Agrippa by the brazen coin and the balance. Whom being yet in their tender years, he employed in the charge of the commonwealth; and no sooner were they consuls-elect but he sent them abroad to the government of provinces and conduct of armies. His daughter and granddaughter above named he brought up and trained so as that he acquainted them with housewifery and set them even to card, spin and make cloth, forbidding them straightly either to say or do ought but openly in the sight and hearing of all men, and that which might be recorded in their day books. Certes, so far forth he prohibited and forwarned them the company of strangers, that he wrote upon a time to Lucius Tucinius, a noble young gentleman and a personable, charging him that he passed the bounds of modesty, in that he came once to Baiae for to see and salute his daughter. His grandsons himself for the most part taught to read, to write and to swim, besides the rudiments and first introductions to other sciences. But in

nothing travailed he so much as in this, that they might imitate his handwriting. He never supped together with them but they sat at the nether end of the table; neither went he any journey but he had them either going before in a wagon or else about him riding by his side.

65. But as joyous and confident as he was in regard both of his issue and also of the discipline of his house, fortune failed him in the proof of all. His daughter and granddaughter, either of them named Julia, stained with all kind of lewdness and dishonesty, he sent out of the way as banished. Gaius and Lucius both he lost in the space of eighteen months: Gaius died in Lycia, Lucius at Massilia. His third grandson, Agrippa, together with his wife's son, Tiberius, he adopted as his sons in the Forum of Rome by an act of the Curia. But of these twain within a small time he cast out of his favor, yea and confined aside into Surrentum, Agrippa, for his base disposition and fell nature. Moreover he took much more patiently the death than the reproachful misdemeanors of his children. For at the misfortune of Gaius and Lucius he was not extremely dismayed and cast down; marry, of his daughter and her lewd pranks he gave notice in his absence to the senate, and that in writing, which his quaestor read openly before them; and for very shame he absented himself a long time and avoided the company of men: yea, and that which more is, he once was of a mind to put her to death. And verily, when as, about the same time a freedwoman of his, named Phoebe, and one of them that were privy to her naughtiness, knit her own neck in a halter, and so ended her days, he gave it out that he wished with all his heart he had been Phoebe's father. Confined thus when she was, he debarred her wholly the use of wine and all manner of delicate trimming and decking her body; neither would he permit any man, one or other, bond or free, to have access unto her without his privity and leave asked, nor unless

he might be certified before of what age, of what stature and color he was, and what marks and scars he carried about him. After five years' end he removed her out of the island into the continent where she abode at more liberty somewhat, and not so straightly looked into. For to call her home again once for all he could by no means be entreated; as who, many a time when the people of Rome besought him earnestly and were very instant with him in her behalf, openly before a frequent assembly of them cursed such daughters and such wives saying, "God bless ye all from the like." The infant that his grand-daughter Julia bore after she was condemned he expressly forbade to be recognized or to be reared. As touching Agrippa, seeing him to prove nothing more tractable, but rather brain-sick every day more than other, he transported him from Surrentum into an island and enclosed him there besides with a guard of soldiers. He provided also by an act of the senate that in the same place he should be kept forever. And so often as there was any mention made either of him or his two Julias, he used to fetch a sigh and groan again, and withal to break out into this speech:

> Would God I never had wedded bride
> Or else without any child had died.

66. Friendship with any person as he did not easily entertain so he maintained and kept the same most constantly, not honoring only the virtues and deserts of every man according to their worth, but enduring also their vices and deliquencies at least if they exceeded not. For out of all that number of his dependents there will hardly be any found during his friend-ship to have been plunged in adversity and thereby over-thrown: except Salvidienus Rufus whom he had before ad-vanced to the dignity of consul, and Cornelius Gallus pro-moted by him to the provostship of Egypt, raised both from

the very dunghill. The one of these for practicing seditiously
an alteration in the state; and the other for his unthankful and
malicious mind he forbade his house and all his provinces.
But as for Gallus, when as both by the menaces of his accusers
and also by the rigorous acts of the senate passed against him,
he was driven to shorten his own life, Augustus commended
verily their kind hearts to him for being so wroth and grieving
so much in his behalf; howbeit for Gallus' sake he wept and
complained of his own hard fortune, in that he alone might
not be angry with his friends within that measure as he would
himself. All the rest of his favorites flourished in power and
wealth to their lives' end as chief persons every one in their
rank; notwithstanding some discontentment and dislikes came
between. For otherwhiles he found a want in Marcus Agrippa
of patience, and in Maecenas of taciturnity and secrecy; when
as the one upon a light suspicion of his cold love and affection,
with a jealousy besides that Marcellus should be preferred before him, left all and went to Mitylene; the other unto his
wife Terentia revealed a secret as touching the detection of
Murena's conspiracy. Himself also required the same mutual
benevolence of his friends, as well dead as living. For although
he was none of these that lie in the wind to mung and catch
at inheritances, as who could never abide to reap any commodity by the last will and testament of an unknown person;
yet weighed he most strictly and precisely the supreme judgements and testimonies of his friends concerning him, delivered
at their deaths, as one who dissembled neither his grief in case
a man respected him slightly and without honorable terms,
nor his joy if he remembered him thankfully and with kindness. As touching either legacies or parts of heritages, as also
portions left unto him by any parents whatsoever, his manner
was either out of hand to part with the same to their children,
or if they were in their minority, to restore all unto them with

the increase, upon the day that they put on their virile gowns, or else whereon they married.

67. A patron he was (to his freedmen) and a master (to his bondservants) no less severe than gracious and gentle. Many of his enfranchised men he highly honored and employed especially: as Licinius Enceladus, with others. His servant Cosmus, who thought and spoke most harshly of him, he proceeded to chastise no farther than with hanging a pair of fetters at his heels. As for Diomedes his steward, who walking together with him, by occasion of a wild boar running full upon them, for very fear put his master between himself and the beast, he imputed unto him rather timidity than any fault else; and although it were a matter of no small peril, yet because there was no prepensed malice, he turned all into a jest. Contrariwise, the selfsame man forced to death Procillus, a freedman of his, and whom he set the greatest store by, because he was detested for abusing men's wives. Gallus, his scribe, had received five hundred denarii for making one privy unto a letter of his hands; he caused his legs to be broken for his labor. The pedagogue and other servitors attendant upon Gaius his son, who taking the vantage of his sickness and death, bore themselves proudly and insolently in his province, and therein committed many outrages, he caused to be thrown headlong into a river, with heavy weights about their necks.

68. In the prime and flower of his youth he incurred in sundry ways the infamous note of a vicious and wanton life. Sextus Pompeius railed upon him as an effeminate person, Marcus Antonius laid to his charge that he earned his uncle's adoption by suffering the filthy abuse of his body. Likewise Lucius, brother to the said Marcus, inveighed against him as if he had abandoned and prostituted his youth (deflowered and tasted first by Caesar) unto Hirtius also in Spain for 300,000 sesterces; and that he was wont to singe his legs with red hot

walnut shells to the end that the hair might come up softer. The very people also in general one time on a day of their solemn stage plays both construed to his reproach and also with exceeding great applause verified of him a verse pronounced upon the stage, as touching a priest of Cybele, mother of the gods, playing upon a timbrel:

Videsne? Cinaedus orbem digito temperat.

See'st thou? A catamite sways the globe with his finger.

69. That he was a common adulterer his very friends do not deny, but they excuse him forsooth, saying that he did it not upon filthy lust, but for good reason and in policy to the end that he might more easily search out the plots and practices of his adversaries by the means of women and wives, it skilled not whose. Marcus Antonius objected against him, besides his over-hasty marriage with Livia, that he fetched a certain noble dame, the wife of one who had been consul, forth of a dining parlor, even before her husband's face, into his own bed-chamber, and brought her thither back again to make an end of the banquet with her hair all ruffled, even while her ears were yet glowing red; also that he put away Scribonia because she was too plain and round with him upon grief she took that a concubine was so great and might do so much with him; also that there were bargains and matches sought out for him by his friends, who stuck not to view and peruse both wives and young maidens of ripe years, all naked, as if Toravius the bawd were a-selling of them. Moreover he writes thus much to Augustus, after a familiar sort, as yet being not fallen out flatly with him, nor a professed enemy: "What has changed and altered you? Is it because I lie with a queen? She is my wife. And is this the first time? Did I not so nine years since? Alas good sir, you that would have me company with Octavia my wife only, tell me true: know you for your part

none other women but Drusilla? Go to; so may you fare well and have your health, if when you shall read this letter, you be not ready to deal carnally with Tertulla, or Rufilla, or Salvia Titisenia, or with all of them. And think you it skills not where and whom you lust after and meddle with?"

70. Moreover, much talk there was abroad of a certain supper of his, more secret than the rest, and which was commonly called "of the twelve gods," at which there sat guests in habit of gods and goddesses, and himself among them adorned like Apollo: not only the letters of Antony who rehearsed most bitterly the names of every one, do lay in his reproach, but also these verses without an author so vulgarly known and rife in every man's mouth:

> Cum primum istorum conduxit mensa choragum
>   Sexque deos vidit Mallia sexque deas,
> Impia dum Phoebi Caesar mendacia ludit,
>   Dum nova divorum cenat adulteria:
> Omnia se a terris tunc numina declinarunt,
>   Fugit et auratos Iuppiter ipse thronos.

When first the table of these guests hired one the dance to lead
  And Mallia six goddesses and gods as many saw;
While Caesar Phoebus counterfeits profanely, and instead
  Of supper, new adulteries makes of gods against all law,
All the heavenly powers then, from the earth their eyes quite
      turned away,
  And Jupiter himself would not in gilt shrines longer stay.

The scandal of this supper was increased by the exceeding dearth and famine at that time in Rome, and the very next morrow there was set up this cry and note within the city, that the gods had eaten up all the corn, and that Caesar was become Apollo indeed, but yet Apollo the Tormentor, under which surname that god was worshipped in one place of the city. Furthermore, taxed he was for his greedy grasping after

precious house furniture and costly Corinthian vessels; as also
for giving himself much to dice play. For, as in the time of the
proscription, there was written over his statue:

Pater Argentarius, ego Corinthiarius

My father was a banking-money changer
And I am now a Corinth-vessel monger,

because it was thought he procured some to be put into the
bill of those that were proscribed, even for the love of their
Corinthian-vessels; so afterwards during the Sicilian war, this
epigram of him went current abroad:

Postquam bis classe victus naves perdidit,
Aliquando ut vincat, ludit assidue aleam.

Since time he lost his ships at sea in fight defeated twice
That win he may sometime, he plays continually at dice.

71. Of these criminous imputations or malicious slanders
(I wot not which), the infamy of his unnatural uncleanness he
checked and confuted most easily by his chaste life both at the
time and afterwards. Likewise the invidious opinion of his
excessive and sumptuous furniture, considering that, when
he had by force won Alexandria, he retained for himself out
of all the king's household stuff and rich implements no more
but one cup of the precious stone myrrh; and soon after, all
the brazen vessels which were of most use, he melted every
one. Marry for fleshly lust otherwise, and wantonness with
women, he went not clear, but was blotted therewith. For
afterwards also, as the report goes, he gave himself overmuch
to the deflowering of young maids whom his wife sought
out for him from all places. As for the rumor that ran of his
dice playing he bashed no whit thereat; and he played simply
without art and openly for his disport, even when he was well
stricken with years, and not only the month of December but

in other holidays as well, yea and on work days too. Neither is there any doubt to be made thereof. For in a certain epistle written in his own hand: "I supped," quoth he, "my Tiberius, with the same men. There came moreover to bear us company these guests: Vinicius and Silius the father. In supper time we played like old men, both yesterday and today. For when the dice were cast whoever threw the chance *Canis* or *Senio*, for every die he staked lay to the stock a denarius, which he took up and swooped all clean whose luck it was to throw Venus." Again in another letter: "We lived full merrily, my Tiberius, during the feast *Quinquatria*; for we played every day: we haunted, I say, and kept the dicing house hot. Your brother did his deed with many great shouts and outcries, howbeit in the end he lost not much; but after his great losses he gathered up his crumbs prettily well by little and little, and beyond his hope and expectation. I, for my part, lost 20,000 sesterces in my own name, but it was when I had been over-liberal in my gaming, as commonly my manner is. For, if I had called for those losing hands which I forgave my fellow gamesters, or kept but that which I gave clean away, I had won as good as 50,000 clear. But I chose rather thus to do. For my bounty exalts me unto celestial glory." Unto his daughter he writes thus: "I have sent unto you 250 denarii, just so many as I had given to my guests apiece, if they would have played together at supper-time either at dice or at odd-and-even." For the rest of his life, certain it is, that in every respect he was most continent, and without suspicion of any vice.

72. He dwelt at first hard by the Forum of Rome, above the winding stairs Anulariae, in an house which had been Calvus the orator's; afterwards in the Palatine hill, although in a mean habitation, belonging sometime to Hortensius, and neither for spaciousness nor stately setting out, nor trim furniture conspicuous; as wherein the galleries were but short,

standing upon pillars made of soft Alban stone; and the reception rooms without any marble or beautiful pavements. For in the space of forty years and more, he kept one bedchamber winter and summer, and albeit he found by experience the city not very wholesome in the winter for his health, yet continually he wintered there. If he purposed at any time to do ought secretly and without interruption, he had a special room alone by itself aloft which he called "Syracuse" or "Technophyon," "little workshop." Hither would he withdraw himself orderly, or else make a step to some country house near the city, of one of his libertines. Was he sick at any time? Then he used to lie in Maecenas' house. Of all his retiring places of pleasure, he frequented these especially, that stood along the Maritime tract, and the isles of Campania; or else the towns near adjoining to the city of Rome, to wit, Lanuvium, Praeneste and Tibur; where also within the porches of Hercules' Temple, he sat very often to minister justice. Large palaces and full of curious works he misliked, and verily, those that were sumptuously built he razed down to the very ground. His own, as little as they were, he adorned and beautified not so much with trim statues and gay painted tables, as with open walks, pleasant groves, and such things as for their antiquity and rareness were notable. Of which sort were at Capri the huge members of monstrous fishes and wild beasts, the bones that are said to be of giants, and the armor of the demigods and worthies in old time.

73. How slenderly provided he was of household stuff and furniture otherwise appears by his dining pallets and tables yet remaining; the most part whereof be scarce answerable to the elegance of a mere private person. Neither slept he, by men's saying, otherwise than upon a low bed, and the same but meanly spread and laid with coverlets. He wore not lightly any apparel but of housewife's cloth, made within house by his

wife, his sisters, his daughter and granddaughters. His gowns were neither straight and scant, nor yet wide and large. His senator's robe neither with overbroad stripes of purple, nor with narrow. His shoes underlaid somewhat with the highest, that he might seem taller than he was. As for the raiment which he used abroad, and his shoes, he had them at all time laid ready within his bed-chamber, against all sudden occurrences and unlooked-for occasions whatsoever.

74. He feasted daily, and never otherwise than at a set table; not without great respect and choice of degrees and persons. Valerius Messalla writes, that he never entertained any of his libertines at supper except Menas, and him naturalized first, even after the betraying of Sextus Pompeius' fleet; himself writes that he invited one in whose farm he would make his abode, and who in times past had been a spy of his. He came to the board himself when he made a feast, sometimes very late, and otherwhiles left the same as soon; and then his guests would both fall to their suppers before he sat down, and also continued sitting still after he was gone. The suppers he made consisted ordinarily of three dishes of meat, and, when he would fare most highly, of six at the most; and as he entertained his guests in no exceeding sumptuous manner, so he welcomed them with all the kindness and courtesy that might be. For he would provoke them, if they either sat silent or spoke softly to the fellowship of discourse and talk; yea and interpose either musicians and players or else clowns out of the circus, but most commonly story-tellers.

75. Festival and solemn days he celebrated sometimes with unmeasurable expenses, otherwhiles with mirth and sport only; at the *Saturnalia*, and at other times when it pleased him, he used to send abroad as his gifts, one while apparel, gold and silver; otherwhile money of all stamps, even old pieces current in the kings' days, and strange coins; sometime nothing but

hair cloth, sponges, coal rakes, tongs and such like stuff, under obscure and doubtful titles symbolizing somewhat else. He was wont also to offer sale, by marting in the time of a banquet to his guests, of such things, as were in price most unequal, yea and to tender blind bargains unto them also of painted pictures, with the wrong side outward, and so by uncertain venturing upon their hap, either to frustrate and disappoint, or fully to satisfy the hope of the chapmen; yet so, as the cheapening of the thing should always pass through the whole company, and the loss or gain grow to them all as common.

76. As touching diet (for I may not overpass so much as this) he was a man of very little meat, and feeding for the most part plain. Coarse bread and small fishes; cheese pressed with the hand; and green figs especially of that kind which bear twice a year, his appetite served unto. His manner was to eat even just before supper, when and wheresoever his stomach called for food. His very words out of his own epistles show no less, which are these, "While we were in a wagon, we tasted of bread and dates." Again, "As I returned homeward in my litter from the Regia, I ate an ounce of bread with a few hard grapes." And once more, "The very Jew, my Tiberius, observes not his fast upon the Sabbath so precisely, as I have this day, who in the baths, not before the first hour of the night was past, chewed two morsels of bread, even before I began to be anointed." Upon this neglect of diet, he used divers times to take his supper alone, either before his other guests were set and fell to meat, or else after all was taken away, and they risen; whereas, at a full board he would not touch a bit.

77. He was by nature also a very small drinker of wine. Cornelius Nepos reports of him that his usual manner was during the time he lay encamped before Mutina to drink at a supper not above thrice. Afterwards, whensoever he drank

most liberally he passed not a pint, or if he went beyond, he cast it up again. Instead of drink he took a sop of bread soaked in cold water, or a piece of cucumber, or a young lettuce head, or else some new gathered apple, sharp and tart.

78. After his noon's repast he used to take his repose, and to sleep awhile, in his clothes as he was, with his shoes on, stretching out his feet, and holding his hand before his eyes. After supper he retired himself into a little study. And there continued he by a candle far in the night, even until he had dispatched the rest of that day's business, either all or the most part. From thence, he went directly to his bed, where he slept at the most not above seven hours; and those verily not together but so, as in that space of time he would awake three or four times; and if he could not recover his sleep thus broken and interrupted (as it happened otherwhiles), he would send for some to read or tell tales, and by their means catch a sleep again, and draw the same out often after day-break. Neither would he ever lie awake without one sitting by his bedside. Much offended he was with want of sleep (or waking) early in a morning; and if he were to be awakened sooner than ordinary, either about some worldly affairs of his friends, or service of the gods, because he would not prejudice thereby his own good or health, he used to stay in some of his familiar friends' upper rooms and loft, next to the place where his occasions lay. And even so, many a time for want of sleep, both as he was carried through the streets, and also when his litter was set down, he would between whiles take a nap and make some stay.

79. He was of an excellent presence and personage, and the same throughout all his age most lovely and amiable; negligent though he were in all manner of pikedness, for combing and trimming of his head so careless, as that he would use at once many barbers, such as came next hand, it skilled not whom;

and one while he clipped, another while he shaved his beard; and yet at the very same time, he either read, or else wrote somewhat. His visage and countenance, whether he spoke or held his peace, was so mild, so pleasant and lightsome, that one of the nobles and potentates of Gaul, confessed unto his countrymen, he was thereby only stayed and reclaimed, that he did not approach near unto him, under color of conference as he passed over the Alps, and so shove him down from a steep crag to break his neck, as his full intent was. He had a pair of clear and shining eyes; wherein also (as he would have made men believe), was seated a kind of divine vigor; and he joyed much, if a man looking wistly upon him held down his face, as it were against the brightness of the sun. But in his old age he saw not very well with the left eye. His teeth grew thin in his head, and the same were small and ragged; the hair of his head was somewhat curled and turning downward; and withal of a light yellow color. His eyebrows met together; his ears were of a mean bigness; his nose both in the upper part, bearing out round, and also beneath somewhat with the longest. Of color and complexion, he was between a brown and fair white. His stature but short (and yet Julius Marathus his freedman writes in the history of his life, that he was five foot and nine inches high). But as low as the same was, the proportionable making and feature of his limbs hid it so, as it might not be perceived, unless he were compared with some taller person than himself standing by.

80. His body, by report, was full of spots, having upon the breast and belly natural marks which he brought with him into the world; dispersed, for the manner, order, and number, like unto the stars of the celestial bear. As also certain hard rising of thick brawny skin, occasioned in divers places by the itching of his body, and the continual and forcible use of the strigil [much like a curry comb] in the baths; which

callosities resembled a ringworm. In his left hip, thigh, and leg, he was not very sound; insomuch, as many times for grief thereof he halted on that side; but by a remedy that he had of sand and reeds, he found ease and went upright again. Also, the forefinger of his right hand he perceived otherwhiles to be so weak, that being benumbed and shrunk by a cramp upon some cold, he could hardly set it to writing, with the help of an hoop and finger-stall of horn. He complained also of the grief in his bladder, but voiding at length little gravel-stones by urine, he was eased of that pain.

81. All his lifetime he tasted of certain grievous and dangerous sicknesses, but especially after the subduing of Cantabria; what time, by reason of his liver diseased and corrupted by distillations, he was driven to some extremity, and thereby of necessity entered into a contrary and desperate course of physic. For, seeing that hot fomentations did him no good, forced he was by the direction and counsel of Antonius Musa his physician, to be cured by cold. He had the experience also of some maladies which came yearly and kept their course at a certain time. For about his birthday, most commonly he was sickish and had a faintness upon him; likewise in the beginning of the spring, much troubled he was with the inflation of the midriff and hypochondrial parts; and whensoever the wind was southerly, with the catarrh. By occasion whereof, his body being so shaken, he could not well endure either cold or heat.

82. In wintertime clad he went against the cold with four coats, together with a good thick gown, and his waistcoat or petticoat body of woollen; well lapped also about the thighs and legs. During summer he lay with his bed-chamber doors open, and oftentimes within a cloister supported with pillars, having water walming out of a spring, or running from a spout in a conduit; or else someone to make wind hard by him. He could not away so much as with the winter sunshine; and

therefore even at home he never walked up and down in the air without a broad brimmed hat upon his head. He traveled in a litter, and never but in the night. The journeys that he made were soft and small; so as if he went from Rome but to Tibur or Praeneste, he would make two days of it. Could he reach to any place by sea, he chose rather to sail thither than go by land. But as great infirmities as he was subject unto, he maintained and defended his body with as much care and regard of himself, but principally by seldom bathing. For anointed he was very often and used to sweat before a light fire; and then upon it to be doused in water lukewarm or else heated with long standing in the sun. And so often as he was to use the sea waters hot, or those of Albula for the strengthening of his sinews, he contented himself with this, namely, to sit in a wooden bathing tub, which himself by a Spanish name called *Dureta*, and therein to shake up and down his hands and feet one after another, by turns.

83. The exercises in Mars field of riding on horseback and bearing arms, he laid aside immediately after the civil wars, and took himself, first, to the little tennis-ball, and the hand-ball blown with wind. Soon after, he used only to be carried and to walk, but so as that in the end of every walk he would take his run by jumps, lapped and wrapped within a light garment or a thin veil and sheet of linen. For his recreation and pastime, his manner was sometimes to fish with the hook, otherwhiles to play with cockle bones, or trundling round pellets, or else with nuts even among little boys; whom he would seek out from all parts, if they were of an amiable countenance and could prattle prettily with a lovely grace. These the Romans called *delicias suas*, their darlings in an honest sense; not such as the Greeks in an unclean signification, named *paidica*, wanton baggages, catamites, but principally those of the Moors' and Syrians' kind. As for dwarfs, crooked

and misshapen elves and all of that sort, he could not abide such, as being the very mockeries of nature's work, and of unlucky presage.

84. Eloquence, and other liberal professions he exercised from his very childhood right willingly, and therein took exceeding great pains. During the war at Mutina, notwithstanding that huge heap of affairs and occurrences, by report, he read, he wrote, he declaimed every day. For afterwards, neither in the senate-house, nor before the people, nor yet to his soldiers made he ever speech, but it was premeditated and composed before; albeit he wanted not the gift to speak *ex tempore*. Now, for fear lest his memory at any time should fail him, lest also he might spend too much time in learning by rote, he began to read and rehearse all out of his written copy. His very speeches also with folk by themselves, even with Livia his wife about any grave and serious matters, were never but penned and put down in writing; out of which he would rehearse the same, that he might not speak otherwise *ex tempore* or more or less than was meet. His pronunciation and utterance was sweet, carrying with it a peculiar and proper sound of his own; and continually he used the help of an elocutionist to moderate his voice; but sometimes when his throat was weakened, he delivered his orations to the people by the mouth of a crier.

85. Many compositions he made in prose, of sundry arguments. Of which he would read some in a meeting of his familiars, as it were in an auditorium; as namely a rejoinder called *Rescripta*, unto Brutus, against Cato. Which volumes, when for the most part, he had rehearsed, being now well stricken in years and growing weary, he made over to Tiberius for to be read through. In like manner he wrote certain exhortations unto philosophy, and somewhat of his own life, which he declared in thirty books, even unto the Cantabrian

war, and no farther. As for poetry he dealt in it but super-
ficially. One treatise there is extant written by him in hexa-
meter verses, the argument whereof, is *Sicily*, and so it is entitled. There is another book also, as little as it, *Of Epigrams*;
which for the most part he devised while he was in the baths.
For, having in a great and ardent heat begun a tragedy [called
Ajax], when he saw his style would not frame thereto and
speed no better, he defaced and wiped it quite out. And when
some of his friends asked him how *Ajax* did? he answered,
that his *Ajax* was fallen upon a sponge [was wiped away or
blotted out with a sponge: alluding to Ajax, that fell upon his
own sword].

86. The eloquence that he followed was of an elegant and
temperate kind; wherein he avoided unapt and unfit sentences,
as also the stinking savors, as himself saith, of dark and obscure
words, but took especial care how to express his mind and
meaning most plainly and evidently. For the better effecting
thereof, and because he would not in any place trouble and
stay reader or hearer, he stuck not either to put prepositions
unto verbs, or to iterate conjunctions very oft; which being
taken away breed some obscurity, although they yield a greater
grace. As for those that affect new-made words, such as also
use old terms past date, he loathed and rejected alike, as faulty,
both the sorts of them in a contrary kind. Those he shook up
divers times, but especially his friend Maecenas, whose po-
maded curls, for these were his terms, he evermore curses and
taxes, yea and by way of imitation merrily scoffs at. Neither
spared he so much as Tiberius for hunting otherwhiles after
old words out of use, and such as be obscure and hardly
understood. As for Marcus Antonius, he rates him as if he were
frantic, for writing that which men may rather wonder at
than understand. And proceeding to mock his lewd and un-
constant humor in choosing a kind of eloquence by himself,

he added thus much moreover: "And are you in doubt to imitate Cimer Annius and Veranius Flaccus so that you might use the words which Crispus Sallustius gathered out of Cato's *Origins*? or rather transfer the rolling tongue of Asiatic orators, full of vain words, and void of pithy sentences, into our language and manner of speech?" And in a certain epistle, praising the ready wit of Agrippina his own granddaughter, "but you have need," quoth he, "to endeavor that neither in writing nor in speaking you be troublesome and odious."

87. In his daily and ordinary talk certain phrases he had which he used very often and significantly, as the letters of his own hand-writing do evidently show, in which, ever and anon, when he meant some that would never pay their debts, he said, "They would pay *ad Kalendas Graecas*, on the Greek Kalends." And when he exhorted men to bear patiently the present state whatever it was, "Let us content ourselves," quoth he, "with this Cato." To express the speedy expedition of a thing done hastily, "Quicker," he would say, "than asparagus can be cooked." He continually put for *stultus*, fool, *baceolus*, dolt; for *pullus*, dark, *pulleiaceus*, darkish; and for *cerritus*, mad, *vacerrosus*, blockhead; and instead of *male se habere*, feel badly, *vapide se habere*, feel flat; and for *languere*, be weak, *betizare*, be like a beet, which vulgarly we call *lachanizare*; similarly, for *sumus*, *simus*, and *domos* in the genitive singular case, for *domus*. And he never used these two words otherwise, that no man should think it was a fault rather than a custom. Thus much also have I observed, especially in his manuscripts, that he never cuts a word in sunder, nor in the end of any line does he transfer the overplus of letters unto those next following, but presently puts them down even there underneath, and encloses them within a circle.

88. Orthography, that is to say, the form and precise rule of writing set down by grammarians, he did not so much observe,

but seems to follow their opinion rather who think that men should write according as they speak. For whereas oftentimes he either exchanges or leaves clean out, not letters only, but syllables also, which is a common error among men. Neither would I note thus much, but that it seems strange to me, which some have written of him, namely, that he substituted another in the place of a consular lieutenant (as one altogether rude and unlearned) because he had marked in his handwriting *ixi* for *ipsi*. And look how often himself writes darkly by way of ciphering, he puts B for A, C for B, and so forth after the same manner, the letters next following instead of the former; and for X a double AA.

89. Neither verily was he less in love with the study of Greek literature, for even therein also he highly excelled as having been brought up and taught under the professed rhetorician Apollodorus of Pergamus: whom, being now very aged, he even took with him in his youthful days from Rome to Apollonia. Afterwards also he became well furnished with variety of erudition and learning through association with the philosopher Areus and his two sons, Dionysius and Nicanor. Yet so as for all that, he could neither speak readily nor durst compose anything in Greek. For if occasion required, he drew it up in Latin and gave it unto another for to be translated into Greek. And as he was not altogether unskillful in poems, so he took delight even in the old comedy also, which he exhibited oftentimes to be acted in his public solemnities. In reading over and perusing authors of both languages he sought after nothing so much as wholesome precepts and examples serving to public or private use; and those, when he had copied them out word for word, he sent either to his inward friends and domestic servants, or to the commanders of armies and governors of provinces, or else for the most part to the magistrates of the city, according as any one of them needed ad-

monition. Moreover, whole books he both read from one end to the other unto the senate, and also published oftentimes to the people by proclamation: as namely, the orations of Quintus Metellus touching upon the propagation and multiplying of children; those likewise of Rutilius concerning the mode and form of buildings: thereby the rather to persuade them that he was not the first that looked into these matters, but that their forefathers in old time had even then a care and regard thereof. The fine wits flourishing in his days he cherished by all means possible. Such as rehearsed before him their compositions he gave audience unto, courteously and with patience; not only verses and histories, but orations also and dialogues. Marry if any thing were written of himself, unless it were done with serious gravity and by the best, he took offense thereat; and he gave the praetors charge not to suffer his name to be made vulgar and stale in the trivial contentions of orators, poets, etc. when they were matched with one another.

90. For religious scrupulosity and superstition, thus by hearsay he stood affected: thunder and lightning he was always afraid of, in so much as always and in every place he carried about him for a preservative remedy a seal's skin; yea and whenever he suspected there would be any extraordinary storm or tempest, he would retire himself into a closed, secret room, underground, and vaulted above head; which he did because once in times past he had been frightened with a flash of lightning, crossing him in his journey by night, as we have before related.

91. As for dreams, neither his own, nor other men's of himself he neglected. At the battle of Philippi, albeit he meant not to step out of his pavilion by reason of sickness, yet he went forth, warned to do so by the dream of his physician. And it fell out well for him, considering that after his camp, forced and won by the enemies, his litter in that concourse of

theirs was stabbed through and all rent and torn, as if he had remained there behind, lying sick. Himself, every spring, was wont to see many visions most fearful, but the same proved vain illusions and to no purpose; at other times of the year he dreamed not so often, but yet to more effect. When as he ordinarily frequented the temple dedicated to Jupiter the Thunderer in the Capitol, he dreamed that Jupiter Capitolinus complained how his worshippers were taken from him perforce, and that he answered he had placed Thundering Jupiter hard by him, as a porter; whereupon soon after he adorned the lanterns of that temple with a ring of bells, because such commonly do hang at men's gates. By occasion of a vision by night, he begged yearly upon a certain day money of the people, and held out his hand hollow to those that brought and offered unto him brazen dodkins called *asses*.

92. Certain foretokens and ominous signs he observed as infallible presages, to wit, if in a morning his shoes were put on wrong, and namely the left for the right, he held it unlucky; again, when he was to take any long journey by land or sea, if it chanced to mizzle of rain, he took that for a lucky sign betokening a speedy and prosperous return. But moved he was especially with supernatural sights. There happened a date tree to spring forth between the very joints of the stones before his door, which he removed and transplanted in the inward court of his domestic gods, taking great care that it might get root and grow there. He joyed so much in the island of Capri that the boughs of a very old oak tree, hanging and drooping now for age down to the ground, became fresh again at his coming hither, that he would needs make an exchange with the state of Naples, and in lieu of that island gave them Aenaria. Certain days also he precisely observed: as for example, he would not take a journey anywhither upon the day after the Nundinae; nor begin any serious matter upon the

nones of a month; herein verily avoiding and eschewing nought else, as he writes to Tiberius, but the unlucky ominousness of the name.

93. Of foreign ceremonies and religions, he entertained with all reverence those that were ancient, and whereof he conceived good reason; the rest he despised. For having been instituted and professed in the sacred mysteries of Ceres at Athens, when afterwards he sat judicially upon the tribunal at Rome to hear and determine a controversy as touching the privilege of Ceres' priests in Attica, and perceived that certain points of great secrecy were proposed there to be debated, he dismissed the assembly and multitude of people standing about in the court, and himself alone heard them plead the case. But contrariwise, not only when he rode in visitation all over Egypt, himself forbore to turn a little out of his way for to see Apis, but also commended his grandson Gaius, because in riding through Judea he did not so much as once make supplication in Jerusalem.

94. And seeing we have proceeded thus far, it would not be impertinent to annex hereto, what befell unto him before he was born, what happened upon his very birthday, and what presently ensued thereupon. Whereby that future greatness and perpetual felicity of his might he hoped for and observed. At Velitrae, part of the town wall in old time had been blasted by lightning, upon which occasion answer was given by the Oracle that a citizen of that town should one day be ruler of the world. The Velitrians, in confidence hereof, both then and afterwards also, many a time warred with the people of Rome, even well near to their own final ruin and destruction. At length (though late it was) by good proofs and evidences it appeared that the said strange accident portended the mighty power of Augustus. Julius Marathus reports that some six months before Augustus' nativity there happened at Rome a

prodigy publicly known whereby foreshown and announced it was that nature was about to bring forth a king over the people of Rome, at which the senate being affrighted made an act, that no man child that year born should be reared and brought up. But they whose wives then were great bellied (for every one was ready to draw the hope unto himself) took care that the said act of the senate should not be brought into the city chamber and there enrolled. I read in the books of Asclepias of Mendes entitled *Theologoumenon* [*Discourses about the Gods*], how Atia, being come at midnight to celebrate the solemn sacrifice and divine service of Apollo, fell fast asleep, while other dames slept also. Suddenly a serpent crept close unto her and soon went forth from her. She therewith being awakened purified herself as she would have done upon her husband's companying with her. And presently there arose to be seen upon her body a certain mark or speck representing the picture of a serpent, which never after could be gotten out, so that immediately thereupon she forbore the public baths forever: in the tenth month after she was delivered of Augustus, and for this cause he was reputed to be the son of Apollo. The same Atia, before she was brought to bed of him, dreamed that her entrails were heaved up to the stars and there stretched forth and spread all over the compass of earth and heaven. His father Octavius likewise dreamed that out of the womb of Atia there arose the shining beams of the sun. The very day on which he was born the conspiracy of Catiline was debated in the senate-house, and Octavius by occasion of his wife's childbirth came very late thither. Well known it is and commonly spoken that Publius Nigidius, understanding the cause of his stay, so soon as he learned the hour also when she was delivered, gave it out confidently that there was born the sovereign lord of the world. Afterwards when Octavius, leading an army through the secret parts of Thracia, inquired in the sacred grove of *Liber Pater* (according to the rites and ceremonies of that barbarous religion), concerning his son, the same answer he received from the priests there. For when the wine was poured upon the altar, there arose from thence so great a shining flame as surmounted the roof of the temple and so ascended to heaven. And in times past the like strange token happened to Alexander the Great, and to none but him, when he sacrificed upon the same altar. Moreover, the night next following, he presently thought he saw his son carrying a stately majesty above the ordinary proportion of a mortal weight, with a thunderbolt and scepter in his hand, wearing also the triumphant robes of Jupiter Optimus Maximus upon his back and a radiant coronet on his head; over and besides, riding a chariot dight with laurel and drawn by twelve steeds exceeding white. While he was yet a very babe (as Gaius Drusus has left in writing extant), being by his nurse laid in the evening within a cradle in swaddling clothes upon the ground floor, the next morning he could nowhere be seen; and after long seeking was found at last upon a very high tower facing the rising sun. So soon as he began to speak he commanded the frogs to keep silence, which about the manor of his grandsire by the city chanced to make a foul noise, and thereupon ever after the frogs in that place are not able to croak. About four miles from Rome, as you go directly to Capua, it fell out that suddenly an eagle snatched a piece of bread out of his hand as he took his dinner within a pleasant grove. And when he had mounted up a very great height, came gently down of a sudden again and restored the same unto him. Quintus Catulus after the dedication of the Capitol dreamed two nights together: in the former, he thought that Jupiter Optimus Maximus, while many young boys, noblemen's sons, were playing about his altar, severed one of them from the rest and bestowed in his bosom the public broad seal of the state to carry in his hand. And the next night following he saw in another dream the same boy in the bosom of Jupiter Capitolinus, whom when he commanded to be pulled from thence, prohibited he was by the admonition of the god, as if the same boy should be brought up for the defense and tuition of the commonwealth. Now the morrow after, chancing to meet with young Augustus (whom erst he had not known before), he beheld him wistly not without great admiration, and withal openly gave it out that he was for all the world like unto that boy of whom he dreamed. Some tell the former dream of Catulus otherwise: Jupiter, when a number of boys required of him a tutor, pointed out one of them, unto whom they should refer all their desires, and then lightly touching the boy's lips with his fingers, brought that kiss back to his own mouth. Marcus Cicero, having accompanied Gaius Caesar into the Capitol, happened to report unto his familiar friends the dream he had the night before: namely how a boy of an ingenious face and countenance was let down from heaven by a golden chain and stood at the door of the Capitol, unto whom Jupiter delivered a whip. Hereupon spying at unawares little Augustus, whom (as yet altogether unknown to most men) his uncle Caesar had sent for to the sacrifice, he avouched plainly that this boy was the very one whose image was represented unto him in a vision as he lay asleep. When he was putting on his virile gown, it fortuned that his broad studded coat with a purple stripe, being unstitched in the seams of both shoulders, fell from about him down to his feet. There were some who made this interpretation, that it betokened nothing else but that the class whereof that robe is a badge would one day be subjected unto him. Julius of sacred memory, being about to choose a plot of ground for to encamp in, about Munda, as he cut down wood chanced to light upon a date tree which he caused to be spared and reserved as the very presage of victory. From the root of it there sprung immediately certain shoots which in a few days grew so fast that they not only equalized but over-topped and shadowed their stock; yea and doves haunted the same, therein to nestle and breed, although that kind of bird cannot of all others abide any hard leaves and rough branches. Upon this strange sight especially, Caesar, by report, was moved to suffer none other to succeed him in the empire but his sister's grandson. Augustus, during the time that he was retired to Apollonia, went up in the company of Agrippa into the gallery of Theogenes the mathematician. Now when Agrippa (who inquired first what his own fortune would be) had great matters and those in manner incredible foretold to him, Augustus himself concealed the time of his own nativity and in no wise would utter the same, for fear and bashfulness, lest he should be found inferior to the other. But when, hardly after many exhortations and much ado, he had delivered the same, Theogenes leapt forth and worshipped him. Augustus then anon conceived so great a confidence in his fortunes that he divulged his horoscope and the ascendant of his nativity; yea and also stamped a piece of silver coin with the mark of the celestial sign Capricorn, under which figure and constellation he was born.

95. After Caesar's death, being returned from Apollonia, as he entered Rome, suddenly when the sky was clear and the weather very fair, a certain round coronet in form of a rainbow compassed the circle of the sun, and therewith soon after, the monument of Julia, Caesar's daughter, was smitten with lightning. Moreover in his first consulship, while he attended to take his augury, there were presented unto him, like as to Romulus, twelve vultures; and as he sacrificed, the livers of all the beasts then killed appeared in open view enfolded double and turned inwardly from the nether fillet. And no man of

skill conjectured otherwise but that prosperity and greatness hereby was portended.

96. Furthermore, the very events also of his wars he foresaw. What time as all the forces of the triumvirs were assembled together at Bononia, an eagle perching over his tent flew at two ravens that assailed and fell upon her on either side, and in the end struck them both down to the ground. Which sight the whole army marked very well, and presaged thereby that one day there would arise between the colleagues of the triumvirate such discord, and the like end ensue thereof, as later followed. At Philippi there was a certain Thessalian who made report of the future victory, alleging for his author Caesar of famous memory, whose image encountered him as he journeyed in a desert and by-way. About Perusia when he offered sacrifice and could not speed, but demanded more beasts still to be killed, behold the enemies made a sudden sally forth and caught up and carried away the whole provision of the sacrifice. The soothsayers then agreed upon this point, that those perilous and adverse calamities which had been threatened and announced to him that sacrificed, should light all and return upon their heads who got the innards; and so it fell out indeed. The day before he fought the battle at sea, near Sicily, as he walked upon the shore, a fish leapt out of the sea and lay at his feet. At Actium, as he was going down to fight the battle, there met him on the way an ass with his driver. The man's name was Eutychus [Fortunate] and the beast's Nicon [Victor]. After the victory obtained, he set up the images of the both in brass, within that temple into which he converted the very place where he encamped.

97. His death also (whereof from hence forth I will write) and his deification after death was known before by many signs most evident. When he had taken a review of the city, and was about the solemn purging thereof within Mars field

before a frequent assembly of people, an eagle there was that soared oftentimes around about him, and crossing at length from him unto a house thereby, settled upon the name of Agrippa, and just upon the first letter of that name. Which when he perceived, he commanded his colleague, Tiberius, to pronounce the vows which the manner was to offer until the next lustrum. For, notwithstanding the tablets containing them were now written and in readiness, yet denied he to undertake those vows which he should never pay. About the same time the first letter of his own name, upon a flash and stroke of lightning went quite out of the inscription that stood upon his statue. Answer was made by the soothsayers that he was to live but just one hundred days after: which number that letter did betoken; and that it would come to pass that he should be canonized and registered among the gods, because *Aesar*, the residue of the name Caesar, in the Etruscan language signified "god." Being about therefore to send Tiberius away into Illyricum and to company him as far as Beneventum, when divers suitors for one cause or another interrupted him, yea and detained him about hearing and determining matters judicially, he cried out aloud (which was also within a while reckoned as a presaging omen) that were he once out of Rome, he would never after be there again what occasion soever might make him stay. And so being entered upon his journey, he went forward as far as to Astura, and so presently from thence (contrary to his usual manner) with the benefit of a forewind and a gentle gale, took ship by night and sailed over.

98. The cause of his sickness he caught by a flux of the belly. And for that time having coasted along Campania and made circuit about the islands next adjoining, he bestowed also four days within a retiring place of pleasure at Capri, where he gave his mind to all ease and courteous affability. It happened as he passed by the bay of Puteoli, certain passengers and

soldiers out of a ship of Alexandria, which then was newly arrived, all clad in white, wreathed also with garlands and burning frankincense, had heaped upon him all good and for-tunate words, chanting his singular praises in these terms, that by him they lived, by him they sailed, by him they enjoyed their freedom, and all the riches they had. At which, he took great contentment and was cheered at the heart, insomuch as thereupon he divided to every one of his train about him forty pieces of gold, but he required an oath again and assurance of each one that they should not lay out that money otherwise than in buying the wares and commodities of Alexandria. For certain days together that remained, among divers and sundry gifts, he distributed as well gowns and cloaks, with this con-dition, that Romans should use the Greek habit and speak likewise Greek; the Greeks likewise should wear the Roman attire and use their language. He beheld also continually Greek youths (of whom there remained yet some store at Capri) exercising themselves according to the ancient custom. And even unto them he made a feast in his own sight, permitting them, or rather exacting of them, their old liberty of sporting, of snatching apples and cates, and of scrambling for such small gifts and favors as were sent or scattered abroad. In one word, he forbore no manner of mirth and pastime. The isle hard by Capri he called Apragopolis [Do-nothing City] from the idleness of such as out of his train retired themselves thither. But one of his beloved minions named Masgabas he had wont merrily to call *Ktistes*, as one would say, in Greek, the Founder of that island. The sepulchre of this Masgabas (who had died the year before) when he perceived one time out of his dining chamber to be frequented with a sort of people and many lights, he pronounced this verse aloud, which he made *ex tempore* in Greek:

I see the tomb of Ktistes all on fire.

And therewith turning to Thrasyllus, a companion of Tiberius sitting over against him, and not knowing what the matter was, he asked him of what poet's making he thought that verse to be. And when he stuck at the question and made no answer, he came out with another to it:

Thou seest with lights Masgabas honored.

Of this verse also he demanded whom he thought to be the maker. But when Thrasyllus returned no other answer but this, that whosoever made them, right excellent they were, he laughed heartily and made himself exceeding merry. Soon after, he crossed over to Naples, albeit even then his guts were greatly enfeebled and the disease grew variable; yet for all that, the quinquennial gymnastic games instituted in his honor, he beheld to the very end, and so together with Tiberius went to the place appointed. But in his return from thence, his disease increased more and more, so as at length he yielded to it at Nola, where having sent for Tiberius and called him back from his journey, he held him a great while in secret talk; neither from that time framed he his mind to any greater affair.

99. Upon his dying day, enquiring ever and anon whether there was as yet any stir and tumult abroad as touching him, he called for a mirror and commanded the hair of his head to be combed and trimmed; his jaws also, ready from weakness to hang or fall, to be composed and set straight. Then, having admitted his friends to come unto him, and asked them whether they thought he had acted well the comedy of his life, he adjoined withal this final conclusion, in Greek:

Now clap your hands and all with joy resound a shout.

After this he dismissed them all, and while he questioned with some that were new come from the city concerning the daughter of Drusus, then sick, suddenly amidst the kisses of

146

The man's name was Eutychus [Fortunate]
and the beast's Nicon [Victor].

Livia and in these words he gave up the ghost, "Live mindful, Livia, of our wedlock, and so, farewell." Thus died he an easy death as he ever wished to have. For lightly, so often as he heard of anybody to have departed this life quickly and without any pangs, he prayed unto the gods that he and his might have the like euthanasia, for that was the very word he was wont to use. One sign only and no more he showed of a mind disquieted and distracted before he yielded up his final breath: in that he suddenly started as in a fright and complained that he was being carried away by forty tall and lusty young men. And even that also was rather a pregnant presage of his mind, than a raving fit and idle conceit of light brain. For so many soldiers they were indeed of the praetorian band who carried him forth dead into the street upon their shoulders.

100. He died in that very bed-chamber wherein his father Octavius left his life before him, when Pompeius and Appuleius, having both their forename Sextus, were consuls: fourteen days before the Kalends of September, at the ninth hour of the day, being seventy-six years old, wanting five and thirty days. His corpse was conveyed and borne by the decurions of the free boroughs and colonies from Nola to Bovillae by night, for it was the hot season of the year; whereas till the daytime it was bestowed in the hall of every town, or else in the greatest temple thereof. From Bovillae the degree of Roman knights took charge of it and brought it into the city of Rome where they placed it within the porch of his own house. The senate both in setting out his funerals and also in honoring his memorials proceeded so far in striving to see who should show greater affection that among many other compliments, some were of a mind that the pomp and solemn convoy of his obsequies should pass forth at the triumphal gate with the image of victory (which is in the courthouse) going before, and the chief noblemen's children of both

147

sexes singing a doleful and lamentable song; others opined that upon the very day of this funeral their rings of gold should be laid away and others of iron put on. Again, divers gave advice that his bones should be gathered up by the priests of the most ancient societies. And one above the rest would have had the name of the month August to be shifted and transferred unto September, for that Augustus was born in this and died in the other. Another urged that all the time from his very birth until his dying day should be named the Augustan Age, and so recorded in the calendars and chronicles. But it was thought best to keep a mean in the honors done unto him. Whereupon twice and in two several places praised he was in a funeral oration: once before the temple of Julius, late deceased, of sacred memory, by Tiberius; and again at the old rostra by Drusus the son of Tiberius; and so upon senator's shoulders was he borne into the Campus Martius, and there committed to the fire and burnt. Neither wanted there a grave personage, one who had been praetor, who affirmed and bound it with an oath that he saw his very image when he was burnt, ascending up to heaven. The chief gentlemen of the knight's order in their single waistcoats, ungirt and barefooted, gathered up his relics together and bestowed them in a stately monument; which piece of work himself had built between the street Flaminia and the bank of the Tiber, in his sixth consulship, and even then given the groves growing about it and the walks adjoining it to be common for the use of the people of Rome forever.

101. His last will and testament made by him when Lucius Plancus and Gaius Silius were consuls, the third day before the nones of April, a year and four months before he died, and the same in two note-books written partly with his own hand, and in part with the hands of Polybius and Hilarius, his freedmen, was brought forth by the Vestal Virgins who had the

keeping thereof upon trust; together with three other rolls or volumes, sealed alike. All which instruments were opened and read in the senate. He ordained for his six heirs: in the first place Tiberius, two-thirds, and Livia, one-third; in the second rank he appointed Drusus the son of Tiberius to inherit one-third part, and Germanicus with his three male children, the other parts remaining. In the third degree he nominated of his own kinsfolk, allies and friends, very many. He bequeathed as a legacy to the people of Rome, forty million sesterces. To the soldiers of the guard, a thousand sesterces apiece. Among the cohorts of the city soldiers, 500, and to those of the legionary cohorts, 300 apiece. Which sum of money he commanded to be paid presently; for he had so much in store at all times (put up in bags and coffers) lying by him. Sundry parcels gave he besides by legacy parole. And of some thereof he deferred the payment, if the same were above 20,000 sesterces. For paying of which he set a year's day at the farthest, alleging for his excuse his mean estate, and protesting that by this account there would not come to his heirs' hands above 150 millions, albeit within the compass of twenty years immediately going before he had received by the wills and testaments of his friends four thousand millions. All which mass of treasure, together with two patrimonies by his two fathers and other inheritances, he had spent well near every whit upon the commonwealth. The two Julias, to wit his daughter and his niece, he forbade expressly (if ought happened to them) to be interred in his own mausoleum. Of those three rolls or instruments above named, in the first he comprised his own directions as touching his funeral; the second contained a register or index of those acts which he had achieved, and his pleasure was that the same should be engraven in bronze tablets and erected before his mausoleum. In the third he represented a breviary and abstract of the whole empire: to wit, how many soldiers were enrolled and in pay in any place whatever; also how much money was in the common treasury of the city and in his own coffers; lastly, what the arrears were of such revenues and tributes as were due to the state and unpaid. Whereto he annexed also a schedule containing the names of freedmen and bond, his receivers from whose hands the reckoning might be exacted.

THE HISTORY OF
TIBERIUS NERO CAESAR

TIBERIUS

THE PATRICIAN BRANCH OF THE CLAUDIAN family (for there was likewise another plebeian branch of that name, neither in power nor dignity inferior) had the first beginning out of Regilli, a town of the Sabines. From thence they came with a great retinue of vassals to Rome newly founded, there to dwell; induced thereto by the counsel of Titus Tatius, fellow in government of the kingdom with Romulus; or (which is more the received opinion) through the persuasion of Atta Claudius, a principal person of that house, about the sixth year after the kings were expelled. And so, by the senators of Rome ranged they were among the patricians. Upon this, soon after, they received by virtue of a grant from the whole city for their clients and vassals, lands to occupy beyond the river Anio; and for themselves a place of sepulture under the Capitol. And so, in process of time, obtained twenty-eight consulates, five dictatorships, censorships seven, triumphs six and two ovations. This family, being distinguished by sundry forenames and surnames both, in a general consent rejected the forename of Lucius, after that two of their lineage bearing that name were convicted, the one of robberies, the other of murder. Among surnames it assumed the addition of Nero, which in the Sabine tongue signifies "strong" or "stout."

2. Many of these Claudii, as they deserved in many ways passing well of the commonwealth, so in as many sorts they faulted and did amiss. But to relate the principal examples only

of both kinds: Appius surnamed the Blind was he who dissuaded the entering into league and society with king Pyrrhus, as prejudicial unto the state; Claudius Caudex was the first man that passed over the narrow seas with a fleet and drove the Carthaginians out of Sicily; Claudius Nero surprised and defeated Hasdrubal coming out of Spain with a great and puissant army, before he could join with his brother Hannibal. Contrariwise, Claudius Appius Regillanus, being decemvir chosen to frame and pen the Roman laws, went about by violence (for the satisfaction of his fleshly lust) to enthrall a virgin freeborn; and thereby gave occasion to the commons for to fall away and forsake the nobles a second time. Claudius Drusus, having his own statue erected with a diadem, in a town called Forum Appii, attempted with the help of his favorites and dependants to take all Italy in his own hands. Claudius Pulcher, when, taking of his auspices before Sicily, the sacred chickens would not feed, caused them, in contempt of religion, to be plunged into the sea that they might drink, seeing that they would not eat; and thereupon began a battle at sea, in which, being vanquished and commanded by the senate to nominate a dictator, scorned, as it were, and made but a jest at the public danger and calamity of the state, and named a base sergeant of his own called Glycia. There stand likewise upon record the examples of women and those as divers and contrary. For two Claudias there were of the same house: both she that drew forth the ship with the sacred images of the Idaean Mother of the Gods, which was stuck fast and grounded within the shoals of the Tiber, having before made her prayer openly that as she was a true and pure virgin, so the ship might follow her, and not otherwise: as also another, who after a strange and new manner, being a woman, was arraigned before the people for high treason, for that when her coach wherein she rode could hardly pass forward by reason of a thick throng and press of people, she had openly wished that her brother Pulcher were alive again and might lose a fleet a second time, to the end that there might be by that means a less multitude at Rome. Moreover, very well known it is that, excepting only that Publius Clodius who for the sake of expelling Cicero out of Rome, suffered himself to be adopted a commoner and one too who was younger than himself, all the Claudii were always aristocrats, the only maintainers or patrons of the dignity and power of the patricians; yea and in opposition to the commons so violently and stubbornly that not one of them, although he stood upon his trial for life and death before the people, could find it in his heart so much as to change his weed or to crave any favor at their hands. Nay, some of them there were, who, in a brawl and altercation stuck not to beat the very tribune of the commons. Furthermore, a virgin vestal there was of that name who when a brother of hers triumphed without a warrant from the people, mounted up with him into the chariot, and accompanied him even into the Capitol: to this end that none of the tribunes might lawfully oppose themselves and forbid the triumph.

3. From this race and lineage Tiberius Caesar derives his genealogy, and that verily in the whole blood and of both sides: by his father from Tiberius Nero; by his mother from Appius Pulcher, who were both of them the sons of Appius the Blind. Incorporate he was besides into the families of the Livii by reason that his grandfather by the mother's side was adopted thereinto; which family, commoners though they were, flourished notwithstanding and was highly reputed. It was honored and graced with eight consulships, two censorships and three triumphs; with a dictatorship also and a mastership of the horse; renowned likewise and ennobled for brave and notable men: Salinator especially, and the Drusi. As for Salinator, in his censorship he noted and taxed all the tribes, every one, and

the whole body of the people for inconstant levity, for that having upon his former consulship condemned him and set a fine upon his head, yet afterwards they made him consul a second time and censor besides. Drusus, upon the killing of one Drausus, the general of his enemies, in close combat and single fight, purchased unto himself and his posterity after him that surname. It is reported also that this Drusus, being propraetor, recovered and fetched again out of his province (Gaul) that gold which in times past had been given unto the Senones when they besieged the Capitol, and that it was not Camillus (as the voice goes) that wrested the same perforce out of their hands. His son in the fourth degree of descent, called, for his singular employment against the Gracchi, patron of the senate, left behind him a son, who in a similar variance and debate, as he was busy in devising and putting into practice sundry plots, was treacherously slain by the adverse faction.

4. But the father of this Tiberius Caesar, being treasurer unto Gaius Caesar and admiral of the fleet in the Alexandrian war, performed very good service for the achieving of victory; whereupon he was both substituted as pontifex in place of Publius Scipio, and also sent with a commission to plant colonies in Gaul, among which were Narbo and Arelate. However, after Caesar was slain when all men for fear of troubles and uproars decreed an amnesty and oblivion of that deed (and all other quarrels thereon depending), he proceeded further and opined that they should consult about the rewards of such tyrant-killers. After this, having borne his praetorship (in the end of which year there arose some discord among the triumvirs) he, retaining by him still the ensigns and ornaments of that office after the time fully expired, and following Lucius Antonius, the consul and the triumvir's brother, as far as to Perusia, when the rest yielded themselves, continued alone fast and stuck to the faction (that sided against Octavius) and first

escaped to Praeneste, then to Naples, where when he had proclaimed (but in vain) freedom for all bondslaves, he fled into Sicily. But taking it to the heart that he was not immediately admitted to the presence of Sextus Pompeius, but debarred from the use of his fasces to be borne afore him, he crossed the sea into Achaea and went to Marcus Antonius. With whom, by occasion that shortly after an atonement and peace was made between all parties, he returned to Rome, and at the request of Augustus, yielded unto him his own wife Livia Drusilla, who both at that time was great with child, and also had already before brought him a son named Tiberius, in his own house. Not long after, he departed from life, and left his children surviving him, namely Tiberius Nero and Drusus Nero.

5. Some have thought that this Tiberius Caesar was born at Fundi, grounding upon a light conjecture because his mother's grandame was a Fundane born; and for that soon after the image of Felicity, by virtue of an act of the senate, was there publicly set up. But as most authors and those of better credit do write, born he was at Rome in the Palatine mount, the sixteenth day before the Kalends of December, when Marcus Aemilius Lepidus was consul the second time together with Munatius Plancus, even after the war at Philippi; for so it stands upon the record and in the public registers. Yet there want not some who write otherwise: partly that he was born a year before in the consulship of Hirtius and Pansa, and partly, the year next following, wherein Servilius Isauricus and Antonius were consuls.

6. His infancy and childhood both were full of toilsome travail and danger, by occasion that everywhere he accompanied his parents still, in their flights and escapes. And verily twice he had like to have betrayed them with his squalling at Naples, a little before the forcible and sudden entry of the enemy while they made shift secretly to get into a ship; once

when he was taken hastily from his nurse's breast; and again when he was taken out of his mother's lap and arms by those who, as the necessity of the time required, did their best to ease the poor women of their burden and load. He was carried away with them likewise through Sicily and Achaea; yea and being recommended to the Lacedaemonians (who were under the protection of the Claudii, their patrons) for to take charge of him in public, he was in danger of his life by reason of a fire which suddenly from all parts arose out of a wood, and encircled all the company in his train so that some part of Livia's apparel and the hair of her head was scorched and singed therewith. The gifts bestowed upon him in Sicily by Pompeia, the sister of Sextus Pompeius, to wit a little cloak with a button, or clasp, on it; likewise studs and bosses of gold, continue and are yet showed to be seen at Baiae. After his return into the city of Rome, being adopted by Marcus Gallius, a senator, in his last will and testament, he accepted the inheritance and entered upon it, but within a while forbore the name because Gallius had sided with the adverse faction and taken part against Augustus. Being nine years old he praised his father, deceased, openly from the rostra. Afterwards, as he grew to be a young man, he accompanied the chariot of Augustus in the triumph after Actium, riding upon the trace horse on the left hand, while Marcellus, the son of Octavia, rode upon the other on the right hand. He was president also at the city festival, yea and took part in the Trojan tournament in the circus, where he led the troop of the bigger boys.

7. After he had put on his virile robe, his whole youth and all the time besides of the age next ensuing, even unto the beginning of his empire, he passed for the most part in these affairs following. He exhibited one sword fight performed by fencers in memory of his father, likewise another in the honorable remembrance of his grandfather Drusus. And those at

sundry times and in diverse places: the former in the Forum of Rome, the latter in the amphitheater. He brought again into the lists even those that were freed before time and discharged from that profession, whom he now hired and bound to fight for the sum of one hundred thousand sesterces. He did set forth stage plays also, but while himself was absent. All was done with great magnificence, and at the expense of his mother and step-father. Agrippina, the daughter of Marcus Agrippa and granddaughter to Pomponius Atticus, a knight of Rome, him I mean unto whom Cicero wrote his epistles, he took to wife. And when he had begotten a son of her named Drusus, albeit she fitted him well enough and was besides with child again, enforced he was to put her away and forthwith to wed Julia, the daughter of Augustus. Not without much grief and heartbreak, considering that he both desired still the company of Agrippina and also disliked the conditions and demeanor of Julia, whom he perceived to have had a mind and fancy unto him while she was the wife of a former husband. Which verily was thought also abroad. But as he grieved, after the divorce, that he had driven away Agrippina, so when he chanced but once to meet her still with his eyes so bent, so swelling and staring that straight order was given and a watch set that she should never after come in his way nor within his sight. With Julia he lived at the first in great concord and mutual love, but afterwards he began to estrange himself, and (which was the more grief) he proceeded to part beds and to lie away from her continually, especially after that the pledge of love, their son begotten between them, was untimely taken away, who being born at Aquileia, died a very infant. His own brother Drusus he lost in Germany, whose body he conveyed to Rome, going before it all the way on foot.

8. In his first rudiments and beginnings of civil offices, he pleaded at the bar in defense of Archelaus, the people of

Tralles and those of Thessaly, on sundry charges, while Augustus sat in judgement to hear their trial. In the behalf also of the Laodiceans, Thyaterenes and Chians, who had suffered great losses by earthquake, and humbly sought for relief, he pleaded before the senate. As for Fannius Caepio who together with Varro Murena had conspired against Augustus, he arraigned for high treason before the judges, and caused him to be condemned. And amid these affairs he executed a double charge and function: to wit, the purveyance of corn and victuals, whereof there happened to be scarcity; and the investigation of work-house prisons; the masters whereof had become odious, because they caught up and held to work not only wayfaring persons, but also those who for fear of taking a military oath and to be enrolled, were driven to shroud themselves in such corners.

9. His first service in the wars was in the expedition of Cantabria, when he had the place of military tribune. Afterwards, having the conduct of an army into the East, he restored the kingdom of Armenia unto Tigranes, and from the tribunal seat did put the diadem upon his head. He recovered also those military ensigns which the Parthians had taken from Marcus Crassus. After this he governed as regent that part of Gaul beyond the Alps, called Comata, which was full of troubles, partly by the incursions of barbarous nations, and in part through the intestine discords of princes and nobles of the country. Then warred he upon the Raeti and the Vindelici, and then in Pannonia he conquered the Breuci and Dalmatians. In the German war he brought over into Gaul 40,000 that yielded unto him and placed them near unto the Rhine bank, where they had their habitations assigned. For which acts he entered the city of Rome both in an ovation (riding on horseback) and also in a triumph, mounted upon a chariot, being the first, as some think, that was honored with triumphant or-

naments, a new kind of honor and never granted to any man before. To bear the magistracy he both began betimes, and also ran through them all, almost without any interval of waiting; namely his quaestorship, praetorship and consulship. After some space between he became consul a second time, yea and also received the tribunician authority for five years together.

10. In this confluence of so many prosperous successes, in the strength also of his years and in perfect health, he had a full purpose, suddenly, to retire himself and remove out of the way as far as he could. Whether it were for the weariness he had of his wife, whom he neither durst plainly charge or put away, nor was able to endure any longer, or to the end that by avoiding the contempt incident to daily and continual residence, he might maintain and increase his authority by absenting himself, should at any time the state stand in need of him, it is uncertain. Some are of the opinion that considering Augustus' children were now well grown, he of his own accord yielded up unto them the place and possession, as it were, of the second degree (in administration of the commonweal), which himself had usurped and held a long time: following herein the example of Marcus Agrippa, who having preferred Marcus Marcellus to be employed in public affairs, departed unto Mitylene, lest by his presence he might seem to hinder or belittle him. Which cause even himself, but afterwards, alleged: Marry, for the present, pretending the satiety that he had of honorable positions, and rest from his travails, he made suit for license to depart; neither gave he any ear to his own mother humbly beseeching him to stay; nor to his step-father, who complained also that he should be forsaken thereby and left desolate in the senate. Moreover, when they were insistent still to hold him back, he abstained from all kinds of meat for four days together. At length, having obtained leave to be gone, he left his wife and son behind him at Rome, and forth-

with went down to Ostia giving not so much as one word again to any that accompanied him thither, and kissing very few of them at the parting.

11. As he sailed from Ostia along the coast of Campania, upon news that he heard of Augustus' weakness, he stayed a while and went not forward; but when a rumor began to spread of him (as if he lingered there, waiting some opportunity of greater hopes) he made no more ado, but even against wind and weather, sailed through and passed over to Rhodes, having taken a delight to the pleasant and healthful situation of that island ever since he arrived there in his return from Armenia. Contenting himself here, with a mean and small habitation, with a farmhouse likewise near the city not much larger nor of greater room, he purposed to lead a very civil and private life, at times walking in the gymnasium without a lictor or other officer, performing acts and duties with the Greeks there almost as an equal. It happened upon a time, when he disposed of the businesses which he wished to dispatch on that day, that he gave it out beforehand that he was desirous to visit all the sick in the city. These words of his were mistaken by those next about him. Whereupon all the lazars and diseased persons were by commandment brought into a public porch or gallery, and placed there in order according to the sundry sorts of their maladies. At which unexpected sight, being much troubled and perplexed, he wist not for a good while what to do. Nevertheless, he went around about from one to another, excusing himself for this that was done even to the meanest poorest and basest of them all. This only thing and nothing else beside was noted wherein he seemed to exercise the power of his tribunician authority: being daily and continually conversant about the schools and auditoriums of professors, on an occasion when there arose a great brawl among the sophists opposite in arguing cases and declaiming

one against another, there chanced to be one who perceiving him coming between and inclining to favor one part over the other, railed bitterly at him. Withdrawing himself therefore by little and little and retiring home to his house, he came forth suddenly again and appeared with his lictors, whereupon he cited by the voice of his crier to appear before his tribunal, that foul-mouthed, railing fellow, and so commanded him to be had away to prison. After this, he had certain intelligence given to him that Julia, his wife, was convicted and condemned for her incontinency and adulteries; also that in his name (by a warrant directed from Augustus) she had a bill of divorce sent unto her. And albeit he was glad of these tidings, yet he thought it his part, as much as lay in him, by many letters to reconcile the father unto his daughter; yea, and however she had deserved badly at his hands, yet to suffer her for to have whatsoever he had at any time given unto her in free gift. Now, after he had passed through the time of his tribune's authority, and confessed at last that by this retiring out of the way he sought to avoid naught else but the suspicion of jealousy and emulation with Gaius and Lucius, he made suit that, seeing he was now secured in this behalf, and they strengthened enough and able with ease to manage and maintain the second place in government, he might be permitted to return and see his friends and acquaintances again, whose presence he missed and longed after. But he could not obtain so much; nay, admonished he was and warned beforehand to lay aside all regard of his friends and kinsfolk, whom he was so willing to leave and abandon before.

12. He abode therefore still at Rhodes, even against his will, and hardly by the means and intercession of his own mother wrought thus much, that, for to cover up his ignominy and shame, he might be absent under this pretense, as if he were Augustus' lieutenant. And then verily lived he not only pri-

vately to himself, but also exposed to danger, and in great fear of some hard measure. He lay close and hid in the upland and inward parts of the island, and avoided the offices of them that made sail by those coasts, but who frequented him continually. Forasmuch as no man went into any province that way as lord general or magistrate, but he struck aside and turned to Rhodes. Besides, other causes there were of greater fear and trouble presented to him. For when as he crossed the seas to Samos for a visit to Gaius, his wife's son, who was president of the Eastern parts, he perceived him to be more estranged than before time through the slanders and criminous imputations which Marcus Lollius, companion and governor to the said Gaius, had put into his head. He was drawn also into suspicion by certain centurions whom his favor had advanced and who were returning to camp after a furlough, that he had delivered to many of them mandates of an ambiguous and double construction, such as might seem to sound the minds of everyone and solicit them to rebellion. Of which suspicion being notified by Augustus, he never rested to call for and require to have someone of any degree and order whatsoever to observe all his deeds and words.

13. He neglected also his wonted exercises of horse and armor; yea, and having laid by the habit of his native country, he betook himself to a cloak and slippers (after the Greek fashion). In such a state and condition as this he continued almost two years throughout, more despised and hateful every day: to the point that the Nemausians overthrew his images and statues; and upon a time, at a certain feast where familiar friends were met together, when mention was made of him, there was one who stood up and promised Gaius that in case he did but command and say the word, he would immediately sail to Rhodes and fetch him the head of that exiled person; for so he was commonly called. And chiefly upon this which

was now no bare fear but plain peril, enforced he was, by most earnest prayers, not only of his own, but also of his mother, to require and seek for to return; which he obtained at length with the help somewhat of good fortune. Augustus had fully set down with himself to resolve upon nothing as touching that point, but with the will and good liking of his elder son, Gaius. Now was he, as it happened, at that time, much offended and displeased with Marcus Lollius, but to his step-father (Tiberius) well affected, and ready to be by him entreated. By the permission therefore and good leave of Gaius, called home he was; but with this condition, that he should not meddle one jot in the affairs of state.

14. Thus in the eighth year after his departure, returned he full of great hopes and nothing doubtful of future fortunes, which he had conceived as well by omens as also by predictions and prophesies even from his very birth. For Livia while she went with child of him, among many and sundry experiments she made and signs she observed (and all to know whether she should bring forth a man child or no) took closely an egg from under a hen that was sitting, and kept it warm sometime in her own, and then in her women's hands by turns one after another, so long until there was hatched a cock-chicken with a notable comb on the head. And when he was but a very babe, Scribonius the astrologer gave out and warranted great matters for him, namely that he should one day reign as monarch, but yet without the royal diadem. For as yet, you must know, the sovereign power of the Caesars was unknown. Also, as he entered into his first expedition, and led an army into Syria through Macedonia, it chanced that the consecrated altars of the victorious legions in time past at Philippi shone out suddenly of themselves, all on fire. And soon after, when in his journey toward Illyricum he went to the oracle of Geryon near unto Padua, and drew forth his lot, whereby

he was advised that for counsel and resolution in such particulars as he required after he should throw golden dice into the fountain Aponus, it fell out so that the dice cast by him showed the greatest number. And even at this very day these dice are seen under the water. Some few days likewise before he was sent for home, an eagle (never seen aforetime at Rhodes) perched upon the very top and ridge of his house; and the very day before he had intelligence given him of his return, as he was changing his apparel, his shirt was seen on fire. Thrasyllus also, the astrologer, whom for his great profession of wisdom and cunning he had taken into his house to bear him company, he made then most trial of; namely, when upon kenning a ship afar off, he affirmed that joyful news was coming, whereas at the very same instant as they walked together, Tiberius was fully purposed to have turned him headlong down into the sea, as being a false prophet (for that things fell out untowardly and contrary to his former predictions) and one besides who chanced for the most part to be privy unto him of all his secrets.

15. Being returned to Rome, and having brought his son Drusus solemnly into the Forum, he removed immediately out of the Carina district and the house of Pompey onto the Esquiline, to the gardens of Maecenas. There he gave himself wholly to quietness, performing private duties only and not meddling at all in public offices. After Gaius and Lucius died, within the compass of three years, he, together with their brother, Marcus Agrippa, was adopted by Augustus, but compelled first himself to adopt Germanicus, his brother's son. Neither did he aught afterwards as the head of a family, nor retained one jot of that right which he had forgone by his adoption. For he gave no donations, he manumitted no slaves, nor yet made benefit of any inheritance or legacies otherwise in nature of a *peculium* (an allowance given and granted unto one

by him under whose tuition he is, be he father or master), and so he did put them down in his book of receipts. But from that time forward was there nothing omitted for the augmentation of his state and majesty; and much more after Agrippa once was in disfavor and sent away. Whereby the world took knowledge for certain that the hope of succession rested only in him.

16. Now was the tribunician authority conferred a second time upon him, and that for the term of five years. The honorable charge and commission likewise, for to pacify the state of Germany was assigned unto him; and the Parthian ambassadors, after they had declared their message at Rome unto Augustus, were commanded to repair unto him also into his province (of Germany). But upon the news that Illyricum revolted, he removed from thence to the charge of a new war which, being of all foreign wars the most dangerous since those with the Carthaginians, he managed with the power of fifteen legions, and equal forces of auxiliaries for the space of three years, in great extremity of all things, but especially in exceeding scarcity of corn. And notwithstanding that he was oftentimes recalled from this service, yet he persisted unto the end, fearing lest the enemy, so near a neighbor and so puissant withal, should make headway and come upon them, if they first should quit the place and retire. And verily, passing well paid and rewarded was he for this perseverance of his, as having thereby fully subdued and brought under his subjection all Illyricum as far as reaches and spreads between Italy, the kingdom of Noricum, Thracia and Macedonia, between the river Danube also and the gulf of the Adriatic sea.

17. Which glorious exploit of his was yet more amplified and increased by the opportunity of an occurrence that fell between. For, about the very same time Quintilius Varus together with three legions was overthrown and defeated in Germany. And no man made any doubt but that the Germans,

following the train of this their victory, would have joined Pannonia, had not Illyricum been subdued before. For these his noble acts, a triumph with many great honors was decreed for him. Some also delivered their sentence that he should be surnamed Pannonicus. Others would have had the addition of Invincible, and some again of Pius in his style. But as touching any such surname, Augustus interposed his negative voice, promising and undertaking in his behalf that he would rest contented with the one which he was to assume after his father's death. As for the triumph, Tiberius himself did put it off until a further day, because the whole state was in mourning for the overthrow and loss above said of Varus. Nevertheless, he entered the city in his rich *praetexta*, or embroidered purple robe, with a chaplet of laurel upon his head, and so mounted up to the tribunal erected for him in the Septa, while the senate stood to give attendance; and there, together with Augustus, in between the two consuls, he took his place and sat down. From whence, after he had saluted the people, he was honorably conducted round about all the temples.

18. The next year following, being returned into Germany, because he perceived that the Varian defeat aforesaid happened through the rashness and negligence of the general, he did nothing at all without the opinion of his council of war. And whereas he had used also before to stand upon his own bottom, and to rest in his self-judgement alone, then, contrary to his manner he conferred with many as touching the management of the war; yea, and he showed more care and preciseness in every point than was his wont afore-time. Being about to pass over the Rhine, all his provision of victuals he strictly reduced to a certain rate and stint, and would not send over the water before he had inspected (standing upon the very bank of the river) the load of every wagon, that no carriages might be discharged or unloaded, but such as were by him

allowed and thought necessary. When he was once on the other side of the Rhine, this course and order of life he held: namely to sit upon a bare bank of turf, and so to eat his meat; to lie abroad all night, and take his rest oftentimes without his tent; to deliver all directions for the day following, as well as whatever matters of emergency were to be enjoined, by writing; with this caveat and admonition, that whereof any man doubted, he should repair unto him at all hours of the night, and seek for no other expositor but himself.

19. Martial discipline he required most sharply, bringing again into use and execution certain kinds of chastisements and ignominious disgraces which had been used in ancient times: insomuch as he branded with open shame the lieutenant of a legion for sending a few soldiers with his own freedman over the other side of the river a-hunting. As for battles, albeit he did put as little as might be upon the hazard of fortune and chance, yet entered he upon them with much more resolution, so often as, while he watched or studied by candle, the light suddenly died down and went out, when nobody forced it, trusting confidently (as he said) upon this sign, which both he and all his ancestors had tried and found infallible during all their warlike conducts and regiments. But howsoever he sped well and had good success in this province, he escaped very fair that he had not been killed by a certain one of the Bructeri, who being among those that were next about his person, and detected by his timorous gestures, was apprehended and with torture forced to confess his prepensed designment.

20. Being after two years returned out of Germany to Rome, he rode in that triumph which he had deferred, accompanied by his lieutenants, for whom he had obtained triumphal ornaments. And ere he turned into the Capitol he alighted from his chariot and bowed himself to the knees of his father, sitting then before him as president. A captain and commander of

Pannonia named Baton, he rewarded first with exceeding great presents, and then removed him to Ravenna, in thankful requital for allowing him upon a time, when with his army he was enclosed within the straights, to pass forward and escape. After this, he bestowed upon the people of Rome a solemn dinner, where they sat at a thousand tables; and gave besides to them three thousand sesterces apiece for a largess. He dedicated also the temple of Concord, likewise that of Pollux and Castor, in his own name and his brother's, all out of the spoil won from the enemies.

21. And not long after, when by virtue of an act preferred by the consul that he should administer the provinces jointly with Augustus, and likewise hold the general review and muster of the people, he performed the latter and finished it with a solemn purging called *lustrum*. Then took he his journey into Illyricum. And being immediately called back out of the very way, he came and found Augustus dangerously sick, howbeit yet breathing and alive, with whom he continued in secret talk one whole day. I know well, it is commonly received and believed that when Tiberius, after private conference was gone forth, these words of Augustus were overheard by the chamberlains: "*Miserum populum Romanum qui sub tam lentis maxillis erit*" ["O unhappy people of Rome, that shall be under such a slow pair of jaws"]. Neither am I ignorant of this also, that some have written and reported of Augustus how openly and in plain terms, without dissimulating, he disliked his churlish behavior and harshness of manners so much that divers times being in pleasant discourse and merry talk, he would break off when Tiberius came in place. Nevertheless, overcome by his wife's entreaty and earnest prayer, he refused not to adopt him, or rather was induced so to do upon an ambitious humor and conceit of his own, that, leaving such a successor, himself might another day be more missed

and wished for again. Yet I cannot be persuaded otherwise, than to think that Augustus, a right circumspect, considerate and prudent prince, did nothing, especially in so weighty a business, hand over head and without advice; but having duly weighed the vices and virtues of Tiberius, esteemed his virtues of more worth, and especially seeing that both he sware solemnly in a general assembly of the people that he adopted him for the good of the commonweal, and also commends him in certain epistles for a most expert and martial valor, yea, as the only defender and protector of the people of Rome. Out of which, I have thought good to quote some places here and there as examples: "Farewell most sweet Tiberius, and god bless your conduct and proceeding, warring as you do for me and the Muses." Again, "O most pleasant, and (as I desire to be happy) right valiant man and accomplished captain, with all perfections, adieu." Also, "As touching the order and manner of your summer camp, for mine own part verily, my Tiberius, I am of this mind, that considering so many difficulties and distresses, in regard also of so great sloth and cowardice of soldiers, no man in the world could perform the service better than you have done. And even they of your train, who were with you, do all confess, that this verse may be applied fitly unto you:

Unus homo nobis vigilando restituit rem.

One man alone by watchful sight
Our tottering state hath set upright.

"And whether," quoth he, "there fall out any occurrence to be considered upon with more care and diligence, or whether I be displeased and angry at anything, I have a great miss, I assure you, of my Tiberius, and evermore that verse of Homer cometh into my remembrance:

While this man bears me company (so well he doth foresee)
We may ev'n out of flaming fire return, both I and he.

"When I hear say and read that you are weakened and grown lean with incessant and continual labor, God confound me, if my body does not quake and tremble. I pray you therefore spare yourself, lest if it come to our ears that you are sick, both I and your mother also die for sorrow, and the people of Rome, besides, hazard the empire. It makes no matter whether I be in health or no, if you be not well. The gods, I beseech to preserve you for us and vouchsafe your health both now and ever, unless they hate the people of Rome to death."

22. The death of Augustus he divulged not abroad, before that young Agrippa was slain. This Agrippa was killed by a military tribune, set and appointed to guard him, so soon as he read the writ whereby he was commanded to do the deed. This writ, whether Augustus left behind him when he died, thereby to take away all matter that might minister tumult after his death, or whether Livia in the name of Augustus wrote it and that with the privity of Tiberius, or without his knowledge, it rests doubtful. Certain it is that when the said tribune brought him word that the thing was dispatched which he had commanded, he made answer that he gave no such commandment, and added moreover that he should answer it before the senate. He was avoiding, no doubt, the envy and hard conceit of men for the present, for within a while after, he buried the matter in silence.

23. Having now assembled the senate by virtue and authority of his tribuneship, and begun to make a speech unto them by way of consolation, all of a sudden, as if unable to master his grief, he fell into a fit of sighing and groaning; yea he wished that not only his voice but his vital breath might also fail him, and therewith gave the book unto his son Drusus to read it out. After this, when the last will and testament of

Augustus was brought in, and none of the witnesses admitted to come in place, but those only who were of senator's degree, the rest standing without the Curia and there acknowledging their hands and seals, he caused it to be read and pronounced by his freedman. The will began in this manner: "Forasmuch as sinister fortune has bereft me of Gaius and Lucius, my sons, I will that Tiberius Caesar be mine heir, in the one half and a sixth part (that is to say, in eight parts of twelve, or two-third parts)." By which very beginning their suspicion was augmented who thought thus, that seeing he forbore not to make his preface after this sort, he ordained Tiberius to be his successor upon necessity, rather than by any judgement and choice.

24. Albeit he made no doubt to enter upon his imperial government immediately, and to manage the same by taking unto him a strong guard of soldiers about his person, that is to say main force and the very form of absolute rule and dominion. Yet, nothwithstanding, he refused the title a long time, and putting on a most impudent and shameless mind, at times he seemed to rebuke his friends that encouraged him thereto as those who knew not what a monstrous and untamed beast the empire was; and at other times with ambiguous answers and crafty deals holding the senate in suspense when they besought him to take it upon him, yea and humbly debased themselves before his knees, with the result that some of them, having their patience moved therewith, could endure him no longer, and one among the rest in that tumult cried aloud: "Let him either do it at once, or else give over quite." And another openly to his face upbraided him in these words, that other men be slack in doing and performing that which they have promised, he was slack in promising that which he did and performed. In the end, as if forsooth he had been compelled and complaining withal that there was imposed upon his shoulders a miserable and burdensome servitude, he

took the empire upon him; and yet no otherwise than giving hope that one day he would resign it up. His very words are these: "Until I come unto that time wherein you may think it meet to give some rest unto my aged years."

25. The cause of this holding off and delay that he made was the fear of imminent dangers on every side, insomuch as he would often say that he held a wolf by the ears. For there was one of Agrippa's slaves, named Clemens, who had levied and gathered together no small power for to revenge his master's death; and Lucius Scribonius Libo, a nobleman, secretly complotted a sedition and rebellion; yea and a two-fold mutiny of the soldiers arose, in Illyricum and in Germany. Both the armies called hard upon him for performance of many matters extraordinarily, but, above all, that they might have equal pay with the praetorian soldiers. And as for the German soldiers, they refused him for their prince and sovereign, as not by them ordained, and with all their might and main urged Germanicus, who was then their general, to take upon him the government of the state, albeit he withstood and denied them stoutly. Fearing therefore the issue and danger of this occurrence most of all, he required for himself to have that part of the commonweal in charge which it should please the senate to lay upon him, seeing that no man was sufficient to wield the whole, unless he had another or many assistants rather joined with him. He feigned himself also to be sickly, to the end that Germanicus might with the better will and more patience abide in expectance either of a speedy succession after him, or at least ways of fellowship in the empire with him. Well, after he had appeased those mutinies, Clemens likewise by a fraudulent wile he overcame and brought him under his power. As for Libo, because he would not be thought at his entrance newly into the empire for to proceed too rigorously, two years after, and not before, he charged and reproved him

before the senate, contenting himself meanwhile to beware of him only, and to stand upon his guard. For, as the said Libo was together with him among other pontifices sacrificing, he took care that instead of the iron cleaver, there should be closely laid for him a chopping-knife of lead. And when the same Libo requested upon a time to have secret talk and conference with him, he would not grant it, unless his son Drusus might be by, and as long as he walked up and down with Libo, he seemed to lean upon his hand; and so, held it sure enough all the while until their communication was ended.

26. But being once delivered from this fear, he carried himself at the beginning very orderly and after a civil sort, yea and somewhat under the port of a private person. Of very many dignities, and those right honorable, which by public decree were presented unto him, he accepted but few, and those of the meanest kind. His birthday, falling out in the time of the plebeian games and plays exhibited in the Circus, he hardly would suffer to be celebrated and honored so much as with the addition extraordinarily of one chariot drawn by two steeds. He forbade expressly any temples, *flamens* or priests to be ordained for him, yea and the erection of statues and images in his honor, without his leave and permission, which was given with this only clause and condition, that they should not be set up among the images of the gods, but stand with other ornaments of the house. He prohibited also by his negative voice the solemn oath of observing and keeping his acts inviolably; also to call the month of September Tiberius, or October Livius. The forename also of Imperator and the surname likewise of *Pater Patriae*; also a civic coronet at the foregate or porch of his palace he refused. Nay, the very name of Augustus, hereditary though it were, he would not put as an addition to any of his epistles, but those only which he sent unto kings and great potentates. Neither bore he more than

three consulships, the first but a few days; the second three months; the third during his absence until the Ides of May.

27. He detested flattery and obsequious compliments so much that he would admit no senator to his litter, either by way of dutiful attendance, or otherwise about any business whatsoever. When a certain consular person was about to make satisfaction unto him, and humbly to entreat and crave pardon by a reverent touching of his knees, he started and fled from him so that he fell therewith and lay along his back. Yea, and that which more is, if in any talk or continued speech there passed words of him smelling of flattery, he would not stick to interrupt the speaker, to check him, and presently to alter and correct such terms. One there was who called him *Dominus*, that is, Lord, but he gave him warning not to name him any more by way of contumely. Another chanced to speak of "his sacred business," and a third again, that he went into the senate by his warrant or authority. He caused them both to change those words, and for "authority" to say "counsel," and instead of "sacred" to put in "laborious and painful."

28. Moreover, against railing taunts, bad reports and rumors, as also slanderous libels, verses and songs cast out either of himself or those about him, he stood so firm and patient, that ever and anon he would give out that in a free state folk ought to have both tongue and thought free. And when upon a time the senate called earnestly unto him that such crimes and the offenders themselves might be brought judicially into question, "we have not," quoth he, "so much leisure as to entangle ourselves in any more affairs. If you open this window once, you will suffer nothing else to be done. For under pretence hereof, you shall have the quarrels of every man preferred unto you." There is besides a passing civil apophthegm of his extant which he uttered in the senate: "If so be," quoth he, "that he speak otherwise of me than well, I will endeavor to give an account

of my deeds and words; but in case he continue so still, I will hate him for it in turn."

29. And these things were so much the more remarkable in him for that in speaking to them either one by one severally, or to all at once in general, yea and in reverencing them, himself exceeded in a manner the measure of all humanity. When he dissented one day in opinion from Quintus Haterius in the senate, "pardon me, I beseech you," quoth he, "if I as a senator shall speak aught over-frankly against you." And then, directing his speech unto the whole house: "both now," quoth he, "and many times else, my Lords, this hath been my saying, that a good and gracious prince, whom you have invested in so great and so absolute a power, ought to serve the senate and all the citizens generally, and oftentimes, yea and for the most part, each of them individually. Neither repent I that I have so said, for I have ever found you, and do so still, to be my good, my gracious and favorable Lords."

30. Furthermore, he brought in a certain show of the common liberty by preserving entire for the senate and magistrates both their ancient majesty and also their authority. Neither was there any matter so small or so great pertaining to public or private affairs but proposed it was at the counsel-table before the senators; namely, concerning tributes, customs and revenues of the state, monopolies, building and repairing any public work, enrolling and discharging soldiers, setting down the number both of legions and auxiliary forces: finally, who should have their place of command and government continued by a new commission, or take charge of extraordinary wars, and also in what form they thought it good to answer letters sent by kings. A certain captain over a troop of horsemen, being accused of an outrage and for robbery, he compelled to make his answer before the senate. He never entered the Curia but alone. And being one time brought in sick

within his litter, he caused all his train and company to leave.

31. That some decrees were enacted against his mind and judgement he never once complained, nor found himself grieved. Notwithstanding he opined that magistrates appointed to any charge ought not to be absent, to the end that by their presence they might the better attend their function and calling. Yet one praetor-elect obtained the favor of free travel privileges. Again, when he advised in the Trebians' behalf a grant that they might bestow the money in paving a highway, which was by legacy given for the building of a new theater, he could not prevail but that the will of the testator should stand and be fulfilled. When it happened upon a time that an act of the senate should pass by walking to a side, and himself went over to the other part where the fewer in number were, there was not one that followed him. Other matters also were handled and debated by the magistrates and by the ordinary course of law, and not otherwise, while the consuls bore so great sway and authority that certain ambassadors out of Africa repaired unto them for dispatch, complaining that they were put off and delayed by Caesar unto whom they had been sent. And no marvel, for evident it was that himself also would arise up unto the said consuls and give them the way.

32. He rebuked generals of armies, even such as had been consuls, for not writing unto the senate of their war exploits; also for consulting with him and asking his advice as touching the granting of military gifts, as if it lay not in their own power to give and dispose all. He commended a praetor for bringing up again the ancient custom, in the entrance of his office, to make an honorable mention and rehearsal of his ancestors before a frequent assembly of the people. The funeral obsequies of certain noble personages he accompanied with the common multitude to the very fire. The like moderation he showed in meaner persons and matters both. When he had

called forth unto him the magistrates of the Rhodians for delivering unto him public letters from the state without the customary conclusion [i. e., prayers for the emperor's welfare], he gave them not so much as one hard word but commanded them to make the addition, and sent them away. Diogenes, the professed grammarian, who was wont to dispute and discourse at Rhodes every sabbath, had put him back and would not admit him into his school, although he had come of purpose extraordinarily to hear him, but by his pages posted him off until the seventh day. Now when this same Diogenes stood waiting before his gate at Rome to do his duty and salute him, he quit him no otherwise than thus, namely by warning him to repair thither again seven years after. When the presidents and governors abroad gave him counsel to burden the provinces with heavy tributes and taxes, he wrote back unto them that it was the part of a good shepherd to shear his sheep and not to flay them.

33. By little and little he put himself forth and showed his princely majesty, however for a long time in some variety, yet for the most part rather mild and gracious than otherwise, and more inclined to the good of the commonwealth. And at the first, thus far forth only interposed he his absolute power, that nothing should be done unjustly. Therefore he both repealed certain constitutions of the senate, and also very often, when the magistrates were sitting judicially upon the bench to decide matters, he would offer himself to join, as it were, in counsel, and to be assistant with them, or else just over against them in the forepart of the tribunal. And if the rumor went that any defendant were likely by favor to escape clear, all on a sudden he would be in place, and either on the ground below, or else from the tribunal seat put the other judges in mind of the laws of their conscience and religion, and of the crime where upon they sat. Also if anything were amiss and faulty in the

public ordinances and manners of the city, forlet by occasion of idleness or taken up through evil custom, he undertook to reform the same.

34. He abridged and restrained the expenses of stage-plays and games exhibited unto the people by cutting short the wages paid to actors upon the stage and reducing the pairs of gladiators to a certain number. That Corinthian vessels and manufactures grew to an exceeding high rate, and that three mullets were sold for 30,000 sesterces, he grievously complained, and gave his opinion that there should be a gauge set and a mediocrity kept in household furniture; also that the price of victuals in the open market should be ordered yearly at the discretion of the senate, with a charge given unto the aediles for to inhibit victualling houses, taverns and the like, that they should not suffer any pastry-works to be set out to sale; and to the end that by his own example also he might put forward the public frugality, himself at his festival suppers caused oftentimes to be served up to the board viands dressed the day before and those half-eaten already, saying that the side of a wild boar had in it all the same that the whole had. He forbade expressly by an edict the usual and daily kisses commonly given and taken; likewise the intercourse of New Year's gifts sent to and fro, namely that it should not continue after the Kalends of January. He had wont to bestow for his part a New Year's gift four-fold worth that which he received, and to give same with his own hand, but being offended that all through the month he was in his other affairs troubled with such as had not been with him, nor felt his liberality upon the holiday, he never gave any again after the said day.

35. Wives of lewd and dishonest life, if there wanted accusers to call them publicly into question, his advice and sentence was that their next kinsfolk should by the ancient custom agree together in common, for to chastise and punish. He

absolved a Roman knight from his oath (who had sworn never to divorce his wife) and gave him leave to put her away, being taken in adultery with her son-in-law. Certain women, infamous for whoredom and filthiness, began to profess bawdery openly, to the end that, having by this base trade and occupation lost the right privilege and dignity of matrons, they might elude the laws and avoid the penalties thereof. Likewise out of the youth of both degrees [senators as well as knights], the lewdest spendthrifts willfully underwent the ignominious note of degradation, because they would not be liable to an act of the senate in that behalf for performing their parts in acting upon the stage, or in the arena. But them, as well as those light women aforesaid, he banished all, that none ever after should by such elusion of the law seek evasion. He took from a senator his robe after he knew that just before the Kalends of July he had removed out of his dwelling-house, into certain gardens outside the city, to the end that when the said day was past, he might take his house again within the city at lower rent. Another he deprived of his quaestorship for that having, as it were, by lottery chosen and married a wife the one day, he dismissed her on another [i. e., the morrow]; his levity was notable as well in making choice so lightly, as in casting her off so quickly, making but a game of marriage.

36. All foreign ceremonies in religion, the Egyptian also and the Jewish rites, he prohibited, compelling those who were given to that superstition for to burn all their religious vestments, the instruments likewise and furniture whatsoever thereto belonging. The serviceable youth of the Jews, under color of a military oath, he sent into sundry provinces which were in a pestilent and unwholesome air above others. The rest of that nation, or such as were addicted to the like religion, he banished out of Rome, upon a pain of perpetual bondage if they obeyed not. He expelled also astrologers, but upon their

earnest entreaty and promise to give over the practice of that art, he permitted them there to remain.

37. A special care he had to keep the peace and to preserve the state from outrages and robberies, also from licentious mutinies and seditions. The set guards and garrisons of soldiers he disposed thicker than the wonted manner was throughout all Italy. He ordained a standing camp at Rome, wherein the praetorian cohorts, wandering up and down before that time, and dispersed in divers inns and hostelries, might be received. All insurrections of the people he punished most sharply; he took likewise much pains to prevent such commotions. There happened upon some discord and variance to be a murder committed in the theater; the principal heads of the faction, as also the actors themselves for whose sake the quarrel and fray began, he exiled, neither could he ever be brought by any prayer and entreaty of the people to restore them. When the commons of Pollentia would not suffer the dead corpse of a certain principal centurion to be carried with funeral obsequies out of their market place, before they had forcibly extorted out of his heir's hands a piece of money to the setting out of a game of fencers with unrebated swords, he took one cohort from Rome, and another out of king Cottius' kingdom, dissembling the cause of his journey, and suddenly revealing their arms and weapons which they closely carried, and giving alarm with the sound of trumpets, all at once he put them into the town with banner displayed at sundry gates, and so cast into perpetual prison the greater part of the commons and decurions. The privilege and custom of sanctuaries, wherever they were, he abolished. The Cyzicenes, who had committed some notorious outrage and violence upon Roman citizens, he deprived generally of their freedom, which in the war against Mithridates they had by their good service gotten. The rebellions of enemies he repressed. He did not undertake any

expedition afterwards himself therefor, but by his lieutenants only, and not even by them without lingering delays and driven thereto of necessity. Kings that rebelliously took up arms, or were suspected to break out, he kept down with threats rather and complaints, than otherwise by force and open hostility. Some of them, whom he had lured out of their own realms unto him with fair words and large promises, he never sent home again: by name, Maraboduus the German, Rhascuporis the Thracian, and Archelaus the Cappadocian, whose kingdom he reduced into the form of a province.

38. For two years together after he came unto the empire, he never set foot once out of Rome gates. And the time ensuing, he absented not himself in no place unless it were in towns near adjoining, or as far as Antium when he travelled farthest; and that was very seldom and for a few days. None the less he promised and pronounced openly oftentimes that he would visit the provinces and armies abroad; yea, and every year almost he made preparation for a journey, taking up all the wagons that were to be gotten, and laying provision of corn and victuals in all the good boroughs and colonies by the way, yea, and at the last suffered vows to be made for his going forth and return home. At last, commonly and by way of a jest and byword, he was called Callippides, who in a Greek proverb is noted to be always running, yet never gains ground one cubit forward.

39. But being bereft of both his sons, of which Germanicus died in Syria and Drusus at Rome, he withdrew himself into Campania, as to a retiring place; and all men well near were fully persuaded that he would never return but die soon after. Both which had like indeed have come to pass. For, in truth, he never came again to Rome; and within some few days later at Tarracina, in a certain part of his manor house (built especially for his own lodging), called Spelunca, as he sat

there at supper, a number of huge stones from above chanced to fall down, whereby many of his guests at the table and servants there waiting were crushed and squeezed to death; but he himself, beyond all hope, escaped.

40. Having made his progress over Campania, when he had dedicated the Capitolium at Capua, and the temple of Augustus at Nola, which he pretended to have been the motive of his journey, he betook himself to Capri, delighted especially with that island because there was but one way of access unto it, and the same by a small shore and landing place, as being otherwise enclosed round about, partly with craggy rocks and steep cliffs of an exceeding height, and in part by the deep sea. But soon after, when the people called him home, and incessantly besought him to return, by occasion of an unhappy and heavy accident, whereby at Fidenae twenty thousand folk and more, at a solemn fight of sword-players, perished by the fall of an amphitheater, he passed over into the mainland, permitting all men to come unto him; the rather for that, when he first set forth and went out of Rome, he had given straight commandment by an edict that no man should trouble him, and all the way avoided as many as were coming towards him.

41. Being retired again into the said isle, he cast aside all care even of the commonwealth; so far forth that never after did he so much as repair and make up the broken decuries of horsemen; he changed no military tribunes nor captains; no, nor any presidents and governors of provinces. He held Spain and Syria both for certain years without consular lieutenants; he neglected Armenia and suffered it to be overrun and possessed by the Parthians; Moesia to be wasted and spoiled by the Dacians and Sarmatians, as also Gaul by the Germans, to the great shame and no less danger of the whole empire.

42. To proceed, having now gotten the liberty of this secret place, and being as one would say removed from the eyes of

people, at length he poured forth and showed at once all those vices which with much ado for a long time he had cloaked and dissembled. Of which I will particularize and make relation from the very beginning. In the camp, when he was but a new and untrained soldier, for his excessive greediness of wine bibbing, he was for Tiberius, named Biberius [Drinker]; for Claudius, Caldius [Hot]; for Nero, Mero [Wine]. After being emperor, even at the very time when he was busy reforming the public manners and the misdemeanor of the city, he spent with Pomponius Flaccus and Lucius Piso one whole night and two days in gluttony and drunkenness. Unto the former of these twain he presently gave the government of the province of Syria; upon the other he conferred the provostship of Rome, professing even in all his letters and writings that they were the most pleasant companions and friends at all assays. To Cestius Claudius, an elderly fornicator and prodigal spendthrift, who had in times past been by Augustus put to ignominy and shame, yea and by himself some few days before rebuked before the senate, he sent word that he would take supper with him, upon this condition that he altered nothing, nor left aught out of his ordinary and customed manner, and namely, that wenches all naked should serve at the table. He preferred one to be a competitor for the quaestorship, who was a most base and obscure person, before others that were right noble gentlemen; only for carousing and drinking up at a banquet a whole amphora of wine when he drank unto him. Unto Asellius Sabinus he gave 200,000 sesterces for a dialogue of his making, in which he introduced a combat or disputation between the mushroom, the fig-pecker, the oyster and the thrush. To conclude, he instituted a new office, forsooth, a master of pleasures, wherein he placed Priscus, a Roman knight, and one who had been censor.

43. But during the time of his private abode in Capri, he devised a room with seats and benches in it, even a place of

purpose for his secret wanton lusts. To furnish it there were sought out and gathered from all parts, a number of young drabs and stale catamites, sorted together; such also as invented monstrous kinds of libidinous filthiness, whom he termed *spintriae* who, being in three ranks or rows linked together should abuse and pollute one another's bodies before his face, that by the very sight of them he might stir up his own cold courage and fainting lust. He had bed-chambers besides, in many places, which he adorned with tablets and petty puppets, representing in the one sort, most lascivious pictures, and in the other as wanton shapes and figures. He stored them likewise with the books of the poetess Elephantis, that none might lack for a pattern of the like form and fashion in that beastly business, performed in every kind. He devised in the woods also and groves here and there, certain places for lechery and venereal acts; and throughout the caves and hollow rocks he had youths of both sexes, in the habit of Pans and Nymphs, ready to prostitute themselves: wherefore now men, in open place, abusing the usual name of the island, termed him the Caprinicus [Goat-like].

44. He incurred yet the infamy of greater and more shameful filthiness, such as may not well be named or heard, or much less believed: to wit, that he should train up and teach fine boys, the tenderest and daintiest that might be had (whom he called his little fishes) to converse and play between his thighs as he was swimming, and prettily with tongue and teeth seem to make unto his secret parts and there to nibble, whom, likewise, as babes of good growth and strength, howbeit as yet not weaned, he would set unto his privy member as unto the nipple of a breast to suck. And verily, both by nature and because of his years, more prone he was and given to lust in this kind. Therefore, whereas a certain painted tablet of Parrasius' making (in which Atalanta yields her mouth unto

Meleager in that beastliness) was given unto him as a legacy, upon condition that if he were offended with the argument or matter represented therein, he might in lieu thereof receive a million sesterces, he not only preferred the said picture before such a sum of money, but also dedicated it in his own bed-chamber. It is reported besides, that being at a sacrifice upon a time, and casting a fancy to the beautiful and well-favored face of a youth as he carried before him the censer, he could not contain himself, but immediately and before the completion of the sacrifice, even there and then took him aside out of the place and so abused his body, and together with him a brother of his who played the flute; yea and soon after, for that they twitted and upbraided one another for this abominable act, he broke their legs both.

45. Moreover, the way in which he was wont to offer abuse unto the very persons of women, and those nobly born and of good reputation, appeared most evidently by the woeful end of one dame named Mallonia. For when she was by force brought unto his bed, and most resolutely refused to suffer any more than naturally a woman was to suffer, he suborned certain promoters falsely to accuse her. And evermore, as she pleaded in her own defense, asked her still whether she repented not yet of her obstinacy: so that at length she left the court, made haste home to her house, and there ran herself through with a sword, after she had openly and aloud reproached the shaghaired and goatish old churl with his filthy and beastly mouth. Whereupon, in an Atellan farce this shameful note, received with exceeding great accord, was rife and current abroad in every man's mouth, that the old he-goat was licking the does.

46. Being very niggard of his purse, and one that would part with nothing, he never maintained those of his train in all his journeys and expeditions with any wages or set salaries,

but found their meat and victuals only. Yet must I needs say that once out of his step-father's indulgence and bounty, he bestowed upon them a piece of liberality, when having arranged them according to the worthiness of every one into three ranks, he dealt among those of the first 600,000 sesterces, of the second 400,000, of the third, 200,000. And the last he called the company not of his friends, but of his Greeks [by way of contempt].

47. All the while he was emperor neither built he any stately works (for the very temple of Augustus and the re-edification of Pompey's theater, which only he and no one else had undertaken, after many years he left unfinished), nor exhibited he so much as one solemn show unto the people, and at those which were by any other set out, he was very seldom present; and all for fear lest some thing or other should be demanded at his hands, especially after that he was compelled once to manumit the comedian Actius. Having relieved the want and poverty of some senators, because he would not help more of them, he denied to succor any other than those, who alleged before the senate good and just causes of their necessities. By which deed of his, he frighted most of them unto a modesty and bashfulness, and among the rest one Hortalus, the grandson of Quintus Hortensius, the professed orator, who being of a very mean estate had begotten four children by the means and persuasion of Augustus.

48. As touching his public munificence, he never showed it but twice: once when he purposed and published a free loan for three years of a hundred millions of sesterces, and again, when unto certain landlords of fair houses and tenements situated upon Mount Caelius which were consumed with fire, he restored the full price and worth of them. One of these boons he was forced to grant, by reason that the people, in great want of money, called earnestly for his help. He had,

by virtue of an act of the senate, ordained that usurers should lay out two-thirds part of their stock in lands, tenements and appurtenances unmovable; the debtors likewise made present payment of two-thirds part of their debts. And yet the thing was not done and dispatched accordingly. The other boon also was to mitigate the grievousness of those heavy times. For then it was that twenty thousand were killed at Fidenae by the fall of a theater. Howbeit this later beneficence of his he so highly prized, that he commanded the name of Mount Caelius to be changed and called Augustus. The legacies given by Augustus in his last will unto the soldiers being once published, he never after bestowed any largess upon them; saving that among those of the praetorian guard he dealt one thousand deniers apiece; in and to the legions in Syria certain gifts, for that they alone among all their ensigns in the field honored no image at all of Sejanus. Moreover, he made very seldom any discharges of old soldiers, as expecting upon age their death, and by death gaping for some gain and vantage. Neither succored he the very provinces with his bountiful hand, except it were in Asia, by occasion that certain cities therein were by earthquake overthrown.

49. Afterwards, and in process of time, he gave his mind wholly even to rapine and plain pillage. It is for certain known, that Gnaius Lentulus the Augur, a man of exceeding great wealth, for very fear and anguish of mind was by him driven to a loathing and weariness of his own life; and at his death to make no other heir but himself. That dame Lepida likewise, a right noble lady, was condemned by him, to gratify Quirinius, one that had been consul, but passing rich and childless withal; who having before time put her away being his wedded wife, twenty years after called her judicially into question, and laid to her charge, that long ago she had bought and provided poison for to take away his life. Besides, as well

known it is, that certain princes and potentates of Gaul, Spain, Syria and Greece, forfeited their estates upon so slight a slander and impudent imputation, that against some of them nought else was objected but this, that they had part of their substance and wealth lying in money, yea and that many cities and private persons lost their ancient immunities and privileges, as also their right in mines and metals, tolls and customs; and finally that Vonones, a king of the Parthians who being driven out of his kingdom by his own subjects, retired himself with a huge mass of treasure into Antioch, under the protection, as it were, of the people of Rome, was perfidiously stripped out of all and killed.

50. The hatred that he bore to his kinsfolk and near allies, he betrayed, first in his brother Drusus by disclosing a letter of his, wherein he dealt with him about compelling Augustus to restore the common liberty; afterwards, in others also. As for his wife Julia, so far was he from showing any courtesy or kindness unto her when she stood confined (which had been the least matter of a thousand) that whereas by an ordinance of her father's, she was shut up within one town, he gave straight order that she should not step out of doors and enjoy the society of people and worldly commerce; nay, he proceeded so far, as to bereave her of that little stock and household stuff which her father allowed her, yea, and defrauded her of the yearly pension and exhibition for her maintenance; and all, forsooth, under a color of common right and law, because Augustus in his last will and testament had not expressly provided in this behalf. Being not well able to endure his mother Livia, as challenging to herself equal part with him in power and authority, he avoided both to keep ordinary and daily company, and also to entertain long speech or secret conference with her; so that he might not be thought ruled and directed by her counsels, which otherwhiles he was wont

both to stand in need of, and also to use. Also, he took to the very heart the passing of this act in the senate, that in his style as he had the title, son of Augustus, so that addition should run withal son of Livia. And therefore it was, that he would not suffer her to be named *Parens Patria* [Mother of her Country], nor to receive any remarkable honor in open place and by public decree. Oftentimes also he admonished her to forbear intermeddling in greater affairs and such as were not meet for women; especially after he perceived once, that when the temple of Vesta was on fire, she also came thither in person among others and there encouraged the people and soldiers both to do their best and help all what they could, as her manner was to do in her husband's days.

51. By these degrees he proceeded even to secret rancor and malice against her, but chiefly upon this occasion, as men report. She had been very earnest with him many a time to enroll one in the decuries of the judges who was made free citizen of Rome; but he denied flatly to choose and admit the party, unless it were upon this only condition, that she would suffer a clause to be written and annexed to the instrument, in these words, This grant was by my mother wrung and wrested from me. Whereat she, highly displeased and offended, brought forth out of her closet certain old letters of Augustus written unto her, as touching his perverse, bitter and intolerable manners; and those she openly read. He again took the matter so grievously, that she had both kept those writings so long by her, and also cast them in his dish so spitefully, that some think this was the greatest cause of his departure from the city. And verily, for the space of three years complete, during which time he was absent and his mother living, he saw her but once; and that was no more than one day, and very few hours of the same. And afterwards as little mind he had to be by her lying sick; and when she was dead, suffering

her corpse by staying so long above ground (while men hoped still of his coming) to corrupt at length and putrefy. After she was interred, he forbade her deification, pretending she herself had given that order. Her will he annulled, all her friends and familiars, even those unto whom upon her death-bed she had committed the charge of her funerals, within a short time he persecuted and plagued, yea and one of them, to wit, a worshipful knight of Rome, he condemned to the treadmill.

52. Of his two sons, he loved neither Drusus that was by nature, nor Germanicus by adoption, as a father should do, as taking offense at the vices of the one [of Drusus]. For Drusus was of an effeminate mind, given to a loose and idle life. There-fore was not Tiberius so nearly touched and grieved for him being dead; but presently after his funeral, returned to his ordinary and accustomed business prohibiting vacation of just-ice [as the manner was in any mournful time] to continue any longer. Moreover, when the Ilian ambassadors came some-what with the latest to comfort him, he (as if now by this time the memory of his sorrow had been clean worn out), scoffed at them and made this answer: That he likewise was sorry in their behalf for the loss they had of Hector, so noble and brave a citizen. As for Germanicus, he disgraced him so, as that not only he did diminish all his worthy exploits as vain and needless, but also blamed his most glorious victories as dangerous and hurtful to the commonwealth. Also, for that without his advice, he went unto Alexandria (by occasion of an extreme and sudden famine) he complained of him in the senate; yea and it is verily believed, he was the cause of his death, and used the means of Gnaius Piso, lieutenant of Syria; who soon after being accused of this crime, would (as some think) have uttered abroad those directions and warrants that he had so to do, but that Sejanus secretly withstood it. They were in secret delivered, and therefore could not be proved.

For which Tiberius was oftentimes and in many places much blamed, and in the night season commonly called upon with this cry and note, *Redde Germanicum* [Give us Germanicus again]. The suspicion whereof himself afterwards confirmed and made good, by afflicting in cruel manner the wife also and the children of the said Germanicus.

53. Furthermore, his daughter-in-law Agrippina, for complaining over-boldly of him after the death of her husband, he took by the hand and recited unto her a Greek verse, to this effect, If thou hast not sovereign rule and dominion, thinkest thou, pretty daughter, that thou art wronged? And so vouchsafed her no speech at all after. Also, because upon a time, when she durst not at supper taste of those apples which he had reached unto her, he forbore to invite her any more; pretending that she charged him with the crime of attempting her with poison; when as indeed, it was of purpose plotted and packed aforehand, both that himself should by the offering of such fruit tempt her, and she again beware most present and assured death. At the last, having untruly accused her as if she minded to fly one while to the statue of Augustus, and another while to the armies, he confined and sent her away to the isle Pandataria; and as she railed at him he by the hands of a centurion with whipping and lashing her over the face struck out one of her eyes. Again, when as she was fully determined to pine herself to death, he caused her mouth perforce to be opened, and meat to be crammed into her throat. Yea, and after that by continuance in this mind she consumed quite away and died in the end, he inveighed against her in most odious and reproachful terms, having opined first in the senate, that her birthday also should be reckoned among the dismal and unlucky days. Furthermore, he expected thanks, as for a high favor done unto her, in that he strangled her not before with a cord, and so flung her to the Mourning Stairs, and in

regard of such a singular clemency as this, he suffered a decree to pass, that thanks should be given unto him, and a present of gold consecrated unto Jupiter Capitolinus.

54. Whereas by Germanicus he had three grandsons, Nero, Drusus and Gaius; by Drusus he had one, to wit Tiberius. When he was left destitute and fatherless by the death of his children, the two eldest sons of Germanicus, namely Nero and Drusus, he recommended to the senate; and celebrated the day of both their commencements with giving a congiarie to the people. But no sooner understood he, that upon New Year's day there had been public vows made by the city for their life also and preservation, but he gave the senate to understand, that such honors ought not to be conferred upon any persons, but those that were experienced and far stepped in years. Thereby, having discovered the inward character and canker of his heart, from that day forward he exposed them to the slanders and imputations of all men. When also, by sundry subtle devices he had wrought so, that they might be both provoked to give railing taunts, and also being so provoked come to mischief and destruction, he accused them in his letters, heaped most bitterly upon them heinous reproaches, caused them to be judged enemies to the state, and so hunger-starved them to death; Nero, within the isle Pontia, and Drusus at the very foot and bottom of the Palatium. Men think that Nero was driven to work his own death [i. e., to commit suicide], what time as the hangman, as sent by a warrant from the senate, presented unto him halters and hooks [to strangle him, and drag him to the *Scalae Gemoniae*]. As for Drusus, kept he was from all food and sustenance, insomuch as he gave the attempt to eat the very flocks that stuffed the mattress whereupon he lay; and the relics of the both, were so dispersed and scattered abroad, that hardly they could be ever gathered together.

55. Over and above his old friends and familiars, he had demanded twenty out of the number of the best and principal citizens, as counselors and assistants unto him in public affairs. Of all these, he could hardly show twain or three at the most alive; the rest, some for one cause and some for another he brought to confusion and killed. Among whom (with the calamity and overthrow of many more) was Aelius Sejanus, whom he had to the highest place of authority advanced, not so much for any good will, as to be his instrument and right hand, by whose ministry and fraudulent practices he might circumvent the children of Germanicus, and so establish as heir apparent in succession of the empire the grandson he had by Drusus, as his natural son.

56. No milder was he one jot unto the Greek professors living and conversing daily with him, and in whom he took most contentment. One of them named Zeno, as he reasoned and discoursed very exactly of a question he asked, What harsh dialect that was, wherein he spoke? and when he answered, It was the Doric, he confined him for his labor into Cynaria, supposing that he twitted and reproached him for his old absence from Rome because the Rhodians spoke Doric. Also, whereas his manner was out of his own daily readings, to propound certain questions as he sat at supper, having intelligence, that Seleucus the grammarian enquired diligently of his ministers and servitors, what authors at any time he had in hand, and so came prepared to assail the said questions, first he forbade him his house and ordinary society, afterwards he forced him even to death.

57. His cruel and unpliable nature was not hidden, no not in his very childhood, the which Theodorus Gadaraeus, his teacher in rhetoric, seemed both at first to foresee most wisely, and also to express as fitly, when by way of chiding and rebuke he called him ever and anon *Pelon Haimati Pephuramenon*, clay

soaked in blood. [Clay so tempered became very strong and tough.] But the same broke out and appeared somewhat more when he became emperor, at the very beginning; what time as yet he lay for to win the love and favor of men, with a pretense of civil moderation. A certain buffoon there was, who as a funeral passed by, had willed the party whose body was carried forth to report unto Augustus, that his legacies were not yet paid and delivered, which he had left for the commons of Rome. Him, he caused to be haled and brought unto his presence, to receive also the debt which was due; and then commanded him to be led to execution and so relate the truth unto his father Augustus. Not long after as he threatened to send unto prison one Pompeius a Roman knight, for stoutly denying something, he assured him, that of a Pompeius he would make him a Pompeianus, glancing by this bitter and biting taunt both at the man's name and also at the old misfortune of that party. [The Pompeiani took part with Pompey against Julius Caesar.]

58. About the same time, when the praetor came to know of him whether his pleasure was to hold the judicial assizes, as touching the case of majesty high treason, or no? he made answer that the laws must have their course and be put in execution; and in very truth he executed them with extreme rigor. There was one who from the statue of Augustus had taken away the head, for to set the same upon the statue of another. The matter was debated in the senate; and because some doubt arose, who did the deed? inquisition was made by torture. The party deliquent being condemned, this kind of calumniation by little and little proceeded so far, that such points as these also were made capital crimes: namely, to have beaten a slave about the image of Augustus, or if a man shifted his apparel there, or brought into any privy or brothelhouse his image imprinted either in money or ring, or to have im-

paired any word or deed of his. To conclude, it cost one his life for suffering in his own colony honors to be decreed unto him upon the same day that they had in times past been decreed for Augustus.

59. Many parts besides under the color of gravity and reformation, but rather indeed following the course of his own nature, he used to play, so cruelly and with such rigor, that some there were, who in verses both upbraided by way of reproach the calamities present, and also gave warning of the future miseries, in this manner:

> *Asper et immitis. Breviter vis omnia dicam?*
> *Dispeream, si te mater amare potest.*

Harsh and unkind (in brief wilt thou I should say all?) thou art;
God me confound, if mother thine can love thee in her heart.

> *Non es eques; quare? non sunt tibi millia centum;*
> *Omnia si quaeras; et Rhodos exilium est.*

No knight thou art; and why? for hundred thousands none;
(Search all) thou hast in store; and now at Rhodes exil'd do'st
wone [dwell].

> *Aurea mutasti Saturni saecula, Caesar;*
> *Incolumni nam te, ferrea semper erunt.*

Of Saturn King thou changed hast that age resembling gold,
For while thou, Caesar, liv'st, the world of iron shall ever hold.

> *Fastidit vinum quia iam sitit iste curorem;*
> *Tam bibit hunc avide, quam bibit ante merum.*

Wine doth he loath, because that now of blood he hath a thirst,
He drinketh that as greedily, as wine he did at first.

> *Aspice felicem sibi non tibi, Romule Sullam;*
> *Et Marium, si vis, aspice; sed reducem,*
> *Nec non Antoni civilia bella moventis;*
> *Nec semel infectas, aspice caede manus.*
> *Et dic, Roma perit. Regnabit sanguine multo,*
> *Ad regnum quisquis venit ab exilio?*

See Sulla, happy for himself, o Romulus not for thee;
And Marius, in case thou wilt, but new returned, see;
Likewise behold of Antony those hands in blood embrew'd
Not once, I mean of Antony, who civil wars renew'd.
Then say, Rome goes to wrack. And he with bloodshed
　　　　　much will reign
Who to a kingdom-state is come, from banishment again.

Which verses at first, he would have had to be taken and construed as made by them who were impatient of any absolute dominion at Rome; and as if they had been framed, not so much with any considerate judgement, as upon choler. And evermore his saying was, *Oderint dum probent* [Let them hate me, so long as they suffer my proceedings to pass]. But afterwards, even himself proved them to be very true and most certain.

60. Within few days after he came to Capri, when a fisherman suddenly and unlooked for, presented unto him (as he was in a secret place doing somewhat by himself) a mullet of an extraordinary bigness, he caused his face to be rubbed all over with the same fish, as put in a fright, no doubt, for that from the back side of that island, he had made means through the rough thickets and by-ways, to creep and get unto him where he was. And when the poor fellow amid this punishment seemed to rejoice yet, and said, It was happy that he had not offered unto him a lobster also which he had caught of an huge greatness, he commanded that his face should be grated and mangled likewise with the said lobster. A soldier, one of his own guard, for filching and stealing a peacock out of an orchard he put to death. In a certain journey that he made, the litter wherein he was carried chanced to be entangled and somewhat stayed with briars and brambles; whereupon a centurion of the foremost cohorts that had in charge to try and clear the ways, he caused to be laid along upon the ground, and

there he beat him with cudgels until he was well-near dead.

61. Soon after, he broke out into all kinds of cruelty, as one who never wanted matter to work upon; persecuting the familiar friends and acquaintance of his own mother first, then, of his grandsons and granddaughter, and at the last of Sejanus; after whose death he grew to be most cruel. Whereby especially it appeared, that himself was not wont so much to be provoked by Sejanus, as Sejanus to serve his turn and feed his humor, seeking as he did all occasions. Howsoever in a certain commentary which he composed summarily and briefly of his own life he durst write thus much, that he executed Sejanus because he had found that he raged furiously against the children of Germanicus his son. Of whom to say a truth, the one himself murdered, after he had first suspected Sejanus, and the other, not before he had killed the latter. To prosecute in particular all his bloody deeds would require a long time. It shall suffice therefore to rehearse in general the patterns as it were and examples of his cruelty. There passed not a day over his head, no not so much as any festival and religious holiday, without execution and punishment of folk. Some suffered even upon New Year's day. Accused and condemned there were many, together with their children, and very wives. Straight commandment and warning was given, that the near kinsfolk of such persons as stood condemned to die should not mourn and lament for them. Especially rewards were by decree appointed for their accusers, otherwhiles for bare witnesses also. No informer and promoter was discredited, but his presentment taken. And every crime and trespass went for capital, and so was received, were it but the speaking of a few simple words. Objected it was against a poet, that in a tragedy he had reviled and railed upon Agamemnon; as also it was laid to an historian's charge, for saying that Brutus and Cassius were the last of all the Romans. Presently were the authors and writers

punished, and their writings called in and abolished, notwithstanding certain years before they had been recited even
in the hearing of Augustus, with his good liking and approbation. Some committed to ward were deprived not only of
their solace and comfort in studying, but also of the very use
of talking with others. Of such as were cited peremptorily by
writ and process to answer at the bar, some gave themselves
mortal wounds at home in their houses, as sure to be condemned, only to avoid torture and ignominy; others in the
open face and midst of the court drank poison; and yet were
they with their wounds bound up and, while they yet panted
between alive and dead, hauled away to prison. There was not
one executed but he was thrown also into the Gemoniae [the
Stairs of Mourning] and drawn away with the drag. In one day
there were twenty so thrown and drawn, and among them
boys and women. As for young girls and maidens of unripe
years, because by ancient custom and tradition unlawful it was
to strangle virgins, first deflowered they were by the hangman
and afterwards strangled. Were any willing of themselves, such
were forced violently to live. For he thought simple death
so light a punishment that when he heard how one of the
prisoners, Carnulus by name, had taken his death voluntarily,
he cried out in these words, "Carnulus has escaped my hands."
Also in overseeing and perusing the prisoners in jail, when one
of them besought to have his punishment with speed, he made
this answer, "Nay, marry, thou art not yet reconciled unto me,
that I should show you such a favor." A certain consular writer
hath inserted this in his annals, that upon a time at a great feast
(where himself was also present), Tiberius was on a sudden
asked, and that openly and with a loud voice, by a dwarf
standing at the table among other buffoons and jesters, wherefore Paconius being attaint of treason lived so long: for that
instant verily he chid the party for his saucy and malapert

. . . he spared not to torment and execute any one whomsoever.

tongue, but after a few days wrote unto the senate to take order
with all speed for the execution of Paconius.

62. He increased and strained still more and more this cruelty
by occasion that he was galled and fretted at the news of his
son Drusus' death. For, having been of opinion that he died
upon some sickness and intemperate life, so soon as he understood at length that he was poisoned and so made away by
the villainous practice of his own wife Livilla and Sejanus
together, he spared not to torment and execute any one
whomsoever. So bent was he and addicted whole days together
to the inquisition and trial of this only matter, that when word
came unto him how an host of his, an inhabitant of Rhodes
(whom by familiar letters he had sent for to Rome), was come,
he commanded him out of hand to be put to torture, as if he
had been some near friend present at the aforesaid examination;
but afterwards, when his error was discovered, and seeing how
he had mistaken, he caused him also to be killed, so that he
should not divulge and make known the former injury. The
place is yet to be seen at Capri of his butcherly carnage, from
which he caused condemned persons, after long and exquisite
torments to be flung headlong before his face, into the sea,
where were ready to receive them a number of mariners, who
with their sprits, poles and oars would beat and bat their carcasses to the end that none of them might have any breath or
wind remaining in their body. He had devised, moreover,
among other kinds of torment, this: what time as men, by
deceitful means, had their load with large drinking of strong
wine, he would suddenly knit fast and tie their privy members
with lute strings, that he might cause them to swell and be
pent in most dolorous pains occasioned at once as well by the
strait strings, as by the suppression and stoppage of urine. And
had it not been that both death prevented, and Thrasyllus also
enforced him of purpose (as men say) to put off some designs

in hope of longer life, he would have murdered a good many more (as it is fully believed) and not spared those very grandsons of his that remained yet alive, considering that he both had Gaius in suspicion, and also cast off Tiberius as conceived in adultery. And so it soundeth to truth that he was minded thus to do. For ever and anon he called Priam happy, in that he overlived all his sons and daughters.

63. But how, amid these pranks he lived not only odious and detested, but exceeding timorous and exposed to the contumelious reproaches of the world, there be many evidences to show. That any soothsayers should be sought unto and consulted with secretly and without witnesses by, he forbade. As for the oracles near adjoining to the city of Rome, he attempted to subvert them all. But being terrified with the majesty of those answers which were delivered at Praeneste, he gave over; especially when he was not able to find them (sealed up though they were and brought down to Rome) within the chest, until the same was carried back again unto the temple. Not daring to send away and dismiss from him one or two consular deputies, after he had offered provinces unto them, he detained them so long, until after certain years expired, he ordained others to succeed them, while they remained present with him, in the meantime, still reserving the title of the office. He assigned unto them many commissions and matters of charge, and they continually gave order for execution thereof, by the ministry of their legates, lieutenants and coadjutors.

64. His daughter-in-law and grandchildren, after they were condemned, he never removed from place to place otherwise than chained and in a close covered litter sewed up fast, setting his soldiers to prohibit all passengers that met with them, and wayfaring persons travelling by, once to look back thither, or to stay their pace and stand still.

65. When Sejanus went about seditiously to work alteration

in the state, although he saw now that both his birthday was publicly solemnized, and also his images of gold worshipped everywhere, he overthrew him (I must needs say) at last, but with much ado, by crafty sleights and guile, rather than by his princely authority and imperial power. For first, to the end that he might dismiss the man in show of honor, he assumed him to be his colleague in the fifth consulship, which in his long absence he had taken upon him for that very purpose. Afterwards when he had deceived him with hope of affinity and the tribunes' authority, he complained of the man (who was looking for no such matter) in a shameful and piteous oration, beseeching the senate, among other requests, to send one of the consuls to conduct him, an aged and desolate man, with some guard of soldiers, into their sight. And yet nevertheless, distrusting himself and fearing an uproar, he had given commandment that his grandson Drusus, whom still he kept in prison at Rome, should be set at liberty (if need did so require) and ordained general captain. Yea and while his ships were ready rigged and prepared to what legions soever he meant for to flee, he stood looking ever and anon from the highest cliff, toward the marks and signs which he had appointed (lest messengers might stay too long) for to be raised a great way off, thereby to have intelligence how any occurrence (good or bad) fell out. Nay, when the conspiracy of Sejanus was now suppressed, he was never again secure and resolute; for the space of nine months next ensuing, he stirred not out of the village called Jovis.

66. Besides all this, divers and sundry reproachful taunts from all parts nettled and stung his troubled mind. For there was not a person condemned that reviled him not in all sorts openly to his face, yea, and discharged upon him opprobrious terms, with libels laid in the very orchestra [where the senators sat to behold the plays]. With these contumelies verily, af-

fected he was after a most divers and contrary manner; so that, one while he desired for very shame of the world, that all such abuses might be unknown and concealed; otherwhiles, he contemned the same, and of his own accord broached and divulged them abroad. Furthermore, rated he was and railed at in the letters also of Artabanus, king of the Parthians, who charged him with parricides, murders, cowardice and luxurious riot, who gave him counsel likewise with all speed possible, to satisfy with a voluntary death the hatred of his citizens, conceived against him in the highest degree and most justly. At the last, being even weary of himself, in the beginning of such an epistle as this, he declared and confessed in manner the very sum of all his miseries. "What shall I write? my lords of the senate, or how shall I write? Nay, what is it, at a word, that I shall not write at this time? The gods and goddesses all plague and confound me utterly at once, feeling as I do myself daily to perish."

67. Some think that he foreknew all this by the skill he had of future events; that he foresaw also long before how great a calamity and infamy both would one day betide him; and therefore it was, that he refused most obstinately to take upon him the empire and the name of *Pater Patriae*, as also stood against the oath to maintain his acts, for fear lest within a while after, to his greater disgrace and shame he might be found inferior and unworthy of such special honors. Which verily may be gathered out of the speech he made as touching both those points, when he said but thus: That he would always like to himself, and never change his manners, so long as he continued in his sound wits. Howbeit, provided it would be that the senate bind not themselves to keep the actions of anyone, who by some chance might be altered. And again, "Marry if at any time," quoth he, "ye shall make doubt of my loyal behavior and devoted mind unto you (which before it

ever happen, I wish my dying day to take me from this opinion of yours, once conceived and afterwards changed) the bare title of *Pater Patriae* will add no honor unto me, but upbraid you either with inconsiderate rashness, for imposing that surname upon me, or else with inconstancy, for your contrary judgements of me."

68. Corpulent he was, big set and strong, of stature above the ordinary, broad between the shoulders and large-breasted; in all other parts also of the body (from the crown of his head to the very sole of his foot) of equal making and congruent proportion. But his left hand was more nimble and stronger than the right; and his joints so firm, that with his finger he was able to bore through a green and sound apple; with a fillip also to break the head of a boy, yea of a good stripling and big youth. Of color and complexion he was clear and white, wearing the hair of his head long behind, insomuch as it covered his very neck; which was thought in him to be a fashion appropriate to his lineage and family. He had an ingenuous and well-favored face; wherein notwithstanding appeared many small tumors, and a pair of very great goggle eyes in his head, such as (whereat a man would marvel) could see even by night and in the dark; but that was only for a little while and when they opened first after sleep; for in the end they waxed dim again. His gait was with his neck stiff and shooting forward; with a countenance bent and composed lightly to severity. For the most part he was silent; seldom or never should you have him talk with those next about him; and if he did, his speech was exceeding slow, not without a certain wanton gesticulation and fumbling with his fingers. All which properties being odious and full of arrogance, Augustus both observed in him, and also went about to excuse and cloak for him before the senate and people, assuring them, they were the defects and imperfections of nature, and not the vices

of the mind. He lived most healthfully and verily all the time well near that he was emperor; albeit from that he was thirty years old he governed his health after his own order and direction, without any help or counsel at all of physicians.

69. As little respect as he had of the gods, or sense of any religion (as one addicted to astrology and calculation of nativities, yea and fully persuaded, that all things were done and ruled by fatal destiny), yet feared he thunder exceedingly; and were the air or weather any whit troubled, he ever carried a chaplet of laurel about his neck, because that kind of green branch is never, as they say, blasted with lightning.

70. The liberal sciences of both Greek and Latin he loved most affectionately. In the Latin speech he followed Corvinus Mesalla, whom being an aged professor he had observed from his very youth; but with overmuch affectation and curiosity he marred all and darkened his style, so that he was thought to do somewhat better *ex tempore*, than upon study and premeditation. He composed also a poem in lyric verses, the title whereof is, *A Complaint of Caesar's Death*. He made likewise Greek poems in imitation of Euphorion, Rhianus and Parthenius; in which poets being much delighted, their writings and images he dedicated in the public libraries among the ancient and principal authors. A number therefore of learned men strove a-vie to put forth many pamphlets of them, and to present him therewith. But above all he studied for the knowledge of fabulous history, even unto mere fooleries, and matters ridiculous. For, the very grammarians (which kind of professors as we have said, he affected especially) he would essay and appose commonly with these and such like questions, namely, "Who was Hecuba's mother? What name Achilles had among the virgins? What it was that the sirens were wont to sing?" The very first day after the death of Augustus that he entered into the Curia, as if he minded once for all to per-

form the duty of piety and religion, following the example of Minos he sacrificed indeed, as the manner was with frankincense and wine, but without a minstrel, as the said Minos sometime did at the death of his son.

71. In the Greek tongue, howsoever he otherwise was ready enough and spoke with facility, yet he used it not everywhere, but most of all forbore it in the senate house; insomuch verily, as when he came to name *Monopolium*, he craved leave beforehand, for that he was to use a strange and foreign word; yea and in a certain decree of the senators, when this word *emblema* was read, he gave his opinion, that the said word should be changed, and instead of that strange term some Latin vocable sought out; and if such an one could not be found, then to utter and declare the thing, though it were in more words and by circumlocution. A certain Greek soldier also, being required for to depose and deliver his testimony, he forbade to make answer unless it were in Latin.

72. All the time that he was retired and lived from the city of Rome, twice and no more he essayed to return thither; once he came by water embarked in a galley, as far as to the gardens adjoining to the *Naumachia*, but he had set guards along the banks of Tiber, for to void and put back such as went forth to meet him. A second time, by the way Appia, so far as the seventh mile's end from Rome; but when he had only seen the walls afar off, without approaching nearer unto the city he returned. For what cause he did so at first, it was not certainly known; afterwards, affrighted he was with a prodigious sight. Among other delights he took great pleasure in a serpent dragon, which, when according to his usual manner, he would have fed with his own hand and found eaten by pismires, he was warned thereupon to beware the violence of a multitude. In his return therefore speedily into Campania he fell sick at Astura; but being eased a little of that malady he went for-

ward as far as to Circeii. And because he would give no suspicion of sickness, he was not only present himself at the games exhibited by the garrison soldiers there, but also, when there was a wild boar put forth into the open showplace for to be baited, he lanced darts at him from above, where he was. And presently therewith, by occasion of a convulsion in his side, and for that he had taken the cold air upon an exceeding heat, he fell back by relapse into a more dangerous disease. Howbeit, he bore it out a pretty while; notwithstanding that he was come down so far as to Misenum, he pretermitted nothing of his ordinary and daily manner, no not so much as his feasting and other pleasures, partly upon an intemperate humor of his own, and in part to dissimule and palliate his weakness. For, when Charicles his physician, who was licensed to depart and be absent, went forth from the table and took hold of his hand to kiss it, he supposing that he had felt his pulse, desired him to stay and sit down again, and so drew out the supper longer. Neither gave he over his usual custom, but even then standing in the midst of the banqueting room with a litter by him he spoke to everyone by name as they took their leave.

73. Meanwhile, when he had read among the acts passed in the senate that certain prisoners were enlarged and dismissed, but not so much as once heard, concerning whom he had written very briefly and no otherwise than that nominated they were by an informer; chafing and frowning hereat, as if he had been held in contempt, he fully proposed to go again into Capri, as one who lightly would attempt nothing, but where he was sure enough and without all danger. But being kept back, as well by tempest as the violence of his disease that grew still upon him, he died soon after in a villa named Lucullus, in the seventy-eighth year of his age, three and twentieth of his empire, and the seventeenth day before the Kalends of

April, when Gnaius Acerronius Proculus and Gaius Portius Niger were consuls. Some think that Gaius had given him a poison of slow operation, which should by little and little consume him. Others are of opinion, that when he desired meat in the remission of an ague fit wherein he had swooned, it was denied him, and therewith a pillow thrown upon his face to smother him and stop his breath. Some again, that it was when coming soon to himself, he called for his ring which was plucked from his finger while he fainted. Seneca writes that perceiving himself drawing on and ready to die, he took off his ring, as if he minded to give it unto someone, and so held it a pretty while; then afterwards did it upon his finger again; and so keeping down and gripping close his left hand, lay still a long time without once stirring. But suddenly calling for his grooms and servitors, when none of them made answer, rose up, and not far from his pallet, his strength failing him, he fell down dead.

74. Upon the last birthday feast of his that ever he saw, he thought as he lay asleep, that Apollo Temenites (an idol of exceeding bigness and most artificially wrought) which was newly brought from Syracuse to be set up in the library of his new temple, assured him, that he could not possibly by him be dedicated. And some few days before his death, the watch-tower that gave light at Capri by an earthquake fell down in the night; and at Misenum, the ashes remaining of the embers and coals brought in to heat his refection parlor, being quenched quite and continuing cold a long time, suddenly broke forth into a light fire, at the shutting in of the evening, and so shone out a great part of the night and gave not over.

75. The people joyed so much at his death, that running up and down at the first tiding thereof, some cried out in this note, "Fling Tiberius into the Tiber." Others in their prayers besought the Mother Earth and the infernal gods to vouchsafe

him now dead no place, but among impious wretches. And a sort there were, who threatened his lifeless carcass the drag and the *Gemonia*; as who, over and above the remembrance of his former cruelty in times past, were provoked to anger with a fresh outrage newly committed. For whereas by an act of the senate it was provided, that the execution of condemned persons should be put off until the tenth day after sentence given, it happened so, that the day on which some of them were to suffer, fell out to be the very same, wherein news came of Tiberius' death. These poor souls, notwithstanding they piteously called for help (because in the absence yet of Gaius no man was known, who might in such a case be repaired unto and spoken with), the jailers, for that they would do nothing against the constitution aforesaid, strangled them and flung their bodies into the *Gemonia*. Hereupon, I say, the people's hatred against him increased, as if the tyrant's cruelty remained still after his death. His corpse, so soon as it began to be removed from Misenum, notwithstanding the most part cried with one voice, to carry it rather to Atella, and there to half-burn it in the amphitheater, yet was brought to Rome by the soldiers and burnt in a public funeral fire.

76. A two-fold will he made two years before; the one written with his own hand, the other by his freedman; but both of them were of the same tenor; and signed he had them with the seals of most base persons. By virtue of which will and testament, he left coheirs and equal in portion Gaius his grandson by Germanicus, and Tiberius by Drusus. These he appointed to succeed one another. He gave legacies also to many more, and among the rest unto the Vestal Virgins, and to the soldiers of all sorts in general, as also to the commons of Rome by the poll; yea and to the masters of every street by themselves severally.

THE HISTORY OF
GAIUS CAESAR CALIGULA

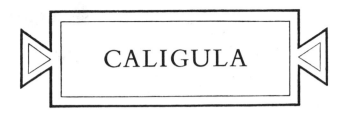

CALIGULA

GERMANICUS, FATHER OF GAIUS CAESAR, SON of Drusus and Antonia, no sooner was adopted by his uncle Tiberius but forthwith he bore the office of quaestor five years before he might by the laws, and after it the consulate. And being sent into Germany to the army when, upon news of Augustus' death, the legions all throughout stood out most stiffly and refused Tiberius for their emperor, offering unto him the absolute government of the state (whether their constant resolution or kind affection herein were greater it is hard to say), he stickled and repressed them, yea and soon after having subdued the enemy, triumphed. After this, being created consul the second time, and driven forth perforce (before he entered into that honorable place) to compose the troubles and to quiet the state in the Eastern parts, when he had deposed the king of Armenia and brought Cappadocia into the form of a province, in the thirty-fourth year of his age, he died of a long disease at Antioch, not without suspicion of poison. For, besides the blackish and swart spots which were to be seen all over his body, and the frothy slime that ran forth at his mouth; his heart also (after he was burnt), they found among the bones all sound and not consumed, the nature whereof is thought to be such that if it be infected with poison, it checks all fire and cannot possibly be burnt.

2. But, as the opinion of the world went, his death was contrived by the wicked plot of Tiberius, and effected by the ministry and help of Gnaius Piso, who about the same time,

being president of Syria, and realizing that he was to offend either Tiberius or Germanicus (as if there were no other remedy, but needs he must do it), made no spare, but beyond all measure dealt with Germanicus, sick as he was, most rigorously, both in word and deed. For which so soon as he was returned to Rome, he had like to have been pulled in pieces by the people; and by the senate he was condemned to die.

3. It is for certain known and confessed that there were in Germanicus all good parts and gifts as well of body as of mind; and those in such measure as never to any man befell the like: to wit, for show, full of passing beauty, favor and feature, with strength and valor answerable thereto; and for wit, excellently well seen in eloquence and learning of both kinds (Greek and Latin). The very attractive object he was of singular benevolence, endowed with a wonderful grace and remarkable desire to win men's favor and deserve their love. The only defect that he had in his making and personage were his slender shanks, and yet the same also by little and little became replenished with continual riding on horseback after his meat. Many a time wounded he his enemy in close fight hand to hand. He pleaded cases of great importance, even after he had won triumphal ornaments. And among other monuments of his studies, he left behind him in Greek, comedies also. Both at home and abroad civil he was, in so much as he would go into free and confederate cities without any lictors. Where ever he knew any sepulchres of brave and worthy men to be, there his use was to offer unto their ghosts. Being purposed to place into one tomb the old relics and bones dispersed of those that were slain in that great overthrow with Varus, he first gave assay with his own hand to gather and carry them together into one place. Moreover, to his slanderers and backbiters (if he lighted upon them), of what quality so ever the persons were, or how great cause soever they gave,

so mild, so remiss and harmless he was that notwithstanding Piso reversed and cancelled his decrees, plagued and persecuted a long time his dependants, yet could he not find in his heart to be angry with him, before he had for certain known that he attempted his person with poisons and sorcerous execrations; and even then he proceeded no farther against him, but by the ancient customs to renounce all friendship with him, and to give his domestic friends charge to revenge him, if ought happened to himself otherwise than well.

4. Of these virtues he reaped most plentiful fruit. So liked and loved of his kinsfolk and friends (for I let pass all other affinities and acquaintance of his), that Augustus after he had continued a long time in suspense, whether he should ordain him for his successor or no, recommended him at last to Tiberius for to be adopted. So highly favored of the common people he was, that many do report and write that whensoever he came unto a place or departed from thence, divers times, by reason of the multitude flocking to meet him and to bear him company, he endangered his own life in the press. As he returned out of Germany, after suppressing the seditious tumults and mutinies there, all the praetorian cohorts every one went out to encounter him upon the way, albeit warning was given beforehand by proclamation that no more than twain of them should go forth. But as for the people of Rome, of all sexes, ages and degrees, they ran out by heaps to meet him twenty miles from Rome.

5. Howbeit far greater and more assured testimonies of men's judgement touching him appeared at, and after his death. The very day wherein he left this life, the temples were pelted with stones, the altars of the gods cast down, the domestic Lares by some flung out of doors into the street; yea, and new-born babies of wedded parents thrown forth to be destroyed. And, that which more is, the report goeth that the very barbarians,

notwithstanding that they were at variance and civil war among themselves, yea and had taken arms against us, yet, as it were in some domestic and common sorrow, agreed all to make truce and cessation of arms for a time. Some of their princes also, and potentates, to declare their extraordinary mourning and regret, did cut off their own beards and shaved their wives' heads. Yea the very king of kings himself gave over his exercise of hunting, and dissolved the society of his great peers and princes at his table; which among the Parthians is as much as public mourning.

6. At Rome, verily, when as the city upon the first rumor of his sickness, in amazedness and heavy cheer, waited for the messengers that came after, all of a sudden in the evening the rumor went current (although the authors were unknown), that now at last he was recovered. Running there was everywhere from all parts with lights and sacrifices into the Capitol; yea the very doors of the temple were like to have been burst open that nothing might stand in their way and hinder them, so desirous and earnestly bent with joy to pay their vows. Tiberius was awakened out of his sleep with the shouts and voices of the people rejoicing and from every side with one accord resounding this note:

Salva Roma, salva patria, salvus est Germanicus.

Safe is Rome, safe is our country, safe is Germanicus.

Also, when now at the last it was known abroad that he was departed from this life, the public sorrow by no comfortable words nor edicts could be repressed, but continued still even during the festival days of the month of December. His glory and the miss of him thus deceased was much augmented also by the outrages of the times ensuing; while all men were of the opinion (and not without good reason) that the fierceness of Tiberius, which soon after broke forth, was held in and kept down by the reverent respect and fear that he had of him.

7. He wedded Agrippina, daughter to Marcus Agrippa and Julia, by whom he had nine children: of which fair issue twain, being yet infants, were taken away by untimely death; one died when he was now waxen a jolly boy, passing full of lovely mirth and pretty talk. Livia dedicated his counterfeit in the habit of Cupid in the chapel of Venus Capitolina; and the same Augustus was wont to kiss while it stood in his bedchamber, so often as he entered into it. The rest survived their father: three of the female sex, Agrippina, Drusilla and Livia, born all one after another in the space of three years; likewise as many male children, Nero, Drusus and Gaius Caesar. As for Nero and Drusus, the senate, upon imputations laid by Tiberius, judged them to be enemies unto the state.

8. Gaius Caesar was born the day next preceding the Kalends of September, when his father and Gaius Ponteius Capito were consuls. The place of his nativity, by the disagreement of writers, is left uncertain. Gnaius Lentulus Gaetulicus writes, that he was born at Tibur; Plinius Secundus, within the country of the Treviri, in a town called Ambiatinum, upon the very confluence of two rivers. For evidence and proof whereof he farther says that certain altars are there to be seen carrying this inscription, "For the childbirth and delivery of Agrippina." But these verses following, divulged soon after that he came to be emperor, do plainly show that born he was in the very camp where the legions wintered.

> *In castris natus patriis nutritus in armis,*
> *Iam designati principis, omen erat.*

Born in the camp, in father's war with soldiers rear'd was he;
A sign, that then ordain'd he was an emperor for to be.

I myself do find among the records, that Antium was the place of his birth. Pliny refutes Gaetulicus, as if he made a lie by way of flattery, because to the praise of a young and glorious prince, he would fetch some argument and matter even out of a city consecrated to Hercules; and was the bolder, as he says, to abuse the said lie, for that, indeed, a year almost before, Germanicus had a son born at Tibur, named likewise Gaius Caesar, of whose amiable childhood and untimely death we have spoken before. And as to Pliny himself, confuted he is by the calculation of the times. For they who have recorded the acts of Augustus do all agree that Germanicus was sent into Germany after the time of his consulship expired, when Gaius was already born. Neither can the inscription of the altar one jot make good his opinion, considering that Agrippina was delivered of daughters twice in that country. And what childbirth so ever it was, without respect and difference of sex, called it is *puerperium*; for that in old time folk used to name little girls also *puerae*, like as little boys *puelli*. There is besides, an epistle of Augustus written, not many months before he died, unto Agrippina his granddaughter as touching this Gaius (for there was not now living any other infant of the like name) in these words, "I have no longer ago than yesterday taken order with Talarius and Asellius, that with the leave of God they bring the boy Gaius upon the fifteenth day before the Kalends of June. I send besides with him of mine own servants a physician whom Germanicus (as I have written unto him) may if he will retain and keep with him still. Farewell my Agrippina and endeavor to come well and in health to thy Germanicus." It appears I suppose sufficiently that Gaius could not in that place be born, unto which he was conveyed from Rome not before he was well near two years old. And as for those verses, these self-same evidences likewise discredit them, and the rather, because they have no author. We are to follow therefore the only authority that remains of the public records, seeing especially that Gaius evermore preferred Antium before all other retiring places, and loved it no otherwise than his native soil; yea, and by report, was fully minded once, upon a tedious weariness that he had of Rome, to transfer thither even the very seat and habitation of the empire.

9. He got his surname Caligula [little boot] by occasion of a merry word taken up in the camp, because he was brought up there in the habit of an ordinary and common soldier among the rest. With whom, how much besides he was able to do in favor by means of his education and daily feeding with them, was most of all known when after the death of Augustus, he only, no doubt, with his very sight and presence quieted them, what time they were in an uproar and at the very point of furious outrage. For they ceased not to mutiny, until they perceived that he was about to be sent out of the way for danger of the sedition, and appointed to the next city adjoining. Then and not before, turning to repentance, they stayed and held back his coach, and so by prayer averted the displeasure that was toward them.

10. He accompanied his father also in the expedition into Syria; from whence being returned, first he abode in house with his mother; and after that she was banished and sent away, he remained with his great-grandmother Livia Augusta; whom deceased he praised in a funeral oration on the rostra when he was yet but a very youth in his *praetexta*. And then removed he to his grandmother Antonia. From her in the twentieth year of his age he was sent for to Capri by Tiberius, and upon one and the self-same day he did don his virile gown and withal cut the first down of his beard, but without any honorable solemnity such as his brethren before him had at their commencements. Here, notwithstanding that he was tempted by all the deceitful trains that they could devise who would have drawn and forced him to quarrels, yet gave he never any occasion, having quite forgotten the fall and cal-

amity of his mother, brethren and near friends, as if nothing had befallen to any of them, and passing over all those abuses which himself had endured with incredible dissimulation; so obsequious and double diligent besides to his grandfather and those about them, that of him it was said and not without good cause, "a better servant and a worse master there never was."

11. Howbeit, his cruel disposition and villainous nature he could not even then bridle and hold in, but both at all castigations and punishments of such as were delivered over to execution, most willing was he to be present. He also would haunt taverns and brothelhouses, going about from place to place disguised under a peruke of false hair and in a long garment; yea, and most studiously gave his mind to learn the artificial feat of dancing and singing upon the stage. And verily Tiberius was well content to wink hereat and suffer all, if haply thereby his fierce and savage nature might have been mollified and become tractable. Which the old man (as he was a prince right prudent and one most quick of scent) had foreseen well long enough before, in that divers times he gave out and said openly that Gaius lived to the destruction of himself and all men, likewise that he cherished and was bringing up a very viper for the people of Rome, and a Phaethon to the whole world.

12. Not long after, he took to wife Junia Claudilla, the daughter of Marcus Silanus, a right noble gentleman. And then, being nominated to succeed as augur in the room of his brother Drusus, before his investiture and installation therein, he was advanced to the sacerdotal dignity of a pontifex: a noble testimony of his piety and towardness, since, the royal line and imperial court being desolate and destitute of all other helps, Sejanus also suspected and soon after overthrown, he thus, by small degrees arose to the hope of succession in the empire. Which hope the rather to confirm, after his wife, the

aforesaid Junia, was dead in childbirth he solicited unto filthy wantonness dame Ennia, the wife of Naevius Macro, then captain of the praetorian cohorts, having promised her marriage also, in case he ever attained to the empire; and for assurance hereof he bound it with an oath and a bill of his own hand. By her means being insinuated once into the inward acquaintance of Macro, he attempted, as some think, to poison Tiberius, and while he was yet living, but laboring for life, commanded his ring to be plucked from his finger, but perceiving that he gave some suspicion of holding it fast he caused a pillow to be forced upon his mouth, and so with his own hands stifled and strangled him; yea, and when his freedman made an outcry at this cruel and horrible act, he gave order immediately to crucify him. And verily this soundeth to truth, considering there be some authors who write that himself afterwards professed, if not the murder done, yet at least his intention one day to do it. For he made his boast continually in reporting his own piety that to revenge the death of his mother and brethren, he entered with a dagger into Tiberius' bed-chamber while he lay asleep; and yet upon mere pity and commiseration bethought himself, flung away the weapon and so went back again. Neither durst Tiberius, although he had an inkling and intelligence of his design, make any inquisition at all of the matter or proceed to revenge.

13. Thus having obtained the empire, he procured unto the people of Rome, or (as I may so say) to all mankind their heart's desire, being a prince of all that ever were most wished for by the greatest part of the provincial nations and of the soldiers, because most of them had known him as an infant; and generally by the whole commonality of Rome, in remembrance of his father Germanicus, and upon compassion they took of that house in manner ruinate and extinct. As he removed therefore from Misenum, albeit he was clad in mourn-

ing weed and reverently did attend the corpse of Tiberius, yet
went he among the altars, sacrifices and burning torches in a
most thick throng and joyful train of such as met him on the
way; who besides other lucky and fortunate names called him
Sidus, "their star," *Pullum*, "their chick," *Pupum*, "their babe"
and *Alumnum*, "their nurseling."

14. No sooner was he entered into the city of Rome, but
incontinently with consent of the senate and the multitude
which rushed into the Curia, after they had annulled the will
of Tiberius who in his testament had adjoined as co-heir unto
him another of his grandsons, under age and as yet in his *praetexta*, permitted he was alone to have the full and absolute
power of all, and that with such a universal joy, that in three
months' space next ensuing and those not fully expired, there
were by report above 160,000 beasts slain for sacrifice. Within
a few days after this, when he passed over by water but to the
islands near Campania, vows were made for his safe return;
and no man there was who did let slip the least occasion to
testify what pensive care he took as touching his health and
safety. But so soon as he was once fallen sick, they all kept
watch by night about the palace; neither wanted some who
vowed to fight armed to the very outrance for his life thus
lying sick, yea and devoted their very lives for him if he recovered, professing no less in written bills set up in public
places. To this surpassing love of his own citizens and countrymen, was adjoined the notable favor also of foreign states.
For Artabanus, king of the Parthians, professing always his
hatred and contempt of Tiberius, sought of his own accord to
him for amity; yea he came in person to a conference with one
of his legates that had been consul, and passing over Euphrates,
adored the eagles and other military ensigns of the Romans, as
also images of the Caesars.

15. Himself also enkindled and set more on fire the affections

of men by all manner of popularity. When he had with many a tear praised Tiberius in a funeral oration before the body of the people, and performed the compliment of his obsequies most honorably, forthwith he hastened to Pandataria and the Pontian islands for to translate from thence the ashes of his mother and brother, and that in foul and tempestuous weather, to the end that his piety and kindness might be the more seen. And being come to their relics, very devoutly himself with his own hands, bestowed them in several pitchers. And with no less show in pageant-wise, having wafted them first to Ostia with a flag pitched in the poop or stern of a galley guided by two ranks of oars, and so forth to Rome up the Tiber, by the ministry of the most worshipful knights of Rome, he conveyed them within two frames devised for the purpose into the Mausoleum, even at noon when people were assembled there in great frequency. In memorial likewise of them he ordained yearly dirges and sacrifices to be performed with religious devotion to their ghosts by the whole city. And more than that, he instituted for his mother solemn games within the Circus, and a sacred chariot withal wherein her image to the full proportion of her body should be carried in the pomp. But in remembrance of his father he called the month September, Germanicus. These ceremonial duties done, by virtue of one sole act of the senate, he heaped upon his grandmother Antonia whatsoever honors Livia Augusta had received in her whole time. His uncle Claudius, a knight of Rome until that time and no better, he assumed unto him for his colleague in the consulship. His brother Tiberius he adopted the very day that he put on his virile gown, and styled him prince of the youth. As touching his sisters, he caused in all oaths this clause to be annexed, "Neither shall I hold myself and children more dear, than I do Gaius and his sisters." Also, he ordained that in moving and propounding of matters by the consuls unto the senators, they should begin in this form, "That which may be to the good and happy estate of Gaius Caesar and his sisters, etc." In the same vein of popularity, he restored all those that had been condemned, confined and exiled, yea he freely dispensed with them, pardoning whatsoever crimes or imputations remained still behind from before time. All the books and registers pertaining to the causes of his mother and brethren, so that no informer or witness should afterwards need to fear, he brought together into the Forum; where protesting beforehand, and calling the gods to record with a loud voice, that he had neither read ought nor meddled once therewith, he burnt them. A certain pamphlet presented unto him concerning his life and safety, he received not, but stood upon this point, that he had done nothing wherefore he should be odious to any person; saying withal, that he had no ears open for informers and tale-bearers.

16. The Spintriae, inventors of monstrous forms in perpetration of filthy lust, he expelled forth of Rome, being hardly and with much ado entreated not to drown them in the deep sea. The writings of Titus Labienus, Cordus Cremutius and Cassius Severus, which had been called in and abolished by divers acts of the senate, he suffered to be sought out again, to be in men's hands extant, and usually to be read; seeing that it concerned him principally and stood him upon most, to have all actions and deeds delivered unto posterity. The breviary of the empire, that by Augustus had been wont to be proposed openly, but was by Tiberius intermitted, he published. Unto the magistrates he granted free jurisdiction, and that there might be no appealing to himself. The knighthood of Rome he reviewed with severity and great preciseness; yet not without some moderation of his hand. He openly took from them their horses [public horses of service], in whom was found any foul reproach or ignominy; as for those, who were

culpable in smaller matters, he only passed over their names in reading the roll. To the end, that the judges might be eased of their labor, unto the four former decuries he added a fifth. He gave the attempt likewise to bring up again the ancient manner of elections, and to restore unto the people their free voices. The legacies due by the last will and testament of Augustus (although the same was abolished), as also of Livia Augusta, which Tiberius had suppressed, he caused faithfully and without fraud to be tendered and fully paid. The exaction called *Ducentesima* of all bargains and sales, he remitted throughout Italy. The losses that many a man had sustained by fire he supplied. And if to any princes he restored their kingdoms, he adjoined withal the fruit and profits also of their rents, customs and imposts growing to the crown in the middle time between; as namely, unto Antiochus Comagenus who had been confiscated and fined in a hundred million sesterces. And that he might the rather be reputed a favorer of all good examples, he gave unto a woman, by condition a libertine, 800,000 sesterces, for that she being under most grievous and dolorous torments, concealed yet and would not utter a wicked fact committed by her patron. For which things, among other honors done unto him there was decreed for him a shield of gold, which upon a certain day every year, the colleges of the priests should bring into the Capitol, with the senate accompanying them, and noblemen's children as well boys as girls, singing the praises of his virtues in musical verse tuned sweetly in meter. Moreover, there passed a decree, that the day on which he began his empire should be called *Palilia,* implying thereby, as it were a second foundation of the city.

17. He bore four consulships; the first, from the Kalends of July for two months; the second from the Kalends of January for thirty days; the third unto the Ides of January; and the fourth unto the seventh day before the said Ides. Of all

these, the last two he held jointly together. The third, he alone entered upon at Lyons, not, as some deem, upon pride or negligence, but because, being absent, he could not have knowledge that his colleague died just against the very day of the Kalends. He gave a largess to the people twice, to wit, 300 sesterces to them apiece, and a most plenteous dinner he made as oft unto the senate and knights as also to the wives and children of them both. In the latter dinner of the twain, he dealt over and above, among the men garments to be worn abroad, unto the women and children, scarves of purple and violet color. And to the end he might augment the public joy of the city with perpetuity, also, he annexed unto the feast *Saturnalia* one day more, and named the same *Juvenalis*.

18. He set forth games of sword-fencers, partly in the amphitheater of Taurus, and partly within the *Septa* in Mars field, into the which he inserted and brought in certain troops of African and Campanian champions to skirmish by companies; even the very best, selected out of both countries. Neither was he always himself president at these public shows, but otherwhiles enjoined the magistrates or else his friends to take the charge of presidency. As for stage-plays, he exhibited them continually in divers places and in sundry sorts; once also in the night season, burning lights throughout the city. He scattered likewise and flung among the common people missiles of many and sundry kinds to scramble for; and dealt man by man baskets with viands therein. At which feasting, to a certain knight of Rome who over against him plied his jaws full merrily, and fed right heartily with a greedy stomach, he sent his own part; as also to a senator for the same cause his letters patents, wherein he declared him extraordinarily praetor. He represented besides, many Circus games, which held from morn to even; interposing one while, the baiting of panthers, another while the Troy-jousting and tournament. But

some especial sports there were above the rest, and then the Circus was laid all over with vermilion and green; where none but senators drove the chariots. Some also he put forth upon a sudden, namely when as he beheld from out of the house Gelotiana the preparation and furniture of the Circus, some few from the next open galleries called unto him for the same.

19. Furthermore, he devised a new kind of sight, and such as never was heard of before. For, over the middle space between Baiae and the huge piles or dams at Puteoli containing three miles and 600 paces well near, he made a bridge; having gotten together from all parts ships of burden, and placed them in a course at anchor, with a bank of earth cast thereupon, direct and straight after the fashion of the highway Appia. Upon this bridge he passed to and fro for two days together; the first day mounted upon a courser richly trapped, himself most brave and goodly to be seen with a chaplet of oak-branches, armed with a battle axe, a light target and a sword, clad also in a cloak of gold; the morrow after he appeared in the habit of a charioteer, riding in a chariot drawn with two goodly steeds of an excellent race; carrying before him Darius a boy, one of the Parthian hostages, with a train of the praetorian soldiers marching after in battle array, and accompanied with the cohort of his minions in wagons. Most men I wote well, are of opinion that Gaius invented such a kind of bridge, in emulation of Xerxes, who not without the wonder of the world, made a bridge of planks over Hellespont, an arm of the sea somewhat narrower than this; others, that by a bruit blazed abroad of some huge and monstrous piece of work, he might terrify Germany and Britain, upon which countries he meant to make war. But I remember well that being a boy, I heard my grandfather report and tell the cause of this work, as it was delivered by his own courtiers, who were more inward with him than the rest, namely, that Thrasyllus the great

astrologer assured Tiberius when he was troubled in mind about his successor, and more inclined to his lawful grandson, that Gaius should no more become emperor than able to run a course to and fro on horse-back, through the gulf of Baiae.

20. He set forth shows also even in foreign parts, to wit in Sicily at Syracuse, the games called *Actiaci*; likewise at Lyons in France, plays of a mixed nature and argument; also a solemn contention for the prize in eloquence, both Greek and Latin. In which trial of masteries, the report goes that those who were foiled and overcome, conferred rewards upon the winners, yea and were forced to make compositions in their praise. But those who did worse, they were commanded to wipe out their own writings, either with a sponge or else with their tongue, unless they would choose rather to be chastised with ferules, or else to be ducked over head and ears in the next river.

21. The buildings left half undone by Tiberius, namely the temple of Augustus and the theater of Pompey, he finished. He began moreover a conduit in the Tiburtine territory and an amphitheater near unto the enclosure called *Septa*; of the two works, the one was ended by his successor Claudius, the other was forlet and given over quite. The walls at Syracuse by the injury of time decayed and fallen down were by him repaired. He had fully purposed also to build anew the palace of Polycrates of Samos; to finish Apollo's temple called Didymeum at Miletus; also to found and build a city upon the top of the Alps; but before all, to dig through the isthmus in Achaea, and thither had he sent already one who had been a principal captain of a cohort to take measure of the work.

22. Thus far forth as of a prince; now forward, relate we must as of a monster. Having assumed into his style many surnames, called he was *Pius*, "kind," *Castrorum filius*, "Son of the [Military] Camp," *Pater Exercitum*, "Father of the Armies," and *Optimus Maximus Caesar*, "Most Gracious and Mighty Caesar."

When he happened to hear certain kings (who were come into the city for to do their duties and to salute him) contend as they sat with him at supper about the nobility of their birth and parentage, he cried forth the line of Homer:

> One sovereign lord, one king let there be.

And there lacked not much but that presently he had taken the diadem upon him and converted wholly the show of empire into the form of a kingdom. But being told that he was mounted already above the height and state both of emperors and also of kings, thereupon from that time forward he began to challenge unto himself a divine majesty; and having given order and commission that the images of the gods which, either for devout worship done unto them, or for curious workmanship seen upon them, excelled the rest (among which was that of Jupiter Olympicus) should be brought out of Greece into Rome, that when their heads were taken off he might set his own in the place, he enlarged the Palace and set out one part thereof as far as to the Forum. Transfiguring likewise and turning the temple of Castor and Pollux into a porch or entry, he stood many times in the middle between the said two gods, and so exhibited himself to be adored by all comers. And some there were who saluted him by the name of Jupiter Latiaris. Moreover he ordained a temple peculiarly appropriate to his own godhead, as also priests and most exquisite sacrifices. In his said temple stood his own image all of gold, lively portrayed and expressing his full proportion, the which was daily clad with the like vesture as himself wore. The masterships of the priesthood by him instituted, the richest men that were, every time of vacancy purchased, such as made the greatest suit and offered most therefor. The victims aforesaid were these fowl: flamingoes, peacocks, woodcocks, guinea hens, and pheasants, and those to be sorted by their kinds and so every day killed. And verily his usual manner was in the night to call unto the moon when she was at full and shining bright out for to come and lie with him in his arms; but in the day time he talked secretly and apart with Jupiter Capitolinus; one while by whispering and rounding one another in the ear, otherwhiles speaking more loud and not without chiding. For he was heard in threatening wise to utter these words (in Greek): "I will remove and translate you into the land of the Greeks." But finally entreated (according as he told the tale himself) and invited first by him for to cohabit, he made a bridge over the temple of Augustus of sacred memory, and so joined the Palace and the Capitol together. And soon after, to the end that he might be nearer unto them, he layed the foundation of a new house in the basement of the Capitol.

23. He could in no wise abide to be either reputed or named the grandson of Agrippa by reason of his base and obscure parentage; yea and angry he would be, in case any man either in oration or verse inserted him among the images of the Caesars. But he gave it out openly that his own mother was begotten by incest which Augustus committed with his own daughter Julia. And not content with this infamous imputation of Augustus, the Actian and Sicilian victories by him achieved he straightly forbade to be celebrated verily with solemn holidays, as being unlucky and hurtful to the people of Rome. As for Livia Augusta his great-grandmother, he called her ever and anon Ulysses in a woman's habit; yea and in a certain epistle unto the senate he was so bold as to lay unto her ignobility, as descended from a decurion of Fundi who was her grandsire by the mother's side, whereas it is evident and certain by public records that Aufidius Lingo bore honorable offices in Rome. When his grandame Antonia requested secret conference with him, he denied her, unless Macro, captain of the guard, might come in between to hear their talk.

And so, by such indignities and discontentments as these, he was the cause of her death; and yet, as some think, he gave her poison withal. Neither when she was dead deigned he her any honor, but out of his dining chamber beheld her funeral fire as it was burning. His brother Tiberius he surprised suddenly at unawares, sending a tribune of soldiers, who rushed in upon him and so slew him. Likewise Silanus his father-in-law he forced to death, even to cut his own throat with a razor, picking quarrels to them both and finding these causes, to wit, that the one [Silanus] followed him not when he took sea being very rough and much troubled, but stayed behind in hope to seize the city of Rome into his own hands, if ought happened but well unto him by occasion of tempests; the other [Tiberius] smelled strongly of antidote, as if he had taken the same to prevent his poisons. Whereas, in very truth Silanus avoided thereby the insufferable pain of being sea-sick and the grievous trouble of sailing; and Tiberius for a continual cough that grew upon him used a medicine. For his uncle Claudius he reserved for nothing else but to make him his laughing stock.

24. With all his sisters, he used ordinarily to be naughty, and at any great feast he placed evermore one or other of them by turns beneath himself, while his wife sat above. Of these sisters, as it is verily thought, he deflowered Drusilla being a virgin, when himself also was yet under age and a very boy; yea, and one time above the rest he was found in bed with her and taken in the manner by his grandmother Antonia, in whose house they were brought up both together. Afterwards also when she was bestowed in marriage upon Lucius Cassius Longinus, a man of consular degree, he took her from him and kept her openly, as if she had been his own lawful wife. Also, when he lay sick, he ordained her to be both heir of all his goods and successor also in the empire. For the same sister deceased, he proclaimed a general cessation of law in all

courts. During which time, a capital crime it was for any man to have laughed, bathed, or supped together with his parents, wife or children. And being impatient of this sorrow, when he was fled suddenly and by night out of the city, and had passed all over Campania, to Syracuse he went; and so from thence returned speedily again with his beard and hair overgrown. Neither at any time ever after, in making a speech before the people or to his soldiers concerning any matters were they never so weighty would he swear otherwise than by the name of Drusilla. The rest of his sisters, Livia and Agrippina, he loved neither with so tender affection nor so good respect, as whom he oftentimes prostituted and offered to be abused by his own stale catamites. So much the more easily therefore condemned he them in the case of Aemilius Lepidus, as adulteresses and privy to his treasons and way-layings addressed against his person. And he not only divulged their handwritings, which were sought out by guile and adulteries, but also consecrated unto Mars Revenger those three daggers prepared for his death, with a title over them, containing the cause of his so doing.

25. As for his marriages, a man may hardly discern, whether he contracted, dissolved, or held them still with more dishonesty. Livia Orestilla, what time she was wedded unto Gaius Piso, himself, being one who came in person to the solemnization of the marriage, commanded to be brought home unto him as his own wife; and having within few days cast her off, two years after he banished and sent her away; because in the middle time between, she was thought to have had the company again of her former husband. Some report, that being an invited guest at the nuptial supper, he charged Piso sitting over against him, in these terms, "Sir, see you sit not too close unto my wife"; and so, presently had her away with him from the table; and the next day published by proclamation, that he had met with a marriage after the example of Romulus and

Augustus. As touching Lollia Paulina, married already to Gaius Memmius, a man of consular degree and ruler of armies; upon mention made of her grandmother as the most beautiful lady in her time, he all of a sudden sent and called her home out of the province [where she was with her husband aforesaid]; and taking her perforce from her husband, wedded her and shortly turned her away; forbidding her straightly forever the use of any man's body whatsoever. Gaesonia, for no special beauty and favor of her own above others, nor yet because she was in the flower of her youth, considering she had been the mother already of three daughters by another man, but only for that she was a most lascivious woman and of unsatiable lust he loved with more ardent affection and constancy; insomuch as many a time he would show her to his soldiers clad in a soldier's cassock with a light target and a helmet riding close unto him; but to his friends, stark naked also. When she brought him a child, he vouchsafed her then the name of his wife and not before; professing and making it known, that in one and the self-same day, he was become both her husband and also father of the infant of her body born. This babe he named Junia Drusilla; whom he carried about with him through the temples of all the goddesses, and bestowed at length in the lap of Minerva, recommending it to her for to be nourished, brought up and taught. Neither had he any surer sign and evidence to believe she was his own and of his natural seed conceived, than her savagery, and that quality had she even then at the first, as that with her violent fingers she would not stick to lay at the face and eyes of other small children playing together with her.

26. Vanity it were and mere folly, to adjoin hereunto, how he served his kinsfolk and friends, to wit Ptolemaeus, king Juba's son and his own cousin removed (for he also was the grandson of Marcus Antonius by his daughter Selena), but especially Macro himself, yea and Ennia likewise, who were his

233

chief helpers and advanced him to the empire. All of them, in right of their near affinity, and in consideration of their good deserts were highly rewarded, even with bloody death. No more respective was he one whit of the senate, nor dealt in gentler wise with them; some, after they had borne the highest honors, he suffered to run by his wagon in their gowns for certain miles together, and as he sat at supper, to stand waiting one while at the head, another while at the foot of the table, girt with a white linen towel about them. Others, whom he had secretly murdered, he continued nevertheless calling for, as if they were alive; giving it out most untruly some few days after, that they had willfully made themselves away. The consuls had forgot by chance to publish by proclamation his birthday; for which he deprived them of their magistracy; and so for three days space the commonwealth was without the sovereign authority. His own quaestor, who happened to be nominated in a conspiracy against him, he caused to be scourged, and the clothes out of which he was stripped to be put under the soldiers' feet, that they might stand more steadily while they were whipping him. In pride and violence he handled other states and degrees of citizens. Being disquieted with the stir and noise that they kept, who by midnight took up their standings in the Circus, he drove them all away with cudgels; in which tumult and hurliburly, there were twenty knights of Rome and above, crowded and crushed to death, as many matrons and wives also, besides an infinite number of the common multitude. At the stage-plays, being minded to sow discord, and minister occasion of quarrel between the commons and knights of Rome, he gave his tickets forth sooner than ordinary, to the end that the equestrian seats might be possessed aforehand by the commoners. At the sword-fight, he otherwhiles commanded the curtains to be folded up and drawn together, during the most parching heat of the sun, and forbade that any person should be let forth; and then, removing and sending quite away the ordinary furniture of shows provided to make pastime, he put forth unto the people for to behold, poor wild beasts and carrion lean, to be baited; the basest sword-fencers also and worn with age, to combat; yea, and appointed householders such as were of quality and well known, but yet noted for some special feebleness and imperfection of body to carry the fight. And divers times he brought a dearth and famine among the people by shutting up the storehouses from them.

27. The cruelty of his nature he showed by these examples most of all. When cattle which were to feed wild beasts prepared for baiting, grew to be sold very dear, he appointed malefactors found guilty to be slaughtered for that purpose. And in taking the review of jails and prisoners therein, as they were sorted according to their offences, he, without once looking upon the cause of their imprisonment, standing only within a gallery, commanded all in the midst, *a calvo ad calvum*, from one bald-pate to another, to be led forth to execution. He exacted of him the performance of a vow, who had promised to do his devoir in public sword-fight for the recovery of the emperor's health; and him he beheld fighting, neither dismissed he him before he was victor, and after many prayers. Another there was, who for the same cause had vowed to die. This man being not very forward to pay his vow, he caused to be dight with sacred herbs, and adorned with fillets, like a sacrifice; and so delivered him into the hands of boys, who calling hard upon him for the discharge of his vow, should course and drive him through the streets of the city, until he were thrown headlong down the steep embankment. Many honest citizens of good calling and estate, after he had first disfigured with marks of branding irons, he condemned to dig in mines, and to make highways or to encounter with beasts;

or kept them creeping with all four like brute beasts within a cage for the nonce; or else slit them through the midst with a saw. And those whom he thus served, were not all of them guilty of any grievous offences; but sufficient it was, if they had a base opinion and spoke but meanly of some show that he exhibited, or because they had never sworn stoutly by his *Genius*. Parents he forced to be present at the execution of their own children. And when one father excused himself by reason of sickness, he sent a litter for him. Another of them immediately after the heavy spectacle of his son put to death, he invited to his own board, made him great cheer, and by all manner of courtesy provoked him to jocundness and mirth. The master of his sword-fights and beast-baitings he caused for certain days together to be beaten with chains in his own sight; but killed him not quite, before himself could no longer abide the stench of his brain by this time putrified. A poet, the author of *Atellane Interludes,* for a verse that he made implying a jest which might be doubly taken, he burnt at a stake in the very middle show-place of the amphitheater. A knight of Rome, whom he had cast before wild beasts, when he cried out, that he was innocent, he commanded to be brought back; and after he had cut out his tongue, sent him among them again, to fight for his life or to be devoured.

28. Having recalled one from exile which had been long banished, he demanded of him, what he was wont to do there, who made answer thus by way of flattery, "I prayed," he said, "to the gods always that Tiberius who had banished him, as now it is come to pass, might perish, and you become emperor." Hereupon Caligula weening that those whom he had banished prayed likewise for his death, sent about into the islands, to kill every one of them. Being desirous to have a senator torn and mangled piecemeal, he suborned certain of purpose, who all on a sudden as he entered into the Curia,

should call him enemy to the state, and so lay violent hands upon him; and when they had with their writing irons all to pricked and stabbed him, deliver him over to the rest, for to be dismembered and cut in pieces accordingly. Neither was he satisfied, until he saw the man's limbs, joints and innards drawn along the streets, and piled all on a heap together before him.

29. His deeds most horrible as they were, he augmented with as cruel words. His saying was, that he commended and approved in his own nature nothing more, than (to use his own term) *adiatrepsian* [unmovable rigor]. When his grandmother Antonia seemed to give him some admonition, he (as though it were not enough to disobey her), said, "Go to, dame; remember I may do what I will against all persons whomsoever." Being minded to kill his own brother, whom for fear of poison he imagined to be fortified aforehand with preservatives; "What," he said, "is there any antidote against Caesar?" When he had banished his sisters, he threatened them in these terms, saying, that he had not islands only at command but swords also. A certain citizen of praetor's degree, desired oftentimes from the retiring place where he was at Anticyra (into which isle he went for his health's sake), to have his leave continued. But he gave order he should be killed outright, adding these words therewith, that blood-letting was necessary for him, who in so long time had found no good by hellebore. Once every ten days, his manner was to subscribe and write down a certain number out of the jail to be executed, and said withal, that he cast up his reckonings, and cleared the book of accounts. When he had at one time condemned a sort of Frenchmen and Greeks together, he made his boast that he had subdued Gallograecia.

30. He would not lightly permit any to suffer death, but after many strokes given and those very softly, with this rule and precept evermore, which now became rife and well

known, "Strike so as they may feel that they are dying." He executed on a time one whom he had not appointed to die, by error only and mistaking his name; "But it makes no matter," he said, "for even he also hath deserved death." This speech of the tyrant out of a tragedy, he often repeated, *Oderint dum metuant* [Let them hate me so long as they fear me]. Many a time he inveighed bitterly against all the senators at once as the dependents and adherents of Sejanus, or the informers against his mother and brethren; bringing forth those evidences which he had made semblance before were burnt. And therewith excused and justified the cruelty of Tiberius as necessary, seeing he could not otherwise choose but believe so many that made presentments unto him. The degree of knights he railed at continually, as devoted wholly to the stage and showplace. Being highly displeased upon a time with the multitude favoring as they did the contrary faction [of charioteers] to his, he said, "Would God that the people of Rome had but one neck." And when Tetrinius Latro was by them called for to fight at sharp he said, that they also who called for him were *Tetrinii*, worthy to be put to sword-fight every one. It fortuned that five of these *Retiarii*, fighting together had without any combat yielded themselves as overcome to as many *Secutores*. Now when commandment was given by the people that they should be killed, one takes me up his trident again and slew all the other five who were thought the conquerors. This slaughter he both bewailed in an edict as most cruel, and also cursed them that endured to see the sight.

31. He was wont moreover to complain openly of the condition of his time wherein he lived, as not renowned by any public calamities; whereas the reign of Augustus was memorable for the overthrow of Varus; that of Tiberius ennobled by the fall of scaffolds in the theater at Fidenae. As for himself, like he was to be forgotten, such was the prosperity in his days.

And evermore he wished the carnage of his armies, famine, pestilence, fires, or earthquake.

32. Even while he was at his recreations and disports, while he set his mind upon gaming and feasting, the same cruelty practiced he both in word and deed. Oftentimes as he sat at dinner or banqueted, were serious matters examined in his very sight by way of torture; and the soldier that had the skill and dexterity to behead folk, then and there used to cut off the heads of any prisoners indifferently without respect. At Puteoli, when he dedicated the bridge, which, as we noted before, was his own invention; after he had invited many unto him from the shore and strand, suddenly he turned them all headlong over the bridge into the water. And seeing some of them taking hold of the helmets for to save themselves, he shoved and thrust them off, with poles and oars into the sea. At a public feast in Rome, there chanced a servant to pluck off a thin plate of silver from the table; and for this, immediately he delivered him to the hangman for to be executed, namely, to have his hands cut off and hung about his neck just before his breast, with a written title carried before him declaring the cause of this his punishment; and so to be led round about all the companies as they sat at meat. One of these fencers called *Mirmillones*, coming out of the fence-school played at wooden wasters with him, and there took a fall for the nonce, and lay along at his feet; him he stabbed for his labor with a short iron; and withal, after the solemn manner of victors, ran up and down with his garland of palm branches. There was a beast brought to the altar ready to be killed for sacrifice; he comes girt in habit of these beast-slayers, and with the axe-head that he lifted up on high, knocked down the minister himself, who was addressed to cut the said beast's throat, and so dashed his brains out. At a plenteous feast where there was great cheer, he set up all at once an immeasurable laughter; and when the consuls who sat

just by him asked gently and with fair language, whereat he laughed so? "At what else," he said, "but this, that with one nod of my head, I can have both your throats cut immediately."

33. Among divers and sundry jests and merry conceits of his, as he stood once hard by the image of Jupiter, he demanded of Apelles, an actor of tragedies, whether of the twain he thought to be the greater and more stately, Jupiter or himself. And while he made some stay ere he answered, he tore and mangled him with whipping, praising ever and anon his voice crying unto him for mercy as passing sweet and pleasant, even when he groaned also under his lashes. So often as he kissed the neck of wife or concubine, he would say withal, "As fair and lovely neck as this is, off it shall go if I do but speak the word." Moreover, he gave it forth many a time, that he would himself fetch out of his wife Caesonia, though it were with torture strings, what was the reason that he loved her so entirely.

34. Neither raged he with less envy and spiteful malice, than pride and cruelty, against persons of all times and ages. The statues of brave and worthy men, brought by Augustus out of the Capitol courtyard for the straightness of the place, into Mars field, he overthrew and cast here and there in such sort as they could not be set up again with the titles and inscriptions whole; forbidding that ever after there should be anywhere statue or image erected unto any person living, without his advice asked and grant passed. He was of mind also to abolish Homer's verses, "For why may not I," he said, "do that which Plato lawfully did, who banished him out of the city that he framed and ordained?" The writings likewise and images of Virgil and Titus Livius, he went within a little of removing out of all libraries. The one [Virgil] of these he carped as a man of no wit and very mean learning; the other [Livy] for his verbosity and negligence in penning his history. Moreover, as touching lawyers (as if he meant to take away

all use of their skill and knowledge), he cast out these words many times, that he would surely bring it to pass, they should be able to give none other answer nor council than according to reason and equity.

35. He took from the noblest personages that were the old badges of their houses; from Torquatus the collar; from Cincinnatus the curled lock of hair; and from Gnaius Pompey, of an ancient stock descended, the surname of Magnus belonging to that lineage. As for king Ptolemaeus (of whom I made report before), when he had both sent for him out of his realm and also honorably entertained him he slew all of a sudden, for no other cause but that as he entered into the theater to see the shows and games there exhibited, he perceived him to have turned the eyes of all the people upon him, with the resplendent brightness of his purple cassock. All such as were fair and carried a thick bush of hair grown long, so often as they came in his way, he disfigured by shaving their heads all behind. There was one Esius Proculus (whose father had been a principal captain of the foremost cohort) for his exceeding tall personage and lovely favor withal named Colosseros. Him he caused suddenly to be pulled down from the scaffold where he sat, and to be brought into the plain within the lists, where he matched him in fight with a sword-fencer of that sort which be called *Threces* and afterwards with another, all armed. Now when he had given the foil twice and gotten the upper hand, he commanded him forthwith to be pinioned and bound fast, and being put into foul and overworn clothes to be led round about the streets to be showed unto women, and so to have his throat cut in the end. To conclude, there was none of so mean and base condition nor of so mean estate, whose commodities and good parts he depraved not. Against the great prelate styled King of Nemi, because he had many years already enjoyed his sacerdotal dignity, he suborned

an adversary mightier than himself. When as upon a certain day of public games there was greater applause and more clapping of hands than ordinary at Popius the fencer, manumitting his slave for joy of the fortunate combat which he had made, he flung out of the theater in such haste that treading upon his own gown skirt he came tumbling down the stairs with his head forward, chafing and fuming, yea and crying out that the people of Rome, lords of all nations, yielded more honor, and that out of a most vain and frivolous occasion, unto a sword-fencer, than to consecrated princes, or to himself there in personal presence.

36. No regard had he of chastity either in himself or in others. Marcus Lepidus, Mnester the pantomime, yea and certain hostages he kept and loved by way of reciprocal commerce in mutual impurity. Valerius Catullus, a young gentleman descended from a family of consul's degree, complained and openly cried out, that he was unnaturally by him abused, and that his very sides were wearied and tried out with his filthy company. Over and above the incests committed with his own sisters, and his love so notorious of Pirallis, that common strumpet and prostitute, there was not lightly a dame or wife of any worship and reputation that he forbore. And those for the most part would he invite together with their husbands to supper; and as they passed by at his feet, peruse and consider curiously; taking leisure thereto after the manner of those that buy wares in open market; yea and with his hand chuck them under the chin and make them to look up, if haply any of them for bashfulness held down their faces. And then so often as he listed, out he goes from the refection room, and when he had called her unto him apart that liked him best, he would within a little after (even while the tokens were yet fresh testifying their wanton work), return and openly before all the company either praise or dispraise her, reckoning up

every good or bad part of body and action in that brutish business. To some of them, himself sent bills of divorce in the name of their husbands absent, and commanded the same to be set upon the file and stand in public record.

37. In riotous and wasteful expense, he outwent the wits and inventions of all the prodigal spendthrifts that ever were; as having devised a new-found manner and use of baths, together with most strange and monstrous kinds of meats and meals; namely, to bathe with hot and cold ointments, to drink off most precious and costly pearls dissolved in vinegar; to set upon the board at feasts loaves of bread and other viands, all of gold, saying commonly withal, that a man must either be frugal or else Caesar. Moreover for certain days together, he flung and scattered among the common people from the gable of the basilica Julia, money in pieces of no mean value. He built moreover tall galleons of cedar timber, with sterns beset with precious stones, carrying sails of sundry colors, containing in them baths, large galleries, walking places, and dining chambers of great receipt, with vines also and trees bearing apples and other fruit in as much variety; wherein he would sit feasting in the very day-time among choirs of musicians and melodious singers, and so sail along the coasts of Campania. In building of stately palaces and manor houses in the country he cast aside all rules and orders as one desirous to do nothing so much as that which was thought impossible to be done. And therefore he laid foundations of piles where the sea was most raging and deep withal, and hewed rocks of most hard flint. Plains also he raised even with mountains and by digging down hilltops levelled them equal with the plains; all with incredible celerity, as punishing those who wrought but slowly even with death. In sum (and not to reckon up everything in particular), that infinite wealth and mass of treasure which Tiberius Caesar left behind him valued at 2700 million sesterces,

he consumed to nothing, before one whole year was gone about.

38. Being exhausted therefore and grown exceeding bare, he turned his mind to rapine by sundry and most nice points; of forged calumny, of sales, of imposts and taxes. He affirmed plainly, that those held not Roman citizenship whose ancestors had obtained the grant thereof in these terms, "to them and their posterity," unless they were sons; for, by *posteri* [posterity], quoth he, ought to be understood none beyond this degree of descent. And when the grants of Julius and Augustus (late emperors of sacred memory) were brought forth as evidences, he bewailed the same as past date and of no validity. He charged those also with false valuation of their estates, unto whom there had accrued afterward (upon what cause soever) any increase of substance. The last wills and testaments of such as had been principal centurions, as many I say, as from the beginning of Tiberius' empire, had left neither the said Tiberius, nor himself heir, he cancelled for their unthankfulness. Of all the rest likewise he held the wills as void, and of no effect in case any person would come forth and say, that they purposed and intended at their death to make Caesar their heir. Upon which fear that he put men in, being now both by unknown persons nominated heir among their familiar friends, and also by parents among their children, he termed them all mockers and cozeners, for that after such nuncupative wills they continued still alive; and to many of them he sent certain dainties empoisoned. Now such causes as these abovesaid he heard judicially debated; having beforehand set down a certain sum of money, for the raising whereof he sat judicially in court, and when that sum was fully made up, then and not before he would arise. And (as he was one who in nowise could abide any little delay) he condemned upon a time by virtue of one definitive sentence above forty persons, liable to judgement for divers and sundry crimes; making his boast

withal unto his wife Caesonia newly wakened out of her sleep, what a deal he had done, while she took her noon's repose. Having published an open auction of the residue remaining of furniture provided to set out all shows and games, he caused the said parcels to be brought forth and sold; setting the prices thereof himself and enhancing the same to such a prick, that some men enforced to buy certain things at an extreme and exceeding rate (whereby they were impoverished and stripped of all their goods) cut their own veins and so bled to death. Well known it is that while Aponius Saturninus took a nap and slept among the seats and stalls where these sales were held, Gaius put the beadle in mind not to let slip and overpass such an honorable person of praetor's degree as he was, considering, quoth he, that with the head he had so often nodded and made signs unto him as it were, to buy this and that, and thus taking that occasion, he never rested raising the price while he sat and nodded still, until there were fastened upon the man (ignorant, God wot, altogether of any such matter) thirteen sword-fencers, at nine million sesterces.

39. In Gaul likewise, when he had sold the jewels, ornaments, and household stuff of his sisters by him condemned; their servants also at excessive high prices; finding sweetness in the gain growing thereupon and thereby drawn on to proceed in that course, whatever furniture belonged to the old imperial court he sent for it all from Rome, for the carriage whereof, he took up even the passengers' wagons that usually were hired, yea the very jades which served mills and bakeries; insomuch as many times there wanted bread in Rome; and a number of termers, such as had matters depending in law, for that they could not make their appearance in court at their days appointed, by absence lost their suits. For the selling of which furniture there was no fraud, no guile, no deceitful allurement to be devised that he used not; one while checking

each one for their avarice, and rating them because they were not ashamed to be richer than he; otherwhiles making semblance of repentance, in that he permitted persons to have the buying of such things as belonged to the empire. Intelligence was given unto him that a certain wealthy man in that province had paid 200,000 sesterces unto his officers (who had the bidding of guests unto his own table) that by some subtle shift, himself might be foisted in among other guests; neither was he discontented that the honor of supping with him was prized so high. The morrow after therefore, as this provincial man was sitting at a public auction, he sent one of purpose to tender unto him some frivolous trifle (I wot not what) at the price of 200,000 sesterces, and withal to say unto him, that take a supper he should with Caesar, as a guest invited by his own self.

40. He levied and gathered new tributes and imposts, such as never were heard of before; at the first by the hands of publicans; and afterward (by reason of the excessive gains that came in) by the centurions and tribunes of the praetorian cohorts. For he omitted no kind of thing, no manner of person, but he imposed some tribute upon them. For all cates that were to be sold throughout the city, there was exacted a certain taxation and set payment. For actions, for suits, for judgements wheresoever commenced or drawn in writing, the fortieth part of the whole sum in suit went to his share in the name of a tribute; not without a penalty in case any one were convicted of compromising or abandoning a suit. The eighth part of the poor porters' and carriers' day's wages; out of the gets also and takings of common strumpets, as much as they earned by once lying with a man, was paid as tax. Moreover to the law, this branch was annexed, that there should be liable to this tribute, not only the parties themselves that by trade of harlotry got their living, but even they likewise who kept houses of bawdry, as also that wedded persons should pay for their use of marriage.

41. After these and such like taxes were denounced by proclamation, but not yet published abroad in writing, when as
through ignorance of the written law many trespasses and
transgressions were committed; at length, upon instant demand of the people, he proposed indeed the act, but written
in very small letter and within as narrow a place, so that no
man might exemplify the same or copy it out. And to the end
that there might be no kind of pillage which he attempted not,
he set up a brothelhouse in the very palace, with many rooms
and chambers therein distinguished asunder, and furnished according to the dignity and worth of that place. In it there stood
to prostitute themselves, married wives, youths and springals
freeborn. Then sent he all about to fora and basilicas, pages to
invite thither young men and old for to satisfy their lust. All
comers at their entrance paid money (as it were) for usury and
interest. Certain persons also were appointed to take note in
open sight, of their names, as of such as were good friends
increasing the revenues of Caesar. And not disdaining so much
as the lucre and advantage arising out of hazard and dice-
play, he gained the more by cogging yea and forswearing of
gamesters. And upon a time, having put over to his next
fellow gamester his own turn, out he goes into the foregate of
the house; where, having espied two wealthy knights of Rome
passing by, he commanded them to be apprehended incontinently, and condemned in the confiscation of their goods.
Which done, he returned in again, leaping for joy and making
his vaunt, that he never had a luckier hand at dice.

42. But when he had once a daughter born, complaining then
of his poverty and the heavy charges that lay upon him not
only as emperor, but also as a father, he took the voluntary
contributions of men toward the finding of the girl her food,
as also for her dowry another day. He declared also by an
edict, that he would receive New Year's gifts; and so he stood

the first day of January in the porch of his house Palatine, ready to take what pieces soever of money came, which the multitude of all sorts and degrees, with full hands and bosoms poured out before him. Finally, so far was he incensed with the desire of handling money, that oftentimes he would both walk barefooted up and down, yea and wallow also a good while with his whole body upon huge heaps of coined gold pieces, spread here and there in a most large and open place.

43. In military matters and warlike affairs he never dealt but once, and that was not upon any intended purpose; but what time he had made a progress to Mevana to see the sacred grove and river of Clitumnus, being put in mind to make up the number of the Batavians whom he had about him for his guard, it took him in the head to make an expedition into Germany. Neither deferred he this design, but having levied from all parts a power consisting of legions and auxiliary forces, and taken musters most rigorously in every quarter, as also raised and gathered together victuals and provision of all sorts in that quantity as never any other before him the like, he put himself on his journey. Wherein he marched, one while in such hurry and haste, as that the praetorian cohorts were forced (against the manner and custom) to bestow their ensigns upon the sumpter-beasts' backs and so to follow after; other-whiles, after such a slow and delicate manner, as that he would be carried in a litter upon eight men's shoulders, and exact of the common people inhabiting the neighbor cities that the highways might be swept and watered for the dust, against his coming.

44. After that he was arrived once at the camp, to the end that he might show himself a sharp and severe captain, those lieutenants who had brought aid with the latest, out of divers and dissituate parts, he discharged with ignominy and shame. But in the review of his army the most part of the centurions who had already served out their complete time, yea and some

whose term within very few days would have fully expired, he deprived of their places, finding fault forsooth with the old age and feebleness of every one. As for the rest, after he had given them a rebuke for their avarice, he abridged the fees and avails due for their service performed; and brought that same down to the value of 6000 sesterces. And having achieved no greater exploit, than receiving the surrender of Adminius the son of Cinobellinus king of the Britains, who being by his father banished, was fled over sea with a small train about him, he sent magnificent and glorious letters to Rome, as if the whole isle had been yielded into his hands; warning and willing the carriers ever and anon, to ride forward in their wagon directly into the market-place and the Curia, and in no wise to deliver the said missives but in the temple of Mars unto the consuls, and that in a frequent assembly of the senate.

45. Soon after, when there failed matter of war, he commanded a few Germans of the corps de guard, to be transported and hidden on the other side of the Rhine, and that news should be reported unto him after dinner in most tumultuous manner, that the enemy was come. Which done, he made what haste he could, and together with some of his friends and part of the praetorian horsemen he entered the next wood; where after he had cut off the branches of trees and adorned their bodies in manner of trophies, he returned into the camp by torch-light. As for those verily who followed him not in this service, he reproved and checked them for their timorousness and cowardice; but his companions and partners in this doughty victory, he rewarded with a new kind (and new name) of coronets, which being garnished with the express form of sun, moon, and stars he called *exploratorias*. Again, when as certain hostages were had away by his means perforce out of the grammar school, and privily sent before, he suddenly left his supper, and with his men of arms pursued them as run-

aways, and being overtaken and caught again he brought them
back as prisoners bound in chains, showing himself even in this
interlude also, beyond all measure insolent and intemperate.
Now after he was come back to supper, those who brought
him word that the battles were come forward, he exhorted to
sit down to meat armed as they were in their corselets; yea
and advertised them out that most familiar line of Virgil:

Durarent, secundisque rebus se servarent.

Still to endure in all assays
And keep themselves for better days.

Moreover, amid these affairs, he rebuked most sharply the
senate and people both, in their absence; for that while Caesar
fought battles and was exposed to so many perils, they could
so unseasonably celebrate feasts, haunt also the Circus, the
theaters, and their retiring places of solace and pleasure.

46. Last of all, as if he meant now to make a final dispatch
forever of the war, having embattled his army upon the ocean
shore, planted his ballasts and other engines of artillery in their
several places (and no man wist the while or could imagine
what he went about), all at once he commanded them to
gather fish-shells, and therewith to fill their headpieces and
laps, terming them the spoils of the ocean, due to the Capitol
and the Palatium. In token also and memorial of this brave
victory, he raised an exceeding high turret, out of which as
from a watchtower, there might shine all night long lights and
fires for the better direction of ships at sea in their course. And
after he had pronounced publicly a donative to his soldiers, even
a hundred deniers apiece; as if thereby he had surmounted all
former precedents of liberality, "Now go your ways," quoth
he, "with joy. Go your ways I say, enriched and wealthy."

47. Turning his mind after this to the care of his triumph,
he selected and set apart for the pomp (over and above the

captives and barbarians) the tallest men of stature also that were to be found in Gaul; and every one that (as he said himself) was worthy to be seen in a triumph, yea and some of the nobles and principal persons of that nation, whom he compelled not only to color the hair of their heads yellow like burnished gold, and to wear the same long, but also to learn the German language, and to bear barbarous names. He gave commandment also, that the galleys with three ranks of oars, wherein he had embarked and entered the ocean, should be conveyed to Rome, a great part of the way by land. He wrote likewise unto his procurators and officers, to provide the furniture of his triumph, with as little cost as might be; but yet the same in as ample manner as never was before the like, seeing they had both might and right to seize all men's goods into their hands.

48. Before his departure out of that province, he intended the execution of a horrible and abominable design; even to put to sword those legions which long ago upon the decease of Augustus had made a commotion because, forsooth, they had beset both his father Germanicus their captain, and himself also, then an infant. And being hardly and with much ado reclaimed from such a rash and inconsiderate project, yet could he by no means be stayed; but stiffly persisted in a full mind and will to tithe them [to kill every tenth man of them]. When he had summoned them therefore to a public assembly, unarmed, and without their swords, he environed them with his cavalry all armed. But seeing once that many of them, suspecting whereabout he went, slipped away in sundry places for to resume their weapons if any violence were offered, himself abandoned the assembly and fled, taking his way directly and immediately to Rome, diverting all his bitterness and cruelty upon the senate; whom, to avert from himself the odious rumors of so great and shameful villainies, he openly threatened; complaining among other matters that he

was by them defrauded of his just and due triumph; whereas, himself but a little before, had intimated and denounced upon pain of death that they should not make nor meddle in any matter about his honors.

49. Being encountered therefore and met upon the way by ambassadors from that most honorable order of senators, entreating him to make speed; with a most loud voice, "Come I will," quoth he, "I will come, I say, and this with me here," beating oft upon the sword's hilt, which he wore by his side. He made it known also by an edict, that he returned indeed, but it was to them alone who wished it, namely, the knights and the common people. For himself would be no longer a citizen or prince to the senate. He commanded moreover, that not one of the senators should meet him. And thus, either omitting quite or putting off his triumph, he entered the city riding in ovation, upon his very birthday; and within four months after came to his end, having attempted and done notable outrages and very great villainies, but plotting still and practicing much greater. For he had purposed to remove his imperial court to Antium, and afterwards to Alexandria; but having massacred first the most choice and chief persons of both degrees. And that no man may seem to doubt hereof, there were in his secret cabinet found two books bearing divers titles. The one had for the inscription *Gladius* [the sword]; the other *Pugio* [the dagger]. They contained both of them the marks and names of such as were appointed to death. There was found besides, a big chest full of divers and sundry poisons, which soon after, being by Claudius drowned in the seas, infected and poisoned the same, not without the deadly bane of fishes killed therewith, which the tide cast up to the next shores.

50. Of stature he was very tall, pale and wan-colored; of body gross and without all good making; his neck and shanks exceeding slender; his eyes sunk in his head, and his temples

hollow, his forehead broad, and the same furrowed and frowning; the hair of his head growing thin, and none at all about his crown; in all parts else hairy he was and shagged. It was therefore taken for an heinous and capital offense, either to look upon him as he passed by from a higher place, or once but to name a goat upon any occasion whatsoever. His face and visage being naturally stern and grim, he made of purpose more crabbed and hideous; composing and dressing it at a looking-glass, all manner of ways to seem more terrible and to strike greater fear. He was neither healthful in body nor stood sound in mind; being a child, much troubled with the falling sickness. In his youth, patient of labor and travail; yet so, as that ever and anon upon a sudden fainting that came upon him, he was scarce able to go, to stand, to arise, to recover himself and to bear up his head. The infirmity of his mind, both himself perceived, and oftentimes also was minded to go aside unto Anticyra, an isle where grew the best hellebore, a purgative meet for lunatic persons, there to purge his brain thoroughly. It is for certain thought that he was poisoned with a potion given unto him by his wife Caesonia; which indeed was a love medicine, but such a one as cracked his wits. He was troubled most of all with want of sleep; for he slept not above three hours in a night; and in those verily he took no quiet repose, but fearful; and scared with strange illusions and fantastic imaginations; as who, among the rest, dreamed upon a time that he saw the very form and resemblance of the sea talking with him. And hereupon for a great part of the night, what with tedious wakefulness and weariness of lying, one while sitting up in his bed, another while roaming and wandering to and fro in his galleries (which were of an exceeding length) he was wont to call upon and look still for the daylight.

51. I should not do amiss, if unto this mind's sickness of his I attributed the vices which in one and the same subject were

of a most different nature; to wit, excessive confidence, and contrariwise, overmuch fearfulness. For, he that set so light by the gods and despised them as he did, yet at the least thunder and lightning used to wink close with both eyes, to enwrap also and cover his whole head; but if the same were greater and somewhat extraordinary, to start out of his bed, to creep and hide himself under the bedstead. During his travel through Sicily, after he had made but a scorn and mockery at the miracles and strange sights in many parts there, he fled suddenly by night from Messana, as affrighted with the smoke and rumbling noise of the top of Aetna. And he that against the barbarians was so full of threats and menaces, when as beyond the river Rhine he rode in a chariot between a defile, and the army marched in thick squadrons together; by occasion only that one said, there would be no small trouble and hurliburly, in case the enemy from any place appeared in sight; forthwith he mounted on horseback and turned hastily to the bridges. But finding them full of camp-slaves and carriages wherewith they were choked, as one impatient of any delay, he was from hand to hand and over men's heads conveyed to the other side of the water. Soon after likewise, hearing of the revolt and rebellion of Germany, he provided to fly; and for the better means of flight, prepared and rigged ships; resting and staying himself upon this only comfort, that he should yet have provinces beyond sea remaining for him, in case the conquerors following the train of their victory, either seized the hilltops of the Alps (as sometimes the Cimbrians), or possessed themselves of the very city of Rome, as the Senones in times past did. Hereupon I verily believe that the murderers of him afterwards devised this shift, namely to hold up his soldiers with a loud lie when they were in an uproar, and to bear them in hand that he laid violent hands on himself, affrighted at the fearful news of the field lost.

His face and visage being naturally stern and grim, he made of purpose more crabbed and hideous; composing and dressing it at a looking-glass, all manner of ways to seem more terrible and to strike greater fear.

52. As for his apparel, his shoes and other habit, he wore them neither after his own country-guise, nor in a civil fashion, no nor so much as in manlike manner, not yet always, I may tell you, sorting with the state and condition of a mortal wight. Being clad oftentimes in cloaks of needlework and embroidered with divers colors, and the same set out with precious stones; in a coat also with long sleeves; and wearing bracelets withal, he would come abroad into the city. Sometime you should see him in his silks, and veiled all over in a loose woman's mantle of fine sendal [lawn] with a train; one while going in Greek slippers, or else in buskins; otherwhiles in a simple pair of brogues or high shoes, such as common soldiers used. Now and then also he was seen shod with women's pumps. But for the most part he showed himself abroad with a golden beard, carrying in his hand either a thunderbolt or a three-tined mace, or else a rod called *caduceus* (the ensigns all and ornaments of the gods) yea and in the attire and array of Venus. Now for his triumphal robes and ensigns he used verily to wear and bear them continually, even before any warlike expedition; and sometime the cuirass withal of king Alexander the Great, fetched out of his sepulcher.

53. Of all the liberal sciences, he gave his mind least to deep literature and sound learning, but most to eloquence; albeit he was by nature fair spoken and of a ready tongue. Certes if it had been to plead and declaim against one, were he angered once, he had both words and sentences at will. His action, gesture and voice also served him well; insomuch as for very heat and earnestness of speech, scarce was he able to stand his ground and keep still in one place, yet might he be heard of them that stood afar off. When he was about to make an oration, his manner was to threaten in these terms, namely, that he would draw forth at his adversary the keen weapon and dart of his night-study; condemning the milder and more

piked kind of writing so far forth, as that he said of Seneca, a writer in those days most accepted, that his compositions were plain exercises to be shown only, and was no better himself than sand without lime. His wont was also, to answer by writing the orations of those orators who had pleaded well; to devise as well accusations and defences of great persons and weighty matters in the senate; and according as his style framed, either to over-charge and depress, or to ease and relieve every man with his sentence; having called thither the knights to hear him speak.

54. The arts moreover and masteries of other kinds he practiced right studiously, even those of most different nature. A professed sword-fencer he was and a good charioteer; a singer withal and a dancer. Fight he would even in earnest with weapons at sharp; and run a race with chariots in the open Circus, which he built in many places. As for chanting and dancing, he was so hotly set thereupon, that he could not forbear so much as in the public theaters but that he would both fall a-singing with the tragedian as he pronounced, and also imitate the gesture of the player, as it were by way of praise or correction. And verily, for no other cause proclaimed he (as it is thought) a vigil all night long, that very day on which he was murdered, but that by taking the opportunity of the night's licentiousness, he might therewith begin to enter upon the stage. And divers times danced he by night; but once above the rest, having raised out of their beds three honorable persons that had been consuls, and sent for them at the second watch into the palace. While they were much afraid and doubted some extremity he caused them to be placed aloft upon a scaffold, and then suddenly with a great noise of hautboys and cymbals, out comes he leaping forth with a pall and cassock reaching down to his ankles; and after he had danced out the measures to a song, vanished and went

his way again. Now this man so apt a scholar as he was to learn all other feats, had no skill at all in swimming.

55. To whom he took a love and liking, he favored them all exceedingly and beyond all reason. Mnester the famous pantomime he affected so much, as that he bashed not to kiss him even in the open theater; and if any while he [Mnester] was dancing or acting a part, made never so little noise and interrupted him, he commanded the party to be pulled out of his place, and with his own hand scourged him. A knight of Rome chanced to keep some stir while the said Mnester was upon the stage; unto him he sent word peremptorily by a centurion to depart without delay, and go down to Ostia, there to take sea, and so to carry unto King Ptolemaeus as far as into Mauritania his letters in writing tablets, the tenor whereof was this, "To this bearer, whom I have sent hither to you, see you do neither good nor harm." Certain fencers called *Thraces* he made captains over those Germans that were of his and squires to his body. As for the *Mirmillones*, he deprived them of their armor. One of them named Columbus, fortuned to foil his concurrent, howbeit he had gotten before some small hurt; he made no more ado but put poison into the wound, which thereupon he called Columbinum. So much addicted and devoted was he to the green faction of charioteers, that day by day he would take his suppers and make his abode in their hostelry. Upon Eutychus, a chariot-driver, he bestowed in gifts at a certain banquet, two millions of sesterces. To one of their chariot-steeds named *Incitatus*, for whose sake (because he should not be disquieted), he was wont the day before the games Circenses, by his soldiers to command the neighbors there adjoining to keep silence, besides a stable all built of marble stone for him, and a manger made of ivory; over and above his caparison also and harness of purple, together with a brooch or pendant jewel of precious stones at

his chest; he allowed a house and family of servants, yea and household-stuff to furnish the same; all to this end, that guests invited in his name might be more finely and gaily entertained. It is reported moreover that he meant to prefer him unto a consulship.

56. As he rioted thus and fared outrageously, many there were who wanted no heart and good will to assault his person. But after one or two conspiracies detected, when others for default of opportunity held off and made stay, two at length complotted and imparted one unto the other their design, yea and performed it; not without the privity of the mightiest freedmen about him, and the captains of his guard. The reason was, for that they also, being nominated (although untruly) as accessory to a certain conspiracy, perceived themselves suspected and odious unto him therefore. For, even immediately, by sequestering them apart into a secret place he brought upon them great hatred, protesting with his sword drawn, that die he would upon his own hand, if they also thought him worthy of death. Neither ceased he from that time forward to accuse one unto the other, and to set them all together by the ears. Now when these conspirators were resolved and agreed to assail him during the Palatine games, as he departed thence out of the theater at noon-tide, Cassius Chaerea, tribune of the praetorian cohort, took upon him to play the first part in this action; even he, whom being now far stepped in years Gaius Caligula was wont to frump and flout in most opprobrious terms as a wanton and effeminate person; and one while, when he came unto him for a watch-word, to give him Priapus or Venus; another while, if upon any occasion he rendered thanks, to reach out unto him his hand, not only fashioned but wagging also after an obscene and filthy manner.

57. Many prodigious signs were seen presaging his future death and murder. The image of Jupiter at Olympia, which

his pleasure was to be disjointed and translated to Rome, did set up all on a sudden such a mighty laughter that the workmen about it let their engines and vices slip and so ran all away. And straightways came there one in place whose name also was Cassius, that avouched, he had warning and commandment in a dream to sacrifice a bull unto Jupiter. The Capitol in Capua upon the Ides of March was smitten with lightning. Likewise at Rome the porter's lodge belonging to the prince's palace. And there wanted not some who gave their conjecture, that by the one prodigy was portended danger to the master of the house from his guard; by the other some notable murder such as in times past had been committed upon the same day. Also, Sulla the astrologer, when Gaius asked his opinion, as touching the horoscope of his nativity, told him plain, that most certain and inevitable death approached near at hand. Likewise, the oracle at Antium gave him a caveat, to beware of Cassius. For which very cause, he had given express commandment that Cassius Longinus, proconsul then in Asia, should be killed; not remembering that the foresaid Chaerea had to name Cassius. The day before he lost his life, he dreamt that he stood in heaven close unto the throne of Jupiter, and that Jupiter spurned him with the great toe of his right foot, and therewith threw him down headlong to the earth. There went also for current prodigies of his fall, even those occurrences that happened unto him that very day, a little before he was murdered. As himself sacrificed, besprewn he was with the blood of the flamingo. And Mnester the skillful actor above named, represented that very tragedy which Neptolemus the tragedian acted at the solemnity of those games wherein Philip king of the Macedonians was killed. And when in the interlude entitled *Laureolus*, wherein the chief player making haste to get away out of the ruin, vomited blood, many more of the actors in a second degree strove a-vie to give some trial and experiment of the like cunning, the whole stage by that means flowed with blood. Prepared there was likewise against night another show, wherein the dark fables reported of Hell and the Infernal Spirits there were to be exhibited and unfolded by Egyptians and Ethiopians.

58. Upon the ninth day before the Kalends of February, about one of the clock after noon, doubting with himself, whether he should rise to dinner or no (for that his stomach was yet raw and weak upon a surfeit of meat taken the day before), at last by the persuasion of his friends he went forth. Now, when as in the very cloister through which he was to pass certain boys of noble birth sent for out of Asia (to sing hymns, and to skirmish martially upon the stage) were preparing themselves, he stood still and stayed there to view and encourage them. And but that the leader and chieftain of that crew said, he was very cold, he would have returned and presently exhibited that show. But what befell after this, is reported two manner of ways. Some say that as he spoke unto the said boys, Chaerea came behind his back, and with a drawing blow grievously wounded his neck with the edge of his sword, giving him these words before, *Hoc age* [Mind this]. Whereupon, Cornelius Sabinus, another of the conspirators, encountered him a front, and ran him through in the breast. Others write, that Sabinus, after the multitude about him was voided by the centurions (who were privy to the conspiracy), called for a watchword, as the manner is of soldiers, and when Gaius gave him the word, "Jupiter," Chaerea cried out aloud, *Accipe ratum* [Here take it sure], and with that, as he looked behind him, with one slash cut his jaw quite through; also as he lay on the ground and drawing up his limbs together cried still, that he was yet alive, the rest of their accomplices with thirty wounds dispatched and made an end of him. For this mot, *Repete* [Strike again], was the signal of them all. Some

of them also thrust their swords through his privy members. At the very first noise and outcry, his litter bearers came running to help, with their litter-staves; soon after, the Germans that were the squires of his body came in; and as they slew some of the murderers, so they killed certain senators also that were innocent.

59. He lived twenty-nine years, and ruled the empire three years, ten months, and eight days. His dead corpse was conveyed secretly into the Lamian gardens, where being half-burnt only in a hasty funeral fire, covered it was with a few turfs of earth lightly cast over it; but afterwards, by his sisters now returned out of exile, taken up, burnt to ashes and interred. It is for certain known and reputed, that before this compliment was performed, the keepers of those gardens were troubled with the walking of spirits and ghosts; and in that very house wherein he was murdered there passed not a night without some terror or fearful object, until the very house itself was consumed with fire. There died together with him both his wife Caesonia, stabbed with a sword by a centurion, and also a daughter of his, whose brains were dashed out against a wall.

60. What the condition and state was of those days, any man may gather, even by these particulars. For neither, when this massacre was divulged and made known abroad, men gave credit by and by thereto; but there went a suspicion, that Gaius himself had feigned and given out a rumor of this murder, by that means to sound men's minds, and find how they stood affected unto him. Nor yet had those conspirators destined the empire to anyone. And the senators in recovering their ancient freedom again accorded so, as that the consuls assembled them not at the first into the Curia, because it bare the name Julia, but into the Capitol. Yea and some of them, when their turns came to speak, opined, that the memory of the

Caesars should be utterly abolished and razed out, giving advice to pull down their temples. Moreover, this hath been observed and noted especially, that the Caesars who had to their forename Gaius, beginning at him first who was slain in those troublesome days of Cinna, died all of them a violent death.

THE HISTORY OF
TIBERIUS CLAUDIUS DRUSUS
CAESAR

CLAUDIUS

DRUSUS, FATHER TO THIS CLAUDIUS CAESAR, was in times past forenamed Decimus and afterwards Nero. Dame Livia wedded unto Augustus even when she was great with child brought him into the world within three months after the said marriage, and folk suspected that begotten he was in adultery by his step-father himself. Certes presently after his birth this verse went rife in every man's mouth:

> On persons great this fortune doth attend,
> That children they may have at three months' end.

This Drusus in the honorable place of quaestor and praetor, being general of the Rhaetian and then of the German war, was the first Roman captain that sailed in the North Ocean; and on the farther side of Rhine he cast those trenches of a strange and infinite work which yet at this day be called Drusinae. Many a time he put the enemy to sword, and when he had driven him as far as the inmost deserts, gave not over chasing and pursuing until there appeared unto him the likeness of a barbarian woman, more portly than a mortal wight, which in the Latin tongue forbade him to follow the train of victory any farther. For which acts achieved, he enjoyed the honor of a petty triumph [called ovation], and had the triumphal ornaments granted unto him. After his praetorship, he entered immediately upon the consulate; and having enterprised a second expedition thither, fell sick and died in his summer camp, which thereupon took the name of *Castra*

265

Scelerata [the wicked camp]. His corpse by the principal citizens and burgesses of the free boroughs and colonies, by the decuries also and orders of the scribes (who met them in the way and received it at their hands) was conveyed to Rome and buried in Mars field. Howbeit the army reared in honor of him an honorary tomb about the which every year afterwards upon a certain set day the soldiers should run at tilt, keep jousting and tournament; the cities likewise and states of Gaul, sacrifice and make public supplications to the gods. Moreover the senate among many other honors, decreed for him a triumphant arch of marble, with trophies thereto in the street Appia; as also the surname of Germanicus to him and his posterity forever. Furthermore he is thought to have carried a mind no less glorious than civil and popular. For over and above the conquests gained of his enemies, he won also from the royal spoils; and oftentimes to the uttermost hazard of his life coursed and chased the general of the Germans all over the field. Neither dissembled he, but gave it out that, one day he would restore unto the commonwealth their ancient state and liberty again. Whereupon, I suppose, some presume to write, that Augustus had him jealousy and suspicion, called him home out of his province, and because he lingered and delayed his return, made him away by poison. Which verily put down I have, because I would not seem to pretermit such a matter, rather, than for that I think it either true or probable; considering that Augustus both loved him while he was alive so entirely, as that he always ordained him fellow heir with his sons (like as he openly professed upon a time in the senate house), and also commended him after his death so highly, that in a solemn oration before the body of the people he prayed unto the gods, to vouchsafe his own Caesars to be like unto him, and to grant himself one day such an end as they had given him. And not contented with this that he had engraven upon his tomb an epitaph in verse which he himself composed, he wrote also the history of his life in prose. By Antonia the younger, he became father verily of many children, but three only he left behind him at his death, namely, Germanicus, Livilla, and Claudius.

2. This Claudius was born at Lyons, in the year when Julius Antonius and Fabius Africanus were consuls, upon the Kalends of August, that very day on which the altar was first dedicated there unto Augustus. And named he was Tiberius Claudius Drusus; and a while after, when his elder brother was adopted into the family Julia, he assumed into his style the surname of Germanicus. Being left an infant by his father, all the time in manner of his childhood and youth, piteously handled he was with sundry diseases, and those tough and such as stuck long by him; insomuch as being dulled and enfeebled thereby both in mind and body, he was not thought in the very progress of riper age, sufficient and capable of any public office or private charge. Yea and many a day after that he came to full years, he was at the dispose of another, even under a pedagogue and governor; whom in a certain book himself complains of, terming him a barbarous fellow, and no better sometime than a mulier, set over him of purpose to chastise and punish him most cruelly for every light cause and occasion whatsoever. By reason of his sickness, both at the sword-play which he and his brother jointly exhibited in memorial of their father, he sat as president (not after the accustomed manner) lapped in a cloak; and also upon his commencement day, when he was to put on his virile gown, about midnight without any honorable attendance and solemn train, brought he was in a litter into the Capitol.

3. Howbeit, from his very childhood, he employed no mean study in the liberal sciences. And oftentimes gave good proof even in public place of his proceedings in them all; yet could

he never for all that reach to any degree of dignity, or yield better hope of himself for the time to come. His mother Antonia was wont to call him *portentum hominis* [the monster and fantastical show of a man], as if he had not been finished but only begun by nature; and if she reproved anyone for his foolishness she would say, he was more sottish than her son Claudius. His grandmother Augusta thought always most basely of him, as who used neither to speak unto him but very seldom, nor to admonish him, unless it were in some sharp and short writing, or else by messengers going between. His sister Livilla, when she heard that he should be one day emperor, openly and with a loud voice detested and wished far from the people of Rome so hard and miserable a fortune.

4. And no marvel, for to the end that it might be more certainly known what opinion his great uncle Augustus had of him both ways [as well good as bad], I have set down certain articles and principal points gathered out of his own epistles. "I have," quoth he, "my good Livia, talked and conferred with Tiberius as you charged me, about this, namely, what is to be done to your grandson Tiberius, at the solemnity of the Martial game [in honor of Mars Revenger]. Now, we are both agreed that it must be determined and set down once for all what course we should take and follow with him. For if he be whole and complete, what doubt need we make but that he is to be trained and advanced by the same opportunities and grades by which his brother was. But if we perceive him stricken and defective in body and mind we must minister matter to men, who are wont to scoff and sniff, to deride both him and us. For we shall ever find trouble and vexation enough if at every occasion presented to us we should deliberate whether we think him able to manage honorable offices in the state or no. Howbeit for the present (concerning such things whereof you ask my advice) I mislike it not that he have the

charge of the priests' dining chamber during the solemnities aforesaid if he will suffer himself to be admonished and schooled by Silvanus' son his kinsman, that he do nothing which may be noted or derided. That he should behold the Circus games from the imperial box in no wise can I allow. For being exposed so in the very forefront of the theater he will be eyed and observed. Neither like we that he should go up the Alban mount or abide at Rome during the Latin holidays. For if he be able to accompany his brother to that mountain, why is he not as well made praefect of the city? Thus, my Livia, you have our opinions delivered, as who are fully resolved that once for all somewhat must be put down as touching the whole matter, lest we be evermore hovering between hope and fear. You may also if it please you impart to Antonia thus much of this our letter." Again, in another epistle: "As for young Tiberius [Claudius], I for my part while you are absent, will daily invite him to supper, that he may not sup alone with his Sulpitius and Athenodorus. And I could wish with all my heart that he would more soundly and less flightily make choice of some special one, whose gesture, habit and gait he might, silly soul as he is, imitate.

> He comes far short, when he is matched, with men of deep understanding.

But look, when his mind is not wandering the generosity of his heart appears sufficiently." Likewise in a third letter: "Your grandson Tiberius, my sweet Livia, if I do not wonder, that when he declaimed that he could please and content me, I pray God I be dead. For how he that in his daily talk speaks so unclearly should be able, when he declaims, to deliver his mind and what he hath to say clearly, I cannot see." Neither is there any doubt to be made but that after all this, Augustus ordained and left him indued with no honorable office, save only the sacerdotal dignity of augurs; nay he nominated him not so much as his heir, but in a third degree and descent, even among those that were well near strangers; and that in a sixth part only of his substance, and by way of legacy bequeathed unto him not above 800,000 sesterces.

5. Tiberius his uncle conferred upon him when he sued for honorable dignities the ornaments of consuls. But when he instantly demanded still, not imaginary but true magistracies indeed, he wrote back unto him in his writing tablets thus much only, that he had sent unto him forty pieces of gold to spend at the feast *Saturnalia,* and to bestow in puppets and trifling gauds, at the same time. Then, and not before, casting aside all hope of preferment and real dignities, he betook himself to rest and quietness of life, lying close, one while within gardens of pleasure and in a manor house without the city; and lurking otherwhiles in a withdrawing place out of the way in Campania. And by his daily acquaintance and company keeping with most base and abject persons besides the old infamous note of sluggardy and foolishness he incurred an ill name for drunkenness and dice-play. Notwithstanding, that all the while he thus led his life, he never wanted the public attendance and reverent regard of men seeking unto him.

6. The order of knights elected him twice for their patron, in an embassage that was to be sent and delivered in their own behalf; once when the consuls required to have the carriage of Augustus' corpse upon their own shoulders to Rome; a second time when they were to congratulate the same consuls for the suppressing of Sejanus. Moreover, they were wont in shows and in the theater, when he came in place, to arise up and lay off their mantles as we used to do of our hats in respective honor of him. The senate also ordained, that to the ordinary number of the priests called *Augustales,* who were by lot chosen, he should be admitted extraordinarily; and soon

after, that his house, which by the misfortune of a fire he had lost, should at the city's charge be re-edified; as also the privilege to deliver his mind and opinion in the senate among those who had been consuls. Which decree of theirs was reversed and annulled, when Tiberius [the emperor] alleged by way of excuse his imbecility, and promised to repair the foresaid loss out of his own private purse and liberality. Yet when he lay upon his death-bed, he both named him among his heirs in a third range and in a third part of his estate, and also bequeathed him a legacy of two million sesterces; yea recommended him besides by name unto the armies, to the senate likewise and the people of Rome in the rank of his especial friends and kinsfolk.

7. At length under Gaius [Caligula], his brother's son, who at his first coming to the empire sought by all manner of enticing allurements to gain the good opinion of a bountiful and gracious prince, he began first to bear office of state, and continued consul together with him for the space of two months. And it fortuned at his first entrance into the Forum with his fasces, that an eagle soaring thereby settled upon his right shoulder. He was pricked also and allotted unto a second consulship, against the fourth year following. Divers times he sat as president of the solemn shows in Gaius' turn; what time the people cried *Feliciter* [All hail or happiness], partly to the emperor's uncle, and in part to Germanicus' brother.

8. Yet lived he nevertheless subject to the contumelious reproaches of the world. For if at any time, he came somewhat with the latest and after the hour appointed to a supper, hardly and with much ado was there any room made for to receive him, and not before he had gone round about the tables where guest were set, for to find a place. Likewise, whensoever he fell asleep after meat (which was an ordinary thing with him), the buffoons and jesters about him made good sport, pelting him with olive and date stones; otherwhiles also

they would by way of merriment awaken him with the clap of a ferula [or lash] of some whip. They were wont likewise to glove his hand (as he lay snoring asleep) with his shoes, that as he suddenly awaked he might rub his face and eyes therewith.

9. Neither verily could he avoid divers dangerous troubles; first in his very consulship, for, being behindhand and over slack in taking order with the workmen for the making and erecting of Nero's and Drusus' statues, who were Caesar's [Gaius Caligula] brethren, he had like to have been removed out of that honorable office. Afterwards, as either any stranger or one of his own house informed ought against him, he was continually and sundry manner of ways molested. But when the conspiracy of Lepidus and Getulicus came to light, being sent among other ambassadors to congratulate Gaius in the name of the city, he was in jeopardy of his very life; while Gaius chafed and fumed with great indignation, that his uncle chiefly of all others was sent unto him, as it were to govern a child; insomuch, as some have not stuck to report in writing, that he was turned also headlong into the river in his clothes and all as he came appareled. From which time forward, never spoke he to any matter proposed in the senate, but last of all those that had been consuls, as being in reproachful wise and to his disgrace asked his opinion after them all. There was received likewise against him the examination of a forged will, wherein himself also had been a witness and put his seal. Last of all, he was forced to disburse eight million sesterces at his entrance into a new priesthood; by occasion whereof, his estate being so much decayed, that for his disability to keep credit and satisfy the debt due unto the treasury by an edict of the treasurers, his property was advertised to be sold.

10. Having passed the greatest part of his time in running through these and such like troubles, at length in the fiftieth year of age, he attained to the empire, and that by a strange

and wonderful hap. Being among others excluded by the conspirators that laid wait for Gaius' life, what time they voided all the company about his person, under a color as if he desired to be apart himself alone in some by-place, this Claudius had stepped aside and retired into a lodging called Hermeum. Not long after, being affrighted at the rumor of that murder, slyly crept forth into a solar or garret next adjoining, and there hid himself between the hangings before the door. While he lurked close there, a common soldier chancing to run to and fro that way, espied his feet, and by earnest enquiry and asking who he was, happened to take knowledge of him; who having drawn him forth of the place (when as for fear he fell down humbly at his feet and took hold of his knees) saluted him by the name of emperor. From thence he brought him immediately to his other fellow soldiers, who as yet stood wavering and wist not what to do but fare and fume. By them was he bestowed in a litter upon their shoulders. And so was he brought into the praetorian camp, all sad and amazed for fear; pitied also by the multitude that met him on the way, as if some innocent had been haled to execution. Being received within the trench and rampart, lodged he was all night among the soldiers' watch with less hope than confidence. For the consuls together with the senate and the cohorts of the city soldiers seized the Forum and the Capitol with a purpose to claim and recover the common liberty; and when himself was sent for by a tribune of the commons into the Curia to sit in consultation and give his advice about those matters that were thought good to be propounded, he made answer that detained he was perforce and by constraint. But the next morrow, when the senate grew more cold and slack in following and executing their foresaid projects (by reason of their tedious trouble and discord who dissented in opinion), while the multitude also standing round about demanded by this time one ruler and

Claudius, by name, he called the soldiers in armor to an assembly and suffered them to take their oath of allegiance and to swear to maintain his imperial dignity. Therewith promised he unto them 1500 sesterces apiece: the first of all the Caesars that obliged unto him the soldiers' fealty by a fee and reward.

11. Having once established his empire, he thought nothing more important than to abolish the remembrance of those two days wherein there was some doubtful question about the change and alteration of the state. Of all deeds and words therefore which had passed during that time, he made an act that there should be general pardon and perpetual oblivion, which also he made good and performed accordingly. Only some few colonels and centurions out of that crew which conspired against Gaius he put to the sword: as well for example's sake as for that he had certain intelligence that they required to have him also murdered. Then presently turning and bending his mind to the duties of piety and kindness, he took up no form of oath, either with more devout religion or oftener, than by the name of Augustus. He gave order that for his grandmother Livia there should by decree be granted divine honors; as also in the stately pomp of the Circus, a chariot drawn with elephants, like unto that of Augustus; likewise for the souls of his own parents departed, public dirges and funeral feasts, and particularly in honor of his father, Circus plays and games every year upon his birthday; and in memorial of his mother, a coach to be led and drawn along through the Circus, and the surname of Augusta which by his grandmother was refused. In remembrance of his brother Germanicus (to celebrate whose memorial he omitted no occasion) he exhibited a Greek comedy at the solemn games held in Naples, where by sentence of the umpires and judges he received a coronet therefor. He suffered not so much as Marcus Antonius to pass unhonored, nor without a thankful

mention and remembrance, protesting one time, and that by an edict, that so much the more earnest he was to have men celebrate the birthday of his father Drusus because upon the same day his grandfather Antonius was also born. The marble arch, decreed verily in times past by the senate to be erected for Tiberius near unto the theater of Pompey but forlet, he finished. And albeit he abrogated and repealed all the acts of Gaius, yet the day of his death, although it were the beginning of his empire, he forbade to be registered among feasts in the calendar.

12. But in honoring himself he was spare and carried a civil modesty. The forename of emperor he forbare; excessive honors he refused; the espousals of his own daughter, the birthday also of his grandson, he passed over in silence, only celebrating it with some private ceremony and religious complements within house. He restored no banished person, but by the authority and warrant of the senate. That he might bring with him into the Curia the captain of the guard and tribunes of the soldiers, also that those acts might be ratified and stand in force which his procurators had set down in judging of cases, he obtained by entreaty. He made suit unto the consuls for a licence to hold fairs and markets for his own private manors and lands. In commissions and examinations of cases held by the magistrates, he would oftentimes be personally present and sit as one of the commissioners. To the same magistrates, when they exhibited any plays or games, himself also with the rest of the multitude would arise up and both with hand and voice do them honor. When the tribunes of the commons repaired unto him before the front of his tribunal, he excused himself unto them for that by reason of straight room he could not give attendance unto them otherwise than standing upon their feet. Therefore, within a small time he purchased so much love and favor, that when news came to Rome that forelaid and slain he was in his journey to

Ostia, the people in a great tumult and uproar fell to banning and cursing both the soldiers as traitors, and the senate also as parricides; neither ceased they thus to force against them until first one messenger and then another, yea and soon after many more were produced by the magistrates to the public rostra, who assured them that he was alive and approached homeward.

13. Yet continued he not for all this, secured every way from the danger of secret practices and way-laying, but assailed he was as well by private persons, as by whole factions and conspiracies, yea and sore troubled in the end with civil wars. For there was a man, one of the commons, taken about midnight near unto his bed-chamber with a dagger. Found there were likewise twain of the knight's degree in the open street with a staff having a blade in it, and a hunter's knife, waiting for him: the one to assault his person when he was gone forth of the theater; the other as he sacrificed at the temple of Mars. Now there had conspired to make an insurrection and to alter the state, Gallus Asinius and Statilius Corvinus, the grandsons of Pollio and Messala, the orators, taking unto them for their accomplices many of his own freedmen and servants. As for civil war, kindled it was and begun by Furius Camillus Scribonianus, lieutenant general of Dalmatia; but within five days quenched quite clean and suppressed, by reason that the legions which had changed their oath of allegiance, in remorse of conscience and touch of religion repented, after that upon signification given of a journey to their new general, neither the eagles could be dight and trimmed, nor the military ensigns plucked up and removed [ominous and unlucky signs].

14. To his first consulship he bore four more: of which the two former jointly and immediately one after another; the rest ensuing with some time between, to wit, each one in the fourth year; and as for the third, he had no precedent for it in any other prince, as being substituted in the place of a consul

deceased. A precise justicer he was, ministering justice both when he was consul, and also being out of that office, most painfully; even upon the solemn days instituted for him and his, yea, and otherwhiles upon the ancient festival days and such as were religious. He followed not always the prescript rule of laws, moderating either the rigor or the lenity of penalties by equity and reason, according as he stood affected to a case: for both unto those he restored their actions and gave leave to commence them anew, who in the court before private judges had once lost their suits by claiming more than was due; and also such as were convict of some greater deceit and cozenage, he condemned to be cast unto wild beasts, exceeding therein the ordinary punishment by law appointed.

15. Moreover, in the examination, trial and deciding of controversies he was wondrous variable: one while circumspect, wary and of great insight; otherwhiles as rash and inconsiderate; now and then also foolish, vain and like to one without all reason. When he reviewed upon a time the decuries of jurors, and put whom he thought good from their jurisdiction, one of them, who had answered to his name and concealed the immunity and privilege that he had by benefit of children, he discharged quite, as a man ambitious to be a juror. Another of them being called into question by his adversaries before him as touching a matter between him and them, and pleading withal for himself that it was a case to be tried not extraordinarily (by Caesar) but by the common course of law, he compelled immediately to handle and decide his own case before him: as who in his proper business should give proof how indifferent a juror he would be hereafter in the matter of another. There was a woman that would not acknowledge her own son. Now when by evidences and arguments alleged *pro et contra* on both sides, the question rested in equal balance doubtful, he awarded that she should be

wedded to the young man, and so forced her to confess the truth and to take him for her child. Most ready he was to give judgement on their side who made appearance in court when their adversaries were absent, without any respect and consideration whether a man slacked and stayed by his own default or upon some necessity. One cried out upon a forger of writings and required that both his hands might be cut off. He made no more ado but forthwith called instantly to have the hangman sent for, with his chopping knife and butcher's block, to do the deed. There happened one to be called judicially to the bar for that being a foreigner he bore himself as a Roman citizen. And when the advocates of both sides grew to some little variance about this circumstance, namely, whether the defendant ought to make his answer and plead his own cause in a Roman gown or a Greek cloak, he then, as if he would make exceeding show of equity, commanded him to shift and change his habit often in the place, according as he was either accused or defended. Moreover, sitting in judgement to decide a certain controversy, when he had heard what could be said, he pronounced sentence out of a written tablet, as it is verily thought, to this effect, that he judged on their side who had alleged the truth. For which pranks he became base and contemptible, so much that everywhere and openly he was despised. One, to excuse a witness whom Caesar had called for out of a province, alleged in his behalf and said he could not possibly come in time and be present, dissimuling the cause thereof a great while. At length, after many long demands what the reason might be, "why," quoth he, "the man is dead at Puteoli." Another when he gave him thanks for suffering a person accused to have the benefit of a trial and to be defended, added moreover these words, "and yet this is a usual and ordinary thing." Furthermore, I myself have heard old folk say that these lawyers and barristers were wont to abuse his patience so much that as he was going down from the tribunal they would not only call upon him to come back again, but also take hold of his gown lappet and skirt, yea and otherwhile catch him fast by the foot, and so hold him still with them. And that no man need to marvel hereat, there was one of these Greek lawyers who pleading before him happened in earnest altercation to let fall these words, "you are both old and a fool besides." And verily it is known that a Roman knight, accused before him for his obscene filthiness and unnatural abuse of women (although untruly), and having an indictment framed against him by his enemies, when he saw common strumpets cited and their depositions heard against him, flung his writing stylus and the books which he had in his hand, with great upbraiding of him also for his foolishness and cruelty, even at his very face, so that he rippled and hurt therewith his cheek not a little.

16. He bore also the censorship, an office that a long time had been discontinued, after Paulus and Plancus the censors; but even in this very place he held with an uneven hand and as variable a mind. In the review taken of Roman knights, he dismissed without shame and disgrace a young man charged with many infamous villainies, howbeit one whom his own father testified upon his knowledge and trial to be right honest, saying withal, that he had a censor of his own. To another youth, who was in a very bad name for spoiling of maidens and adulteries committed with wives, he did no more but give warning, either more sparingly to spend himself in those young and tender years of his, or else more warily at leastwise, to go to work; adding thus much besides, "For why know I," quoth he, "what wench thou keepest?" And when upon the entreaty of his familiar friends he had taken off the infamous note which was set upon the name of one, "Well," quoth he, "let the blot yet remain still to be seen." An honorable man

and a principal personage of the province Greece, howbeit ignorant in the Latin tongue, he not only erased out of the roll of jurors, but also deprived of his citizenship and made him a mere alien. Neither suffered he any man to render an account of his life otherwise than with his own mouth, as well as everyone was able, and without an advocate to speak for him. He noted many with disgrace, and some of them without their knowledge, as expecting no such thing; yea, and for a matter that had no precedent, namely, because without his privity and a passport obtained they went forth of Italy; one among the rest for that in the province he accompanied a king in his train: alleging as an example that in his ancestor's days, Rabirius Postumus for following king Ptolemaeus into Alexandria to save and recover the money which he had lent him, was accused before the judges of treason to the state. Having assayed to put many more to rebuke, with great imputation of the inquisitor's negligence, but with greater shame of his own, whomsoever he charged with single life, with childless estate, or poverty, those easily were able to prove themselves husbands, fathers and wealthy. Certes, one there was who being accused to have laid violent hands upon himself and wounded his own body with a sword, stripped himself naked and showed the same whole and sound, without any harm in the world. Many other acts he did of special note while he was censor as namely these: he commanded a silver chariot sumptuously wrought and set out to sale in the street Sigillaria, for to be bought and broken all to pieces openly. Also, in one day he published twenty edicts or proclamations, and these two among the rest: in the one he gave the people warning that when their vineyards bore grapes plentifully, they should pitch their vessels very well within; in the other he did them to understand that there was nothing so good against the stinging of a viper as the juice of the yew tree.

17. One expedition and no more he undertook, and that was very small. When the senate had by decree allowed him triumphal ornaments, he, supposing that a bare title of honor was inferior to the majesty of a prince and emperor, willing also to enterprise some exploit whereby he might win the due glory of a complete triumph, made choice, before all other provinces, of Britain; attempted by none since Julius Caesar of famous memory, and at that time in a tumultuous uproar for that certain revolts and rebels fled from thence and were not returned. As he sailed from Ostia thitherward, twice had he like to have been cast away and drowned by reason of the strong blustering southern wind near unto Liguria, hard by the islands Stoechades. Having therefore travelled by land from Massilia as far as to the Cape Gessoriacum, he crossed the seas from thence into Britain. And in very few days, without battle or bloodshed, part of the island yielded to his devotion. So in the sixth months after his first setting forth he returned to Rome and triumphed with most sumptuous pomp therefor prepared. To the sight of which solemnity he suffered not only the presidents and governors of provinces to have recourse into the city, but also certain banished persons. And among the enemies' spoils he set up a naval coronet and fastened it to the gable of his palatine house, hard by another civic garland in token and memorial of the ocean by him sailed over and subdued. After his triumphant chariot rode Messalina his wife in a coach; then followed those gallants also who in the same war had attained to triumphal ornaments; the rest went on foot and in their rich robes bordered with purple. Only Crassus Frugi mounted upon a brave courser trimly trapped, and arrayed himself in a triumphant mantle of estate for that now twice he had achieved that honor.

18. He was at all times most careful and provident for the city especially that the market might be well served with

victuals. When the Aemilian edifices (or tenements) were on fire and continued still burning, he remained two nights together in the place called Diribitorium; and when the multitude of soldiers and household servants failed, he called together by means of the magistrates the commons of the city out of all the streets and parishes to come in and help, setting before him his chests full of money exhorting them to do their best for the quenching of the fire, and ready for to pay presently every one a good reward according to the pains he took. Now, when corn and victuals were grown very scarce (such was the continual unseasonable weather that brought barrenness), he was upon a time in the midst of the market place detained by the multitude and so assailed and pelted with reviling taunts and with pieces of broken bread, that hardly and with much ado he was able to escape, and no otherwise than by a postern gate, into the palace. Whereupon he devised all the means he possibly could to bring into the city provision of corn and victuals, even in the winter season. For he not only proposed certain set gains to all corn masters that would venture for grain, undertaking himself to bear all the loss that should happen to any of them by tempest, but ordained also great fees and avails for those that would build ships for such traffic and merchandise, according to the condition and quality of each one:

19. Namely for every Roman citizen, exemption from the Law Papia Poppaea; for enfranchised Latins, the freedom of Roman citizens, and for women, the privilege and benefit of those that had four children, which constitutions stand in force and be observed at this day.

20. Many works he finished and those rather for greatness, huge, than for use, needful. But the chief and principal were these: the conduit of water begun by Gaius; also a sluice to let out and drain the lake Fucinus; and the haven at Ostia; although he knew well enough that the one (of the twain)

Augustus had denied unto the Marsians who continually entreated him about it; and the other intended oftentimes in the designs of Julius Caesar of sacred memory, was for the difficulty thereof laid aside. The two cold and plenteous fountains of the water Claudia, of which the one bears the name of Caeruleus, the other of Curtius or Albudignus, as also the new river of Anio he conveyed and brought to Rome all the way, within stone-work; and then derived and divided the same into many and those right beautiful pools. He went in hand with the lake Fucinus in hope of gain as well as of glory, inasmuch as some there were who would have bound themselves in covenant and promise to drain the said marsh at their own private charges, in case the ground being once made dry might be granted unto them in freehold. Now for the length of three miles, partly by digging through the hill, and partly by hewing out the rock before him, he finished the channel at last with much ado and after eleven years' labor, albeit thirty thousand men were at work continually about it and never rested between. The harbor at Ostia beforesaid he made by drawing an arm of the sea about on the left and the right hand both. And withal at the mouth and entrance thereof, where now the ground lay deep, he raised a huge dam or pile against it. For the surer foundation of which pile, he drowned beforehand that ship wherein the great obelisk had been transported out of Egypt. And when he had supported it with buttresses of many stones, he planted aloft upon the same an exceeding high watch-tower to the pattern of that Pharus at Alexandria, to the end that by the fires burning there in the night season, vessels might direct their course.

21. He dealt often among the people great congiaries. Many shows likewise he exhibited, and those magnificent; not such only as were usual and in accustomed places, but those that were both newly devised and also brought into use again,

whereas they had of ancient time been discontinued: yea and where no man else before him had ever set forth any. The games for the dedication of Pompey's theater, which being half burnt he had re-edified, he gave a signal to begin from out of his tribunal erected in the *orchestra*, seeing that before time, when he had sacrificed and done his devotions in the houses above and came down from thence through the midst of the theater and assembly, not one would once arise and give applause, but sat still and kept silence. He set out also the secular games and plays, as if they had been exhibited by Augustus over-soon [they were solemnized once in the revolution of one hundred years or one hundred and ten, as some write], and not reserved unto their full and due time. And yet himself in his own histories writes, that whereas the said solemnities had been intermitted, Augustus long after by a most exact calculation of the years reduced them into order again. By occasion where-of, the voice of the crier was then ridiculous and laughed at, when after the solemn manner he called the people to behold those games and plays which no man had once seen already, or should ever see again; whereas there survived yet many who had seen them before, yea and some of the actors who in times past had been produced, were then likewise brought forth upon the stage. Oftentimes also he represented games in the Vatican Circus, and otherwhiles after every five courses of chariot-running he brought in the baiting of wild beasts. But in the great Circus which was beautified with bar-gates of marble and goals all gilded (whereas beforetime they had been made of soft sandstone and wood), he appointed proper and peculiar places for the senators, who had wont beforetime to behold the same sports here and there. Beside the races for the prize of chariots drawn with four steeds, he represented also the warlike Troy pastime and the baiting of leopards, which the troop of the praetorian horsemen slew, having for their leaders the tribunes and the captain himself. Moreover, he brought into the showplace Thessalian men of arms, whose manner is to chase about the circus wild bulls, until they be tired; then to mount them, and by the horns to force them down to the ground. As for shows of sword-fencers, he exhibited them in many places, and after divers and sundry sorts. One, that was kept every year within the praetorian camp, without any baiting and sumptuous provision of furniture. As for that, which was ordinarily set out and formally with baiting and other preparation in Mars field at the *Septa*; in the same place likewise, another extraordinary one and of short continuance, which he began to call *Sportula*, because he proclaimed at first when he exhibited it, that he invited the people thereto, as it were to a sudden supper and short pittance. And in no kind of sport represented unto them was he more civil, familiar and better disposed to pass the time away; insomuch as putting forth his left hand, he together with the common sort would both by word of mouth tell, and with his fingers also number the pieces of gold as he tendered them unto the winners; and many a time by way of exhortation and entreaty provoke the people to mirth; ever and anon calling them Sirs, yea, and between whiles intermingling bald and far-fetched jests. As for example, when the people called for one Palumbus [a fencer] to play his prizes, he promised to let them have him, if he were once caught. This also was but a simple plain jest although to good purpose and in season delivered; when he had by a special indulgence, granted unto a champion who fought out of a British chariot (for whom his four children made earnest suit and entreaty) that he should be freed from that profession of sword-fight; and that with the great favor and liking of all men, he sent presently an admonition in writing; wherein he advertised the people, how much they should endeavor to get children, seeing, as they did, in what good stead they served, and how they procured grace even unto a sword-fencer. He represented also in Mars field a war-like show of the winning and sacking of a town; likewise the yielding of the princes of Britain; where he sat himself as president in his rich coat-armor. When he was about to let out the water of the lake Fucinus, he exhibited it in a naval fight before; and as they who were to fight this battle cried out unto him, "*Ave Imperator*," etc. [All hail O emperor; they salute thee and wish thy life who are ready to die]; and he again made answer, "*Avete vos*" [Farewell ye]. After which word given, as if he had pardoned them this skirmish, there was not one of them would fight; he sitting a good while in doubt and suspense within himself, whether he should destroy them all with fire and sword, at length leapt forth of his throne, and running to and fro about the circuit of the said lake (not without foul faltering of his legs under him) partly with threats, and in part by way of exhortation, constrained them to skirmish. At this brave show, the Sicilian and Rhodian fleets encountered; either of them consisting of twelve galleys ruled with three ranks of oars apiece. To give the signal of battle, there was a Triton of silver arising out of the midst of the lake by a machine artificially devised, to sound the trumpet and set them together.

22. Certain points about religious ceremonies, touching the state likewise of civil and military affairs, as also concerning all degrees of persons both at home and abroad, he either reformed, or after long disuse forgotten, brought into practice again, or else instituted and ordained new. In the election and admission of priests throughout their several colleges, he nominated not one but he took his oath first. He observed also precisely that so often as there was an earthquake in the city, the praetor for the time being should call a public assembly of the people and proclaim certain holidays; likewise, that upon the prodigious sight of an unlucky fowl in the Capitol,

there should be held a solemn procession and supplication; wherein himself personally in the right of high priest, after warning given unto the people from the rostra, did read and pronounce a form of prayers and they say after him. But from this congregation he sequestered and removed the base multitude of mechanical laborers and slaves.

23. The handling of causes and judicial pleading in courts, divided beforetime into certain months for winter and summer, he conjoined altogether. The jurisdiction as touching feoffments upon trust which was wont year by year and only within the city to be committed unto the magistrates, he ordained to hold by patent forever; and betook the charge thereof unto the governors also of state in every province. That branch annexed to the Law Papia Poppaea [that a woman under fifty years of age, should not be wedded to a man that was threescore], which implies that men three score years of age are disabled for generation, he altered by an edict. He ordained that unto wards, the consuls should extraordinarily appoint tutors and guardians. That they also who by the magistrates were forbidden to make abode within any provinces, should be debarred likewise from the city of Rome and Italy. Himself confined some after a strange fashion and without any precedent, inhibiting them to depart above three miles from the city. When he was to treat of any great affair in the Curia, his manner was to sit in the tribunes' pew just in the midst between the consuls' chairs. As for passports which the consuls were wont to be sued unto for, he would have the citizens to be beholden unto himself only therefore, and to crave the same at his hands.

24. The badges and ornaments belonging unto the consuls he granted unto the procurators also. From as many as refused the honorable dignity of senators he took away also the knight's degree. The right to wear the laticlave [the senator's

robe] studded with purple (although he promised at first not to choose anyone senator who could not reckon four lineal descents from a citizen of Rome), he allowed also to a libertine's son. But with this condition, if he were adopted before by a knight of Rome. And fearing for all that, lest he should be blamed, he showed, that even Appius Caecus the chief ancestor and author of his own race, being censor, admitted into the senate the sons of libertines; ignorant as he was that in the days of the said Appius and in the times long after ensuing, those were called libertines, not only who themselves were manumitted and enfranchised, but such also as were freeborn of their progeny. The college of quaestors, instead of paving the streets and highways he enjoined to exhibit a game or show of sword-fencers; and in the lieu of the provinces, Ostia and Gaul which he took from them, he restored the charge of the public treasure in the temple of Saturn; which office in the mean space between from Augustus' days the praetors for the time being or those verily who had been praetors before, had borne. Unto Silanus espoused and betrothed unto his daughter, before he was fourteen years of age, he granted triumphal ornaments; but of elder persons to so many, as there is an epistle extant written in the common name of the legions wherein they make petition, that unto the consular lieutenants there might be granted together with the conduct of the army, the said triumphal honors, to the end that they should not pick quarrels and seek occasions of war. Moreover to Aulus Plautius he gave by decree an ovation; and as he entered so into the city himself met him upon the way, and both when he went into the Capitol and returned also from thence again, walked on his left side. Unto Gabinius Secundus, who had vanquished the Cauci, a nation in Germany, he permitted and gave leave to assume the surname Caucius in his style.

25. The knights' service and their places he ordered so by

degrees, as that after the charge of a cohort, he granted the leading of a wing, and after the command thereof, the tribuneship of a legion. He ordained their stipends also and a kind of imaginary warfare called *Supra-Numerum* (which they that were absent might execute) and in name or title only. By virtue of a decree that passed even from the nobles themselves, he prohibited all soldiers professed, to enter into any senators' houses for to do their duty and salute them. Those libertines who bare themselves for Roman knights he caused to forfeit their goods and bodies to the state. Such of them as were unthankful and of whom their patrons complained, he deprived of freedom and made them bound again. Yea and denied unto their advocates for to hear any plea and to sit in judgement against their own freedmen. When some masters there were, that put forth their sick and diseased slaves into the Isle of Aesculapius for to avoid the tedious trouble of their cures at home, he made an act and ordained, that all such slaves should be free and not return again into the hands of their masters, in case they ever recovered; and if any master chose to kill them outright rather than thus to put them forth, they should be guilty of murder. He gave warning by an edict, that no wayfaring men should travel through any town in Italy, but either on foot or borne in a chair, or else carried in a litter. In Puteoli and in Ostia he placed several cohorts to put by all mischances of fires. He forbade all persons by condition aliens to take upon them Roman names; those I mean only that distinguished houses and familes. As many of them as usurped the freedom of citizenship he beheaded in the Esquiline field. The two provinces Achaia and Macedonia, which Tiberius had appropriated to himself [and his successors], he yielded up again into the hands of the senate. The Lycians he deprived of their freedom, by occasion of the mortal discord and variance among them. To the Rhodians, who repented for their old trespasses he restored their liberty which they had lost. He forgave all tributes to the Ilienses forever, as to the first founders and stock-fathers of the Roman nation; and to that purpose he read an old letter in Greek written unto king Seleucus by the scnate and people of Rome; wherein they promised to entertain amity and league with him upon this condition, that he would grant unto the Ilienses, their natural kinsfolk, immunities from all taxes and tributes. The Jews who by the instigation of one Chrestus were evermore tumultuous, he banished Rome. The ambassadors of the Germans he permitted to sit in the *orchestra* (with the senators) being moved so to do at their simplicity and confident boldness, for that being brought into the *Popularia* and perceiving Parthians and Armenians sitting among the senators, they of their own accord had removed and passed to that quarter, giving out these words withal, that their valor and condition of estate was nothing inferior to the others. The religion of the Druids among the Frenchmen, practicing horrible and detestable cruelty and which under Augustus Roman citizens were forbidden to profess, he quite abolished. Contrariwise, the sacred rites and holy ceremonies of Ceres called *Eleusinia*, he attempted to transfer out of Attica to Rome. The temple likewise of Venus Erycina in Sicily, which in continuance of time was decayed and fallen down, he caused to be repaired and built again at the common charges of the people of Rome. He made covenants and league with foreign kings, by the complements of killing a sow in the Forum, and using withal the sentence or preface that the heralds in old time pronounced. But both these affairs and others besides, the whole empire also in a manner or a great part thereof, he managed not so much after his own mind, as by the direction and will of his wives and freedmen, being verily affected and framed for the most part so as stood either with their profit or good pleasure.

26. When he was a very youth, he had espoused two maidens, namely Aemilia Lepida great-granddaughter to Augustus, likewise Livia Medullina, surnamed also Camilla, a lady descended from the ancient house of Camillus the dictator. The former of these twain, because her parents had offended Augustus he cast off remaining as yet a virgin; the latter, he lost by occasion of sickness, upon that very day which was appointed for the marriage. After this, he wedded these wives, to wit, Plautia Herculanilla, whose father had triumphed; and not long after, Aelia Paetina, whose father had been consul. Both these he divorced, Paetina upon light offenses and small displeasures; marry, Herculanilla he put away for her filthy lust and whorish life; as also for suspicion of a murder. After these he took to wife Valeria Messalina, the daughter of Barbatus Messalla his cousin, whom when he found once, over and beside the rest of her abominable vices, to have been wedded to Gaius Silius [while she was empress and wife to Claudius], and that with a dowry assured unto her and signed among the auspices, he put her to death. And in a speech that he made openly before his praetorian soldiers, avowed that because his marriages proved so bad, he resolved to remain unmarried and live a single life; and if he did not continue so forever he would not refuse to be stabbed by their very hands. Neither could he endure, but forthwith treat upon conditions of marriage even with Paetina, whom long before he had put away; yea and with Lollia Paulina, wife sometime to Gaius Caesar. But through the enticing allurements of Agrippina, the daughter of Germanicus his own brother, what by the means of kissing courtesies, what by the opportunities of other dalliances, being drawn into love and fancy with her, at the next session of senate he suborned certain of purpose to opine and give advice, to compel him for to make her his wife, as being a matter of right great con-

sequence, and which most of all concerned the state; that other men also might be dispensed with and licensed to contract the like marriages which until that time were reputed incestuous. And so, himself stayed hardly one day between before he dispatched the wedding; but none were found that followed the precedent, except one libertine and another who had been a principal centurion in the foremost cohort, at whose marriage even himself in person together with Agrippina was present to do him credit and honor.

27. Children he begat of three wives. By Herculanilla he had Drusus and Claudia; by Paetina he was father of Antonia; and Messalina bare unto him Octavia and a son, whom first he named Germanicus and afterwards Britannicus. As for Drusus, he lost him at Pompeii before he was fourteen years of age by occasion that he was choked with a pear which in play being tossed aloft into the air, fell just into his mouth as he gaped wide for it; unto whom also but few days before, he had affianced in marriage the daughter of Sejanus; which makes me more to marvel that some have written that he was treacherously killed by Sejanus. His supposed daughter Claudia, who indeed was conceived by his freedman Boter, although she was born before the fifth month after the divorce, and began to be nursed and reared, yet he commanded to be laid at her mother's door and stark naked to be cast forth. Antonia his daughter, he gave in marriage to Gnaius Pompey Magnus; afterwards to Faustus Sulla, right noble young gentlemen; and Octavia he bestowed upon Nero emperor after him his wife's son, notwithstanding she had been promised and betrothed before unto Silanus. His son Britannicus, whom Messalina bore unto him the twentieth day after he came to the empire and in his second consulship, being yet a very babe he recommended continually both to the soldiers in open assembly, dandling him in his own hands, and also to the common people

Being desirous upon a time to behold an execution performed after the ancient manner at Tibur, when as (the malefactors standing bound already to a stake) there wanted the butcherly executioner to do the feat, he stayed there still in the place, and waited until evening, for one that was sent for out of Rome.

at the solemnities of games and plays, holding him either in his bosom or just before him, while the multitude with great acclamations, all good words, and fortunate auspices seconded him. Of his sons-in-law who matched with his daughters, he adopted Nero; Pompey and Silanus he not only cast off and rejected but murdered also.

28. Of all his freedmen he esteemed especially Posides the eunuch, unto whom also in his triumph over Britain, among martial men and valiant soldiers, he gave a spear without an iron head for his great valor. And no less account made he of Felix, whom first he ordained captain over the cohorts of horsemen, yea and ruler of the province, the husband of three queens. As also of Harpocras, unto whom he granted a privilege to be carried in a litter throughout the city of Rome, and to set out the games and plays in public. And besides these, he affected with much respect Polybius, the guide and director to him in his studies, who oftentimes would walk cheek by jowl between the two consuls. But above all these, he held in greatest esteem Narcissus his secretary, and Pallas the keeper of his books or accounts; whom by virtue of a decree also which went from the senate, he suffered willingly to be not only rewarded with rich fees, but also to be adorned with the honors of quaestor and praetorship; likewise to get, by hook and crook so much, as that when himself complained upon a time how little treasure he had in his coffers, one made answer unto him not absurdly, that he might have store enough and plenty, in case his two freedmen would admit him to share with them.

29. To these freedmen and to his wives as I said before, being wholly addicted and enthralled, he bore himself not as a prince, but as their minister and servitor. According as it was commodious to any of these, or stood with their affection and pleasure, he granted honorable dignities, conferred the conducts of armies, and awarded impunities and punishments;

yea and for the most part, I assure you, when himself was altogether ignorant and wist not what he did. And not to reckon up particularly every small thing, to wit, his liberalities and gifts revoked, his judgements reversed, his patents and writings concerning the grants of offices either foisted in or plainly altered or changed by them. He slew his father-in-law Appius Silanus; the two Julias, the one daughter of Drusus, and the other of Germanicus, upon bare imputation of a crime, without any ground, not allowing them so much as lawful trial and liberty to plead in their own defense. Likewise Gnaius Pompey, husband to his elder daughter, and Lucius Silanus espoused to the other, and all through their suggestions and informations. Of which, Pompey was stabbed even as he lay in bed with a beloved youth and catamite of his; Silanus was forced to resign up his praetorship four days before the Kalends of January, and to lose his life in the beginning of the year, on the very wedding day of Claudius and Agrippina. To the execution of thirty-five senators, and above that a hundred Roman knights so easily was he induced, as that, when the centurion brought word back, as touching the death of one who had been consul, he flatly denied that he gave any such warrant. Nevertheless the thing he allowed, while his freedmen aforesaid standing by, avouched, that the soldiers had done their devoir, in that they ran willingly of their own heads to revenge their emperor. For, it would be thought incredible if I should relate how even for the very marriage of Messalina with the adulterer Silius, his own self sealed the writings for assurance of the dowry, being persuaded and brought thereunto, as though the said wedding was but colorably, of purpose pretended to avert forsooth and translate the danger, that by certain prodigies were portended to hang over his head.

30. Right personable he was, and carried a presence not without authority and majesty, whether he stood or sat; but

especially when he was laid and took his repose. For, of stature he was tall and not lank and slender. His countenance lively, his gray hairs became him well, with a good fat and round neck. Howbeit, both as he went his hams, being feeble, failed him; and also while he was doing ought, were it remissly or in earnest, many things disgraced him; to wit, indecent laughter and unseemly anger, by reason that he would froth and slaver at the mouth, and had evermore his nose dropping. Besides, his tongue stammered. His head likewise at all times, but especially if he did anything were it never so little, used to shake and tremble very much.

31. Concerning his bodily health, as beforetime he used to be grievously sick, so being once emperor exceeding healthful he was and stood clear of all diseases save only the pain of the stomach, in a fit whereof he said, he thought to have killed himself.

32. He made feasts, and those very great and ordinarily; yea, and in most open and large places, such as for the most part would receive six hundred guests at one sitting. He feasted also even upon the sluice of the lake Fucinus, what time he had like to have been drowned, when as the water let out with a forcible violence reflowed back again. At every supper his manner was to have also his own children, who together with other noblemen's children, as well boys as girls, should after the old manner sit and feed at the table's feet. One of his guests, who was thought to have closely stolen away a cup of gold the day before, he reinvited against the morrow, and then he set before him a stone pot to drink in. It is reported moreover, that he meant to set forth an edict, wherein he would give folk leave to break wind downward and let it go even with a crack at the very board; having certain intelligence, that there was one who for manners' and modesty's sake, by holding it in, endangered his own life.

33. For appetite to meat and drink his stomach served him passing well always, and in every place. Sitting upon a time judicially in Augustus' Forum to hear and determine causes, and scenting there the steam of a dinner, there was a dressing and serving up for the priests *Salii* in the temple of Mars next adjoining, he forsook the tribunal, went up to the said priests, and there sat down with them to meat. Lightly you should never have him go out of any dining room, but with his belly strutting out, well whittled also and drenched with wine; so as straightways, while he lay down along upon his back and took a sleep gaping, there was a feather put ordinarily into his mouth wide open for to discharge his stomach. He took very short sleeps, for commonly before midnight he awaked; yet so, as otherwhiles he would catch a nap in the daytime, as he sat to minister justice, and scarcely could be awakened by the advocates at the bar, who of purpose raised their voices and pleaded the louder. He was excessively given to the wanton love of women. As for the preposterous abuse of male-kind, he was altogether unacquainted therewith. He played at dice most earnestly (concerning the art and skill whereof, he published also a little book), being wont to play that game even while he was carried up and down, having his carriage and dice-board so fitted, as there might be no confusion nor shuffling at all in play.

34. That cruel he was and given to bloodshed naturally appeared in great and very small matters. As for tortures used in examinations, and the punishments that parricides suffered, he exhibited and exacted the same to be done without delay, and openly in his own presence. Being desirous upon a time to behold an execution performed after the ancient manner at Tibur, when as (the malefactors standing bound already to a stake) there wanted the butcherly executioner to do the feat, he stayed there still in the place, and waited until evening, for

one that was sent for out of Rome. At all sword-fights, whether they were set forth by himself or by others, he commanded as many of the champions as chanced only but to stumble and fall therewith, to have their throats cut, especially the fencers called *Retiarii*. And why! because forsooth he would see their faces as they lay gasping and yielding up their breath. It fortuned, that a couple of these fighting at sharp wounded and killed one another; thereupon he commanded little knives to be made of both their blades, for his own proper use. He took such pleasure in those that fought with wild beasts, as also in the sword-fights ordinarily about noon, that he would by break of day go down to the theater for to behold the one; and at noon dismiss the people to their dinners, and sit it out himself to see the other. Yea, and besides those that were appointed to such combats, upon any slight and sudden occasion set some to fight for their lives, even out of the number of carpenters, servitors, and such like employed about these games; if haply any of those artificial motions that go by devices, or a pageant in frame proved not well. He fetched in also one of his own pages even in his gown, as he went to fight for his life.

35. But it passed, how timorous and diffident he was. At his first coming to the empire (however as we said before, he bragged and stood upon his civil and familiar behavior), he durst not for certain days go to any feast, dinner or supper, without pensioners standing about him with their spears and javelins, and his soldiers waiting at the table. Neither visited he any sick person, unless the bed-chamber where the party lay, were first searched; the beds, bolsters, pillows, coverlets and other clothes were groped, felt, and thoroughly shaken beforehand. All the time after, he appointed evermore certain searchers for them all that came to salute him, sparing not one, and such searchers as were most cruel. For, long it was first, and that with much ado, ere he granted that women, young

boys in their embroidered coats, and maidens, should not be handled and felt in this manner; that any man's attendants likewise or clerks might not have their pen-sheaths and penknife-cases taken from them. In a civil commotion, when Camillus (making no doubt but that without any war at all he might be terrified) willed him in a contumelious, menacing, and malapert letter, to resign up the empire and to lead a quiet life in private estate, he called his nobles and chief personages about him to counsel and put to question, whether it were best to hearken unto him or no.

36. At the headless report and flying news of some treason that should be practiced against him, he was so affrighted, that he went about to lay down his imperial dignity. By occasion, that one, as I related before, was taken with a weapon upon him about his person as he sacrificed, in all haste he sent out the beadles and called the senate together, before whom, with tears and loud outcries, he bewailed his own piteous case, as who nowhere could make account of any safety; and thereupon for a long time forbore to come abroad. His affectionate love also to Messalina, most fervent though it were he renounced and cast clean from her, not so much for any indignity of the dishonorable wrongs she offered unto him, as upon every fear of danger, as fully persuaded that she practiced to bring the empire into Silius the adulterer's hands. At which time in a great fright he fled in shameful manner to the camp, asking and inquiring all the way nothing else, but whether the empire remained still safe to his behoof.

37. There arose no suspicion, there came forth no author so light and vain, but gave him a bone to gnaw upon, and put not small toys in his head whereby he was forced to beware and seek revenge. One of those that had a matter depending in court before him, taking him aside, when he came by way of salutation, avowed unto him, that he dreamed, how he was

killed by one. Then within a while after, the same party, as if he had now taken knowledge who that one was that should murder him, pointed unto Claudius, and said, "This is he." Whereupon immediately apprehended he was, and haled to execution. After the same manner by report, came Appius Silanus to his death. For, when Messalina and Narcissus had conspired to work his overthrow and final destruction, they complotted thus, that Narcissus betimes in a morning before daylight rushed like a man amazed and astonished into the bed-chamber of his patron Claudius relating unto him his dream, namely that Appius had laid violent hands upon him; and Messalina for her part, composing and framing herself as if she wondered greatly thereat, reported, how she likewise had seen already the same vision for certain nights together. And not long after this, word came, as it was before agreed between them, that Appius was coming to rush in among them; who had indeed been bidden the day before to be present at the same instant. Whereupon, as if the said dream had now proved true and been plainly represented in effect, order was given for Appius to be indicted, arraigned, and to suffer death. Neither doubted Claudius the morrow after to report the whole story and the order thereof unto the senate, and withal to give thanks unto his freedman Narcissus, for being so vigilant and watchful in his very sleep for his sake.

38. Being privy to himself of passionate anger and bearing malice, he excused them both in an edict, distinctly promising that the one of them verily should be but short and harmless, the other not unjust nor causeless. Having sharply rebuked the men of Ostia because they had not sent boats and barges to meet him as he came upon the river Tiber, and that in such odious terms as these, that he was now become base and abject in their eyes. All of a sudden he pardoned them upon the submission and readiness to make satisfaction. Some there were,

whom in the very open street he thrust from him with his own hand, coming unto him somewhat out of season. Similarly, he confined and banished a scribe of a quaestor and a senator that had borne the praetorship, both of them without their cause heard and altogether guiltless, for that the one pleading as an advocate against him when he was a private person had carried himself not so modestly as he should; and the senator in his aedileship had amerced and fined certain tenants of his for selling boiled meats contrary to the law expressly fobidding so to do, and withal whipped his bailiff coming between to intercede for them. For which cause also, he took from the aediles their authority to punish the disorder of those that kept taverns and victualing houses. But as touching his own foolishness, he concealed it not, but gave it out and protested in certain short orations, that he counterfeited himself a fool for the nonce during Gaius' days; because otherwise he should not have escaped, nor attained to that imperial place which he was now entered upon. Howbeit, he could not make the world believe so much, until there was a book put forth within a short time after, entitled *Exaltation of Fools*. The argument and matter whereof was, that no man feigns folly.

39. Among other things, men wondered at him for his oblivion and unadvisedness. When Messalina was by his own commandment killed, within a while, after he was set in his dining parlor, he asked why his lady came not. Many of those whom he had condemned to death, the very morrow immediately after, he commanded to have warning both to sit in counsel with him, and also to bear him company at diceplay; yea, and by a messenger chid and checked them as drowsy and slothful for staying so long and making no better haste. Being minded to take Agrippina to wife against all law of god and man, he ceased not in all his speech to call her his daughter and nurseling, to give out also, that she was born

and brought up in his bosom. Having a purpose to admit Nero into the very name of his own house and family, as if he had not incurred blame enough already for adopting him his wife's son, having a natural son of his own who was now of ripe years, he eftsoons divulged, that never anyone had been by adoption inserted or incorporated into the family of the Claudii.

40. He showed ofttimes so great negligence and careless-ness what he said or did, that he was thought not to know nor consider, either who made any speech, or among whom, or at what time, and in what place? When there was some question and debate about butchers and vintners, he cried out in the senate house, "I beseech you, my masters, who is able to live without a little piece or morsel of flesh?" and withal described the abundance of the old taverns, from whence himself also in times past was wont to be served with wine. As touching a certain quaestor who was a candidate of his and by him re-commended; among other reasons why he favored him he alleged this, because his father had in due time given him, lying sick, cold water to drink. Having in the senate brought in a woman to depose, "This," quoth he, "was my mother's freedwoman, and she that used to deck and dress her; but she always took me for her patron. This have I delivered of pur-pose, because there be some yet in mine house, who think me not to be a patron." Moreover, sitting upon the tribunal when he was in a great chafe, and the men of Ostia requested at his hands (I wot not what) in the name of their town, he cried out aloud, that he knew nothing wherefore he should oblige them unto him. "And if any man else," quoth he, "I also am free and at mine own liberty." As for these words of his which now I will relate, they were rife in his mouth daily, yea every hour and minute thereof: "What, dost thou take me for Theogonius?" besides many such foolish terms, not beseeming private persons, much less a prince otherwise not uneloquent

nor unlearned; nay, rather one eagerly given to his book, and a great student in the liberal sciences.

41. In his youth, he attempted to write a history, exhorted thereto by Titus Livius; and having the help besides of Sulpitius Flavus. And when he put the same first to the trial and judgement of men in a frequent auditorium, hardly and with much ado he read it through, being often in the while coldly heard, by an occasion that himself gave. For when as he began his reading, there was set up a laughter, by reason that many of the seats broke with the weight of a certain corpulent and fat swad, he was not able to hold, no not after the tumult appeased, but eftsoons ever and anon call to mind that accident and fall afresh to unmeasurable laughing. During his empire likewise he both wrote much and also rehearsed the same continually by his reader. The beginning of his foresaid history he took from the time ensuing the murder of Caesar dictator; but he passed over to the latter days and began again at the civil pacification; perceiving that it was not in his power and liberty to write of the occurrences in those former times, as who was often checked both by his mother and also by his grandame. Of the former argument he left behind him two volumes; of the later, forty-one. He compiled of his own life eight books: a report not so wisely and discreetly put down, otherwise elegantly penned. Also, an *Apology of Cicero against the books of Asinius Gallus*: a piece of work full enough of learning. He devised moreover three new characters or letters in the Latin alphabet, and put them to the number of the old as most necessary. And having published while he was yet a private person concerning the reason of those letters, one book, soon after being emperor he easily effected that they should be brought into use also indifferently with the rest. And verily such manner of writing with those characters is now extant to be seen in many books, in journals, and inscriptions of buildings.

42. With no less diligence studied he the Greek disciplines, professing as any occasion was offered his affectionate love to that tongue, and the excellency thereof. When a certain barbarian discoursed in Greek and Latin, "See you be skillful," quoth, he, "in both our languages"; and in recommending Achaia unto the senate, he said it was a province that he affected well and delighted in, for the society of studies common to him and them; and many a time he answered their ambassadors in the senate, with a long and continued oration in Greek. But upon the tribunal he used very much verses also out of Homer. Certes whensoever he had taken revenge of enemy or traitor, he lightly gave unto the tribune over the guard of his person, calling unto him after the usual manner for a watchword, none other than this:

> Resist, revenge with main and might,
> When one provokes thee first to fight.

To conclude, in the end he wrote Greek histories also, to wit twenty books of Etruscan history and eight of Carthaginian. In regard of which histories, into the ancient school at Alexandria he adjoined another bearing his own name, and ordained it was, that every year in the one of them his books on Etruscan history, and in the other his Carthaginian history, upon certain days appointed therefore should (as it were in a frequent auditorium) be read whole through by several single readers in their turns.

43. Toward the end of his life, he showed certain signs, and those evident enough, that he repented both his marriage with Agrippina, and the adoption also of Nero. For by occasion that his freedmen made mention and gave their commendation of a judicial proceeding of his, wherein he had condemned the day before a woman in the case of adultery, he avouched that the destinies likewise had so ordained that all

his marriages should be unchaste howbeit not unpunished; and soon after, meeting his son Britannicus and embracing him more closely than his manner was, "Grow apace," quoth he, "and take account of me for all that I have done." Using withal these Greek words, "What inflicted the wound will heal it." And when he had fully purposed to give him, being as then very young and of tender years, his virile robe, seeing that his stature and growth would bear and permit it, he uttered these words moreover, "To the end that the people of Rome may yet at last have a true and natural Caesar."

44. And not long after this he wrote his will and signed it with the seals of all the head-magistrates; whereupon before that he could proceed any further, prevented he was and cut short by Agrippina. Whom they also who were privy to her and of her counsel, yet nevertheless informers, accused besides all this of many crimes. And verily it is agreed upon generally by all, that killed he was by poison; but where it should be, and who gave it, there is some difference. Some write, that as he sat at a feast in the Castle with the priests, it was presented unto him by Halotus the eunuch his taster; others report that it was at a meal in his own house by Agrippina herself, who had offered unto him a mushroom empoisoned, knowing that he was greedy of such meats. Of these accidents also which ensued hereupon, the report is variable. Some say, that straight upon the receipt of the poison he became speechless, and continuing all night in dolorous torments, died a little before day. Others affirm that at first he fell asleep; and afterwards, as the meat floated aloft vomited all up, and so was followed again with a rank poison. But whether the same were put into a mess of thick gruel (considering he was of necessity to be refreshed with food being emptied in his stomach) or conveyed up by a clyster, as if being overcharged with fullness and surfeit, he might be eased also by this kind of egestion and purgation, it is uncertain.

45. His death was kept secret until all things were set in order about his successor. And therefore, both vows were made for him as if he had lain sick still, and also comical actors were brought in place colorably to solace and delight him, as having a longing desire after such sports. He deceased three days before the Ides of October, when Asinius Marcellus and Acilius Aviola were consuls; in the sixty-fourth year of his age, and fourteenth of his empire. His funerals were performed with a solemn pomp and he was enrolled among the gods, which honor forlet and abolished by Nero he recovered afterwards by the means of Vespasian.

46. Especial tokens there were presaging and prognosticating his death: to wit, the rising of a hairy star which they call a comet; also the monument of his father Drusus was blasted with lightning; and for that in the same year most of the magistrates of all sorts were dead. But himself seems not either to have been ignorant that his end drew near, to have dissimuled so much, which may be gathered by some good arguments and demonstrations. For both in the ordination of consuls he appointed none of them to continue longer than the month wherein he died; and also in the senate, the very last time that ever he sat there, after a long and earnest exhortation of his children to concord, he humbly recommended the age of them both to the lords of that honorable house. And in his last judicial session upon the tribunal once or twice he pronounced openly, that come he was now to the end of his mortality; notwithstanding they that heard him grieved to hear such an omen, and prayed to the gods to avert the same.

THE HISTORY OF
NERO CLAUDIUS CAESAR

NERO

OUT OF THE DOMITIAN STOCK AND NAME, there spring two famous families, the Calvini and the Aenobarbi. These Aenobarbi have for the first author of their origin and surname Lucius Domitius who, as he returned in times past homeward out of the country, encountered, by report, two young twin men, carrying with them a venerable presence more than ordinary, who commanded him to relate to the Senate and people of Rome news of that victory of which they as yet were in doubt. And for the better assurance of their divine majesty they stroked his cheeks, so that therewith they made his hair of black, red, and a color like brass. Which mark and badges continued also in his posterity; and most of his descendants have very red beards. Moreover, having borne seven consulships, triumphed likewise and been censor twice, and therewith having been chosen into the rank of patrician, they all remained in the same surname. Neither were they known by any other forenames than Gnaius and Lucius or the variety thereof which is worthy of note: For some continued either of the said names in three persons together; others changed one after another in alternation in every descent. We have heard say that the first, second, and third of these Aenobarbi were forenamed Lucii. And again, the next three following them in order were Gnaei. All the rest, no otherwise than by their turns one after another had their forenames, first Lucii and then Gnaei. That many persons descended of this house should be known, I suppose it very pertinent and material; whereby it might the better appear that Nero degenerated from the virtues of his ancestors, and as yet he carried away and resembled the vices of them all, as though inbred by nature.

2. To fetch the beginning therefore of this our discourse somewhat farther back, his great grandfather's grandfather Gnaius Domitius, being in his tribunate much offended at the pontiffs for electing any other but himself into his father's place, transferred the right of subrogating priests in the place of those that were deceased, from their college to the body of the people. But in his consulship, having vanquished the Allobroges and the Arverni, he rode through his province mounted upon an elephant, while the whole multitude of his soldiers attended upon him in a train after the manner of a solemn triumph. This Domitius it was, of whom Licinius Crassus the orator said, in a certain declamation, it was no marvel that he had a brazen beard, since his face was made of iron, and his heart of lead. His son, being praetor, was the man, who as Caesar went out of his consulship (which he was thought to have borne against the auspices and the laws) summoned him before the Senate to be examined, tried and censured by them. Afterwards when he was consul, he attempted to fetch Caesar back, who was then general of an army, from his forces in Gaul; and being by the adverse faction nominated Caesar's successor in that province, was taken prisoner in the beginning of the civil war before Corfinium. From whence being dismissed and set at liberty, after he had, by his coming, much strengthened the Massilians who were then under siege, he forsook them and, in the end, at the battle of Pharsalia lost his life. He was a man not very constant and resolute, but withal of a savage nature. Being driven to utter despair, he was so much afraid of death, which for fear he had desired, that after a draught of poison he repented the taking thereof and

cast it up again; and he enfranchised his physician, who of purpose had so tempered it that it might do him no great harm. And when Gnaius Pompey put to question what should be done to those neutrals who stood indifferent, he alone opined that they were to be reckoned enemies and proceeded against them accordingly.

3. He left behind him a son, worthy without question to be preferred before all others of his name and lineage. This man being among those that were implicated in Caesar's death, and of that conspiracy, stood condemned (though guiltless) by the law of Paedia. When he had betaken himself to Cassius and Brutus his near kinsfolk, after the death of them both, he held still in his hand the fleet committed before to his charge, and augmented it. Neither did he yield it up to Marcus Antonius before his own side was everywhere quite overthrown; and he then did it of his own accord, so that Antony took himself highly beholden unto him therefore. He only also of all those who by virtue of the like law stood condemned was restored into his native country, and went through the most honorable offices of state. Soon after, when civil dissension was renewed, being in quality of lieutenant to the said Antony, when the sovereign empire was offered to him by those who were ashamed of Cleopatra, he did not dare to accept it nor yet to refuse it resolutely, by reason of sudden sickness, and went and sided with Augustus, and within a few days departed this life. And he was also noted with some infamy; for Antony gave it forth commonly that for the love of one Servilia Nais whom he kept, he fled to Augustus' side.

4. From him came that Domitius, who soon after had the name abroad to have been the executor of Augustus' goods and substance left by his will. He was a man no less renowned in his youth for good skill in the ruling of chariots, as he was afterwards for the triumphant ornaments achieved by the

German war. But he was arrogant of spirit, wasteful in expense, and therewith cruel. When he was aedile he forced Lucius Plancus that had been censor, to give way to him on the street. Bearing the honorable offices of praetor and consul, he produced upon the stage the gentlemen and dames of Rome, to act a comical and wanton interlude. He exhibited baiting of wild beasts both in the circus and also in every quarter of the city, and a show of sword-fight. But this he did with so great cruelty that Augustus was compelled of necessity to restrain him by an edict, since no secret warning nor admonition at his hands would prevail.

5. Of Antonia the elder, he begot the father of Nero, a man in all the parts of his life ungracious and detestable. For accompanying Gaius Caesar in his youth into the East, he killed a freedman of his own, because he refused to quaff as much as he was commanded. Being discharged therefore out of the cohort of his friends, he led his life never a whit more modestly; but both within a village standing upon the street Appia suddenly put his horses to gallop, and not unwittingly rode over a little child and trod him to death; and also at Rome in the midst of the Forum plucked a Roman knight's eye out of his head, for chiding him somewhat over boldly. He was so false and perfidious besides, that he defrauded not only the money-changers of the prices of such commodities as they had brought up, but also when he was praetor cheated the chariot runners of the prizes of their victories. For which pranks he was reproved in jest even by his own sister (Lepida), and upon complaint made by the masters of the four factions he enacted, that from thenceforth ever after, the said prizes should be presently paid. Being accused likewise for treason to the state and many adulteries, as also for incest committed with his sister Lepida a little before the decease of Tiberius, he escaped the law by the alteration of the times, and died at Pyr-

gae of the dropsy, when Agrippina daughter to Germanicus had brought him a son named Nero.

6. This Nero was born at Antium, nine months after that Tiberius departed this world, eighteen days before the Kalends of January, just as the sun was newly risen, so that its beams were well near upon him before he could touch the earth. As touching his horoscope, many men straightways gave many guesses and conjectures of fearful events. And even a very word that his father Domitius spoke was taken to be a presaging omen. For when his friends by way of congratulation wished him joy of his son newborn, he said, that of himself and Agrippina there could nothing come into the world but accursed, detestable and to the hurt of the public welfare. Of the same future infortunity there appeared an evident sign upon his naming day. For when his sister (Agrippina) requested Gaius Caesar (Caligula) to give the infant what name he would, looking wistly on Claudius his uncle (who afterwards, being emperor, adopted Nero), said he gave him his name. Neither spoke he this in earnest, but in jest; and Agrippina scorned and rejected it, for at that time Claudius went for a fool and the laughing stock of the court. At three years of age Nero became fatherless. And being his father's heir but of one third part, yet he could not touch so much as that, full and whole, by reason of Gaius his co-heir, who had seized upon all the goods. And his mother also was soon after confined and packed away; he, being in manner destitute of all help and very needy, was fostered in his Aunt Lepida's house under two pedagogues, a dancer and a barber. But when Claudius was come once to the empire, Nero not only recovered his patrimony, but also was enriched by the inheritance of Crispus Passienus, his mother's husband, that fell unto him. And verily through the grace and power of his mother now called home again and restored to her estate, he flourished and grew so great, that

commonly it was bruited abroad, that Messalina the wife of Claudius sent some of purpose to take the opportunity of his noon's sleep, and so to strangle him, as the only rival of Britannicus, and one that eclipsed the light of his glory. Now in the tale it went besides, that the said parties took a fright at a dragon issuing out of his pillow, whereupon they fled back, and forsook the enterprise. Which fable arose upon this, that there was indeed found the slough of a serpent in his bed about the bolsters. And yet, this slough he enclosed within a bracelet of gold (as his mother willed him) and wore it a good while after, upon his right arm; and at length, weary of any memorial of his mother's, flung it away. But in the extremity and despair of his estate he sought for the same again in vain.

7. In his tender years, and while he was yet a boy of no full growth, he acted at the circus the warlike Troy fight most resolutely, with great favor and applause of the people. In the eleventh year of his age he was adopted by Claudius and put to school unto Annaeus Seneca, even then a senator. The report goes that Seneca, the next night following, dreamed as he lay in bed that he was teaching Gaius Caesar; and shortly after Nero proved his dream true, betraying the fell stomach and shrewd nature of the said prince, by the first experiments that he could give thereof. For when his brother Britannicus saluted him after he was once adopted (as his wonted manner was before) by the name of Aenobarbus, he went about to lay this imputation upon Britannicus before his father, that he was some changeling. His aunt Lepida likewise being in trouble, he deposed against in the open face of the court, thereby to gratify his mother, who followed the suit hotly against her. Being honorably brought into the Forum, the day of his first plea and commencement, he promised publicly for the people a congiary and donative for the soldiers. Having proclaimed also a solemn jousting, he himself rode before the praetorian soldiers

bearing a shield in his own hand. After this he solemnly gave thanks to his father in the senate. Before whom being then consul, he made a Latin oration in the behalf of the Bononians, and another in Greek for the Rhodians and inhabitants of Ilium. His first jurisdiction he began as provost of the city, during the celebration of the Latin holidays; what time the most famous advocates and patrons in those days strove a-vie, who could bring before him most accusations and longest – not (as the manner was) such as were ordinary and brief; notwithstanding the express commandment of Claudius forbidding the same. Not long after, he took to wife Octavia; and for the good health of Claudius, exhibited the circus games and baiting of wild beasts.

8. Being seventeen years old, so soon as it was known abroad that Claudius was dead, he came forth to those of the praetorian cohort that kept watch between the sixth and the seventh hour of the day; for by reason that the whole day besides was ominous and dismal, there was no time thereof thought more auspicious and convenient than it to enter upon the empire. And so being proclaimed and saluted emperor before the palace stairs, he was in a litter brought to the camp; and hastily from thence, after a short speech made unto the soldiers, was conveyed into the Curia. From whence he departed home in the evening; and of those exceeding and infinite honors which were heaped upon him, he refused only the title of *Pater Patriae*, in regard of his young years.

9. Beginning then with a glorious show of piety and kindness at the funerals of Claudius, which were most sumptuously performed, he praised him in an oration and consecrated him a god. In the memorial of his own father Domitius, he did him right great honor. His mother he permitted to have the whole regiment of all matters as well public as private. The very first day also of his empire, when the tribune of the sentinels asked

of him a watchword, he gave unto him this word, *Optima mater* (my best mother), and afterwards many a time she accompanied him through the streets in his own litter. He planted a colony at Antium, enrolling therein the old soldiers out of the praetorian cohort, and joining with them (by translating their habitations) the richest centurions; here also he made a harbor, a most sumptuous piece of work.

10. And to show a surer proof still of his towardness, after profession made to govern the empire according to the prescript rule of Augustus, he omitted no occasion to show either bountifulness or clemency, no nor so much as to testify his gentleness and courtesy. Those tributes and taxes which were anything heavy he either abolished or abated. The rewards due unto informers as touching the Law Papia he reduced to the fourth part only of the penalty. Having dealt among the people four hundred sesterces for every poll, he allowed yearly salaries to as many senators as were most nobly descended (howbeit decayed and weakened in their estates), and to some of them 500,000 sesterces. Likewise for the praetorian cohorts he ordained an allowance of corn monthly gratis. And whensoever he was put in mind to subscribe and set his hand to a warrant (as the manner is) for the execution of any person condemned to die, he would say, "Oh, that I knew not one letter of the book." Many times he saluted all the degrees of the city one after another, by rote and without book. When the senate upon a time gave him thanks, he answered, "(Do so) when I shall deserve." To his exercises in Mars field he admitted the commons also, yea and declaimed often publicly before them. He rehearsed his own verses likewise, not only within house at home, but also in the theater; and that with so general a joy of as many as heard him, that for the said rehearsal there was a solemn procession decreed; and some of his said verses written in golden letters were dedicated to Jupiter Capitolinus.

11. Many and sundry kinds of shows he set forth, to wit, the Juvenile sports, the Circeian games, and the stage plays; also a sword-fight. In the Juvenile pastimes, he admitted old men, even those of consul's degree; aged women also and matrons to disport themselves. At the *Circenses*, he appointed places for the knights of Rome apart by themselves, where he put also, to run a race for the prize, chariots drawn with four camels. In the stage plays (which, being instituted for the eternizing and perpetuity of his empire, he called *Maximi*), very many of both degrees [knights and senators] and sexes played their parts upon the stage. A Roman knight of very good note and especial mark mounted upon an elephant and ran down a rope. There was brought upon the stage to be acted the Roman comedy of Afranius entitled *Incendium*; and granted it was unto the actors therein to rifle all the goods and implements of the house as it burned, and to take the same as their own. Scattered also abroad there were for the people missiles, during the whole time of those plays, to wit, a thousand birds every day of all kinds, viands manifold, tickets and tallies for corn, apparel, gold, silver, precious stones, pearls, pictures, slaves, draught animals and beasts also tamed; last of all ships, isles, and lands.

12. These games he beheld from the top of the *proscenium*. At the sword-fight which he exhibited in the amphitheater built of timber in one year's space within the ward of Mars field he suffered not one man to be killed, no not so much as a guilty malefactor. Moreover, he brought into the lists for to fight even four hundred senators and six hundred knights of Rome. Some of good wealth and reputation, out of the same degrees, he caused to come forth into the show-place, for to kill wild beasts and perform sundry services thereto belonging. He represented also a naval fight upon salt water from the sea, with a device to have sea beasts swimming therein. Also certain Pyrrhic [warlike] dances in armor, sorted

out of the number of young men; and after their devoir done, he gave freely unto every one of them patents to be enfranchised citizens of Rome. Between the arguments of these Pyrrhic dances, it was devised that a bull should mount Pasiphae, hidden within a frame of wood resembling an heifer, which was acted so lively that many of the beholders believed verily it was so indeed. As for Icarus, at the first attempt to fly, he fell presently down hard by Nero's own couch, so that he besprent him with blood. For very seldom had he used to sit as president at these games; but his manner was to behold them as he lay upon his bed; first through little peep-holes, but afterwards setting the whole gallery open from whence he looked. He was the first moreover that instituted at Rome, according to the Greek fashion, quinquennial games of three kinds, to wit, of music and poetry, of gymnic masteries, and of horsemanship; which games he called Neronia. After he had dedicated the baths and a place therein for gymnic exercises, he allowed the oil that went thereto both for the senate and also for the knights. He ordained wardens of all this solemnity, especial persons of consular degree, chosen by lot to sit as overseers in the place of praetors, and then he came down himself into the *orchestra* and the senators' quarter. And verily the victorious coronet for the Latin tongue, both in prose and verse, about which the best and most worshipful persons had contended, when it was granted unto him with their own consents he received; and the harp presented unto him by the judges he adored and commanded that it should be carried to the statue of Augustus. At the gymnic games which he exhibited in the *Septa*, during the solemn preparation of the great sacrifice of oxen, he cut off the first beard that he had, which he bestowed within a golden box, adorned it with most precious pearls, and then consecrated it in the Capitol [to Jupiter Capitolinus]. To the show of wrestlers and other athletes he called also the Vestal Virgins, because at Olympia the priestesses likewise of Ceres are allowed to see the games there.

13. I may by good reason, among other shows exhibited by him, reckon also the entrance into Rome of Tiridates, whom, being the king of Armenia, Nero had solicited by large promises. Now when he meant to show him unto the people upon a set day appointed by an edict, and was driven to put it off (the weather being so cloudy), he brought him forth before them to be seen upon the best and most opportune day that he could find. Having bestowed about the temples situated in the Forum cohorts of armed soldiers, he himself sat upon his ivory curule chair of estate before the rostra in triumphal habit, among the military ensigns, banners, and streamers. And as the king came up towards him by the ascent of the steep pulpit, he admitted him first to his knees; and then raising up with his right hand kissed him. Afterwards as he was making his prayer unto him, having taken off his tiara, he put on the diadem. While one who had been practor pronounced unto the multitude the suppliant's words, as they were delivered unto him by an interpreter. Being brought after this into the theater and making supplication again, he placed Tiridates on his right side next to himself. For which Nero was with one accord saluted emperor; and so bringing with him the laurel branch into the Capitol, he shut both doors of double-faced Janus' temple, as if no relic of war remained behind.

14. Four consulships he bore; the first for two months, the second and last for three, the third for four. The middle two he continued without any intermission; the rest he varied with a year's space between.

15. In his ordinary jurisdiction, he lightly gave no decision before the day following, and that was by writing. In trials this course he held, namely, to decide every cause by itself one after another, upon certain days of the session; and to cease

the huddling up and debatements of matters. So often as he went aside to consult, he deliberated and asked advice of nothing either in common or openly; but reading secretly to himself the opinions written by every counselor, he pronounced what liked his own self, as if many more thought well of the same. For a long time he admitted not the sons of libertines into the Curia; and to those that were admitted by the emperors his predecessors he denied all honorable offices. If there sued for magistracies more than there were places void, he gave unto them the conduct of legions, to comfort their hearts again for delaying and making them to stay longer. He granted for the most part all consulships for six months' term. And if one of the two consuls happened to die about the Kalends of January, he substituted none in his stead; as misliking altogether the old precedent of Caninius Rebilus, who was consul but one day. Triumphal ornaments he gave even unto those that had born quaestor's dignity only, yea and to some of the knight's degree, and verily not always for any military service. His orations sent into the senate concerning certain matters, he caused for the most part to be read and rehearsed by the consuls, passing by the quaestor's office [unto whom properly it appertained].

16. He devised a new form of the city buildings, and namely, that before the edifices there should be porches. From the roofs whereof, all fires might be put out: and those he built at his own charges. He had an intention once to set out and enlarge the walls of Rome, even as far as to Ostia; and from thence by a canal to let the sea into old Rome. Many matters under him were both severely punished and also restrained, yea and likewise newly ordained. Expenses in his days had a gauge set upon them. The public suppers were brought down to small collations. It was forbidden that anything cooked, but only pulse and vegetables should be sold in taverns and cook's

houses; whereas before time, there was no manner of viands but it was set out to sale. The Christians, a kind of men given to a new and wicked superstition, were put to death with grievous torments. The sports of charioteers, wherein by an old and licentious custom they had been allowed to range up and down, to beguile folk, to pilfer in merriment, were prohibited. The factions of the mimes together with the actors themselves were banished and sent away.

17. Against forgers of writings, then first came up this invention, that no books or instruments should be signed unless they were bored and had a thread three times drawn through the holes. Provided it was that in wills the two first parts thereof should be showed as blanks, unto those that came to seal the same, having the testator's name only written therein. Also, that no clerk who was to draw and write another man's will should put down any legacy for himself. Also, that they who had suits pending in court, should pay the certain due fee set down by law, for pleading of their causes; but for the benches nothing, considering the city allowed the same gratis. Also, that in the pleading and deciding of controversies all causes debated aforetime before the treasury should be removed unto the Forum, to be tried before the arbiters. Finally, that all appeals from the judges should be made unto the senate.

18. Having no will, no motion, nor hope at any time to propagate and enlarge the empire, he thought once to have the forces withdrawn even out of Britain; neither gave he over that intent of his, but only for very shame lest he might be thought to deprave the glory of his father (Claudius). Only the realm of Pontus with the leave of Polemon, as also the kingdom of the Alps, by the death of king Cottius, he reduced into the form of a province.

19. Two voyages and no more he undertook, the one to Alexandria, the other into Achaia. But his journey to Alexan-

dria he gave over the very day of his setting forth; by occasion that he was disquieted at once, both with a religious scruple and also with some peril. For when he had gone in procession about all the temples, and had sat down within the chapel of Vesta, as he was rising up, first the hem of his gown stuck to the seat, and after this there arose so dark a mist before his eyes, that he could see nothing. In Achaia he attempted to dig through Isthmus, and made a speech unto the praetorian soldiers, exhorting them to begin the work; and having given the signal by sound of trumpet, he himself first broke up the earth, carried it forth upon his own shoulders in a scuttle. He prepared also an expedition to the Caspian gates, for which he enrolled a new legion of Italian soldiers six feet high; this legion he called the Phalanx of Alexander the Great. These particulars premised, partly deserving no blame, and in part worthy even of no mean praise, I have collected together, that I might sever and distinguish them from Nero's villainies and wicked acts, whereof from henceforward I will make report.

20. Among other arts and sciences, he was in his childhood trained in the skill also of music. And he no sooner attained to the empire, but he sent for Terpsus the harper, renowned in those days for his cunning above all other. Sitting by him as he played and sung, day by day after supper until it was far in the night, Nero himself likewise by little and little began to practice and exercise the same. And he let no means pass that expert professors in that kind were wont to do, either for preserving or the bettering and fortifying of their voices, even to wear before him upon his breast a thin plate of lead, to purge by clyster or vomit, to abstain from apples and fruit, withal such meats as were hurtful to the voice; so long, until his proceedings still drawing him on (a small and rusty voice though he had), he desired to come forth and show himself upon the open stage, having among his familiar companions

this Greek proverb evermore in his mouth, that hidden music was nought worth. The first time that he mounted the stage was at Naples, where he gave not over singing (albeit the theater was shaken and ready to fall by a sudden earthquake), before he had finished the song begun. In the same place he chanted often and many days together. Moreover, after some short time between taken to repair his voice (as one impatient of keeping within house), from the baths there he passed directly to the theater; and having in the midst of the orchestra before a multitude of people feasted and banqueted, made promise in the Greek tongue that if he had sipped a little and wet his whistle, he would ring out some note more fully and with a stronger breast. Now, being much delighted with the Alexandrines' praises of him in song, who newly in a second voyage had with their fleet conflowed to Naples, he sent for more of them out of Alexandria. And never the later he chose from all parts youths of knights' degree, and not so few as five thousand of the lustiest and strongest young men out of the commons, who, being sorted into factions, would learn certain kinds of shouts and applauses, which they termed bees, tiles, and bricks [from the sounds produced by the humming of bees, or the clapping together of the hands, held round like tiles, or flat like bricks]; also that deft and trim boys, such as had the thickest bush of hair upon their heads, and were set out in most excellent apparel, and not without a ring on their left hands, should give their attendance upon him as he sung. The leaders of these had for their stipend 400,000 sesterces.

21. Esteeming so highly as he did of singing, he solemnized at Rome also again the foresaid games called *Neroneum* before the day and time by order appointed. And when all the people called upon him for his celestial voice, he made answer, that he verily would do them that pleasure (being so willing and desirous as they were to hear him); but it should be in his

gardens. Howbeit, when the corps de guard seconded the prayers of the common people, willingly he promised to fulfill their minds out of hand in the very place; and without any further delay caused his own name to be written in the roll of other professed minstrels and singers to the harp. Thus having put his lot into the pitcher with the rest, he entered the stage when his turn came, and withal the captains of the guard supporting his harp; after them the tribunes military, and close unto them his most inward friends. Now when he had taken up his standing, and ended his poem, he gave public notice and pronounced by the voice of Cluvius Rufus (no meaner man than of consul's degree) that he would sing and act the story of Niobe, and so continued he well near unto the tenth hour of the day; which done he deferred the music coronet due for the present victory, together with the residue of that gaming unto the next year following, and all because he might have occasion oftener to chant. But bethinking himself that the time was long, he ceased not to come ever and anon abroad to show his skill in open place. He stuck not also in private shows and games to do his devoir, even among common actors and stage players; and namely, when one of the praetors made offer of a million sesterces. He sung moreover, disguised, tragedies of the worthies and gods, of noble ladies likewise in old time and of goddesses, having their visards framed and made to the likeness of his own face and of some woman whom he loved. Among the rest he chanted the tale of Canace travailing in childbirth, of Orestes who killed his own mother, of Oedipus that plucked out his own eyes, and of Hercules enraged. In the acting of which tragedy, the report goes that a novice placed to guard the entry of the stage, seeing him dressed and bound with chains (as the argument of the said tragedy required) ran in a good haste to help him.

22. Exceedingly given he was of a boy to delight in horse-

manship, and with the love of charioting mightily inflamed; and very much would he be talking (forbidden though he were) of the Circeian games. And one time as he was bewailing among his school-fellows the hard fortune of a chariot driver, and of one of the greencoat faction who was drawn and dragged by his steeds, being chidden therefor by his school-master, he had a lie ready, and said that he spoke of Hector. But, as about his first entrance to the empire, his custom was daily to play upon a board with ivory horses drawing chariots, so he used to resort from his retiring place to all the circus games, even the very least and meanest of them. First by stealth and privily; afterwards in open sight; so as no man made doubt, but at such a day he would be sure always there to be. Neither dissimuled he that he was willing to augment the number of the prizes. And therefore the show of chariot-running was drawn out in length and held until late in the evening, by oc-casion of many more courses than ordinary; so as now the masters of every faction deigned not to bring forth their crews and companies unless they might run the whole day through. Soon after, he himself also would needs make one and be seen ofttimes to play the charioteer. And when he had tried what he could do, and performed, as it were, his first acts in private gardens among very slaves and the base commons, he pro-ceeded to show himself in the Circus Maximus in all men's eyes, appointing one of his freedmen to put out a white towel for a signal from the place where magistrates are wont to do it. But not content with this, that he had given good proof of his progress in these feats at Rome, he goes, as I said before, into Achaia, moved especially upon this occasion. Those cities and states where solemn gamings of music are usually held, had brought up a custom to send all the coronets of harp-players unto him. This he accepted so kindly, that he not only ad-mitted at the very first to his presence the ambassadors who

325

brought the same, but also placed them among his familiar guests at the table. And being requested by some of them to sing at supper time, and highly praised with excessive applause, he came out with this speech, that Graecians were the only skillful hearers, and the men alone worthy of his studies. Neither made he any longer stay, but took his voyage; and no sooner was he passed over the sea to Cassiope, but presently he began to sing at the altar there of Jupiter Cassius.

23. After this, he went to all the games of prize, one after another; for even those that usually are celebrated at most remote and distant times he commanded to be reduced all into one year, and some of them also to be iterated [solemnized twice in the same year]. At Olympia likewise he caused (contrary to the manner and custom of that place) a game of music to be held. And lest while he was busied about these matters, anything might either call him away or detain him; when he was advertised by his freedman Helius, that the city affairs required his presence, he wrote back unto him in these words, "Albeit your counsel to me and your willing desire is that I should return with all speed, yet ought you to advise me and wish rather that I may return worthy of myself, that is to say Nero." All the while he was singing, lawful it was not for any person to depart out of the theater, were the cause never so necessary. Whereupon reported it is, that some great-bellied women falling into travail were delivered upon the very scaffolds; yea and many men besides, weary of tedious hearing and praising him, when the town gates were shut, either by stealth leapt down from the walls, or counterfeiting themselves dead were carried forth as corpses to be buried. But how timorously, with what thought and anguish of mind, with what emulation of his concurrents and fear of the umpires he strove for the mastery, it is almost incredible. His manner was to deal with his adversaries as if they had been but his

equals and of the same condition with him, in this sort;
namely, to observe, watch and mark their behaviors; to de-
fame them underhand; otherwhiles to rail at them and give
them hard terms as they came in his way; yea and to corrupt
with bribes and gifts such as excelled in skill and cunning. As
for the judges and umpires aforesaid, he would speak unto them
in all reverence before he began to sing, using these terms –
that he had done whatsoever was to be done; howbeit, the
issue and event was in the hand of fortune; they therefore, as
they were wise men and learned ought to except and bar all
chances and mishaps. Now upon their exhortations unto him
for to be bold and venturous, he would indeed go away from
them better appeased, but yet for all that not without pensive
care and trouble of mind. Finding fault also with the silence
and bashful modesty of some, as if the same argued their discontented heaviness and malicious repining, he said withal that
he had them in suspicion.

24. During the time that he strove for to win any prize, so
strictly obeyed he the laws of the game, that he never durst
once spit and reach up phlegm; and the very sweat of his
forehead he wiped away with his arm only. Moreover in the
acting of a tragedy, when he had quickly taken up his staff
again, which he happened to let fall, being much dismayed
and in great fear, lest for that delinquency he should be put
from the stage, by no means took he heart again, until an
under actor or prompter standing by swore an oath that it
was not espied and marked for the shouts and acclamations of
the people beneath. Now, whensoever he won the victory, he
used to pronounce himself victor. For which cause he contended also in every place for the crier's coronet [due to him
that had the loudest voice]. And to the end that there should
remain extant no memorial or token of any other victors in
these sacred games beside himself, he commanded all their

statues and images to be overthrown, drawn with a drag, and so flung into sinks and privies. Furthermore, he ran with chariots for the best game in many places, and at the Olympic solemnities with one that had a team of ten steeds, notwithstanding he reproved the very same thing in king Mithridates, as appeared by certain verses of his own making. But being once shaken and hoisted out of his chariot and set therein again, howbeit not able to hold out, he desisted and gave over, before he had run the race through. Yet was he crowned nevertheless. After this, at his departure from thence, he enfranchised the whole province throughout; and withal, the judges of these games he endowed with citizenship, and rewarded with great sums of money. Which benefits of his he himself published with his own voice from the middle of the race, upon a day of the Isthmian games.

25. Being returned out of Greece he entered Naples mounted upon a chariot drawn with white horses; for that in the said city he had made profession first of his skill in music; and a part of the wall was cast down against his coming (as the manner is of all victors in those sacred games). In like manner he rode into Antium, and from thence into Albanum and so forward into Rome. But he entered Rome in the very same chariot wherein sometime Augustus had ridden in triumph, clad in a purple cloak, and the same garnished with stars embroidered in gold, wearing upon his head the Olympic coronet, and bearing in his right hand the Pythian, with a pomp and gallant show of the rest before him, together with their titles and inscriptions testifying where, and whom, in what kind of song or fabulous argument, he had won; not without a train also of applauders, following his chariot, after the manner of those that ride escorting a petty triumph, crying with a loud voice that they were Augustines, and the soldiers of his triumph. From thence he rode forward, and having thrown

down the arch of the Circus Maximus, he passed on through the Velebrum and Forum, up to the Palatium and so to the temple of Apollo. To do him honor all the way as he went, were beasts killed for sacrifice, and saffron eftsoons strewed along the streets. Birds were let fly, ribbons also and labels yea and sweetmeats cast among. As for the sacred coronets and garlands aforesaid, he bestowed them in his own bed-chamber round about his beds; likewise his own statues portrayed in the habit of an harper, and with that mark stamped he his money. And after all this (so far was he from letting slack and remitting one jot his ardent study of his music profession), that for the preservation of his voice he would never make speech unto his soldiers, but in absentia, or having another to pronounce his words for him [when he himself was present]. Nor yet would he do ought in earnest or mirth without his elocutionist by, to put him in mind to spare his pipes and hold his handkerchief to his mouth; and to many a man he either offered friendship, or denounced enemy, according as everyone praised him more or less.

26. His unruly wildness, unbridled lust, wasteful riotousness, avarice and cruelty, he practiced verily at first by leisure closely, as the tricks of youthful folly; yet so, as even then no man might doubt that they were the inbred vices of nature, and not the errors of young age. No sooner was it twilight and the evening shut in but presently he would catch up a cap on his head, and so disguised, go into taverns and victualing houses, walk the streets playing and sporting all the way, but yet not without shrewd turns and doing mischief. For he used to fall upon those that came late from supper and knock them soundly; yea and (if they struggled with him and made resistance) to wound and drown them in the town ditches; to break into petty shops also, and rifle them. For he had set up in his house at home a fair, there to receive the price of the booty which

he had gotten, and was to be sold to who would give most and bid best therefor. But many a time at such brawls and scufflings aforesaid, he endangered his eyes, yea and his life too; being once beaten well near to death by a certain young gentleman of senator's degree, whose wife he had misused with unclean handling. Whereupon, never after durst he go abroad into the streets at that hour of the night without his military tribunes following after him aloof and secretly. In the daytime also, being carried close in a chair into the theater, he would be present in person, and from the upper part of the *proscenium* [the forestage] both give a signal to the seditious factions of players (setting them together by the ears) and also behold them how they bickered. Now when they were come once to plain fight, skirmishing with stones and fragments of broken seats, scaffolds, himself stuck not to fling apace at the people, in so much as once he broke the praetor's head.

27. But as his vices grew by little and little to get head, he laid aside these wild tricks by way of sport and in secret; and without all care of concealing and dissimuling the matter, broke out openly to greater outrages. His meals he drew out at length, eating and drinking from noon to midnight, doused and fomented oftentimes in cisterns of hot waters, and in summer season within baths made cold with snow. His suppers he took divers times abroad also in public place, to wit, in the Naumachia shut up and enclosed, or in Mars field, or else in the Circus Maximus, where he was served and attended upon by all the common queans of the city and strumpets of the stews. So often as he went down the river Tiber to Ostia, or sailed along the Baian Bay, there were provided in divers places of the banks booths to bait in, conspicuous brothel houses and taverns; where stood married dames after the manner of hostesses and victualling wives on both sides of the banks, entreating him to land and turn in to them. His manner was

also to give warning unto his familiar friends, and bid himself to supper; and one of them it cost in sweetmeats four million sesterces; and another a good deal more in rose water and odoriferous oils.

28. Over and besides the unnatural abusing of boys freeborn, and the keeping of men's wives as his concubines, he forced also and deflowered Rubria, a Vestal Virgin. Acte, a freed-woman, he went very near to have wedded as his lawful wife, suborning certain men who had been consuls to avouch and forswear that she was of royal blood descended. A boy there was named Sporus, whose genitals he cut out, and essayed thereby to transform him into the nature of a woman. Him he caused to be brought unto him as a bride, with a dowry, in a fine saffron veil, after the solemn manner of marriage; not without a frequent and goodly train attending upon him; whom he maintained as his wife. Hereupon there goes abroad a pretty jest of a pleasant fellow, that it might have been well and happy with the world, if his father Domitius had wedded such a wife. This Sporus trimly set out with the jewels, decked with the ornaments of the empresses, and carried in a litter, he accompanied all about the shire-towns of great resort and market of Greece; yea and afterwards at Rome, up and down the street Sigillaria, many a time sweetly kissing him by the way. For, that he had a lust to lie with his own mother, and was frightened from it by some depraving back-friends of hers; for fear, lest the proud and insolent dame might by this kind of favor grow too mighty, no man ever made doubt; especially after that he entertained among his concubines a harlot, most like in all points (by report) unto Agrippina. It is affirmed moreover, that in times past, so often as he rode in a litter together with his mother, he played the filthy wanton, and was betrayed by the stains appearing upon her vesture.

29. As for his own body, certes, he forfeited the honor

thereof, prostituting it to be abused so far forth, as having defiled in manner all the parts of it, at the last, he devised a kind (as it were) of sport and game, that being covered all over in a wild beast's skin, he should be let loose forth of a cage and then give the assault upon the privities of men and women both as they stood tied fast to a stake; and when he had showed his rage to the full, be killed, forsooth, by Doriphorus his freedman, unto whom himself also was wedded like as Sporus unto him; insomuch as he counterfeited the noise and cries of maidens, when they be forced and suffer devirgination. I have heard of divers that he was fully persuaded, no man nor woman was honest, or in any part of their bodies pure and clean, but most of them dissimuled their uncleanliness and craftily hid it. As many therefore as professed unto him their obscene filthiness, he forgave all other faults and trespasses whatsoever. ["I wish that both Suetonius and Dio had in this place and such like been altogether silent." – Translator].

30. The fruit of riches and use of money he took to be nothing else but lavish expense; thinking them to be very base niggards and mechanical pinch-pennies, that kept any account or reckoning what they spent and laid out, but such only passing rich and right magnificos, who misspent and wasted all. He praised and admired his uncle Gaius in no respect more, than for that he had lashed out and consumed in a short space an huge mass of wealth, left unto him by Tiberius; he kept therefore no mean, nor made any end of prodigal giving and making away all. He allowed unto Tiridates (a thing almost incredible) 800,000 sesterces, day by day, for his expenses, and at his departure bestowed upon him not so little as one hundred million. Menecrates the harper, and Spicillus the sword-fencer he gave patrimonies and houses equal to those of right noble personages who had triumphed. Cercopithecus, whom he had enriched with the lands and houses (as well within the city as

country) of Panercos the usurer, he honored like a prince at his funerals; and interred with the charges well near of a royal sepulture. No garments put he on his back twice; at hazard when he played, he ventured no less than 400,000 sesterces at a cast, upon every point or prick of the chance. He fished with a golden net (drawn and knit) with cords twisted of purple and crimson silk in grain. He never by report when he made any journey, had under a thousand carriages in his train. His mules were shod with silver. His muleteers arrayed in fine red Canusme cloth; and attended he was with a multitude of Mazaces horsemen of Africa and Cappadocia and couriers gaily set out with their bracelets and rich trappings.

31. In no one thing was he more wasteful and prodigal than in building. He made a house, that reached from the Palatine to the Esquiline, which at first he called his Transitory; but when it had been consumed with fire and was re-edified he named his golden edifice. As touching the large compass and receipt, the rich furniture and setting out whereof, it may suffice to relate thus much. The porch was of such a height as therein might stand upright the giant-like image representing his own person, a hundred and twenty feet high. So large was this house, as that it contained three galleries of a mile apiece in length. Also, a standing pool like unto a sea, and the same enclosed round about with buildings in form of cities. It received moreover granges with cornfields, vineyards, pastures and woods to them stored with a multitude of divers and sundry beasts both tame and wild of all sorts. In all other parts thereof, all was laid over with gold, garnished with precious stones and shells of pearls. As for the parlors, framed they were with bowed roofs, ceiled with panels of ivory devised to turn round and remove so as flowers might be scattered from thence; with a device also of pipes and spouts to sprinkle sweet oils from aloft. But of all these parlors and banqueting rooms, the prin-

cipal and fairest was made round, to turn about continually both day and night, in manner of the world. The baths within this house flowed with salt water derived from the sea, and with fresh from the rivers Albulae. This edifice finished after such a fashion, when he dedicated it, thus far forth only he deigned to say: that, he now at length began to dwell like a man. Furthermore, he began a pool reaching from Misenum to Lake Avernus, covered all above head, enclosed and environed with cloisers; into which all the hot waters that were in the baths of Baiae might be conveyed. Likewise he cast a fosse from the said Avernus as far as to Ostia, and the same navigable, that men forsooth might sail in ships, and yet not be upon the sea. This carried in length 160 miles, and bore that breadth, as galleys with five ranks of oars might pass to and fro thereupon. For the performance of these works, he had given commandment that all prisoners wheresoever should be transported into Italy, and that no person convict of any wicked act should be condemned otherwise but to work thereat.

32. To these outrageous expenses, beside the trust and confidence he had in the revenues of the empire, put forward he was upon a certain unexpected hope also that he conceived, of finding a world of wealth; and that through intelligence given unto him by a knight of Rome, who assured him upon his knowledge that the rich treasure and old store of silver and gold both, which queen Dido flying out of Tyre carried away with her, lay buried in Africa within vast caves under the ground, and might be gotten forth with some small labor of those that would go about it. But when this hope failed him and came to nothing, being now altogether destitute, and so far exhausted and bare of money, that of necessity even soldiers' pay, and the fees due unto old servitors in the wars for their service must be deferred, he bent his mind to promoting of false imputations, to pilling also and polling.

First and foremost he brought up this order, that out of the goods of freedmen deceased instead of the one half, three fourth parts should be exacted and gathered for him, of as many, I say, as without public cause bore that name which any of those families did, whereunto himself was allied. Afterwards, that their wills should be forfeit and confiscated who were unthankful to the prince [remembered him not in their wills]. Also, that lawyers should not escape free and go clear away who had drawn and written such wills; and also, that all deeds and words should be brought within the compass of treason if there could be found but any promoter to give information. He called moreover after a long time passed for the rewards and coronets due to victors, which ever at any time the city and state had presented or decreed unto him at the games of prize. And wheareas he had prohibited the use of the amethyst and purple colors, he suborned one of purpose underhand to sell upon a market day some few ounces thereof, and thereupon made stay of all occupiers and chapmen whatsoever, and laid them fast. Furthermore, having espied once (as he was singing) a dame of Rome from the scaffolds in the theater, arrayed in purple forbidden by the law, himself pointed at her (as it is verily thought) and showed her to his procurators; and presently caused the woman to be hailed from thence and turned out, not only of her garments but also of all the goods she had. He assigned an office to no man, but he used these words withal, "thou knowest what I have need of." Also, "let us look to this, that no man may have anything." To conclude, he robbed the temples of many gifts and oblations; the images likewise therein made of gold or silver he melted into a mass; and among the rest, even those of the tutelar gods of Rome, which soon after Galba restored and erected again in their places.

33. As touching his parricides and murders he began them

first with Claudius, of whose death although he were not principal author, yet he was privy and accessory thereto. Neither dissimuled he so much, as who afterwards was wont by a Greek by-word to praise mushrooms (in which kind of meat Claudius had taken his bane) as the food of the gods. Certes, he abused him after he was dead in most spiteful and contumelious manner, both in word and deed, every way, taunting and twitting him, one while with his folly, another while with his cruelty. For in scoffing wise he would say of him that he had ceased *morari* any longer among mortal men, using the first syllable of the said word long [*morari*, to linger or delay; *mōrari*, to play the fool]. And many of Claudius' decrees and constitutions he annulled as the acts of a doltish and doting man. Finally, he neglected the place of his funeral fire, suffering it to be empaled, but with slight stuff and low rails of timber.

As for Britannicus, not so much for envy that he had a sweeter and pleasanter voice than himself, as for fear lest another day he should be more gracious than he among men, in remembrance of his father, he attempted to make him away by poison. This poison, Nero had received at the hands of one Locusta, a woman who appeached and brought to light divers confectioners of poisons; and seeing it wrought later than he looked it should do, and proved not to his mind, by reason that it moved Britannicus to the stool only, he sent for the said woman, and beat her with his own hands; laying hardly to her charge that instead of a poison she had given him a remedy and wholesome medicine. Now when she alleged for her excuse that she gave him the lesser dose, thereby to color and cloak the odious fact, which would have bred much anger and hatred, he said, "Why! then belike I am afraid of the Law Julia." And so he forced her before his face in his own bed-chamber to compound and seethe a poison that should be most quick and of present operation. And then having made trial thereof in a kid, after he saw once that the beast continued five hours before it died, he caused the same to be boiled again and many times more, and so he set it before a pig. And when the pig died presently upon the taking thereof, he commanded it should be brought into his refection chamber, and given unto Britannicus as he sat at supper with him. No sooner had he tasted it but he fell down dead. Nero readily made a lie and gave it out among the guests that Britannicus was surprised by a fit of the falling sickness, as his manner was to be. But the next morrow, in all haste, he took order for his corpse to be carried forth in an exceeding great storm of rain. Unto the said Locusta, for her service done, he granted impunity; he endued her also with fair lands; yea and allowed her to have scholars for to be trained up under her in that feat.

34. His own mother, for looking narrowly into him, and examining his words and deeds somewhat straitly; for seeming also to correct and reform the same, thus far forth only at the first he was grieved and offended with, as that eftsoons he made her odious to the world, pretending that he was about to resign up the empire and depart to Rhodes. Soon after, he deprived her of all honor, dignity, and authority; and removing from about her the guard of German soldiers that attended upon her person, he banished her out of the same house with him, and so forth out of the precincts of the palace. Neither cared he what he did, so he might molest and trouble her, suborning some of purpose both to disquiet her while she abode in Rome with suits and actions; and also when she was desirous of repose and ease in a retiring place out of the way, to course her with reproachful taunts and flouting scoffs as they passed that way either by land or sea. But being terrified with her threats and violent shrewdness, he determined to kill her at once. Having attempted it with poison thrice, and perceiving that she was defended with antidotes, he provided a bed-

chamber for her, with so ticklish an arched roof over her head, as being easily unjointed, the frame thereof might fall in pieces in the night, and light upon her as she lay asleep. When this design could not be kept close, but was revealed by some of the complices privy thereto, he devised a ship, so made as that quickly it should cleave asunder; that either by the wrack, or fall of the fore-deck aloft, she might come to a mischief and perish. And so, making a semblance of a love-day and reconciliation, he sent for her by most sweet and kind letters, training her unto Baiae, there to celebrate with him the solemnity of the *Quinquatrian* [a feast in honor of Minerva, in March]. And having given order beforehand to certain masters of galleys for to split the foist wherein she was embarqued, as if by chance they were run full upon her, he made it late ere he went to the feast, and sat long at it. Now when she was to return back again unto Bauli, in lieu of that vessel thus shaken and cracked, he put unto her the other abovesaid made with joints and vices, easy to fall in pieces; and so, with a cheerful countenance accompanied her to the water side and at the parting also kissed her paps. All the time after, he lay awake in great trouble and fear, waiting for the issue of these enterprises. But when he understood that all went cross, and that she was escaped to land by swimming, being altogether to seek what course to take, as Lucius Agerinus, her freedman, brought word with great joy, how she was escaped alive and safe, he conveyed privily a dagger close by him; and as if he had been suborned and hired secretly by her to kill him, caused the said Agerinus to be apprehended and bound with chains; and withal, his mother aforesaid, to be murdered, pretending as if by voluntary death she had avoided the odious crime thus detected, and so made herself away.

Worse matter yet than all this and more horrible, is reported beside, and that by authors of good credit and who will stand

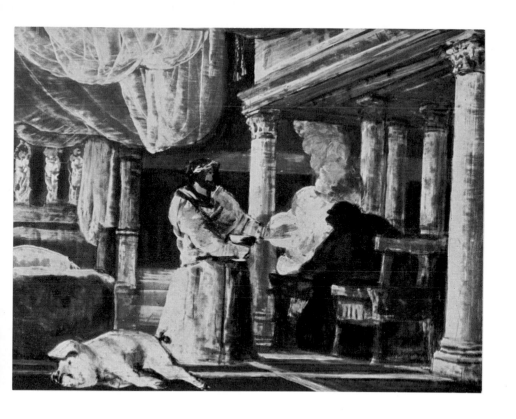

*And so he forced her before his face in his own bed-chamber to compound
and seethe a poison that should be most quick and of present operation. And
. . . he caused the same to be boiled again and many times more,
and so he set it before a pig.*

to it; namely, that he ran in all haste to view the dead body
of his mother when she was killed; that he handled every part
and member of it; found fault with some, commended others;
and being thirsty in the meantime took a draught of drink.
Howbeit, notwithstanding he was heartened by the joyous
congratulation of soldiers, senate, and people, yet he could not
either for the present or ever after endure the sting of conscience for this foul fact, but confessed many a time that haunted
and harried he was with the apparition of his mother's ghost;
tormented also with the scourges and burning torches of the
furies. Moreover, with a sacrifice made by direction of ma-
gicians, he essayed to raise up her soul and spirit, and to entreat
the same to forgive him. Verily as he traveled throughout
Greece, at the sacred Eleusine ceremonies (from the institution
and professing wherein all impious, godless, and wicked persons
are by the voice of a crier debarred) he durst not be present.
To this parricide of his mother, he adjoined also the murder
of his aunt. For when upon a time he visited her lying sick of a
costive belly, and she a woman now well stepped in years, in
handling the tender down of his beard new budding forth,
chanced (as the manner is) by way of pleasing speech, to say,
"Might I but live to take up this soft hair when it is false, I
might see thee once a man grown, etc." He, turning to those
that stood next unto him, in derision and scoffing manner said,
"Marry and even straightways I will cut it off for her sake," and
so made no more ado but gave order unto the physician to ply
the sick woman still with stronger purgatives. For, even before
she was thorough dead he laid sure hold of her goods, and
suppressed her last will, that nothing might escape his clutches.

35. Besides Octavia, he married afterwards two wives, to
wit, Poppaea Sabina the daughter of one who had been quaestor, and the wedded wife before of a Roman knight; then
Statilia Messalina, niece in the third degree removed of Taurus,

twice consul, who had once triumphed. For to have and enjoy Messalina, he murdered her husband Atticus Vestinus, then consul, even during the time of that honorable magistracy. Soon weary he was of Octavia's company and forsook her bed. And when some friends reproved him for it he made answer, that the jewels and ornaments only of a wife ought to content her. Soon after, when he had essayed many times (but in vain) to strangle her, he put her away, pretending she was barren. But when the people misliked this divorce, and forbore not to rail upon him for it, he proceeded even to confine and banish her quite. In the end he murdered her, under a colorable imputation of divers adulteries, charged upon her so impudently and falsely, that when all generally who were by torture examined upon the point, stood stoutly to the very last in denial, he suborned and brought in Anicetus, his own pedagogue, against her, who should slander himself with her and confess that by a wile he had abused her body. The twelfth day after the said divorce of Octavia, he espoused and married the aforesaid dame Poppaea, whom he loved entirely; and yet even her also he killed with a kick of his heel, for that, being big with child and sickly withal, she had reviled him and given him shrewd words for coming home so late one night after his running with chariots. By her he had a daughter named Claudia Augusta, whom he buried when she was a very infant. There was no kind of affinity and consanguinity were it never so near, but it felt the weight of his deadly hand. Antonia, the daughter of Claudius, refusing after the death of Poppaea to be his wife, he slew, under a pretense as if she went about to conspire against him and to alter the state.

Likewise, he killed all the rest, that were either allied unto him or of his kindred. Among whom, Antonius Plautius a young gentleman was one. Whose body, after he had by force filthily abused before his death: "Let my mother go now," said he, "and kiss my successor's sweet lips," giving it out that Plautius was her well-beloved darling, and by her was set on to hope and gape after the empire. His stepson Rufinus Crispinus, the son of Poppaea, being yet of tender years, because the report went of him that in game he would play for dukedoms and empires, he gave order unto his own servants for to drown in the sea, while he was there fishing. Tuscus, his nurse's son, he confined and sent away, for that being his procurator in Egypt, he had bathed in those baths which were built against Nero's own coming. His preceptor and schoolmaster Seneca he compelled to die; albeit Seneca had sworn unto him very devoutly (when he made suit many times for a license to depart the court, had yielded up therewith all his goods into Nero's hands) that he had no cause to suspect him, for he would rather lose his own life than do Nero any hurt. Unto Burrus, captain of the guard, he promised a medicine to heal his swollen throat, and sent him the rank poison toxicum for it. His freedmen that were rich and old, whose favor, friendship and directions had stood him in good stead for procuring unto him in times past adoption, and afterwards the imperial rule, he cut short every one by poison, partly put into their meats and partly mingled with their drinks.

36. With no less cruelty raged he abroad even against strangers and mere foreigners. A blazing hairy star, commonly thought to portend death and destruction to the highest powers, began to arise, and had appeared many nights together. Being troubled therewith, and informed by Babilus the astrologer, that kings were wont to expiate such prodigious signs with some notable massacre, and so divert the same from themselves and turn all upon the heads of their peers and nobles, he thereupon projected the death of all the noblest personages in the city. And verily, so much the rather, and, as it were, upon just cause, by reason of two conspiracies by him pub-

lished and divulged abroad; of which the former and the greater, bearing the name of Piso, was plotted and detected at Rome; the latter going under the name of Vinicius at Beneventum. The conspirators had their trial, and pleaded bound with threefold chains; and as some of them confessed the action of their own accord, so others said moreover that he was beholden unto them for it, because they could not possibly do a cure upon him by any other means (stained as he was and dishonored with all kind of wicked acts), but only by death. The children of the condemned were expelled from the city, and then dispatched with poison or hunger-starved. It is for certain known that some of them with their pedagogues and book-keepers took their bane all at one dinner together; others were restrained for seeking and earning their daily food.

37. After this without all choice and respect, without all measure in his hand, he spared none; he put to death whomsoever it pleased him, and for what cause it skilled not. But not to make long relation of many, it was laid to Salvidienus Orcitus' charge that he had let three shops out of his house about the Forum unto the states abroad for their ambassadors to make their abode and converse in. To Cassius Longinus the lawyer (a man bereft of both his eyes) objected it was, that in the ancient pedigree of his own house and lineage, he had set up again the images of Gaius Cassius, one of them that murdered Caesar. To Paetus Thraseas, for having a stern and severe countenance like a pedagogue. When these with others were appointed once to die, he allowed them no more than one hour's respite to live after, and so that no further delay might come between, he put unto them surgeons (in case they lingered and made no haste) to cure them out of hand (for that was the term he used), meaning thereby, to cut their veins and let them bleed to death. It is verily thought also, that to a certain great eater (an Egyptian born) that used to feed on raw

flesh and whatsoever was given him, he had a great desire to cast men alive, for to be quartered, cut in pieces and devoured by him. Being lifted and puffed up with these, as it were, so great successes, he said that no prince ever knew what he might do; and oftentimes he cast out many words betokening very significantly, that he would not spare the senators remaining behind, but one day utterly erase that order out of the commonwealth, and permit the knights of Rome and his freedmen only to rule provinces and have the conduct of armies. Certes, neither at his coming home nor going forth any whither, vouchsafed he to kiss any one of them, no nor so much as once to resalute them. And when with formal compliments he entered upon his work of digging through Isthmus, he wished and prayed aloud before a frequent audience, that the enterprise might speed well and turn to the weal of himself and the people of Rome, concealing and suppressing all mention of the senate.

38. But yet for all that, he spared not the people nor forbore the very walls and buildings of his country, the city. When one in common talk upon a time chanced to say,

> When vital breath is fled from me,
> Let earth with fire immingled be;

"Nay rather," said he, "While vital breath remains in me, etc." And even so he did indeed; for being offended, as it were with the ill-favored fashion of the old houses, as also with the narrow, crooked and winding streets, he set the city of Rome on fire so openly that many citizens of consul's degree, taking his chamberlains in the manner with matches, touchwood and hurds in their estates, would not once lay hand on them but let them alone; yea and certain store-houses about his golden edifice (for that plot of ground on which they were situated his mind stood most unto) were by war-engines forcibly shaken, thrown down and fired, by reason they were built with stone walls. For six days and seven nights together raged he in this wise making havoc of all, and driving the common people to show themselves the while about the tombs and monuments of the dead. During this time, beside an infinite number of houses standing apart from others, the goodly edifices and building of noble captains in old time, adorned still and beautified with the spoils of enemies, the stately temples also of the gods, vowed and dedicated by the ancient kings first, and afterwards in the Punic and French wars he burned all, on a light fire. And in one word, whatsoever remained from old time worth the seeing and memorable, was consumed. This fire beheld he daily out of Maecenas' high tower; and taking joy (as he said himself) at the beautiful flame that it made, chanted the winning and destruction of Troy, in that musician's habit wherein he was wont to sing upon the stage. And because he would not miss, but lay fast hold upon all the booty and pillage which possibly he could come by, even from thence also, having promised free leave to cast forth dead carcasses, and rid away the rammel of the ruins, whatever relics remained of all their goods and substance unburnt, he permitted not one to go unto it. Finally, not only by receiving, but also by exacting contributions from all parts, he beggared well near the provinces and consumed the wealth of private persons.

39. To amend the matter well, unto these harms and reproachful dishonors of the state, so great as they were arising from the prince, there happened also some other calamities by chance and fortune; to wit, a pestilence continuing one autumn, whereby thirty thousand burials were reckoned in the record of Libitina; and an unfortunate loss in Britain, wherein two principal towns of great importance were sacked, with great slaughter besides of Roman citizens and allies; a

shameful disgrace received in the East by reason that the
Roman legions in Armenia were put under the yoke as slaves,
and Syria was hardly and with much ado kept in terms of
allegiance. But a wonder it was to see, and a thing especially
to be noted, that amid all these infortunities he took nothing
less to the heart than the shrewd checks and reviling taunts of
men; and he was to none more mild, than to such as had provoked him, either with hard speeches, or opprobrious verses.
Many infamous libels and defamatory words, both in Greek
and Latin, were publicly written, or otherwise cast and spread
abroad against him, as for example these:

Nero, Orestes, Alcmaeon, did shorten mother's life;
Nero slew his, when newly her he wedded as his wife.

Quis neget Aeneae magna de stirpe Neronem?
Sustulit hic matrem, sustulit ille patrem.

Who can deny, of great Aeneas our Nero sprung to be,
That rid his mother of her life, as sire from fire did he?

Dum tendit citharam noster, dum Cornua Parthus,
Noster erit Paean, ille Hecatebeletes.

While our Nero bendeth his harp, while Parthian his bow;
Our prince shall be Paean, he Hecatebeletes.

Roma domus fiet; Velos migrate Quirites
Sinon et Veios occupet ista domus.

Rome will become a dwelling house; to Veii flit apace,
Quirites, lest this house before ye come take up the place.

But no search made he after the authors hereof, and some of
them being by the informer convented before the senate, he
would not suffer to sustain any grievous punishment. As he
passed by in the open street, Isidorus the Cynic had checked
him aloud in these terms, that he used to chant the calamities
of Nauplius very well, but disposed he of his own goods as

badly. And Datus, a player of the Atellan Comedies [which were very licentious], in a certain sonnet singing these words, Farewell father, farewell mother, had acted the same so significantly, as that he feigned the one drinking and the other swimming, to express thereby the end of Claudius and Agrippina; and in the last conclusion of all, with these words:

Orcus vobis ducit pedes,

Now Pluto leads forth your feet,

in plain gesture noted the senate. The actor and philosopher Nero did no more unto, but banish them Rome and Italy; either for that he set light by all shame and infamy; or else lest in betraying any grief, he might stir up and provoke pregnant wits to work upon him.

40. Well, the world having endured such an emperor as this little less than fourteen years, at length fell away and forsook him clean. And first the French began, following as the ringleader of their insurrection Julius Vindex, who that very time governed the province as propraetor. Foretold it had been long ago unto Nero by the astrologers that one day he should be left forlorn. Whereupon this saying was most rife in his mouth,

An artisan of any kind
In every land will living find,

so that he might the better be excused and borne withal for studying and practicing the art of minstrelsy and singing to the harp, as a skill delightful unto him now a prince, and needful for him another day a private person. Yet some there were who promised unto him so forsaken, the government of the East parts; and others by special name the kingdom of Jerusalem; but most of them warranted him assuredly the restitution of his former estate. And being inclined rather to rest upon this hope, when he had lost Britain and Armenia, and recovered them both again, he thought himself discharged then and quit from the fatal calamities destined unto him. But sending one time to the oracle of Apollo at Delphi, and hearing this answer from thence, that he must beware of the year seventy-three, as who would say, he was to die in that year of his own age and not before; and divining no whit of Galba's years, with so assured confidence he conceived in his heart not only long life but also a perpetual and singular felicity, that when he had lost by shipwreck things of exceeding price, he stuck not to say among his familiars, that the fishes would bring the same again unto him [as they did to Polycrates, that mighty tyrant of Samos – but it was not long before Polycrates' fall and destruction]. At Naples advised was he of the rebellion in Gaul. Which fell out to be the very same day of the year on which he had killed his mother. But he took this news so patiently and carelessly, that he gave suspicion even of joy and contentment; as if occasion had been offered and presented thereby to make spoil (by the law of arms) of those most rich and wealthy provinces; and straightways going forth into the gymnasium, he beheld with exceeding great earnestness and delight the wrestlers and champions striving for the prize. At supper time also, being interupted with letters importing more tumults and troubles still; thus far forth only he grew into choler and indignation, as that he threatened mischief to them who had revolted. To conclude, for eight days together he never went about to write back unto any man nor to give any charge or direction at all, but buried the matter quite in silence.

41. At last, thoroughly moved and nettled with the contumelious edicts of Vindex coming so thick one in the neck of another, he exhorted the senate, in a letter written unto them, to revenge him and the commonwealth, alleging for an excuse the quinsy [an inflammation in the throat] whereof he was sick, and therefore could not himself be present in person.

But nothing vexed him so much as this, that he was by him blamed for an unskillful musician, and because instead of Nero, he called him Aenobarbus. And verily as touching this name appropriate to his house and family, wherewith he was thus in contumelious manner twitted, he professed to resume the same, and to lay away the other that came by adoption [Nero Claudius Drusus]. All other reviling taunts and slanders, he confuted as mere false, by no other argument than this, that unskillfulness, forsooth, was objected unto him in that very art which he had so painfully studied and brought to so good perfection; and therewith asked them eftsoons one by one, whether they had ever known a more excellent musician than himself. But when messengers came still one after another, in great fear he returned to Rome. And he had his heart lightened but a little in the way, with a vain and foolish presage by occasion that he espied and observed upon a monument a certain French soldier with a Roman knight overmatched in fight and trailed along by the hair of the head; he at this sight leapt for joy and worshipped the heavens. Neither then verily, did he so much as consult in public with the senate, or assemble the people; but only call forth home to his house some of the chief and principal persons among them. And having dispatched in great haste this consultation, the rest of that day he led them all about to his musical water instruments of a strange device and fashion, not known before; and showing every one by itself unto them, discoursing also of the reason and difficult workmanship of each one, he promised even anon to bring them all forth into the open theater, if Vindex would give him leave.

42. After that he understood besides, how Galba likewise and the provinces of Spain were revolted, he fell down at once; his heart was then daunted and clean done. And so he lay a good while speechless in a trance, and ready, as one would

say, to go out of the world. And so soon as he came again to himself, he rent his clothes, beat and knocked his head, saying plainly, that he was utterly undone; yea and when his nurse came about him to comfort his poor heart, telling him that the like accidents had befallen to other princes also before him, he answered again, that he above all the rest suffered miseries never heard of nor known before – thus in his lifetime to forgo and lose his empire. Neither yet for all this struck he sail one whit in laying away or leaving out one jot of his ordinary riot and supine slothfulness. Nay when some little inkling was given of good news out of the provinces as he sat at a most sumptuous and plentiful supper, he pronounced even with express gesture like a player certain ridiculous rhymes, and those set to lascivious and wanton measures, against the chieftains of rebellion – and what were those? even stale stuff and commonly known already. Being also secretly conveyed into the theater he sent word unto a certain player acting his part with great contentment of them that saw and heard him, that he did but abuse his occupations [in that Nero himself, but for his business, would have played with him and put him down].

43. Immediately upon the beginning of this fearful tumult, it is credibly thought that he intended many designs and those very cruel and horrible, yet such as agreed well enough with his natural humor, namely, to send underhand successors and murderers of all those that were commanders of armies and regents of provinces, as if they all had conspired and drawn in one and the self-same line. Also, to massacre all banished persons wheresoever, and the Frenchmen every one that were to be found in Rome; those because they should not band and combine with them that revolted; these, as complices with their own countrymen, and their abettors. Also, to permit the armies to make spoil and havoc of the provinces in Gaul. Also, to poison all the senate generally at some appointed feast.

Last of all, to fire Rome and let wild beasts loose among the people, that thereby there might be more ado and greater difficulty to save the city. But being scared from these designments, not so much upon any repentance, as despair of their accomplishment, and persuaded withal that necessary it was to make a voyage and warlike expedition, the consuls then in place he deprived of their government before the due time, and himself alone entered upon the consulship in their places, as if forsooth, the destinies had so ordained, that Gaul could not be subdued but by a sole consul. Having then taken into his hands the fasces [the symbol of consular authority], when after meat he withdrew himself aside out of his dining chamber, leaning upon the shoulders of his familiar friends, he protested that so soon as ever he was come into the province he would show himself unarmed before the armies, and do nothing else but weep; and after he had once brought them to repentance, sing merrily, the day following, songs of triumph with them that rejoiced with him. "Which songs," quoth he, "ought with all speed even now to be composed for me."

44. In the preparation of this warlike voyage, his special care was to choose forth meet wagons for the carriage of his musical instruments, to cut and poll the concubines which he carried out with him like men, and to furnish them with battle-axes and little bucklers after the Amazonian fashion. This done, he cited the city tribes to take the military oath [enlist], and when no serviceable men would answer to their names, he enjoined all masters to set forth a certain number of bond-servants, neither admitted he out of the whole family and household of every man but such only as were most approved, excepting not so much as their stewards or clerks and secretaries. He commanded likewise all degrees to allow and contribute towards this expedition part of their estate according as they were valued in the censor's book; and more than so,

the tenants inhabiting private estates and great houses, to pay out of hand in yearly pension to his exchequer. He exacted also with great scornfulness and extremity, good money rough and newly coined, refined silver, gold pure and red as fire. Insomuch as most men openly refused the payment of all contributions, demanding in a general consent, that whatever monies promoters had received for their information, should rather be required back again at their hands.

45. By the dearth likewise of corn, whatever hatred was conceived against the gainers thereof, the same grew heavy upon him. For it fell out by chance that in this public famine word came of a ship of Alexandria, how it was arrived carrying a kind of dust for the wrestlers of Nero's court. Having thus stirred up and kindled the hatred of all the world against him, there was no contumelious despite but he sustained. To one statue of his, just behind the crown of the head, was set a curl with an impress in Greek to this effect, "Now in truth, and not before is the combat." And again, "Now or never hale and draw." To the neck of another, there was tied a leather bag, and therewith this title, "What could I do? But thou hast deserved a very leather bag indeed." This writing also was fastened upon the columns, "Now with his chanting he hath awakened the French." And by this time many there were who in the night season making semblance of chiding and brawling with their servants, called often for a *vindex* [= lit., vindicator].

46. Besides all this, he took affright at the manifest portents as well new as old, of dreams, of prodigies and of omens. For whereas before time, he was never wont to dream, when he had murdered his mother, once there appeared visions in his sleep, him thought he saw the helm of a ship wrested out of his hand as he steered it, and that by his wife Octavia he was haled into a very narrow and blind place; one while that he was covered all over with a multitude of winged ants; another

while, that the images of brave men descended of noble houses dedicated to Pompey's theater, went round about him, and debarred him from going forward. Also, that his Spanish steed, wherein he took most delight, was in most parts transfigured into the form of an ape; but having his head only sound and entire, did set up a loud and shrill voice neighing. Out of the Mausoleum [the sepulchre of Augustus], when all the doors thereof flew of their own accord open, a voice was heard calling him by name. Upon the Kalends of January, his domestic gods, garnished and adorned as they were, at the very time when the sacrifice was in preparing, fell all down. And as he was observing the signs by bird flight, Sporus presented him with a ring for a New Year's gift; in the precious stones whereof was engraven the ravishing and carrying away of Proserpina. At the solemn pronunciation of his vows, when as a great and frequent number of all degrees were already assembled together, the keys of the Capitol could hardly be found. What time as out of his invective oration against Vindex these words were rehearsed in the senate, that such wicked persons should suffer punishment, they all cried out with one voice, "*Tu Facies Auguste.*" [Thou shalt do so, O Augustus.] This also had been observed, that the last tragedy which he acted and sung in public place was *Oedipus the Banished,* and just as he pronounced this verse,

> How can I choose but death desire,
> Thus bidden by wife, by mother, and sire?

he fell down.

47. In this meanwhile, when news came that all the other armies also rebelled, the letters delivered unto him as he sat at dinner he tore in pieces, overthrew the table, and two cups of crystal out of which he took the greatest pleasure to drink, and which he called Homericos, for certain verses of Homer engraved and wrought upon them, he dashed against the paved

floor. Then, after he had received a poison of Locusta and put it up in a golden box, he went directly into the gardens of the *Servitii*; where, having sent before his most trusty freedman unto Ostia for to rig and prepare a fleet to sea, he sounded the tribunes and centurions of the guard, whether they would bear him company and fly with him, or no. But when some of them made it coy, others in plain terms refused; and one also cried out aloud,

Usque adeone mori miserum est?
What? is it such a misery
To leave this life and so to die?

he cast about, and thought of many and sundry shifts. Whether he should go as an humble suppliant unto the Parthians or to Galba, or whether it were best for him, arrayed all in black to come abroad into the city, and there in open place before the rostra, with all the rueful and piteous moan that he could possibly make, crave pardon for all that was past, and unless he could turn the people's hearts unto mercy, make suit to have if it were but the deputyship of Egypt granted unto him. Certes, found there was afterwards in his cabinet a speech of his own penning, as touching this argument. But men think he was scared from this enterprise, as fearing lest before he could thither come he should be pulled in pieces. Thus, putting off all farther cogitation of this matter unto the next day, and awakened about midnight when he understood that the guard of his soldiers was retired and gone, he leapt forth from his bed, and sent all about to his friends. But because no word was brought back from any of them, himself accompanied with a few about him went to every one of their lodgings; where finding all doors shut, and nobody to make him answer, he returned to his bed-chamber. By which time, his keepers also and wardens were slipped from thence; but they had stolen away first the hangings and furniture of his chamber, yea and set out of the way the box aforesaid with the poison. Then straightways he sought for Spicillus the sword-fencer, or any other common hackster he cared not who, by whose hand he might receive his death's wound. But finding none, "Well," quoth he, "and have I neither a friend nor a foe?" And so he ran forth, as if he would have thrown himself headlong into the Tiber.

48. But having reclaimed once again that violent mood, he desired some more secret retiring place, wherein he might lurk awhile and recall his wits together. And when Phaon his freedman made offer unto him of a farmhouse of his, that he had outside the city about four miles off, between the highway Salaria and the highway Numentana, barefooted as he was and in his shirt, he cast over it a cloak all sullied and which had lost the color. And so covering his head, and holding an handkerchief before his face, to horseback he went, having not above four persons in his company, of which Sporus made one. And being by and by affrighted with an earthquake and lightning that flashed against his face, he heard withal, as an outcry and shout (from the camp nearby), of the soldiers prophesying all mischief at him and all good unto Galba; yea and one of the passengers that he met, saying, These be they that pursue Nero, as also another asking, What news in Rome of Nero? Now by occasion that his horse under him scenting a dead carcass that was thrown out in the way, started and flung at one side, his face was discovered, and himself known of one Missicius a praetorian soldier, who saluted him by name. When they were come to the next lane, turning out of the roadway, their horses they forsook and turned them loose; and so among thickets of shrubs, rough bushes and briers, with much ado through a narrow path within a reed plot, and not without clothes spread under foot, he got at

length as far as to the wall of the country house abovesaid over and against him. There, when the said Phaon persuaded him to bestow himself the meanwhile, within a pit, from whence sand had been cast forth, "Nay," he said, "I will never go quick underground." And so, after he had stayed a little (while there was a secret way a-making to let him into the farmhouse), he ladled up water with his own hand out of a ditch under him, minding to drink, "And this," he said, "is Nero's cooked water." After this, because his cloak was torn among the bushes and briers aforesaid, he rid it from the pricky sprigs that were run through and stuck therein, and so creeping upon all fours through a straight and narrow hole dug in the wall for him, received he was into the next back room; where he laid him down on a pallet made of a simple scant mattress, and an old over-worn cloak cast over it for a coverlet. Now when hunger came upon him, and thirst withal the second time the brown and coarse bread verily which was offered unto him he refused; but of warm water he drank a pretty draught.

49. When as each one called then instantly on every side upon him, to deliver himself with all speed from the reproachful contumelies and abuses whereto he was hourly subject, he commanded a grave to be made before his face, and gave a measure therefore according to the just proportion of his body; and therewith, if any pieces of marble stone might be found about the house, to be laid in order; that water also and wood should be gotten together for his dead body to be washed anon therewith; weeping at every word he spoke, and inserting ever and anon this pitiful speech, *Qualis artifex pereo!* [What an excellent artist here dies!] While some stay was made about these complements, Phaon's courier brought certain letters which he intercepted and snatched out of his hands. And reading therein that he had his doom by the senate, to be an enemy of the state, that he was laid for all about to be

punished, *more maiorum*, "*more maiorum?*" he said, "what kind of punishment is that?" And when he understood that it implied thus much, that the man so condemned should be stripped all naked, his head locked fast with a fork, and his body scourged with rods to death, he was so terrified therewith, that he caught up two daggers which he had brought with him; and trying the points of them both how sharp they were, he put them up again, making this excuse, that the fatal hour of his death was not yet come. And one while he exhorted Sporus to begin to lament, weep, and wail; another while he entreated hard, that some one of them would kill himself first, and by his example help him to take his death. Sometimes also he checked and blamed his own timorousness in these words, "I live shamefully." And in reproach, "It becomes not Nero; it becomes him not. In such cases as these he had need to be wise and sober; go to, man, pluck up thy heart and rouse thyself." Now by this time approached the horsemen near at hand, who had a warrant and praecept to bring him alive. Which when he perceived, after he had with trembling and quaking uttered this verse,

The trampling noise of horses swift resoundeth in mine ears,

he set a dagger to his throat, while Epaphroditus his secretary lent him his hand to dispatch him. When he was yet but half dead, a centurion broke in upon him, and putting his cloak upon the wound, made semblance as if he came to aid and succor him; unto whom he answered nothing but this, "Too late. And is this your loyalty and allegiance?" In which very word he yielded up his breath, with his eyes staring out and set in his head, to the great fear and horror of all that were present. He had requested of the company which attended upon him, no one thing more earnestly than this, that no man might have his head severed from the body, but that in any

wise he might be burnt whole. And Icelus, a freedman of
Galba, who not long before was delivered out of prison (into
which he was cast by Nero at the beginning of the first tumult)
permitted so much.

50. His funerals were performed with the charges of 200,000
sesterces; his corpse was carried forth to burial enwrapped
within white cloths of tinsel, woven with gold wire between,
the very same that he had worn upon the Kalends of January.
His relics, Ecloge and Alexandra his two nurses, together with
Acte his concubine bestowed within the monument belonging
to the house of the Domitii his ancestors which is to be seen
out of Mars field, situated upon the nap of an hill within their
gardens. In which sepulchre his chest, made of porphyrite
marble, with an altar (as it were) or table of white marble of
Luna standing upon it, was enclosed round about with a fence
of Thasian marble stone.

51. He was for stature almost of complete height within a
little of six feet. His body full of specks and freckles, and foul
of skin besides. The hair of his head somewhat yellow, his
countenance and visage rather fair than lovely and well-
favored. His eyes gray and somewhat with the dimmest. His
neck full and fat. His belly and paunch bearing out, with a pair
of passing slender spindle legs; but withal, he was very healthful. For, being as he was so untemperate and most riotously
given, in fourteen years' space, he never fell sick but thrice;
yet so, as he neither forbore drinking of wine, nor anything
else that he used to do. About the trimming of his body and
wearing of his clothes so nice, as it was shameful; insomuch as
he would always have the bush of his head laid and plaited
by curls in tiers; but what time as he traveled in Achaia, he
drew it backward also from the crown of his head and wore
it long. For the most part, he wore a dainty and effeminate pied
garment called Synthesis [worn at dinner at the Saturnalia,

and by women at all other times]. And with a fine lawn necker-
chief bound about his neck he went abroad in the streets, ungirt, untrussed, and unshod.

52. Of all the liberal sciences in manner, he had a taste when
he was but a child. But from the study of philosophy his mother
turned his mind, telling him that it was repugnant to one who
another day was to be a sovereign; and from the knowledge
of ancient orators, his master Seneca withdrew him, because
he would hold him the longer in admiration of himself. And
therefore, being of his own accord readily inclined to poetry,
he made verses voluntarily and without pain. Neither did he
(as some think) set forth other men's poems as his own. There
have come into mine hands writing tables and books, containing verses very famous and well known abroad, written with
his own hand, so as a man may easily see that they were not
copied out of other books, nor yet taken from the mouth of
any other that indited them, but plainly penned, as a man
would say, by one that studied for them, and as they came in his
head, so put them down, so many blots and scrapings out, so
many dashes and interlinings were in them.

53. No small delight he had besides in painting; and most of
all in forging and molding counterfeits. But above all, he was
ravished and lifted up with popularity and praise of men, and
desirous therefore to imitate and equal them, who by any
means pleased the humors and contented the minds of the
common people. There went an opinion of him, that after
he had gained the coronets for his musical feats performed
upon the stage, he would at the next five years' revolution, go
unto the Olympic games, and contend for the prize among the
champions there. For, he practiced wrestling continually. Neither beheld he the gymnic games throughout all Greece otherwise than sitting below within the stadium, as the manner of
the judges and umpires of such masteries; and if any pair of

them drew too far back out of the appointed place, he plucked them with his own hands into the middle again. He had intended moreover (since he was reputed to have equalled Apollo in singing and matched the sun in charioting) to imitate also the worthy acts of Hercules. And men say there was a lion prepared, which he, all naked, should either with his club brain, or else with strait clasping between his arms throttle and crush to death within the amphitheater, in the sight of all the people.

54. Certainly, a little before his end he had openly made a vow, that in case he continued still in good and happy estate, represent he would likewise at the games, in his own person after victory obtained, an organist and player upon water instruments, upon the flute also and hautboy, yea and a bagpiper, and on the last day (of the said games) an actor of interludes; what time he would dance and gesture Turnus in Vergil. And some write, that Paris the actor was by him killed, as a rival that stood in his way and eclipsed his light.

55. A desire he had (foolish and inconsiderate though it were) of eternity and perpetual fame. And therefore, abolishing the old names of many things and places, he did upon them new, after his own. The month of April also he called Neroneus. He meant moreover to have named Rome Neropolis.

56. All religions wheresoever he had in contempt, unless it were that only of the Syrian goddess. And yet soon after, he despised her so far, that he polluted her image with urine; by occasion that he was wonderfully addicted to another superstition, wherein alone he continued and persevered most constantly. For he received in free gift a little puppet representing a young girl, at the hands of a mean commoner and obscure person, as a remedy, forsooth, against all treacheries and secret practices; and thereupon straightways chancing to discover a conspiracy, he held it for the sovereign deity above all, and persisted honoring and worshipping it every day with

three sacrifices. Nay he would have men believe that he foreknew things to come by advertisement and warning given from her. Some few months before he lost his life, he took regard also of the skill in prying into beasts' entrails. Which he observed indeed, but never sped well therewith, nor gained thereby the favor of the gods.

57. He died in the two and thirtieth year of his age; that very day of the year, on which in times past he had murdered his wife Octavia; and by his death brought so great joy unto the people generally, that the commons wore caps [to testify freedom recovered], and ran sporting up and down throughout the city. Yet there wanted not some, who a long time after decked his tomb with gay flowers that the spring and summer do afford; and who, one while brought forth his images clad in robes embroidered with purple before the rostrum; otherwhile, published his edicts, as if he had been yet living and would shortly return to the great mischief of his enemies. Moreover, Vologesus, king of the Parthians, when he sent his ambassadors unto the senate for to treat about the renewing of alliance with them, requested this also very earnestly, that the memorial of Nero might be still solemnized. To conclude, when twenty years after his decease (while I myself was but a young man) one arose among them (no man knew from whence, nor of what condition) who gave it out, that he was Nero (so gracious was his name among the Parthians), he was mightily upheld and maintained, yea and reluctantly delivered up again.

THE HISTORY OF
SERVIUS SULPICIUS GALBA

GALBA

THE PROGENY OF THE CAESARS ENDED WITH
Nero. Which, that it would so come to pass, appeared
verily by many signs, but by two of all the others most
evident. As Livia in times past immediately after her marriage
with Augustus went to see a manor house and land of her own
in the Vcientane territory, it fortuned that an eagle soaring
over her head let fall into her lap a white hen, holding in her
bill a laurel branch even as she had caught it up. And thinking
it good to have both the fowl kept and the said branch set in
the ground, behold there came of the one such a goodly brood
of chickens that even at this day the very house aforesaid is
called *Ad Gallinas*; and sprung of the other so fair a row of bay
trees that all the Caesars when they were to ride in triumph,
gathered from thence their laurel garlands. And as the manner
was that when any of them triumphed, they should prick
down straightways others in the same place. So it was observed
likewise that a little before the death of each one the tree by
him planted did wither and die. In the last year, therefore, of
Nero, not only the whole grove of trees withered to the very
root, but all the hens there died every one. And anon, after
the temple of the Caesars being struck by lightning, the heads
withal of their statues fell down all at once, and the scepter
of Augustus was shaken out of his hands.

2. After Nero succeeded Galba, in no degree allied unto
the house of the Caesar, but without all question a right noble
gentleman of a great and ancient race, who in the titles and

inscriptions over his own statues wrote himself always the great-grandson of Quintus Catulus Capitolinus. And being once emperor did set up also in his hall the lineal process and race of his house, wherein he derives his descent by the father side from Jupiter, and by his mother from Pasiphae, the wife of King Minos.

3. To prosecute the images and laudatory testimonials belonging to the whole stock and lineage in general were a long piece of work; those only of his own family will I briefly touch. The first of all the Sulpicii, why and wherefore he bore the surname Galba, there is some doubtful question. Some think it came by occasion of a town in Spain, which after it had been a long time in vain assaulted, he at length set on fire with burning brands besmeared all over with galbanum; others, for that in a long sickness which he had, he used continually galbeum, that is to say a cure with remedies wrapped in wool; some again, because he seemed to be very fat, and such a one the French do name Galba; or, contrariwise, that he was slender, as are those creatures (or worms) which breed in oak trees, and be called galbae. This family, one Servius Galba who had been consul, and in his time most eloquent, ennobled first and made renowned, who by report, ruling the province of Spain as praetor, having treacherously put to sword 30,000 Lusitanes, was the cause of the Viriatine war. His grandson being maliciously bent against Julius Caesar (whose lieutenant he had been in Gaul) for a repulse that he took in suing to be consul, joined in the conspiracy with Cassius and Brutus, for which condemned he was by the Law Paedia. From this man descended immediately the grandsire and the father of this Galba the emperor. His grandfather for his learning was more famous than for any dignity in the commonweal that ever he attained unto. For he arose no higher than to the degree of a praetor, but many histories he wrote and those not slightly

nor negligently composed. His father bore the honorable office of consul, a man of very low stature and withal crouch-backed; and having but a mean gift in oratory yet used he to plead cases industriously. Two wives he had, Mummia Achaica, the niece of Catulus, and once removed of Lucius Mummius, who razed and destroyed Corinth; likewise Livia Ocellina, an exceeding wealthy lady and a beautiful one. Of whom for his noble blood's sake, it is thought he was wooed; yea, and somewhat the more hotly after that (upon her importunate suit) he stripped himself once out of his clothes in a secret place before her, and revealed the imperfection of his body, because he would not seem to deceive her for want of knowledge. By Achaica he had issue Gaius and Servius. Of whom Gaius, the elder, having wasted his estate and spent all, left the city of Rome and was by Tiberius prohibited to put in his lot for to be chosen proconsul in his year. Whereupon he voluntarily killed himself.

4. To come now unto Servius Galba the emperor, born he was when Marcus Valerius Messalla and Gnaius Lentulus were consuls, the ninth day before the Kalends of January, in a country house situated under a little hill near unto Terracina, on the left hand as men go to Fundi. Being adopted by his step-mother, he assumed the name of Livius and the surname Ocella, changing his forename withal. For, afterwards even unto the time of his empire, he was forenamed Lucius instead of Servius. It is for certain known that Augustus (when little Galba among other boys like himself saluted him), took him by his pretty cheek and said, in Greek: "And thou also, my child, shall have a taste one day of our sovereign rule." Tiberius likewise, when he had knowledge once that he should be emperor, but not before old age, "go to," quoth he, "let him live, then seeing it is nothing to us." Also, as his grandfather was sacrificing for the expiation of an adverse flash of lightning,

and an eagle caught out of his hands the innards of the beasts, carried them away and bestowed them in an acorn-bearing oak (for some be fruitless), answer was given unto him by the soothsayers out of their learning that thereby was portended and foreshadowed unto his house, sovereign government, but it would be late. Then he again, by way of derision, "you say very true indeed. That will be," quoth he, "when a mule shall bring forth a foal." Afterwards, when this Galba began to rebel and aspire unto the empire, nothing heartened him in this design of his so much as the foaling of a mule. For when all men besides abhorred this foul and monstrous prodigy, he alone took it to be most fortunate, calling to remembrance the aforesaid sacrifice and the speech of his grandfather. When he had newly put on his virile gown he dreamt that fortune spake these words unto him, namely that she stood before his door all weary, and unless she were let in the sooner, she would become a prey unto whomsoever she met. No sooner awakened he and opened his hall door, but he found hard by the entry a brazen image of the said goddess, about a cubit long, which he carried away with him in his bosom to Tusculum where he was wont to summer and having consecrated it in one part of his house there, worshipped the same from that time forward with monthly supplications and a vigil all night long every year. And albeit he was not yet come to his middle and staid age, yet retained he most constantly this old manner of the city (which was now worn out of use, but that it continued still in his house and lineage): his freedmen and bondservants would duly twice a day present themselves all together before him, and one by one in the morning salute him with good morrow, and in the evening take their leave likewise with a farewell and also good night.

5. Among the liberal sciences he gave himself to the study of the civil law. He entered also into the state of wedlock,

but, having buried his wife Lepida and two sons that he had by her, he led always after a single life. Neither could he ever by any offer or condition be persuaded to marriage again, no not by dame Agrippina, who by the death of Domitius [the father of Nero] became a widow and had by all means so-licited Galba even while he was the husband of a wife, and not yet a single man; so much that at a great meeting of ladies and matrons, the mother of his wife Lepida shook her up roundly, yea and knocked her well for it with her own fists. He honored and affected above all others Livia Augusta, the empress, through whose grace and favor while she lived he became mighty, and by whose will and testament when she was dead he had like to have been enriched. For whereas among others whom she remembered in her will he had a special legacy to the value of fifty million sesterces bequeathed unto him; because the said sum was set down in figures and ciphers and not written out at large, her heir Tiberius brought it down to one half million, and yet even that he never received.

6. Having entered upon the honorable offices of state before due time by law set down, when he was praetor during the plays and games called Floralia, he showed a new and strange kind of sight, to wit, elephants walking upon ropes. After that, he governed the province Aquitaine almost one whole year. Soon after, he bore the ordinary consulship in its due time for the space of six months. And it fell out so that as himself therein succeeded Domitius, the father of Nero, so Sylvius, the father of Otho, followed immediately after him, a very presage of the event ensuing whereby he came to be emperor just in the middle between the sons of them both. Being by Gaius Caesar substituted lord general for Getulicus, the very next day after he was come to the legions, when as the soldiers at a solemn show which happened then to be exhibited, clapped their hands, he restrained them with this precept,

that they should keep their hands within their cloaks; whereupon this byword anon ran rife through the camp:

Disce miles militare
Galba est, non Getulicus.

Learn, soldiers, service valorous
Galba is here, and not Getulicus.

7. With similar severity he inhibited all petitions for furloughs. The old soldiers as well as the new and untrained, he hardened still with continual work and labor. And having soon repressed the barbarians who by their inroads and incursions had now by this time broken in violently and set foot within Gaul, he quit himself so well and showed such good proof of his arms unto Gaius (also then and there present in proper person), that among an infinite number of forces levied and assembled out of all the provinces, there were none that went away with greater testimonies of prowess, nor received larger rewards than he and his regiments. Himself above them all was most bravely distinguished in this, that marching with his target before him he marshalled the gallants, jousting and running at tilt in the plain field; and for that he ran also by the emperor's chariot side for the space of twenty miles. When tidings came that Gaius was murdered, and many pricked him forward to take the opportunity then offered, he preferred quietness and rest. For which cause he stood in especial favor with Claudius, and was admitted into the rank of his inward friends, a man of that worth and reputation that when he fell suddenly sick (although not very grievously), the day appointed for to set forth in the British expedition was deferred. He governed Africa as proconsul for two years, being elected without lots drawing for to settle and bring into order that province far out of frame and disquieted as well with the civil mutinies among the soldiers, as tumultuous commotions of the

barbarous inhabitants. Which commission he discharged with great regard of severe discipline and execution of justice, even in very small matters. A soldier of his there was who during the expedition abovesaid, in a great dearth and scarcity of corn, was accused to have sold a residue remaining of his own allowance, to wit, a peck of wheat, for one hundred denarii; whereupon he gave straight commandment that when the said soldier began once to want food, no man should be so hardy as to relieve him. And so for hunger he pined to death. As for his civil jurisdiction and ministering justice, when there grew some question and debate about the propriety and right owner of a laboring beast, and slight evidences and presumptions on both sides were alleged, and simple witnesses also produced, so that it was hard to divine and guess the truth, he made this decree, that the beast should be led hoodwinked unto the pool where it was wont to be watered, and when it was unhooded again, he awarded and pronounced the said beast to be his unto whom of its own accord he returned directly after he had drunk.

8. For his brave exploits, achieved both in Africa then and also in Germany aforetime, he received the honor of triumphal ornaments and a triple sacerdotal dignity, being admitted among the quindecemvirs, into the guild and confraternity of the Titii, and into the college or society of the Priests Augustales. And from that time unto the midst well near of Nero's empire he lived for the most part private in some retiring place out of the way, never going forth on any journey (were it but for exercise) but he took forth with him in a wagon going hard by to the value of a million sesterces; until that time, while he was making his abode in a town called Fundi, the regency of a province in Spain named Tarraconensis was offered unto him. And it fortuned that when he was newly arrived and entered into that province, as he sacrificed within a public temple, a boy among other ministers holding the censer,

suddenly had all the hair of his head turned gray. Now there wanted not some who made this interpretation, that thereby was signified a change in the states, and that an old man should succeed a young, even in Nero's stead. And not long after, there fell a thunderbolt into a lake of Cantabria; and found there were immediately twelve axes: a doubtless token presaging sovereign rule.

9. For eight years' space he governed that province variably and with an uneven hand. At the first, sharp he was, severe, violent, and in chastising verily of trespasses beyond all measure extreme. For he caused a banker, for unfaithful handling of money, to lose both his hands and to have them nailed fast unto his own shop board. A guardian also he crucified for poisoning his ward, whose heir he was in remainder. Now as the party delinquent called for the benefit of law and avouched in his plea that he was a Roman citizen, Galba, as if he would allay his punishment with some comfort and honor, commanded the cross already made to be changed and another to be reared far higher than the ordinary, and the same laid over with a white color. By little and little he grew to be slothful, careless and idle, because he would minister no occasion unto Nero of jealousy; and because (as himself was wont to say) no man was compelled to render an account of his own idleness. As he held the judicial assizes at New Carthage, he had intelligence that Gaul was in a tumult. And while the ambassador of Aquitaine besought him earnestly to send aid, the letters of Vindex came in the very nick exhorting him to frame and carry himself the deliverer and protector of mankind, even to take upon him to be their general captain. He, making no longer stay upon the point, accepted the offer, partly for fear and in part upon hope. For he had both found out the warrants of Nero, sent privily unto his agents and procurators there, as touching his death; and also much confirmed and streng-

thened he was as well by most lucky auspices and omens, as by the prophecy of an honest virgin; so much the rather because the very same verses containing the prophecy the priest of Jupiter at Clunia had two hundred years past (by warning and direction given him in a dream) fetched out of an inward and secret vault of the temple, delivered then likewise by a maiden which had the spirit of prophecy. The meaning and effect of which verses was that one day there should arise out of Spain the sovereign prince and lord of the whole world.

10. Therefore, when he had mounted the tribunal, as if he intended then the manumitting of slaves, and set before him in open sight very many portraits and images of such as had been condemned and killed by Nero; while there stood also in his presence a boy of noble blood, whom he had sent for on purpose out of one of the Balearic islands hard by where he was exiled: he bewailed the state of those times. Whereupon, being with one accord saluted emperor, yet he professed himself to be lieutenant only of the senate and the people of Rome. After this, having proclaimed a cessation of judicial pleas for the time, out of the commons verily of that province he enrolled both legions and auxiliaries, over and above the old army, which contained one legion, two cornets of horsemen and three cohorts; but out of the better sort, to wit, the nobility and gentry, and such I mean as for wisdom and age went before the rest, he ordained a body of a senate, unto whom men should have recourse touching matters of greater importance, as need required. He chose forth also young gentlemen for the knight's degree, who continuing still the wearing of gold rings should be called volunteers, and kept watch and ward instead of sworn soldiers about his lodging and bedchamber. He sent out his edicts also in every province, counseling and persuading all and some to join with him in these designs, and (proportionally to the means that every one had)

to help and promote the common cause. Much about the same time, in the fortification of a town which he had chosen to be the capital seat of the war, a ring was found of antique work, in the gem or stone whereof was engraven the express resemblance of Victory together with a trophy; and soon after a ship of Alexandria, fraught with armor, arrived at Dertosa without a pilot, without mariner or passenger, so that no man might make any doubt but that this war was just, lawful and undertaken with the favor and approbation of the gods. But lo, suddenly and unlooked for, all in manner was dashed and put out of frame. One of the two cornets of horsemen above mentioned, bethinking themselves and repenting that they had changed their military oath, was at the point to fall away and forsake him as he approached the camp, yea and hardly kept in their allegiance to him; certain slaves also, whom (being prepared aforehand to do him a mischief) he had received as a present at the hands of a freedman of Nero's, missed but little of killing him as he passed through a cross-lane to the bath. And surely done the deed they had, but that, as they exhorted and encouraged one another not to overslip the opportunity presented, they were overheard; who, being examined and asked upon what occasion they spoke such words, were by torture forced to confess the truth.

11. Besides these dangers so great, there fell out (to help the matter well) the death of Vindex; wherewith being most of all amazed and like to a man utterly forlorn, he went within a little of renouncing this world and forgoing his own life. But by occasion of messengers coming with news from the city in the very instant, no sooner understood he that Nero was slain, and all men in general had sworn allegiance unto him, but he laid away the name of lieutenant and took upon him the style of Caesar. So he put himself on his journey, clad in his coat armor, with his dagger hanging down from about his

neck just before his breast; neither took he to the use of a gown and long robe again before they were surprised and suppressed who made insurrections and rose up in arms against him: namely, at Rome, Nymphidius Sabinus, captain of the praetorian guard; in Germany, Fonteius Capito, and in Africa, Clodius Macer, both lieutenants.

12. There had a rumor been raised before of his cruelty and covetousness both: for punishing the cities of Spain which were somewhat slack in coming to side with him, by laying very heavy tributes and taxes upon them; some of them also by dismantling and razing their walls; likewise for putting to death certain presidents and procurators together with their wives and children; also for melting a coronet of gold weighing fifteen pounds which the men of Tarracon from out of the old temple of Jupiter had presented unto him, and for commanding that the three ounces which wanted of the full weight should be exacted and made good. This report was both confirmed and also increased upon his first entrance into Rome. For when he would have compelled the servitors at sea (whom Nero had made from mariners and oarsmen, full and lawful soldiers) to return again to their former state and condition, and when they made refusal, and besides called malapertly for their eagle and other military ensigns, he not only sent in among them a troop of horsemen, and so trod them under foot, but also executed with death every tenth man of them. Similarly the cohort of Germans which in times past had been by the Caesars ordained for the guard of their persons, and by many good proofs were found most trusty, he dissolved, and without any recompense for their service sent them home again into their country, pretending that they stood better affected unto Gnaius Dolabella (near unto whose gardens they quartered) than to him. Moreover, these reports also (whether truly or falsely, I wot not) went commonly of him by way

of mockery: that when there was a more plentiful supper than usual served up before him, he gave a great groan thereat; that when his duly appointed steward cast up his books and rendered unto him a breviary of all reckonings and accounts, for his great care and serviceable diligence he reached unto him a dish of pulse. But when Gaius the minstrel played upon the hautboy and pleased him wondrous well, he bestowed liberally upon him for his labor five good denarii, and those he drew with his own hand, out of his privy purse.

13. At his first coming, therefore, he was not so welcome. And that appeared at the next solemnity of public shows. For when, in the Atellan comedies, some had begun a most vulgar canticle with this verse

Venit, Io Simus a villa, etc.
See, our Simus that country clown
Is from his farm now come to town,

the spectators all at once with one accord and voice, sang out the rest in manner of a respond; and repeating withal the said verse oft, as the foreburden of the song, acted (and with gesture) noted him.

14. Thus verily with far greater favor and authority obtained he the empire than managed it when he was therein; notwithstanding, he gave many proofs of an excellent prince; but nothing so acceptable were his good acts, as those were odious and displeasant wherein he faulted and did amiss. Ruled he was according to the will and pleasure of three persons, dwelling as they did together and that within the Palatium (ready evermore at his elbow and in his care), men commonly called his pedagogues. These were Titus Junius, his lieutenant in Spain, a man infinitely covetous; Cornelius Laco, who being of his counsel and assistance was advanced by him to be captain of the guard; and a freedman of his, Icelus, who but a

little before, being honored with the golden ring [knighthood], and endowed with the surname Martianus, looked now for to be the provost and captain of the praetorian gentlemen and knight's degree. Unto these men, I say, playing their parts and committing outrages correspondent to their vices in divers kinds, he yielded and wholly gave himself to be abused so much, that scarcely he was like himself, but always variable: one while precise and stingy, otherwhiles as remiss and careless, more than became a prince elected and a man of these years. Some honorable persons of both degrees he condemned upon the least suspicion, before their case was heard. Roman citizenship he seldom granted to any. The privilege and immunity due to those who had three children, he gave to one or two at most with much ado, and even to them only for a certain time, limited and set down. The judges, making suit for to have a sixth decury adjoined unto them, he not only denied flatly, but also this benefit of vacation granted unto them by Claudius he took from them: that they should not be called forth to sit in the winter season, nor at the beginning of the year.

15. It was thought also that he purposed to determine and limit the offices belonging to senators and knights to within the compass of two years, and not to bestow the same but upon such as were unwilling and refused to take them. The liberalities and bountiful donations of Nero he undertook, aided by a commission of fifty Roman knights, to have revoked; yea, and the same to be exacted for his behoof, allowing out thereof not above the tenth part to be retained; moreover, with this straight condition, that if actors upon the stage, or wrestlers and champions otherwise, had sold any such donation given unto them aforetime, the same should be taken from the buyers, since that the parties who had sold the same had spent the money and were not sufficient to repay it. Contrariwise,

there was not anything, but by the means of his followers, favorites and freedmen he suffered either to be purchased for money, or granted freely for favor: as for example, customs, imposts, immunities, punishments of the innocent and impunity of malefactors. Moreover, when the people of Rome called upon him for justice, namely to have Halotus and Tigellinus executed, the only men of all the blood-hounds and instruments of Nero that wrought most mischief, he saved them from danger, and, besides, advanced Halotus to a most honorable procuratorship; and in the behalf of Tigellinus rebuked the people by an edict for their cruelty unto him.

16. Having thereby given offense and discontentment to the states and degrees in manner all, yet he incurred the displeasure and ill-will most of the soldiers. For when his provosts had promised and pronounced unto them (when they swore allegiance unto him), a greater donative than usually had been given, he would not make good and ratify the same, but eftsoons gave it out that his manner had ever been to choose and buy his soldiers. And just as upon that occasion verily he angered all his soldiers wheresoever, so the praetorians and those of his guard he provoked moreover with fear and nettled with offering them indignities: namely, by removing and displacing most of them one after another, as suspected persons and the adherents of Nymphidius. But the forces of higher Germany grumbled and fumed most of all for being defrauded of their rewards for service performed against the French and Vindex. They were the first therefore that durst break out into open disobedience; and upon New Year's day they refused to take an oath and bind themselves in allegiance unto any other than the senate of Rome. They intended also to dispatch forthwith an embassy unto the praetorian guard with these advertisements and messages from them, namely, that they were displeased with an emperor made in Spain, and therefore themselves

... *it chanced that a bull, maddened by the stroke of the butcher's axe,*
broke the bond wherewith he stood tied and ran full upon his chariot, and
rising up with his forefeet drenched it with blood.

should elect one whom all the armies in general might allow and approve.

17. No sooner heard he this news, but, supposing that he was become contemptible, not so much for his old age, as his childless estate, he presently out of the thick throng and middle multitude that came to salute him, caught hold of Piso Frugi Licinianus, a noble young gentleman and of excellent parts, one whom in times past he had made right great account of, and always in his will remembered as an inheritor to succeed in his goods and name. Him he now called son, him he presented unto the praetorian camp, and there, before a public assembly, adopted. But of the aforesaid donative not a word all this while, no not at that very time. Whereby he ministered unto Marcus Salvius Otho better occasion and readier means to accomplish his enterprise within six days after the adoption.

18. Many prodigious sights, and those presented continually even from the very first beginning, had portended unto him such an end as ensued. When all the way as he journeyed, beasts were sacrificed to do him honor in every town on both sides, it chanced that a bull, maddened by the stroke of the butcher's axe, broke the bond wherewith he stood tied and ran full upon his chariot, and rising up with his forefeet drenched it with blood. As he alit out of it, one of the guard and pensioners about him, with the thrusting of the throng had like with his spear to have wounded him. As he entered also the city of Rome and so passed forward up to the Palatium, he was welcomed by an earthquake and a certain noise resembling the lowing of a beast. But there followed after these greater prodigies still and more fearful. He had selected and laid by itself out of all his treasure a jewel set thick with pearl and precious stones for to beautify and adorn his goddess Fortune at Tusculum. This jewel (as if it had been worthy of a more stately and sacred place), all of a sudden he dedicated to Venus

in the Capitol, and the next night following he dreamt that he saw Fortune making her moan and complaining how she was defrauded of the gift intended and meant unto her, threatening withal that she herself also would take away what she had given him. Now, being affrighted with this vision, when in great haste he was gone apace to Tusculum and had by break of day sent certain before of purpose to provide an expiatory sacrifice for this dream, he found nothing there but warm embers upon the altar hearth and an old man all in black sitting hard by, holding in a dish of glass, frankincense, and in an earthen cup, wine. Observed also it was that upon the Kalends of January while he sacrificed his coronet fell from his head. As he took the auspices, the pullets flew away. And upon the solemn day of the aforesaid adoption, when he would make a speech unto the soldiers, the camp-throne stood not (as the manner was), before his tribunal (such was the forgetfulness of his ministers), and in the senate his curule chair was placed wrong, with the back toward him.

19. But before he was slain, as he sacrificed that morning, the soothsayer oftentimes warned him to beware of danger, for murderers were not far off. And not long after he took knowledge that Otho was possessed of the camp. And when most of those about his person persuaded him still to make what speed he could and go forward thither (for by his authority and presence he might bear sway and prevail), he resolved to do no more but to keep close within the house, to stand upon his guard and to fortify himself with the strength of his legionary soldiers, in many and divers places quartered. Howbeit, he put on a good linen cuirass, although he seemed to acknowledge that in small stead it would stand him against so many sword-points. But, being borne in hand and seduced with rumors which the conspirators had of purpose spread abroad to train him out into the open street, while some few rashly

affirmed that all was dispatched, the rebels and seditious persons defeated and the rest coming in great frequency with joy and gratulation, ready for to do him all the obsequious service they could, he to meet them went forth; and that with so great confidence as that unto a soldier who made boast that he had slain Otho, he answered, "and by whose warrant?" Thus advanced he as far as into the Forum. There the horsemen having commission and commandment to kill him, when they had voided the common people out of the way and put their horses forward through the streets, and espied him afar off, stayed awhile; but afterwards, setting spurs to again, fell upon him and slew him outright, forsaken as he was of all his train and followers.

20. There be that report that at the first uproar he cried out aloud, "what mean you, my fellow soldiers? I am yours and you are mine"; and withal promised to pay the donative. But many more have left in writing that of himself he offered them his throat and willed them (since they thought so good), to mind that only which they came for, even to strike and spare not. A strange and wonderful thing it was that of those who were there present, not one went about to help their emperor; and all that were sent for rejected the messenger saving only a company of German horsemen. These, in regard of his fresh merit (in that he had tenderly cherished and made much of them being sick and feeble), hastened to the rescue, howbeit they came too late, because, being ignorant of the streets and places, they took a wrong way and were hindered. Killed he was at the Lake Curtius, and there left lying even as he was until such time as a common soldier, as he returned from foraging and providing of corn, threw down his load and cut his head off. Now because he could not catch hold of the hair of his head (so bald he was) he hid it in his lap, and anon thrust his thumb into his mouth and so brought it to Otho, who gave it to the scullions, lackies and varlets that

follow the camp. These, sticking it upon a spear, carried it, not without reproachful scorn, all about the camp, setting up ever and anon this note: "Galba, thou lovely cupid, take thy time and make use of thy fresh and youthful years." Provoked they were especially to such malapert frumps and flouts because some days before there ran a rife report abroad that unto one who commended that visage and person of his as continuing still fresh, fair and vigorous, he made this answer from Homer's Iliad:

> I have yet still
> My strength at will.

At their hands, a freedman of Patrobius Neronianus bought the aforesaid head for one hundred pieces of gold, and flung it into that very place where beforetime his patron, by the commandment of Galba, had been executed. At length (though late it was) his steward Argius buried both it and the trunk of his body within his own private gardens in the way Aurelia.

21. Of full stature he was; his head bald, his eyes gray and his nose hooked; his hands and feet by reason of the gout were grown exceeding crooked: so much so that he was unable to abide shoes on the one, or to turn over or so much as hold books with the other. There was an excrescence also of flesh in the right side of his body; and the same hung down so much that it hardly could be tied up with a truss.

22. A great feeder and meat-man by report he was. For in winter time he used to eat before daylight, and at supper to be served so plentifully that the relics and reversion of the board being gathered together into heaps, he commanded to be carried round about and distributed among those that stood waiting at his feet. Given he was overmuch to the unnatural lust of male-kind, but such chose he (and none else) for his darlings as were stale thick-skins and past growth. It was re-

ported that in Spain, when Icelus, one of his old catamites, brought him word of Nero's end, he not only received him in open sight with most kind kisses, but entreated him without delay to be plucked, and so led him at one side out of the way.

23. He died in the seventy-third year of his age, and seventh month of his empire. The senate, as soon as lawfully they might, had decreed for him a statue standing upon a column adorned with the stems and beak-heads of ships in that part of the Forum of Rome where he lost his life, but Vespasian repealed that decree, as being thus conceited of him that he had suborned and sent under hand out of Spain into Judea certain of purpose to murder him.

THE HISTORY OF
MARCUS SALVIUS OTHO

OTHO

THE ANCESTORS OF OTHO HAD THEIR BEGIN-
ning in a town called Ferentinum, extract out of an
ancient and honorable family, even from the princes
of Etruria. His grandfather Marcus Salvius Otho, having for
his father a Roman knight and for his mother a woman of base
condition (and whether she was freeborn or no, it is uncertain),
through the favor of Livia Augusta, in whose house he had his
rising and growth, was made a senator, and exceeded not the
degree of praetor. His father Lucius Otho, by his mother's side
of right noble blood descended and thereby allied to many great
kindred, was so dear and in face so like unto Tiberius the
emperor that most men believed verily he was his own son.
The honorable offices within the city, the proconsulship of Asia
and other extraordinary places of conduct and command he
managed most severely. He adventured also in Illyricum to
proceed so far as to put certain soldiers to death for that in the
commotion of Camillus, upon a touch of conscience, they had
killed their captains and provosts as authors of the revolt and
rebellion against Claudius; and verily this execution himself in
person saw performed in the camp, even before the headquarters; notwithstanding that he knew they were for that service
advanced to higher places by Claudius. By which act of his as
he grew in glory so he decreased in favor. And yet the same
he soon recovered again by detecting the perfidious plot of a
Roman knight whom, by the impeachment of his own son,
he found to have attempted the death of Claudius. For both

the senate endowed him with an honor most rare and seldom seen, to wit his own statue erected in the Palatium; and also Claudius, when he ranged him among the patricians and in most honorable terms praised him, added these words withal, "he is a man than whom I would not wish, I assure you, to have better children than mine own." Of Albia Terentia, a right noble and gallant lady, he begat two sons, Lucius Titianus, and a younger forenamed Marcus and carrying the surname of his father; a daughter also he had by her, whom as yet not marriageable he affianced unto Drusus, the son of Germanicus.

2. This Otho the emperor was born the fourth day before the Kalends of May, when Camillus Arruntius and Domitius Ahenobarbus were consuls. From the very prime of his youth he was riotous, wild and wanton; so much so that his father flogged him well and soundly for it. He was reported also to use night walking, and if he met anyone either feeble or cupshotten or overcome with drink he would catch hold of him, lay him upon a soldier's blanket and so toss and hoist him up into the air. Afterwards, upon his father's death, a certain libertine woman of the court, a dame very influential (in order to make the more benefit by following and courting her as his mistress) he pretended love unto, albeit an old trot she was in manner doting for age. By her means winding himself into the favor of Nero, he easily obtained the chief place among his minions and favorites (such was the congruence of their humors and dispositions), and as some write by mutual abusing of one another's bodies. But so mighty he waxed and bore such a side, that in consideration of a great piece of money agreed upon he presumed to bring into the senate house for to give thanks a man of consular degree who stood condemned for extortion, even before he had fully obtained his restitution.

3. Being now, as he was, privy to all the counsels and secret

designs of Nero, he, to avert all manner of suspicion, on that very day which Nero had appointed for the murdering of his mother, entertained them both at supper with the most exquisite and kindest welcome that might be. Also, dame Poppaea Sabina, being as yet but the paramour of Nero, whom he had newly taken from her husband [Rufius Crispus], and committed in the meanwhile unto himself upon trust for to keep, under a color of marriage he received her. And not content herewith that he alienated her heart from Nero, and used her body, he loved her so entirely that he could not endure Nero himself to be his corrival. Certes, it is thought of a truth that not only the messengers who were sent to fetch her came again without her, but also that one time he kept Nero himself without doors standing there and cooling his heels, with threats also and prayers intermingled, demanding his pawn which he had left with him, but all in vain. Whereupon after the said marriage was broken and dissolved, sent out of the way he was under a pretense of an embassage into Portugal. Which course was thought sufficient for fear least his proceeding to any sharper punishment might have told tales abroad and marred all the play. Howbeit as secretly conceived as it was, out it came and was made known by this distich:

> *Cur Otho mentito sit quaeritis exul honore?*
> *Uxoris moechus coeperat esse suae.*

> Exil'd in show of embassage was Otho. Ask you why?
> With his own wife begun he had to act adultery.

Having been aforetime in no higher place than quaestor, yet governed he a province for the space of ten years with singular moderation and abstinence.

4. As occasion at length and opportunity of revenge was offered, he was the first that combined with Galba in his attempts. At which very instant himself also conceived hope

of the empire; and great the same was, no doubt, considering the condition and state of those times, but greater somewhat by reason of Seleucus the astrologer's words: who, having long before warranted him that he should survive Nero, was then of his own accord come unlooked for, and promised again that shortly also he should be emperor. Omitting therefore no kind of obsequious office and ambitious popularity even to the very meanest: as often as he invited the emperor to supper he would deal throughout the cohort that then warded, to every man a piece of gold; and no less careful was he to oblige unto him one way or other the rest of the soldiers. And when one of them went to law with his neighbor about a parcel of ground in the skirts and confines of both their lands, he, being chosen arbitrator, bought the whole land for the said soldier and enfeoffed him in it. So as now by this time there was scarce one but both thought and said that he alone was worthy to succeed in the empire.

5. Moreover he had fed himself with hopes to have been adopted by Galba, and that looked he for daily. But after that Piso was preferred and himself disappointed of his hope, he turned to plain violence, pricked thereto, over and besides the discontentment of his mind, by occasion that he was so deeply indebted. For he stuck not to profess that he was not able to stand unless he were emperor, and that it skilled not whether he were overthrown by his enemy in the field, or fell under his creditor's hands in the Forum. Some few days before he had fetched over from one of Caesar's servants a million sesterces for the obtaining of a stewardship; and with the help of this sum of money, enterprised he so great a project. At first he committed the matter to five soldiers employed in his bodyguard, then to ten others whom they had brought forth with them, to wit every man twain. To each one of these he paid in hand ten thousand sesterces, and promised 50,000

Wakening then at last about daylight and not before, with one only thrust under his left pap he stabbed himself.

more. By these were the rest solicited, and those not very many, as making no doubt but presuming confidently of this that a number besides would be ready in the very action to second it.

6. He had minded once, presently after the adoption (of Piso) to seize their camp into his own hands and so to set upon Galba as he sat at supper in the Palace. But because of the respective regard of the cohort which then kept watch and ward he checked this intent of his, for fear lest the same should incur the intolerable hatred of the world, considering that, by the guard of that very cohort, Gaius had been slain before, and Nero perfidiously betrayed afterwards. Moreover, exception was taken against the middle time between, partly upon a superstition that he had, and in part by direction from Seleucus. Well then, upon a day appointed, after warning given aforehand unto those that were privy to the conspiracy for to attend him in the Forum at the golden milepost under the temple of Saturn, he saluted Galba in the morning, and (as the manner was) being received with a kiss, was present also as he sacrificed and heard the soothsayers' prediction. Which done, a freedman of his brought him word that the architects were come (this was the watchword agreed upon between them), whereupon as if forsooth he were to look upon a house that was to be sold, he departed, gat him quickly away through the back side of the Palace and hied apace toward the place appointed. Others say that he feigned himself to have an ague, and willed those that stood next to him to make that excuse in case he were asked for. Then, lying hidden within a woman's litter, he hastened to the camp; and because the litter bearers were tired and faint he alighted on the ground and began to run afoot, but by occasion that his shoe's latchet was slack, he stayed behind until such time as, without any further delay, he was taken up on men's shoulders and by the train and company there present saluted emperor, and so with lucky

acclamations among drawn swords came as far as to the head-quarters, while everyone along the way he went adhered unto him as if they had been all privy and party in the conspiracy. There, after he had dispatched certain away to kill both Galba and Piso, he, to win the soldiers' hearts by fair promises, protested before them all assembled together that himself would have and hold no more, than just that which they would leave for him.

7. This done, as the day drew toward evening, he entered into the senate; and, briefly laying before them a reason of his proceeding, as if he had been carried away perforce out of the Forum and compelled to take the empire upon him (which he would administer according to the general will and pleasure of them all), to the palace he goes. Now when as besides other sweet and plausible words delivered by such as did congratulate and flatter him, he was by the base common people called Nero, he gave no token at all that he refused it; nay, rather, as some have reported, ever in his patents, grants and missives which he first wrote unto certain presidents and governors of provinces, he added unto his style the surname of Nero. This is certain, he both suffered Nero's images and statues to be erected again in their own places, and also restored his procurators and freedmen to the same offices that they had enjoyed before. Neither by his imperial prerogative and absolute power subscribed he anything before a warrant for fifty million sesterces to the finishing of Nero's golden house. It is said that the same night being affrighted in his sleep he groaned very sore and was by his servitors that ran thick into the chamber found lying on the bare floor before his bed; also that he assayed by all kinds of propitiatory sacrifices and peace offerings to appease the spirit of Galba, whom he had seen in his sleep to thrust and drive him forth; also the morrow after, as he was taking his auspices, there arose a sudden tem-

pest, whereupon he caught a grievous fall, and oftentimes he mumbled this unto himself (in Greek):

For, how can I (whose blast is short)
With these long hautboys fitly sort?

8. And verily about the same time, the forces and armies in Germany had sworn fealty and allegiance unto Vitellius, which when he understood he propounded unto the senate that an embassage might be sent thither to advertise them that there was an emperor chosen already and advise them withal to peace and concord. Yet, by intercourse of messengers and letters between them, he made no offer unto Vitellius to partake equally with him in the empire and accept of a marriage with his daughter. But when there was no way but one and that by open war, seeing that now already the captains and forces which Vitellius had sent before approached, he had good proof what loyal and faithful hearts the praetorian soldiers carried towards him, even unto the utter ruin and destruction well near of the most honorable degree of senators. Now decreed it had been that by the marines armor should be conveyed over and sent back to Ostia by shipping. And as the said armor was in taking forth out of the armory in the camp at the shutting of the evening, some soldiers, suspecting treachery and treason, raised a tumult and gave an alarm. Wherewith suddenly all of them without any certain leader to conduct them ran to the palace, calling hard to have the senate massacred. And when they had repelled some of the tribunes who assayed to repress their violence, and killed other of them, all embrued in blood as they were and asking where the emperor was, they rushed in as far as into his banqueting room and never rested until they had seen him. Then set he forward his expedition lustily and began with more haste than good speed, without any care at all of religion and the will

of God: as having only stirred and taken those sacred shields called *Ancilia* and not bestowed them quietly again in their due place (a thing in old time held ominous and ever presaging ill luck). Besides, the very same day it was upon which the priest and ministers of Cybele, the mother of the gods, begin to lament, weep and wail. To conclude, all signs and tokens were as crossed as possibly they might be. For not only in the beast killed for sacrifice unto Father Dis he found the innards propitious (whereas in such a sacrifice the contrary had been more acceptable), but also at his first setting out stayed he was by the inundation and swelling of the river Tiber. At the twenty miles' end, likewise, he found the highway choked and stopped up against him with the ruins of certain houses fallen down.

9. With like inconsiderate rashness, albeit no man doubted but that in good policy the war ought to have been protracted because the enemy was distressed as well with famine as the straits wherein he was pent, yet resolved he with all speed to hazard the fortune of the field and to try it out by fight, either impatient of longer thought and pensiveness and hoping that before the coming of Vitellius most part of the business might be dispatched, or else because he could not rule his soldiers calling so hotly upon him to give battle. Yet he was not present in that conflict but stayed behind at Brixellum. And verily in three several skirmishes, which were not great, to wit, upon the Alps, about Placentia and at Castoris (a place so called) won the victory; but in the last battle of all (which was the greatest), he lost the day and was by a treacherous practice vanquished, namely, when upon hope of a parley pretended, as if the soldiers had been brought out of the camp to treat of conditions of peace: suddenly and unlooked for, even as they saluted one another, there was no remedy but fight it out they must. And straightways in a melancholy he conceived a re-

solution to make himself away (as many are of opinion and not without cause) rather for shame that he would not be thought to persevere in the maintenance of his dominion with so great jeopardy of the state and loss of men, than upon any despair or distrust of his forces. For still there remained a puissant army, whole and entire, which he had detained with him for trial of better fortune, and another power was coming out of Dalmatia, Pannonia and Moesia. Neither verily were they discomfited or so much daunted and dejected, but that for to be revenged of this disgrace and ready they were of themselves, and alone without the help of others, to undergo any hard adventure whatsoever.

10. In this war served mine own father Suetonius Laetus in quality of a tribune of the thirteenth legion, and by degree a knight. He was wont afterwards very often to report that Otho, even when he lived a private person, detested all civil wars so far forth, that, when one related at the table the end of Cassius and Brutus, he fell a-quaking and trembling thereat. Also that he never would have been Galba's rival, but that he confidently thought the quarrel might have ended without war. Well then, upon a new accident incited he was to the contempt of this present life, even by the example of a common and ordinary soldier, who, reporting this overthrow of the army, when he could of no man have credit but was charged one while with the lie, another while for his fear and cowardice (as one who was run away out of the battle), fell upon his own sword at Otho's feet. At which sight he cried out aloud and said that he would no more cast so brave men and of so good desert into danger. Having exhorted therefore his own brother, his brother's son and every one of his friends severally to make what shift they could for themselves, after he had embraced and kissed them each one, he sent them all away, and retiring himself into a secret room, two letters he wrote full of con-

solation to his sister, as also to Messalina, Nero's widow whom he had purposed to wed, recommending the relics of his body and his memorial. And what epistles soever he had in his custody, he burnt them all, so that they should breed no man any danger, loss or displeasure with the conqueror. And out of that store of treasure which he had about him, he dealt money to his domestic servants.

11. Being now thus prepared and fully bent to die, perceiving by occasion of some hurliburly which, while he made delay, arose, that those who began to slip away and depart were (by his soldiers) rebuked as traitors and perforce detained, "let us," quoth he, "prolong our life yet this one night." Upon which words and no more he charged that no violence should be offered to any, but suffering his bed-chamber door to stand wide open until it was late in the evening, he permitted all that would to have access unto him. After this, having allayed his thirst with a draught of cold water, he caught up two daggers, and, when he had tried how sharp the points of both were and laid one of them under his pillow, and so the doors being fast shut, he took his rest and slept most soundly. Wakening then at last about daylight and not before, with one only thrust under his left pap he stabbed himself. And when at the first groan that he gave his servants broke in, he, one while concealing and another while discovering the wound, yielded up his vital breath, and quickly (as he had given charge before) was brought to his funeral fire: in the year of his age thirty-eight, and the ninety-fifth day of his empire.

12. Unto so great a mind and generous courage of Otho, neither was his person nor his habit answerable. For he was by report of a mean and low stature. Feeble feet he had besides, and as crooked shanks. As for his manner of attire, as fine and nice he was well near as any woman: his body plucked and made smooth, wearing by reason of thin hair a peruke so

fitted and fastened to his head that no man there was but would have taken it for his own. Nay his very face he was wont every day to shave and besmear all over with soaked bread. Which device he took when the down first began to bud forth, because he would never have a beard. It is said, moreover, that many a time he openly celebrated the divine service and sacred rites of Isis in a religious vestment of linen. Whereby, I would think it came to pass that his death, nothing all consonant to his life, was the more wondered at. Many of his soldiers who were present about him, when, with plentiful tears they had kissed his hands and feet, dead as he lay, and commended him withal for a most valiant man and the only emperor that ever was, presently, in the place and not far from his funeral fire, killed themselves. Many of them also who were absent, hearing of the news of his end, for very grief of heart ran with their weapons one at another to death. Finally most men who in his life time cursed and detested him, now when he was dead, highly praised him, so that it came to be a common and rife speech abroad that Galba was by him slain, not so much for that he affected to be sovereign ruler as because he desired to restore the state of the republic, and recover the freedom that was lost.

THE HISTORY OF
AULUS VITELLIUS

VITELLIUS

AS TOUCHING THE ORIGIN AND BEGINNING of the Vitelli, some write this, others that, and all as contrary as may be: reporting it partly to be ancient and noble, and in part new start up and obscure, and very base and beggarly. Which I would suppose to have happened by means of the flatterers and backbiters both, of Vitellius the emperor, but that I see there is some variance and diversity about the very condition of that family. A little book there is extant of one Quintus Eulogius' making, written unto Quintus Vitellius, quaestor unto Augustus Caesar of sacred memory; wherein is contained thus much, that the Vitellii descended from Faunus, king of the Aborigines, and lady Vitellia (who in many places was worshipped for a goddess), and that they reigned over all Latium; that the offspring remaining of them removed out of the Sabines' country to Rome and were taken into the ranks of the patricians; that many monuments giving testimony of this race continued a long time, to wit, the highway Vitellia, reaching from Janiculum to the sea, and likewise a colony of the same name, the defense and keeping whereof against the Aequicoli they in times past requested, with the strength only and the puissance of their own family; moreover, that afterwards in the time of the Samnite war, when a garrison was sent into Apulia, some of the Vitellii remained behind at Nuceria, and their progeny many a year after returned to Rome and recovered their senator's degree.

2. Contrariwise, more authors there be who have left upon

record that their stock-father was a freedman. Cassius Severus, and others as well as he do write that the same man was also a very cobbler, whose son, having gotten more by chaffering at a price for the confiscate goods of men condemned, and by gains arising out of undertaking men's suits; that of a common naughty pack, the daughter of one Antiochus, a baker, he begat a son who proved afterwards a knight of Rome. This dissonance of opinions I leave indifferent, for men to believe which they will. But, to the purpose: Publius Vitellius, born in Nuceria (whether he were of that ancient lineage or descended from base parents and grandfathers), a Roman knight doubtless, and a procurator under Augustus of his affairs, left behind him four sons, men of quality all and right honorable persons; bearing also their father's surname, and distinguished only by their forenames, Aulus, Quintus, Publius and Lucius. Aulus died even when he was consul, which dignity he had entered upon with Domitius, the father of Nero Caesar; a man very sumptuous otherwise in his house and much spoken of for his magnificent suppers. Quintus was displaced from his senator's estate when, by the motion and persuasion of Tiberius, there passed an act that such senators as were thought insufficient should be culled out and removed. Publius, a companion and dependant of Germanicus, accused and convicted Gnaeus Piso, his mortal enemy and the man who murdered him. And after the honorable place of praetor, being apprehended among the accomplices of Sejanus' conspiracy and committed to the keeping of his brother, with a penknife cut his own veins; and after that, not so much repenting that he sought his own death as overcome with the earnest entreaty of his friends about him, suffered his wounds to be bound up and cured, but in the same imprisonment he died of sickness. Lucius, after his consulship being provost of Syria, with passing fine slights and cunning devices trained and enticed forth

Artabanus king of the Parthians, not only to parley with him, but also to worship and adore the standard of the Roman legions. Soon after, together with Claudius the emperor, he bore two ordinary consulships, one immediately upon the other, and the censorship also; likewise the charge of the whole empire, while Claudius was absent in the expedition of Britain, he sustained: a harmless person, active and industrious, howbeit blemished with a very bad name for the love he bore unto a freedwoman whose spittle mixed with honey he used as a remedy (and that not closely and seldom but every day and openly), washing therewith his pipes and throat. He was besides of a wonderful glavering nature and given unto flatteries. He it was that first by his example brought up the order to adore Gaius Caesar as a god, when, being returned out of Syria, he durst not come into his presence otherwise than with his head covered, turning himself about and then falling down prostrate before him at his feet. And because he would omit no artificial means to curry favor with Claudius, a prince so addicted to his wife and freedmen, he made suit unto Messalina, as if it had been for the greatest gift she could bestow upon him to do him the grace that he might have the doffing of her shoes; and the right foot pump which he had drawn off he carried in his bosom continually between his gown and inward clothes; yea, and many times would kiss the same. The golden images also of Narcissus and Pallas he reverently honored among his domestic gods. This was a word likewise of his, when he did congratulate Claudius at the exhibiting of the secular plays [so called because they were solemnized but once in a hundred, or a hundred and ten years], "*saepe facias*," i. e., "many a time may you this do." He died of a palsy the very next day after it took him, leaving behind two sons whom Sextilla, his wife, a woman for her virtue highly approved and of no mean parentage descended, bore unto him.

Them he saw both consuls and that in one year, yea and the same throughout, for that the younger succeeded the elder for six months. When he was departed from this life, the senate granted unto him the honor of a public funeral, and a statue likewise before the rostra with this inscription: "*Pietatis immobilis erga principem*," i. e., "Of constant devotion and irremovable piety to his prince."

3. Aulus Vitellius, the son of Lucius and emperor, was born the eighth day before the Kalends of October, or as some will have it, the seventh day before the Ides of September, when Drusus Caesar and Norbanus Flaccus were consuls. His nativity, foretold by the astrologers, his parents had in such horror that his father endeavored always what he could that no province while he lived should be committed unto him; and his mother, when he was both sent unto the legions and saluted lord general, straightway lamented as if then he had been undone for ever. His childhood and flower of youth he spent at Capri, among the strumpets and catamites that Tiberius kept there. Himself, noted always with the surname of Spintria [a deviser of new fashions and forms of filthy uncleanness], was thought also, by suffering the abuse of his own body, to have been the cause of his father's rising and advancement.

4. All the time also of his age ensuing, stained as he was with all manner of reproachable villainies, he carried a principal sway above others in the court, grown into familiar acquaintance with Gaius for his love of chariot running, and with Claudius for his affection to dice play. But in greater favor he was a good deal with Nero, both in the selfsame regard aforesaid, as also for this especial merit, in that, being president at the solemnity called Neronia, when Nero was desirous to strive for the prize among the harpers and musicians, but yet durst not promise to do so (notwithstanding all the people called insistently upon him) and thereupon went out of the

theater, he, pretending that he was sent ambassador unto him from the people persisting still in their earnest request, had called him back and so brought him in the end to be entreated.

5. Through the favorable indulgence therefore of three emperors, being advanced not only to right honorable offices of state, but also to as high sacerdotal dignities, he managed after all these the proconsulship of Africa and executed the charge of suveying and supervising the public works, but with mind and reputation both, far unlike. For in his province he demeaned himself for two years together with singular innocence and integrity, for, after his brother succeeded in his stead, he stayed there still in quality of his lieutenant. But in his office within the city he was reported to have secretly stolen away the oblations, gifts and ornaments of the temples; to have embezzled and changed some of them; yea, and in lieu of gold and silver to have foisted tin and copper.

6. He took to wife Petronia, the daughter of one that had been consul, by whom he had a son with one eye, named Petronianus. Him, being by his mother ordained her heir upon condition that he were freed once out of his father's power, he manumitted indeed, but soon after (as it was thought) killed, having charged him besides with parricide and pretending withal that the poison which was provided to work that mischief, he upon remorse of conscience had drunk himself. After this, he wedded Galeria Fundana, whose father had been praetor, and of her body also begat children of both sexes, but the male child had such an impediment of stutting and stammering that little better he was than dumb and tongueless.

7. By Galba sent he was contrary to all expectation into Lower Germany, furthered as it is thought by the voice and favor of Titus Vinius, a man in those days most mighty, and unto whom long before he had been won by favoring the faction unto which they were both equally affected. But since

Galba professed plainly that none were less to be feared than those who thought of nothing but their victuals only, and that his greedy appetite and hungry belly might be satisfied and filled with the plenteous store that the province did yield. So that evident it was to every man that he chose him in contempt rather than upon any special grace. This is for certain known, that when he was to go forth, he wanted provision for his journey by the way; and that for the maintenance of his family was driven to such hard shifts and extremities, that mewing up his wife and children (whom he left at Rome) in a little upper lodging that he rented, he let out his own dwelling house for the rest of the year; yea, and took from his mother's ear a pearl which he pawned, and all for to defray the charges of that voyage. As for a number verily of his creditors who waited for him as ready to stay his passage, and among them the Sinuessans and Formians whose public imposts, tollage and revenues he had intercepted and converted to his own use, he could not be rid of, but by terrifying them with an action at law: serving one of them, and namely a freedman (who very eagerly demanded a debt) with process upon an action of battery, alleging he had stricken him with his heel, and would not withdraw the suit before he had extorted from him fifty thousand sesterces. In his coming toward the camp, the army, maliciously bent against the emperor and ready to entertain any revolt and change of state, willingly and with open arms received him, as a gift of the gods, presented unto them from heaven above: the son of one thrice consul, a man in the vigor and strength of his years, of a gentle disposition besides, and of a frank and prodigal heart. Which opinion and persuasion being of old conceived and settled in men's minds, Vitellius had augmented by some fresh proofs lately given of himself: kissing all the way as he went along every mean common soldier that he met; so courteous and affable above all measure to the very muleteers and wayfaring passengers in every inn and posthouse, that he would in a morning betimes ask them one by one whether they had yet broken their fast and show unto them even by his belching that he had been at breakfast already.

8. Now when he was entered once into the camp, no suit denied he to any man; nay, of his own accord he took off their marks of ignominy who stood in disgrace, dispensed with those that were obnoxious to the laws for wearing poor and sullied garments, and forgave condemned persons their punishments. Whereupon, before one month was fully come and gone, without all respect either of day or time, when the very evening was now shooting in, suddenly by the soldiers called forth he was out of his bed-chamber, and clad as he was in his domestic and home apparel, saluted by the name of Imperator, and carried round about the most frequented and populous towns, holding in his hand the naked sword of Julius the dictator, of sacred memory, which being taken out of the temple of Mars was at the first gratulation presented by one unto him. Neither returned he into the praetorium [the lord general's lodging] before the dining room was caught on fire by occasion of the chimney there, where it first caught. And then verily, when all besides were amazed and in great perplexity upon this adverse and ominous accident, "be of good cheer," quoth he, "it hath shined fair upon us"; and no other speech at all made he unto his soldiers. After this, when the army also of the upper province consented now by this time with the other (that army I mean which had revolted before from Galba and sided with the senate), the surname of Germanicus, generally offered unto him, he gladly accepted; the addition of Augustus he put off, and the style of Caesar he utterly for ever refused.

9. And soon after, when news came unto him that Galba was slain, having settled the state of Germany, he divided his forces thus: sending one part thereof before against Otho, and mind-

ing to lead the rest himself. Unto the army which was sent before there happened a fortunate and lucky sign. For on the right hand all on a sudden flew an eagle toward them, and when she had fetched a compass round about the standards and ensigns, hovered softly before them as they marched on the way. Contrariwise, as himself removed and set forward, the statues on horseback erected in many places for him, all at once suddenly broke their legs and tumbled down, and the garland of laurel which most devoutly he had done about his head fell from it into a running river. Within a while after, as he sat judicially upon the tribunal to minister justice at Vienna, a cock first settled upon his shoulder and anon perched upon his very head. Upon which prodigious sights ensued an event correspondent thereto. For the empire which by his lieutenants was confirmed and established unto him, he by himself was not able to hold.

10. Of the victory before Betriacum and the death of Otho, he heard while he was yet in Gaul. And without delay, whosoever belonged to the praetorian cohorts, he by virtue of one edict cashed and discharged them all for the most dangerous precedent and example that they had given, commanding them to yield up their armor into the marshal's hands. As for those hundred and twenty whose supplications exhibited unto Otho he had found, such I mean as claimed rewards for their good service in killing Galba, he gave commandment that they should be sought out and executed every one. A worthy beginning I assure you and a magnificent: such as might give good hope of an excellent prince, had he not managed all matters else according to his own natural disposition and the course of his former life, rather than respecting the majesty of an emperor. For no sooner put he himself in his journey, but he rode through the midst of cities in triumphant wise, and passed along the great rivers in most delicate barges, garnished

and adorned with coronets of sundry sorts, faring at his table most sumptuously and served with all manner of dainty viands. He observed no discipline either of household servitor or of soldier, but turned the outrages, villainies and licentious pranks of them all to a jest. Who, not content with their ordinary diet allowed and provided for them in every place where they came, at the common charges of the state, whatever slaves or aliens it pleased them, they manumitted and made free, but paid as many as withstood them with whipping cheer, blows, knocks, bloody wounds, oftentimes, yea, and otherwhiles with present death. When he came into the fields where the battle was fought, and some of his train loathed and abhorred the putrefied corruption of the dead bodies, he stuck not to hearten and encourage them with this accursed speech, that an enemy slain had a very good smell, but a citizen far better. Howbeit, to qualify and allay the strong savor and scent that they cast, he poured down his throat before them all exceeding great store of strong wine, and dealt the same plentifully about. With as much vanity as insolent pride, when he beheld the stone under which Otho lay interred with an inscription in his memorial, "worthy was he of such a monument," quoth he. And the very same dagger wherewith he had killed himself he sent to Cologne for to be dedicated unto Mars. Certes upon the top of the Apennine hill he celebrated a sacrifice with a vigil all night long.

11. At length he entered the city with a warlike sound of trumpet, in his coat-armor and with a sword girt unto him, among ensigns, banners and flags: his followers and dependants clad in military cassocks and the armor of all his fellow soldiers discovered in open view. Thus neglecting more and more from time to time all law of God and man, upon the very disastrous day of the Allia he was installed in the sacerdotal dignity of a high priest. He ordained that the solemn assembly

for election of magistrates should be held every tenth year, and himself be perpetual dictator. And to the end that no man might doubt what pattern he chose to follow for government of the commonweal, calling a frequent number of the public priests about him in the middle of Mars field, he sacrificed to the spirit and ghost of Nero. And at a solemn feast he requested a favored flautist to perform something of the master's; and when he began a piece of Nero's, Vitellius was the first to applaud and even leapt up for joy.

12. Having in this manner begun his empire, a great part thereof he administered no otherwise than according to the advice and pleasure of the basest stage-players and charioteers that could be found, but especially of Asiaticus, a freedman of his own. This Asiaticus when he was a very youth had in mutual filthiness with him abused his own body, and afterwards, loathing that abominable sin, ran away. Now, finding him once at Puteoli selling a certain drink made of water and vinegar, first he laid him by the heels and hung a pair of fetters at his feet, but forthwith loosened him and entertained him as his darling again. After which a second time being offended with his contumacy and malapert stubbornness, he sold him to one of these common fencers that went from market to market. And by occasion that he was upon a time put off to the last place in a sword fight for to play his prize, at unawares he privily stole him away; and no sooner was he gone into his province but he manumitted him. The first day of his empire, as he sat at supper, he dubbed him knight of Rome and gave him the golden ring, notwithstanding that the very morning before, when all the soldiers entreated in his behalf, he detested so foul a blot, to stain and discredit the worshipful degree of knighthood.

13. But being given most of all to excessive belly cheer and cruelty, he divided his repast into three meals every day at

the least, and sometime into four, to wit, breakfast, dinner,
supper and drinking parties, able to bear them all very well,
so ordinarily he used to vomit. Now his manner was to send
word that he would break his fast with one friend, dine with
another, etc., and all in one day. And every one of these
refections, when it stood them in least, cost them 40,000
sesterces. But the most notorious and memorable supper above
all other was that which his brother made for a welcome at his
first coming to Rome, at which by report were served up to
the table before him two thousand several dishes of fish, the
most dainty and choicest that could be had, and seven thousand
of fowl. And yet, even this (as sumptuous as it was), himself
surpassed at the dedication of that platter which for the huge
capacity thereof he used to call the target of Minerva and the
shield of the city's protectress. In this he huddled and blended
together the livers of pike, the delicate brains of pheasants and
peacocks, the tongues of flamingoes and the tender small guts
of sea-lampreys, fetched as far as from the Carpathian Sea
and the straits of Spain by his captains over galleys. And, as a
man that had not only a wide throat of his own to devour
much but also as greedy a stomach to feed both unseasonably
and also grossly of whatever came next to hand, he could not
so much as at any sacrifice whensoever, or in any journey
wheresoever, forbear but among the altars snatch up by and by
the flesh, the parched corn also and meal even from the very
hearth, and eat the same; yea, and at every victualling house
by the wayside fall to viands piping hot, yet reeking, and not
cooled one jot; and not to spare so much as meats dressed the
day before and half-eaten already.

14. Being forward enough to put to death and punish any
man what cause soever was pretended, noblemen, his school
fellows and playmates in time past (whom by all fair means
and flattering allurements he had enticed and drawn to the

partnership, as it were, of the empire with him), he killed and one above the rest he made away with poison which he wrought unto him with his own hand in a draught of cold water that he called for, lying in a fit of ague. Of usurers, takers of bonds and obligations, and publicans who ever at any time had demanded of him either at Rome debt, or by the way as he travelled toll and custom, he hardly spared one. And one of them, whom, even as he came to salute him and do his duty, he had delivered over to the executioner for to suffer death, he called straightways back again. And when all that were by praised him for his clemency, he commanded the said party to be killed before his face, saying withal that he would feast his eyes. At the execution of another he caused two of his sons to bear him company for nothing in the world but because they presumed to entreat for their father's life. There was besides a Roman knight who being haled away to take his death, cried aloud unto him, "Sir, I have made you my heir." Him he compelled to bring forth the writing tablets containing his last will; and so soon as he read therein that a freedman of the testator's was nominated fellow heir with him, he commanded both master and man to be killed. Certain commoners also, for this only that they had railed aloud upon the faction of the Blues, he slew, opining that in daring so to do they had him in contempt and hoped for a change. Yet was he to none more spitefully bent than to the wizards and astrologers. Was any of them presented and informed against, he made no more ado, but without hearing what he could say for himself, bereaved him of his life. Nettled he was and exasperate against them for that after an edict of his wherein he gave commandment that all judicial astrologers should depart out of Rome and Italy before the first of October, presently there was a writing, or libel, set up in open place to this effect, that the Chaldeans made this edict as follows, "We give

warning by these presents unto Vitellius Germanicus that by
the Kalends of the said October he be not extant in any place
wheresoever." Suspected also he was to be consenting unto his
own mother's death, forbidding that any food should be ministered unto her, lying sick: induced thereto by one of the
Chatti, a wise woman, on whom he relied as an oracle, that
then and not before he should sit sure in his imperial throne
and continue very long, if he overlive his mother. And others
report how his mother herself, weary of the present state and
fearing what evil days were toward, obtained at her son's hand
poison, and that without any great entreaty.

15. In the eighth month of his empire, the armies of Moesia
both the one and the other, as also at Pannonia, revolted from
him; likewise, of the forces beyond the sea, those of Judea
and of Syria, and some of them swore allegiance unto Vespasian who was present among them. To retain therefore the love
and favor of all other men, he cared not what largesses he made
both in public and in private, beyond all measure. He mustered
also and levied soldiers within the city, with this covenant and
fair condition, that all volunteers should by virtue of his
promise have not only their discharge from service after
victory, but also the avails and fees due unto old soldiers for
serving out their full time. But afterwards, as the enemy came
hotly upon him both by land and sea, on the one side he
opposed his brother with the fleet and young, untrained soldiers, together with a crew of sword fencers; on the other,
what forces he had about Betriacum and the captains there.
And in every place being discomfited in open field or privily
betrayed, he capitulated and covenanted with Flavius Sabinus,
brother of Vespasian, to give up all, reserving his own life
and a hundred million sesterces. And forthwith upon the very
stairs of the palace professing openly before a frequent assembly
of his soldiers how willing he was to resign up that imperial

dignity which he had received against his will, when they all
gainsaid it, he put off the matter for that instant; and but one
night between, even the next morning, by break of day he
came down in a poor and simple array to the rostra where
with many a tear he recited the same words out of a little
written scroll. Now as the soldiers and people both interrupted
him a second time and exhorted him not to cast down his
heart, promising also with their utmost endeavor, and striving
a-vie who should do best to assist him, he took courage again
and plucked up his spirits, so that now fearing nothing at all
he came with a sudden power and violently chased Sabinus
and the rest of the Flavians into the Capitol; and there, having
set fire the temple of Jupiter Optimus Maximus, vanquished
and slew them, while himself beheld both the fight and the
fire out of Tiberius' house, sitting there at meat and making
good cheer. Not long after, repenting what he had done, and
laying all the fault upon others, he called a public assembly
where he swore and compelled all the rest to take the same
oath that he and they would respect nothing in the world
before the common peace. Then loosened he his dagger from
his side and reached it first to the consul, then upon his refusal
to the other magistrates, and anon to the senators one after
another. But when none of them all would receive it he departed, as if he meant to bestow it in the chapel of Concord.
Now when some cried out to him that himself was Concord, he
came back again and protested that he not only retained still the
blade with him, but also accepted the surname of Concord.

16. Hereupon he moved and advised the senate to send
ambassadors together with the Vestal Virgins to crave peace,
or else some longer time to consult upon the point. The next
morrow, as he stood expecting an answer, word was brought
unto him by his espial that the enemy approached. Immediately therefore shutting himself close within a bearing chair,

*. . . he stuck not to hearten and encourage them with this accursed speech,
that an enemy slain had a very good smell, but a citizen far better. Howbeit,
to qualify and allay the strong savor and scent that they cast, he poured down
his throat before them all exceeding great store of strong wine . . .*

accompanied with two persons only, his baker and his cook [that made his dainty pastry works and sweet meats: meet grooms to accompany such a glutton], secretly he took his way to the Aventine hill and his father's house, minding from there to make an escape into Campania. Soon after, upon a flying and headless rumor that peace was obtained, he suffered himself to be brought back to the palace. Where, finding all places solitary and abandoned, and seeing those also to slink from him and slip away who were with him, he did about him a girdle full of golden pieces of coin and fled into the porter's lodge, having first tied a dog at the door and set against it the bedstead and bedding thereto.

17. By this time had the advance guard of the Flavians' main army broken into the palace, and, meeting nobody, searched as the manner is every blind corner. By them was he plucked out of his lurking hole. And when they asked him who he was (for they knew him not) and where, upon his knowledge, Vitellius was, he shifted them off with a lie. After this, being once known, he entreated hard (as if he had somewhat to deliver concerning the life and safety of Vespasian) to be kept sure in the mean season, even though it were in some prison; and desisted he not until such time as having his hands pinioned fast at his back, a halter cast about his neck and his apparel torn from his body, he was haled half-naked into the Forum. Among many scornful indignities offered unto him both in deed and word throughout the spacious street, *sacra via*, from one end to the other, while they drew his head backward by the bush of his hair (as condemned malefactors are wont to be served) and set a sword's point under his chin and all to the end that he might show his face and not hold it down: while some pelted him with dung and dirty mire, others called him with open mouth incendiary and glutton, and some of the common sort twitted him also with faults and deformities of

413

his body: (for, of stature he was beyond measure tall; a red face he had, occasioned for the most part by swilling in wine, and a grand fat paunch besides; he limped somewhat also by reason that one of his thighs was enfeebled with the rush of a chariot against it, what time he served Gaius as his henchman at a chariot running), and at the last, upon the Stairs of Wailing, with many a small stroke all mangled he was and killed in the end, and so from thence drawn with a drag into the river Tiber.

18. Thus perished he with his brother and son together, in the fifty-seventh year of his age. Neither falsified he their conjecture who had foretold him that by the prodigious sign which befell unto him (as we have said) at Vienna, but that he should fall into the hands of some Frenchman. For dispatched he was by one Antonius Primus, a captain of the adverse part: who being born at Tolosa, was in his childhood surnamed Beccus [or Becco, a beak in English, which may somewhat confirm the learned conjecture of him who guesses that both our ancient nation and language were extract from Gaul] which in the French tongue signifies a cock's bill.

THE HISTORY OF
FLAVIUS VESPASIANUS AUGUSTUS

VESPASIAN

THE EMPIRE STANDING THUS A LONG TIME in doubtful terms, unsettled and wandering (as it were) by occasion of the rebellious broils and bloody slaughter of three princes, the Flavii at length took into their hands and established a house: one, I must needs say, of obscure descent and not able to show any pedigree and images of ancestors to commend their race; howbeit, such as the commonwealth had no cause to dislike and be ashamed of, although it be well known that Domitian suffered condign punishment for his avarice and cruelty. Titus Flavius Petro, a burgess of the free borough of Reate, and a centurion, siding in time of the civil wars with Pompey (but whether he served voluntarily or was called forth and pressed it is uncertain), fled out of the battle in Pharsalia and went home to his house. Where afterwards, having obtained his pardon and discharge from warfare, he became a bailiff under the bankers and money-changers to gather up their monies. This man's son, surnamed Sabinus, did nothing martial or skillful in feats of arms (although some write that he had been a principal leader of the foremost cohorts; and others that while he led certain companies he was acquitted from his military oath by occasion of sickliness), came to be a publican in Asia and gathered the custom or impost of fortieths for the state. And there remained certain images which the cities in that province erected for him with this title and superscription, "To a good and faithful publican." After this he put forth money to usury among the

Helvetians, where he ended his life, leaving behind him his wife Polla Vespasia and two children which he had by her. The elder of which, named Sabinus, was advanced to the provostship of the city; the younger, called Vespasianus, attained to the dignity imperial. This dame Polla, born at Nursia and descended of worshipful parentage, was the daughter of Vespasius Pollio, one that had been a military tribune thrice and provost marshal of the camp besides; she was sister to a man of senator's degree and promoted to the dignity of praetor. There is a place moreover even at this day, six miles from Rome (as men go to Spoletium from Nursia), upon the hilltop, bearing the name of Vespasiae, where many monuments of the Vespasii are to be seen: a great evidence to prove the nobleness and antiquity of that family. I cannot deny that some have given out how the father of that Petro came out of the Transpadane region and was a contractor; he would hire those laborers and hinds which were wont yearly to repair out of Umbria into the Sabine country for to till their grounds; and that he planted himself and stayed in the town of Reate aforesaid, and there married a wife. But myself could never find (make what search I could) any sign of trace to lead me thereto.

2. Vespasian was born in the Sabine territory beyond Reate within a small village named Falacrina, the fifteenth day before the Kalends of December, in the evening, when Quintus Camerinus and Gaius Poppaeus Sabinus were consuls: five years before that Augustus departed out of the world. His bringing up he had under Tertulla his grandmother by the father's side, in the land and living that she had about Cosa. Whereupon, when he was emperor he both frequented continually the place of his birth and breeding, the manor remaining still as it had been in former times, nothing altered (because forsooth, his eyes should have no loss nor miss of that which they were wont to see there), and loved also the memorial of his grandmother

418

so dearly that on all solemn and festival days he continued ever drinking out of a silver pot that was hers and out of none other. After he had put on his virile gown, he refused a long time the senator's robe, although his brother had attained thereto. Neither could he be forced to seek for it at last but by his own mother. She in the end wrought perforce so much from him by way of reproachful taunts more than by fair entreaty or reverent authority, while, ever and anon, she called him in taunting wise, his brother's usher. He served as tribune military in Thracia; and in quality of quaestor had the government of Crete and Cyrene, provinces by lot fallen unto him. When he sued to be aedile, and afterwards praetor, he hardly attained to the former offices (and not without some repulse) even in the sixth place; but presently at his first suit and with the foremost he was chosen praetor. Upon displeasure maliciously affected against the senate, because he would by any means win the favor of Gaius the emperor, he earnestly demanded extraordinary plays and games in honor of him for his victory in Germany; and gave opinion in the senate house that to augment the punishment of certain conspirators (against the emperor), their dead bodies should be cast forth and left unburied. He gave him also solemn thanks before that right honorable body for vouchsafing him the honor to be a guest of his at supper.

3. Amid these occurrences he espoused Flavia Domitilla, the freedwoman of Statilius Capella, a Roman knight of Sabrata in Africa; at first of Latin rank, she was afterwards pronounced a freeborn citizen of Rome by decision of arbiters at the suit of her father, Flavius Liberalis, born at Ferentum and only a quaestor's clerk. By her he had issue, Titus, Domitianus and Domitilla. His wife and daughter he overlived, and buried them while he was yet in state of a private person. After his foresaid wife's decease, he called home again to cohabit with

419

him in his house Caenis, a freedwoman of Antonia, and her secretary, whom he had fancied in former time. And he kept her while he was emperor, almost as his true and lawful wife.

4. Under the emperor Claudius, by especial favor of Narcissus, sent he was into Germany as lieutenant of a legion. From thence, being removed into Britain, he fought thirty battles with the enemy. Two most mighty nations, and above twenty towns, together with the isle of Wight lying next to the said Britain, he subdued, under the conduct partly of Aulus Plautius, lieutenant to the consul, and in part of Claudius himself, for which worthy acts he received triumphal ornaments, and in short space two sacerdotal dignities with a consulship besides which he bore the last months of the year. For the middle time between, even until he was proconsul, he led a private life in a retiring place out of the way, for fear of Agrippina who as yet bore great stroke with her son and hated to the heart all the friends of Narcissus, even though he was deceased. After this, having the province of Africa allotted unto him, he governed the same with singular integrity and not without much honor and reputation, but that in a seditious commotion at Hadrumentum there were turnips flung at his head. Certain it is that from thence he returned nothing richer than he was; so that, unable to keep credit, but grown almost bankrupt, he was driven to mortgage all his houses and lands unto his brother, and, of necessity for the maintenance of his estate and dignity, went so low as to make gains by huckster's trade, pampering beasts for better sale. Whereupon he was commonly named Mulio, "the Muleteer." It is also said that convicted he was for extorting from a young man two hundred thousand sesterces, in consideration that by his means he had obtained for him a senator's stripe, even against his father's will, for which he had sore rebuke. While he traveled through Achaia in the train and inward company of Nero, he

incurred his heavy displeasure in the highest degree, for that while he was chanting, either he made many starts away out of the place, or else slept if he stayed there still. And being forbidden not only to converse in the same lodging with him, but also to salute him publicly with others, he withdrew himself aside into a small city which stood out of the way, until such time as lying close there, and fearing the worst, the government of a province with the command of an army was offered unto him. There had been spread throughout all the East parts an opinion of old, and the same settled in men's heads and was constantly believed, that by the appointment of the destinies about such a time there should come out of Judea those who were to be lords of the whole world: which being a prophecy (as afterwards the event showed), foretelling of the Roman emperor, the Jews, drawing to themselves, rebelled, and having slain the governor there, put to flight also the lieutenant general of Syria (a man of consular degree) coming in to aid, and took away from him the eagle. To repress this insurrection, because there was need of a greater army and a valiant captain, yet such a one to whom a matter of so great consequence might safely be committed, himself was chosen above all others, as a man of approved valor and industry; howbeit no way to be feared for the meanness of his birth, lineage and name. Having therefore under his hand an addition to the former power, of two legions, eight coronets of horse and ten cohorts of foot; taking also unto him among other lieutenants, his elder son [Titus], no sooner arrived he in that province, but the other states likewise next adjoining he brought into admiration of him for reforming immediately at his first coming the discipline of the camp, and giving the charge in one or two battles with such resolution as that in the assault of a castle he caught a rap with a stone upon his knee and received in his target some shot of arrows.

5. After Nero and Galba, while Otho and Vitellius strove for sovereignty, he had good hope of the empire, conceived long before by these presaging tokens (which I will now relate): within a country farm by the city, belonging to the Flavii, there stood an old oak consecrated unto Mars, which at three childbirths of Vespasia suddenly did put forth every time a bough from the stock, undoubted signs fore-showing the destiny and fortune of each one. The first was small and slender, which quickly withered (and therefore the girl at that time born lived not one year to an end); the second grew very stiff and long withal, which portended great felicity; but the third came to the bigness of a tree. Whereupon Sabinus, the father of Vespasian, being confirmed besides by the answer of a soothsayer, brought word back (by report) unto his own mothers that she had a grandson born who should be Caesar: whereat she did nothing else but set up a laughter, marveling that her son should have a cracked brain and fall a-doting now, since that his mother had her wits still whole and sound. Soon after, when Gaius Caesar, offended and angry with him for that being aedile he had not been careful about sweeping and cleaning the streets, commanded that he should be all bedaubed with mire that the soldiers gathered up and threw into the lap of his embroidered robe, some were ready to make this interpretation thereof, that the commonwealth trodden one day under foot and forlorn by some civil troubles, should fall into his protection and, as it were, into his bosom. As he was at his dinner upon a time, a strange dog brought into his dining room a man's hand and laid it under the board. Again, as he sat another time at supper, an ox, having been at plough and shaken off his yoke, rushed into the parlor where he was at meat, and when he had driven the waiters and servitors out, as if all on a sudden he had been weary, laid him down along at his feet where he sat, and gently put his neck under him.

A cypress tree likewise in his grandfather's land without any force of tempest plucked up by the root and laid along, the very next day following rose up again greener and stronger than before. But in Achaia he dreamed that he and his should begin to prosper so soon as Nero had a tooth drawn out of his head. Now it fortuned that the morrow following, a surgeon that came forth into the courtyard showed unto him a tooth of Nero's, newly drawn. In Judea, when he consulted with the Oracle of the god of Carmel, the answer which was given assured him in these terms that whatsoever he thought upon and cast in his mind (were it never so great) it should so come to pass. And one of the noblemen of that country taken captive, named Josephus, when he was cast into prison, avouched and said unto him most constantly that he should shortly be set at liberty even by him, but he should be emperor first. There were moreover significant tokens, presaging no less, reported unto him out of the very city of Rome: namely, that Nero in his latter days, a little before his death, was warned in a dream to take the sacred chariot of Jupiter Optimus Maximus forth of the chapel where it stood into Vespasian's house, and so from thence into the Circus. Also, not long after, as Galba held the solemn election for his second consulship, the statue of Julius, late Caesar of famous memory, turned of itself into the East. And at the field fought before Betriacum, ere the battle joined, two eagles had a conflict and bickered together in all their sights; and when one of them was foiled and overcome, a third came at the very instant from the sun rising and chased the victress away.

6. Yet for all this attempted he no enterprise (notwithstanding his friends and soldiers were most pressed and forward, yea and urgent upon him) before that he was solicited by the unexpected favor of some who, as it fell out, were both unknown to him and also absent. Two thousand drawn out of the

three legions of the Moesian army and sent to aid Otho, when
they were upon the way marching (albeit news came unto
them that he was vanquished and had laid violent hands upon
himself), held on their journey nevertheless as far as to Aquileia, giving small credit to that rumor; where, after they had
by vantage of opportunities offered, and uncontrolled liberty,
committed all manner of robberies and outrageous villainies,
fearing lest, if they returned back again they should answer
for their misdemeanors and abide condign punishment therefor; they laid their heads together and consulted about the
choosing and creating of an emperor. For, worse they took not
themselves nor inferior, either to the army in Spain that had
set up Galba, or to the praetorian bands which had made Otho,
or to the German forces who had elected Vitellius, emperors.
Having proposed therefore and nominated of the consular
lieutenants as many as they could in any place think upon,
when they misliked all the rest, taking exceptions against one
for this cause and another for that, while some again of that
third legion which a little before the death of Nero had been
translated out of Syria into Moesia, highly praised and extolled
Vespasian, they all accorded thereto, and without delay wrote
his name upon their flags and banners. And verily, for that
time this project was smothered, the companies for a while
reclaimed and all brought into good order. But when the
said fact was once divulged, Tiberius Alexander, provost of
Egypt, was the first that forced the legions to swear allegiance
unto Vespasian, upon the Kalends of July which ever after was
celebrated for the first day and beginning of his empire. After
them, the army in Judea took the same oath before Vespasian
himself, the fifth day before the Ides of July. These enterprises
were very much furthered by the copy of a letter that went
commonly through men's hands (true or false, I wot not) of
Otho, now deceased, to Vespasian, charging and willing him

now at the last cast to revenge his death and wishing him withal to relieve the distressed state of the commonwealth; by a rumor also spread abroad that Vitellius upon his victory meant fully to make an exchange of the legions in winter harbors: namely, to remove those that wintered in Germany into the East provinces, as to a more secure service and easier warfare. Moreover, among the governors of provinces, Licinius Mucianus, and of the kings, Vologesus of Parthia, had promised, the one (laying down all grudge and enmity which unto that time he openly professed upon a humor of emulation) the Syrian army; and the other, forty thousand archers.

7. Vespasian therefore, having undertaken a civil war and sent before him his captains and forces into Italy, passed over in the meantime to Alexandria, for to be possessed of the frontier straights and avenues of Egypt. Here when he had voided all company from him and was entered alone into the temple of Serapis, after he had, upon much propitious favor of that god obtained, devoutly at length turned himself about, he thought he saw Basilides, one who was known to have had access unto no man, and long since for the infirmity of his sinews scarce able to set one foot before another, and withal to be absent a great way off, to present unto him vervain and sacred herbs, garlands also and loaves of bread (as the manner is in that place). And hereupon immediately letters came unto him, importing thus much, that the forces of Vitellius were discomfited before Cremona; reporting besides that himself was killed at Rome. The only thing that he wanted (being as one would say a prince unlooked for and as yet new come to the empire) was countenance, authority and a kind, as it were, of royal majesty. But even that also came on apace (by this occasion). It fortuned that a certain mean commoner, stark blind, another likewise with a feeble and lame leg, came both together unto him as he sat upon the tribunal, craving that help

and remedy for their infirmities which had been showed unto them by Serapis in their dreams, that he should restore the one to his sight if he did but spit into his eyes; and strengthen the other's leg if he vouchsafed only to touch it with his heel. Now when as he could hardly believe that the thing any way would find success, and therefore durst not so much as put it to the venture, at the last through the persuasion of friends, openly before the whole assembly he assayed both means, neither missed he of the effect. About the same time, at Tegea in Arcadia, by the instinct and motion of prophets, there were digged out of the ground in a consecrated place, manufactures and vessels of antique work: and among the same an image, resembling for all the world Vespasian.

8. Thus qualified as he was and graced with so great fame, he returned to Rome, and after his triumph over the Jews, he added eight consulships more to that which of old he had borne. He took upon him also the censorship, and all the time of his empire esteemed nothing more than first to establish and afterwards to adorn the commonwealth brought almost to utter decay and at the point to fall down. The soldiers, some presuming boldly of their victories, others in grief for their shameful disgrace, were grown to all manner of licentiousness and audacity. The provinces likewise and free states, yea and some kingdoms, fell to discord and seditious tumults among themselves. And therefore of the Vitellians he both discharged and also chastised very many. As for the partners with him in victory, so far was he from allowing them any extraordinary indulgence, that their very due and lawful rewards he payed not but slackly. And because he would not let slip any occasion of reforming military discipline, when a certain gallant youth smelling hot of sweet perfumes came unto him to give thanks for an office obtained at his hands, after a strange countenance showing his dislike of him, he gave him also in words a most

. . . craving that help and remedy for their infirmities which had been showed unto them by Serapis in their dreams, that he should restore the one to his sight if he did but spit into his eyes . . .

bitter and grievous check, saying, "I would rather you had stunk of garlic," and so revoked his letters patent for the grant. As touching the mariners and sea servitors, such of them as are wont to pass to and fro on foot, by turns from Ostia and Puteoli to Rome, who were petitioners unto him that some certain allowance might be set down for to find them shoes, he thought it not sufficient to send them away without answer, but commanded that forever after they should run up and down between unshod. And so from that time they use to do. Achaia, Lycia, Rhodes, Byzantium and Samos, having lost their liberty: likewise Thracia, Cilicia and Commagene, subject until that time to kings, he reduced all into the form of a province. Into Cappadocia, for the continual inroads and incursions that the barbarians made, he brought additional legions, and in lieu of a Roman knight, he placed there for a ruler, a man who had been consul. The city of Rome by reason of old fires and ruins was much blemished and disfigured. He permitted therefore any man to seize as his own all vacant plots of ground, and to build thereupon, in case the owners and land-lords were slack in that behalf. Himself took upon him the re-edifying of the Capitol, and was the first man that did set his hand to the ridding of the rubbish, yea and upon his own neck carried some of it away. Three thousand tables of brass also, which were burnt with the said temples, he undertook to make and set up again, having searched and sought out from all places the patterns and copies thereof. A most beautiful instrument and right ancient record of the whole empire he compiled and finished, wherein were contained from the first beginning well near of the city, all acts of the senate, all deeds passed by the communality as concerning leagues, alliances and privileges granted to any soever.

9. He built also new works: the temple of peace, situated next unto the Forum; that likewise of Claudius, late emperor

of sacred memory, seated upon the mount Caelius, which verily had been begun by Agrippina, but almost from the very foundation destroyed by Nero. Also a most stately amphitheater in the heart of the city, according as he understood that Augustus intended such a one. The two orders, wasted by sundry massacres and sullied through the negligence of former times, he cleansed and supplied by a review and visitation of senate and knights both; wherein he removed the unworthiest persons and took in the most honest that were to be found, either of Italians or provincial inhabitants. And to the end it might be known, that both the said orders differed one from another not so much in liberty as in dignity, he pronounced in the case of a certain brawl between a senator and a knight of Rome that senators might not be provoked first with foul language; marry to answer them with evil words again was but civility and a matter allowed.

10. Suits in law depending one upon another were grown in every court exceeding much: while the old actions by the interruption of jurisdiction hung still undecided, and new quarrels arose to increase them, occasioned by the tumultuous troubles of those times. He chose therefore certain commissioners by lot, some by whom goods taken and carried away perforce during the wars might be restored; and others who extraordinarily should determine and judge between party and party in Centumviral cases [which pertained to the Centumvir's court: to wit, civil cases between private persons, as probates of testaments, etc.] which were so many that the parties themselves, as it was thought, could hardly by the course of nature live to see an end of them: these all were to be reduced to as small a number as possibly might be.

11. Wanton lust and wasteful expense, without restraint of any man, had gotten a mighty head. He moved the senate therefore to make a decree that what woman soever joined

herself in wedlock unto another man's bondservant, should be reputed a bondwoman. Also that it might not be lawful for usurers to demand any debt of young men while they were under their father's tuition for money credited out unto them: I mean, not so much as after their decease. In all other matters, from the very first beginning of his empire unto the end, he was courteous enough and full of clemency.

12. His former mean estate and condition he dissimulated not at any time; nay, he would often of himself profess the same and make it known openly. Yea, and when some went about to fetch the original of the Flavian lineage, from as far as the founders of Reate and the companion of Hercules whose monument is to be seen in the way Salaria, he mocked and laughed them to scorn for their labors. And so far was he from desiring any outward ornaments in show of the world, that upon his triumph day, being wearied with the slow march and tedious train of the pomp, he could not but say plainly that he was well enough served and justly punished who being an aged man had so foolishly longed for a triumph, as if forsooth it had of right been due unto his forefathers, or ever hoped for by himself. Neither accepted he so much as the tribune's authority or addition of *Pater Patriae* in his style, until later. For he had forlet altogether the custom of scarching those that came in duty to salute him, even while yet the civil war continued.

13. The frank speech of his friends, the figurative terms and quips of lawyers pleading at the bar, and the unmannerly rudeness of philosophers he took most mildly. Licinius Mucianus, a man notorious for preposterous wantonness but (presuming confidently of his good deserts) not so respective of him as reverent duty would, he could never find in his heart to gird and nip again but in private, and thus far forth only as in complaining of him unto some good friend of them both to knit up all with these words, "Yet I am a man." When

Salvius Liberalis, pleading in the defense of a rich client, was so bold as to say, "what is that to Caesar if Hipparchus be worth a hundred million sesterces?" himself also commended and thanked him for it. Demetrius the Cynic, meeting him in the way after he was come to his sovereign dignity, and not deigning once to rise up nor salute him, but rather barking at him, I wot not what, he thought it enough to call cur-dog.

14. Displeasures to him done, and enmities, he never carried in mind nor revenged. The daughter of Vitellius his enemy he married into a most noble house. He gave unto her a rich dowry withal, and furniture accordingly. Whenas, by reason that he was forbidden the court under Nero, he stood in great fear and was to seek what to do and whether to go: one of the gentlemen ushers, whose office it was to admit men into the presence, in thrusting him out had bidden him "to be gone in a mischief." When this fellow afterwards came to ask forgiveness, he proceeded no further in heat of anger, but to words only, and to quit him with just as many and almost the very same. For, so far was he from working the overthrow and death of any person upon any suspicion or fear conceived, that when his friends admonished him to beware of Mettius Pompusianus because it was generally believed that the astrologers had by the horoscope of his nativity assured him to be emperor another day, he advanced the same Mettius to the consulship, presuming and promising in the man's behalf that he would be one day mindful of this benefit and good turn of his.

15. There is not lightly found an innocent person to have been punished, but when he was absent and not aware thereof; or at leastwise unwilling thereto and deceived. With Helvidius Priscus, who only saluted him after his return out of Syria by his private name, plain Vespasian; and being praetor, in all his edicts and proclamations passed him over without any honor at all, or once naming him, he was not angry and displeased,

until he had with his most insolent altercations made him in manner contemptible and little better than an ordinary person. Him also, notwithstanding he was first confined to a place and afterwards commanded to be killed, he would have given a great deal to have saved by all means possible; he sent certain of purpose to call back the murderers, and saved his life he had, but that false word came back that he was dispatched already. Otherwise he never rejoiced in the death of any, but rather when malefactors were justly punished and executed he would weep and groan.

16. The only thing for which he might worthily be blamed was covetousness. For, not content with this, to have revived the taxes and payments omitted by Galba, to have enhanced also the tributes of the provinces, yea and of some doubled the same, he fell openly to negotiate and deal in certain trades which, even for a private person, were a shame to use: buying up and engrossing some commodities for this purpose only to put the same off afterwards at a higher price. Neither did he hesitate to sell either honorable places unto suitors for them, or absolutions and pardons to men in trouble, whether they were innocent or guilty it skilled not. Furthermore it is verily thought that of his procurators, if any were greedy and given to extortion more than other, his manner was to promote such for the nonce to higher offices, to the end that when they were more enriched he might soon after condemn them. And commonly it was said that those he used as sponges, for that he did wet them well when they were dry and press them hard when they were wet. Some write that he was by nature most covetous and that an old neatherd upbraided him once therewith, who being at his hands denied freedom without paying for it (which he humbly craved of him now invested in the empire), cried out in a loud voice and said, the wolf might change his hair but not his qualities. Contrariwise there be again who

are of opinion that he was driven to spoil of necessity, even for extreme want both in the common treasury and also in his own exchequer: whereof he gave some testimony in the beginning immediately of his empire, professing that there was need of forty thousand millions to set the state upright again. Which also seems to sound more near the truth, because the money by him ill gotten, he used and bestowed passing well.

17. To all sorts of men he was most liberal. The estate and wealth of senators he made up to the full. To decayed men that had been consul he allowed five hundred thousand sesterces by the year. Very many cities throughout the world by earthquake or fire ruined, he re-edified better than they were before.

18. Fine wits and cunning artisans he set much store by, and cherished them above all others. He was the first that out of his own coffers appointed for professed rhetoricians, as well in Latin as in Greek, a yearly salary of a hundred thousand sesterces apiece. Upon excellent poets, as also actors, also upon the workman who repaired and set up again the giantlike image called Colossus, he bestowed a notable congiary, and endowed them with a great stipend beside. To an engineer also, who promised to bring into the Capitol huge columns at small charges, he gave for his device no mean award, but released him from his labor in performing that work, saying withal that he should suffer him to feed the poor commons [to allow them wages for their painful labor in such works rather than to have the same done without them: and as we say, to keep poor people at work].

19. At those plays during which the stage of Marcellus' theater, newly re-edified, was dedicated, he had brought into request and use again even the old musical entertainments. To Appelles the tragedian he gave four hundred thousand sesterces. To Terpnus and Diodorus, two harpers, two hundred thousand apiece; to some one hundred, and to whom he gave

least, forty thousand, over and above a great number of golden coronets. He feasted continually, and for the most part by making full suppers, and those very plentiful: for why? His meaning was to help the butchers and such as sold victuals. As he delivered forth gifts unto men at the Saturnalia, so he did to women upon the Kalends of March. Yet verily for all this, could he not avoid the infamous name of his former avarice. The men of Alexandria termed him still Cybiosactes after the surname of one of their kings given to most base and beggarly gain. And even at his very funerals, Favor the mimic, representing his person and imitating (as the manner is) his deeds and words while he lived, when he asked the procurators openly what the charges might be of his funeral and the pomp thereto belonging, no sooner heard that it would arise to ten million sesterces but he cried, "give me one hundred thousand and make no more ado, but throw me into Tiber."

20. Of a middle stature he was; well set, his limbs compact and strongly made, his countenance as if he strained hard for a stool. Whereupon one of these wits came out with a pretty conceit. For when Vespasian seemed to request the fellow for to break a jest upon him also, as well as upon others, "That I will," quoth he, "if you had done relieving yourself." His health he had, no man better, although for the preservation thereof he did no more but rub his own jaws and other parts of the body to a certain just number, within the tennis courts; and withal, monthly interpose abstinence from all food for one whole day.

21. This course and order of life for the most part he held. While he was emperor he waked always very early, and before daybreak. Then, having read through all missives, and the breviaries of every office, he admitted his friends, and while he was saluted, he both put on his own shoes, and also apparelled and made himself ready. After dispatch of all cur-

rent business, he took a ride, and so to rest: having one of his concubines lying by his side, of whom he had appointed several in stead of Caenis deceased. From his privy closet he passed into his bath, and so to his refection room. Neither was he, by report, at any time fuller of humanity or readier to do a pleasure. And such opportunities of time as these his domestic servants waited for especially, to prefer their petitions in.

22. At his suppers and otherwise at all times with his friends being most pleasant and courteous, he dispatched many matters by way of mirth. For given exceedingly he was to scoffs, and those so scurrile and filthy that he could not so much as forbear words of ribaldry. And yet there be many right pleasant conceited jests of his extant. Among which this also goes for one. Being advertised by Mestrius Florus, a man of consul's degree, to pronounce *plaustra* rather than *plostra*, he saluted him the next morrow by the name of Flaurus. Having yielded at length to a certain woman enamored of him, and ready as it were to die for pure love, when she was brought to his bed he gave her forty thousand sesterces for lying with him. When his steward came to him to put him in mind what manner and form he would have this sum of money to be set down in his book of accounts. "Marry thus," quoth he, " 'item, given to Vespasian beloved.' "

23. He used Greek verses also in good season and aptly applied: as namely of a certain fellow, tall and high of stature but monstrously endowed, thus, "of great stride and brandishing a far-shadowing weapon." Of Cerylus, his freedman: upon whom, for that being exceeding rich, yet to avoid a payment sometime to his exchequer, he began to give it out that he was freeborn, and so changed his name and called himself Laches, Vespasian played in these terms:

O Laches, Laches wert thou once dead in grave:
Thine old name Cerylus again thou shalt have.

434

Howbeit, most of all he affected a kind of raillery in his unseemly gain and filthy lucre: to the end, that by some scoffing cavil he might put by and do away the envy of the thing, turning all to merry jests. A minister and servitor about him, whom he loved deeply, made suit in the behalf of one as his brother for a stewardship. When he had put him off to a farther day, he called unto him the party himself, and having exacted so much money at his hands as he had agreed for with the mediator aforesaid, without more delay, he ordained him steward. Soon after, when the servitor interposed himself, "Go your way," quoth he, "seek you another to be your brother: for this fellow whom you think to be yours is become mine." Suspecting that his muleteer who drove his carriage alighted one time, as it were to shoe his mules, thereby to win some delay for one that had a matter in law and was coming unto him, he asked the muleteer what the shoeing of his mules would bring in, and so covenanted with him to have part of his gains. When his son Titus seemed to find fault with him for devising a kind of tribute even on urinals, the money that came unto his hand of the first payment he put unto his son's nose, asking withal whether he was offended with the smell or no; and when he answered, no, "And yet," quoth he, "it comes out of urinals." Certain ambassadors brought him word that there was decreed for him at the common charges of the state, a giant-like image that would cost no mean sum of money. He commanded them to rear the same immediately, showing therewith his hand hollow. "Here is the base," quoth he, "and pedestal for it, ready." And not so much as in the fear and extreme peril of death forbore he scoffing. For when as among other prodigious signs, the mausoleum of the Caesars opened suddenly, and a blazing star appeared: the one of them, he said did concern Junia Calvina, a gentlewoman of Augustus Caesar's race, the other had reference to the king of the Par-

435

thians who wore his hair long. In the very first access also and fit of his disease, "Methinks," quoth he, "I am a-deifying."

24. In his ninth consulship, after he had been assayed in Campania with some light motions and grudgings of his sickness, and thereupon returned forthwith to the city, he went from there to Cutilae and the lands he had about Reate, where every year he was wont to summer. Here, having (besides the malady still growing upon him) hurt also his guts and bowels with the use of cold water, and yet nevertheless executed the functions of an emperor, after his accustomed manner, to the point that lying upon his bed, he gave audience to ambassadors. All of a sudden he fell into a looseness of the belly, so that he fainted and was ready to swoon therewith. "An emperor," quoth he, "ought to die standing." As he was arising therefore, and straining still to ease his body, he died in their hands that helped to lift him up, on the sixth day before the Kalends of July: when he had lived threescore years and nine, seven months and seven days over.

25. All writers agree in this, that so confident he was always of his own horoscope and his children's, that after so many conspiracies continually plotted against him, he durst warrant and assure the senate that either his own sons should succeed him or none. It is said, moreover, that he dreamed upon a time that he saw a pair of scales hanging in the midst of the porch and entry of his house Palatine, with the beam thereof even balanced, so as in the one balance stood Claudius and Nero, in the other, himself and his sons. And it fell out so indeed: for they ruled the empire on both sides so many years, and the like space of time just.

THE HISTORY OF
TITUS FLAVIUS VESPASIANUS
AUGUSTUS

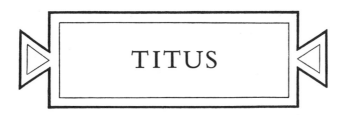

TITUS

TITUS, SURNAMED AS HIS FATHER WAS,
Vespasianus, the lovely darling and delightful joy of
mankind (so fully was he, either endued with good
nature and disposition, or enriched with skillful cunning, or
else graced with fortune's favor; and that – which is hardest
of all – in his imperial state, considering that while he lived as
a private person under the emperor his father, he could not
avoid the very hatred and much less reproof of the world).
This Titus, I say, was born the third day before the Kalends
of January: in that year which was remarkable for the death
of Gaius the emperor, near unto the Septizonium, within a
poor ill-favored house, in a very little chamber and dark
withal; it remaineth yet to be seen.

2. His education he had in the court, together with Britannicus, trained up in the like arts and disciplines under the same
teachers. At which time verily, men say, that a fortune-teller,
whom Narcissus the freedman of Claudius brought to see
Britannicus, after inspection, affirmed most constantly that by
no means he, but Titus, who then stood hard by, should surely
be emperor. Now were these two so familiar that (as it is verily
thought) of the same cup of poison whereof Britannicus drank
and died, Titus also, sitting near unto him, tasted: whereupon
he fell into a grievous disease, that held him long and put him
to great pain. In memorial of all which premises, he erected
afterwards for him one statue of gold in the Palatium; also
another of ivory on horseback (which at the Circus games is

439

even at this day carried before in the solemn pomp) he dedicated, and accompanied accordingly.

3. At the very first, even in his childhood, there shone forth in him the gifts both of body and mind; and the same more and more still by degrees as he grew in years: a goodly presence and countenance, wherein was seated no less majesty than favor and beauty; a special lean strength, albeit his stature was not tall, but his belly bore out somewhat with the most. A singular memory, and aptness to learn all the arts, as well of war as of peace. Most skillful he was in handling his weapon, and withal a passing good horseman. For his Latin and Greek tongue, whether it were in making orations or composing poems, prompt and ready even to the performance thereof *ex tempore*. Neither was he unseen in music, as who could both sing and also play upon instruments sweetly and with knowledge. I have also heard many men say that he was wont to write shorthand most swiftly, striving by way of sport and mirth with his own clerks, whether he or they could write fastest; likewise to imitate what hand soever he had seen: yea, and to profess many a time that he would have made a notable forger and counterfeiter of writings.

4. In quality of tribune military he served in the war both in Germany and also in Britain, with exceeding commendation for his industry and no less report of modesty, as appears by a number of his images and titles to them annexed throughout both provinces. After this warfare of his, he pleaded cases in court, which he did rather to win credit and reputation than to make it an ordinary practice. At which very time he wedded Arrecina Tertulla, daughter of a knight of Rome, but captain of the praetorian bands. And in the room of her deceased he took to wife Martia Furnilla, and from her, when she had borne unto him a daughter, he divorced himself. After this, upon his quaestorship, being commander of a whole legion, he brought

. . . as he consecrated at Memphis the ox Apis, he wore a diadem: which he did indeed according to the custom and rites of the ancient religion there.

under his subjection Tarichaeae and Gamala, two most puissant cities of Judea: where, in a certain battle having lost his horse under him (by a deadly wound) within his flanks, he mounted another whose rider in fight against him had been slain and was fallen.

5. Afterwards, when Galba was possessed of the state, being sent to congratulate his advancement, what way soever he went he turned all men's eyes upon him, as if he had been singled forth to be adopted. But so soon as he perceived all to be full of troubles again, he returned back out of his very journey and visited the oracle of Venus Paphia. Where, while he asked counsel about his passage at sea, he was confirmed withal in his hope of the empire. Having attained thereto within short time, and being left behind to subdue Judea thoroughly, in the last assault of Jerusalem he slew twelve enemies that defended the wall with just so many arrows shot. He won the city upon the very birthday of his daughter, with so great joy and favorable applause of all his soldiers, that in their gratulation they saluted him emperor; and soon after, when he was to depart out of that province, detained him, in humble manner, yea and eftsoons in threatening wise insistently calling upon him to stay or else to take them all away together with him. Whereupon arose the first suspicion that he revolted from his father, and had attempted to challenge the kingdom of the East parts for himself. Which surmise himself made the more, after that in his way to Alexandria, as he consecrated at Memphis the ox Apis, he wore a diadem: which he did indeed according to the custom and rites of the ancient religion there. But there wanted not some who construed it otherwise. Making haste therefore into Italy, after he was arrived first at Rhegium, and from thence at Puteoli, embarked in a merchant's ship of burden. To Rome he goes directly with all speed and most lightly appointed, and unto his father

looking for nothing less, "I am come," quoth he, "father, I am come," checking thereby the rash and inconsiderate rumors raised of him.

6. From that time forward he ceased not to carry himself as partner with his father, yea and protector also of the empire. With him he triumphed; with him he jointly administered the censorship. His colleague he was in the tribune's authority, his companion likewise in seven consulships. And having taken to himself the charge well near of all offices, while he both dictated letters and penned edicts in his father's name, yea and read orations in the senate, and in the quaestor's place. He assumed also the captainship of the guard, an office never to that time executed but by a knight of Rome. In this place he demeaned himself nothing civilly, but proceeded with much violence. For ever as he had any in suspicion, he, by sending secretly certain men, who in the theaters and camps should require to have them punished (as though it were with his father's consent), made no more ado but brought them all to their end. As for example among these, he commanded Aulus Caecina, a man of consular degree, and a guest by him invited to supper, when he was scarce gone out of the banqueting parlor, to be stabbed. I must needs say, that driven he was to this violent proceeding upon an extremity of danger: considering that he had found out his handwriting bearing evidence of a conspiracy that he plotted with the soldiers. By which course, as he provided well and sufficiently for his own security another day, so, for the present time he incurred very much displeasure and hatred of the world: so much that no man lightly, when so adverse a rumor was on foot, and that which more is, against the wills of all men, could have stepped to the imperial throne.

7. Beside his cruelty, suspected he was also for riotous life: in that he continued banqueting until midnight with the most

profuse and wasteful spendthrifts of his familiar minions; for wanton lust likewise, by reason of a sort of stale catamites and gelded eunuchs that he kept about him, and the affectionate love that he was noted to bear to queen Berenice, unto whom also, as it was said, he promised marriage. Suspicion there was moreover of his avarice. For certain it was that in the commissions and hearings of cases which his father held, he was wont to sell the decision of matters and to make a gain thereby. After this, men both reputed and also reported him to be even another Nero. But this name that went of him proved good for him and turned to his greatest commendation, considering that no gross vice could be found in him, but contrariwise many excellent virtues. The feasts that he made were pleasant merriments, rather than lavish and sumptuous. He chose for his friends such as in whom the emperors who succeeded him also reposed themselves, and whom they used especially as necessary members both for them and also for the commonwealth. As for queen Berenice, he sent her quickly away from the city of Rome, but full loath they were both of them to part asunder. Certain of his minions and darlings whom he favored and fancied most, albeit they were such artistic dancers, that within a while after, they carried the greatest praise and prize upon the stage, he forbore quite not only to huggle and embrace, but to behold so much as once in public meeting and assembly. From no citizen took he ought, and from other men's property he abstained if ever any did. Nay, he received not even the contributions granted and usually paid. And yet, being inferior to none of his predecessors in munificence, as having dedicated an amphitheater, and built the baths hard by, with great expedition he exhibited a spectacle of sword-fencers, with all kinds of furniture thereto belonging in most plentiful manner. He represented also a naval fight in the old naumachia, in which very place he brought forth likewise his sword-fencers. And in that one day he put out to be baited five thousand wild beasts of all sorts.

8. Furthermore he was of his own nature most kind and gracious: whereas by a constitution and order that Tiberius began, all the Caesars, his successors, held not the benefits granted by former princes good and in force unless they also themselves made new grants of the same again: he was the first that by virtue of one sole edict ratified and confirmed all that had passed before, neither suffered he any petition to be made unto him for them. In all other suits and requests he evermore held most constantly men's minds at this pass, that he would send none away without hope. And when his domestic ministers about his person would seem to tell him that he promised more than he was able to perform: "What!" quoth he, "there ought no man to depart from the speech of a prince, sad and discontented." Calling to mind one time, as he sat at supper, that he had done nothing for any man that day, he uttered this memorable and praiseworthy apophthegm, "My friends, I have lost a day." The people especially in general he entreated on all occasions with so great courtesy, that, having proposed a solemn sword-fight, he made open profession that he would set it forth, not to please himself, but to content the beholders. And verily, even so he did it. For neither denied he aught to them that would call for it, and of his own accord willed them to ask what their minds stood to. Moreover, showing plainly, that he stood well affected to the manner of the Thracian sword-fencers' fight and their armature, he would many times even with the rest of the people, both in word and gesture (as a favor of that kind), jest and make sport; yet so, as he kept still the majesty of an emperor; and withal he judged with equity indifferently. And because he would omit no point of popularity, sometimes, as he bathed in his own baths, he admitted the commons thither unto him. There fell

out in his reign certain mischances and heavy accidents: as, the burning of the mountain Vesuvius in Campania; a fire at Rome which lasted three days and three nights; also a pestilence the like whereof had not lightly been known elsewhere at any other time. In these calamities so many and so grievous, he showed not only a princely care, but also a singular fatherly affection: sometimes comforting his people by his edicts, otherwhiles helping them so far forth as his power would extend. For repairing the losses in Campania he chose by lot certain commissioners to look thereto, even out of the rank of those who had been consuls. The goods of such as perished in the said mount, whose heirs could not be found, he awarded to the re-edification of the ruined cities adjoining. And having made public protestation that in the said fire of the city there was no loss at all but to himself, what ornaments were in any of his own palaces and royal houses, the same he appointed to the city buildings and the temples: for which purpose he made divers of knight's degree supervisors, to the end that everything might be dispatched with greater expedition. To cure the sickness and mitigate the fury of those contagious diseases, he used all help of God and man, having sought out whatsoever kinds of sacrifices and remedies might be found. Among the adversities of those times may be reckoned these promoters and informers, with such as underhand set them a-work, occasioned all by old licentiousness and impunity. And those he commanded to be whipped and beaten with cudgels soundly in the open Forum; and last of all, they were brought in a show through the amphitheater, partly to be sold for slaves, and in part to be carried away into the roughest and bleakest islands that were. And because he would forever restrain such as at any time should dare to do the like, he made an act, among many others, prohibiting one and the same matter to be tried under many statutes and laws enacted in that behalf; or to make inquisition as touching the estate of any man deceased, after the term of certain years.

9. Having professed that he took upon him the high-priesthood in this regard, because he would keep his hands pure and innocent, he made good his word. For, after that time, never was he the principal author of any man's death, nor privy and accessory thereto (albeit he wanted not sometimes just cause of revenge), but swore devoutly that he would rather die himself than do others to death. Two noble men of the patrician rank, convicted for affecting and aspiring to the empire, he proceeded against no farther than to admonish them to desist and give over, saying that sovereign power was the gift of destiny and divine providence. If they were petitioners for anything else, he promised to give it to them. And verily, out of hand, to the mother of the one, who was then far off (woeful and pensive woman as she was), he dispatched his own courtiers and footmen to carry word that her son was safe. As for themselves, he not only invited them to a familiar and friendly supper that night, but also the next day following, at the fight of sword-fencers, he placed them near his own person, and when the weapons to be used were presented to him, he reached them to these men for to view and peruse. It is said, moreover, that having knowledge of both their horoscopes, he avouched that danger was toward them both and would light upon their heads one day, but from some other; as it fell out indeed. His own brother never ceasing to lay wait for his life, but professedly in manner soliciting the armies against him, plotting also and intending thereupon to fly and be gone, he could never endure either to kill or to sequester and confine, no, nor so much as to abridge of any honor. But, as he had always done him from the first day of his imperial dignity, persevered to testify and declare that partner he was with him in the sovereign government, and his heir apparent to succeed him;

446

otherwhiles secretly with tears and prayers beseeching that he would vouchsafe him yet at length mutual love and affection.

10. Amid this blessed course of life, cut short he was and prevented by death, to the greater loss of mankind than of himself. After he had finished the solemn shows and games exhibited to the people, in the end and upshot whereof he had shed tears abundantly, he went toward the Sabines' territory somewhat more sad then usually he had been: by occasion that as he sacrificed, the beast broke loose and got away; also because in fair and clear weather it had thundered. Hereupon, having gotten an ague at his first lodging and baiting place, when he was removing from thence in his litter, it is said that, putting by the curtains of the window, he looked up to heaven and complained very piteously that his life should be taken from him who had not deserved to die: for there was no fact of his extant of which he was to repent, save only one. Now what that one should be, neither uttered he himself at that instant, neither is any man able readily to guess thereat. Some think he called to mind the over-familiar acquaintance that he had with his brother's wife. But Domitia devoutly swore that he never had such dealing with her: who no doubt would not have denied it if there had been any folly at all between them. Nay, she would rather have made her vaunt thereof, so ordinary a thing it was with her to glory in all naughtiness and shameful deeds.

11. He departed this world in the very same country house wherein his father died before him, upon the Ides of September, two years, two months and twenty days after that he succeeded his father, and in the two and fortieth year of his age. Which being once notified and known abroad, when all men throughout the city mourned no less than in some domestic occasion of sorrow and lamentation, the senate, before they were summoned and called together by any edict, ran to the

Curia, finding as yet the doors fast locked; but when they were set open, they rendered unto him now dead so much thanks, and heaped upon him so great a measure of praises as they never did before at any time while he was living and present among them.

THE HISTORY OF
FLAVIUS DOMITIANUS

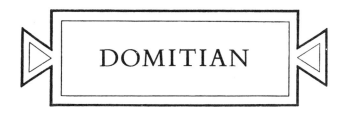

DOMITIAN

OMITIAN WAS BORN THE NINTH DAY BE-
fore the Kalends of November, what time his father
was consul-elect and to enter upon that honorable place
the month ensuing, within the sixth region of Rome city, at
the Pomegranate, and in that house which afterwards he converted into the temple of the Flavian family. The flower of his
tender years and the very prime of youth he passed, by report,
in so great poverty and infamy withal, that he had not one
piece of plate or vessel of silver to be served with. And full
well it is known that Claudius Pollio, a man of praetor's
degree (against whom there is a poem of Nero's extant, entitled *Luscio*, or "The One-eyed Man"), kept by him a scroll
of his own handwriting, yea and otherwhiles brought the same
forth to be seen, wherein he promised him the use of his body
one night. Neither wanted some who constantly avouched that
Domitian was in that sort abused, even by Nerva, who soon
after succeeded him. In the Vitellian troubles he fled into the
Capitol with his uncle Sabinus and part of the forces which
were then present. But when the adverse faction broke in, and
while the temple was on fire, he lay close all night in the
sexton's lodging; and early in the morning, disguised in the
habit of a priest of Isis, and among the sacrificers belonging to
that vain superstition, after he had passed over Tiber, accompanied with only one person, to the mother of a school fellow
of his, he lurked there so secretly that, albeit the searchers
traced him by his footing, yet could he not be found. At last,

451

after victory obtained, he went forth and showed himself; and being generally saluted by the name of Caesar, the honorable dignity of the city praetor, with consular authority, he took upon him; but in name and title only: the jurisdiction whereof he made over to his next colleague. But in all power of lordly rule he carried himself so licentiously and without controlment that he showed even then betimes what a one he would prove hereafter. And not to handle every particular: having with unclean hands offered dishonor to many men's wives, he fled away and married also Domitia Longina, the wedded wife of Aelius Lamia; and in one day gave and dealt above twenty offices, within the city and abroad in foreign provinces: insomuch as Vespasian commonly said that he marvelled why he sent not one also to succeed in his place.

2. He enterprised moreover a voyage into Gaul and Germany, notwithstanding the same was needless, and his father's friends dissuaded him from it; only because he would equalize his brother both in works and reputation. For these pranks of his rebuked he was; and to the end he might the rather be put in mind of his young years and private condition, he dwelt together with his father. In a litter he attended the curule chair of father and brother, whensoever they went forth; and being mounted upon a white courser, accompanied them both in their triumph over Judea. Of six consulships he bore but one ordinary, and the same by occasion that his brother Titus yielded unto him his own place and furthered him in his suit. Himself likewise made wonderful semblance of modesty. But above all, he seemed outwardly to affect poetry (a study which he was not so much acquainted with before time, but he despised and rejected it as much afterwards) and recited his own verses even in public place. Yet nevertheless, when Vologesus, king of the Parthians, required aid against the Alani, and one of Vespasian's sons to be the general of those forces, he labored

with might and main that himself before all others should be sent: and because the quarrel was dispatched already, he assayed by gifts and large promises to solicit other kings of the East to make the same request. When his father was dead, standing in doubtful terms with himself a long time whether he should offer unto the soldiers a donative double to that of his brother Titus, he never stuck to give out and make his boast that left he was to be partner with him in the empire, but that his father's will was very much abused. Neither would he give over from that time forward both to lay wait secretly for his brother, and also to practice openly against him, until such time as he gave commandment when he was stricken with grievous sickness that he should be left for dead before the breath was out of his body: and after he was departed indeed, vouchsafing him no other honor but his consecration, he carped also at him many a time as well in glancing figurative speeches as in open edicts.

3. In the beginning of his empire his manner was to retire himself daily into a secret place for one hour, and there to do nothing else but to catch flies and with the sharp point of a bodkin or writing stylus prick them through: insomuch as when one enquired whether anybody were with Caesar within, Vibius Crispus made answer not impertinently, "no, not so much as a fly." After this, Domitia, his own wife, who in his second consulship had borne him a son, and whom two years after he had saluted as empress, by name of Augusta, her I say, falling in fancy with Paris the stage player and ready to die for his love, he put away; but within a small while after (as impatient of this breach, and divorce) took her home and married her again, as if the people had insistently called upon him to do so. In the administration of the empire he behaved himself for a good while variable, as one made of an equal mixture and temper of vices and virtues, until at length he turned his

virtues into vices: being (so far as we may conjecture), over and above his natural inclination, for want, covetous and greedy, for fear, bloody and cruel.

4. He exhibited ordinarily magnificent and sumptuous shows, not only in the amphitheater but in the Circus also. In which, besides the usual running of chariots, drawn as well with two steeds as four, he represented likewise two battles of horsemen and footmen both; and in the amphitheater a naval fight. For baitings of wild beasts and sword-fencers he showed in the very night by cresset and torch lights; and he brought into the place not men only to fight, but women also to encounter wild beasts. Furthermore, at the games of sword-fight set out by the quaestors (which, having in times past been discontinued and forlet, he brought into use again) he was always present in person, so that he gave the people leave to choose two pair of sword-fencers out of his own school, and those he brought in royally and courtlike appointed, in the last place. And at all sights of sword players, there stood ever at his feet a little dwarf arrayed in scarlet with a wonderfully small head, with whom he used to talk and confer otherwhiles of serious matters. Certes, overheard he was when he demanded him of what he knew and what he thought of the last appointment to the provinces, and namely of ordaining Mettius Rufus lieutenant general of Egypt. He exhibited naval battles performed in manner by full fleets and complete navies: having digged out a great pit for a lake and built a stone wall round about it, near unto Tiber, those he would behold in the greatest storms and showers that were. He set forth also the secular plays and games, making his computation from the year, not wherein Claudius, but Augustus long before had made them. During these, upon the day of the Circus solemnities, to the end that there might be a hundred courses the sooner run, he abridged the laps of everyone, to wit, from

454

seven to four. He ordained moreover in the honor of Jupiter Capitolinus quinquennial games of threefold masteries: music, horse-riding and gymnastic exercises; and in the same, rewarding victors with coronets, more by a good many than now they be. Herein the concurrents strove also for the prize in prose, both Greek and Latin; and besides single harpers, there were sets of those also that played upon the harp, yea and consorts of such as sung thereto in a choir. In the running place, virgins also ran for the best games. At all these masteries and solemnities he sat as president in his pantoffles [or slippers], clad in a robe of purple after the Greek fashion, and wearing on his head a golden coronet with the image of Jupiter, Juno and Minerva; the priest of Jupiter and the college of the religious called the Flaviales sat by him in like habit, saving that in their coronets there was his image also. Similarly he celebrated every year upon the Alban mount the Quinquatria of Minerva, in whose honor he had instituted a college, out of which there should be chosen by lot, masters and wardens of that solemnity who were to exhibit peculiar and especial beast-baitings and stage plays, yea and contentions for the prize of orators and poets besides. He gave a largess to the people thrice: to wit, three hundred sesterces apiece; and at the show of the sword-fight, a most plenteous dinner. At the solemn Septimontial sacrifice, he made a dole of viands, allowing to the senators and knights fair large baskets; to the commons, smaller ones with cates in them: and was the first himself that fell to his meat. The next day after he scattered among them missiles of all sorts, and because the greater part thereof fell to the ranks of the common people, he pronounced by word of mouth for every scaffold of senators and knights, five hundred tickets.

5. Many buildings and those most stately which had been consumed with fire, he re-edified; and among them the Capitol

which had been fired again; but all under the title of his own name, without any memorial of the former founders. Marry, he founded a new temple in the Capitol to the honor of Jupiter Custos; also the Forum which is now called Nerva's Forum; likewise the temple of the Flavian family, a showplace for running and wrestling, another for poets and musicians to contend in, and a naumachia for ships to encounter. From its stone the Circus Maximus was afterwards rebuilt, by occasion that both sides thereof had been burnt down.

6. Expeditions he made, some voluntary, some upon necessity: of his own accord against the Chatti; upon constraint, one against the Sarmatians, by occasion that one whole legion together with their lieutenant fell by the sword; two against the Daci: the former because Oppius Sabinus, a man of consul's degree, was defeated and slain; the second for that Cornelius Fuscus, captain of the praetorian bands (unto whom he had committed the whole conduct of that war), lost his life. Over the Chatti and Daci (after sundry fields fought with variety of fortune), he triumphed twice. For his victory of the Sarmatians he presented only Jupiter Capitolinus with his laurel garland. The civil war stirred up by Lucius Antonius, governor of Upper Germany, he dispatched and ended in his absence: and that by a wonderful good hap, when, as at the very hour of conflict, the Rhine swelling and overflowing suddenly stayed the barbarians' forces as they would have passed over to Antonius. Of which victory he had intelligence by presages before the news by messengers came. For upon that very day when the battle was fought, an eagle after a strange manner having overspread his statue at Rome and clasped it about with her wings, made a great flapping noise in token of much joy; and within a little after, the bruit was blown abroad so rife and common of Antonius' death that many avouched confidently they had seen his head also brought home to Rome.

7. Many new orders besides in matters of common use he brought up. The dole of viands given and distributed in little baskets in lieu of a public supper he abolished, and restored the ancient custom of complete and formal suppers. Unto the four factions [white, blue, red, green] of former times of several crews running with chariots at the Circus games, he added twain, to wit, the golden and the purple livery. Players and actors of interludes he forbade the open stage, but within house verily, he granted free and lawful exercise of their art. He gave commandment that no males should be gelded, and of such eunuchs as remained in the hands of hucksters, he abated the price and brought it down to a meaner. By reason one time of an exceeding plentiful vintage, and as much a scarcity of corn, supposing that by the immoderate care employed upon vineyards tillage was neglected, he made an edict that no man in all Italy should plant any new young vineyards, and that in foreign provinces they should cut them all down, reserving at the most but the one half. Howbeit, he continued not in the full execution of this act. Some of the greatest offices he communicated indifferently between freedmen and soldiers. He prohibited that there should be two legions in one camp. Also that any man should lay up more than a thousand sesterces about the headquarters. For that Lucius Antonius, intending rebellion in the wintering harbor of two legions, was thought to have taken heart and presumed more confidently upon the great sums of money there bestowed in stock. He added a fourth stipend also for soldiers, to wit, three pieces of gold each year.

8. In ministering justice precise he was and industrious. Many a time, even in the Forum, sitting extraordinarily upon the tribunal, he reversed the definitive sentences of the Centumvirs, given for favor and obtained by flattery. He warned eftsoons the commissioners not to accommodate themselves and give care unto persuasive and rhetorical assertions. The judges

that were bribed and corrupted with money he noted and disgraced every one, together with their assessors upon the bench. He moved also and persuaded the tribunes of the commons to accuse judicially for extortion, and to force unto restitution, a base and corrupt aedile; yea, and to call unto the senate for to have a jury impaneled upon him. Moreover, so careful was he to chastise as well the magistrates within Rome as the rulers of provinces abroad of their misdemeanors, that never at any time were they either more temperate or just in their places. The most part of whom, after his days, we ourselves have seen culpable, yea and brought into question for all manner of crimes. Having taken upon him the censuring and reformation of manners, he inhibited that licentious liberty taken up in theaters, of beholding the plays and games pell-mell one with another, in the quarter and ranks appointed for knights. Defamatory libels written and divulged, wherein men and women of good mark were touched and taxed, he abolished not without shame and ignominy of the authors. A man of quaestor's degree, because he took pleasure in puppet-like gesturing and dancing, he removed out of the senate. From women of dishonest carriage he took away the privilege and use of their litters; he made them incapable also of legacies and inheritances. A gentleman of Rome he struck out of the roll of judges for receiving his wife again into wedlock, whom he had before put away and sued in an action of adultery. Some of both degrees, senators as well as knights, he condemned by virtue of the Law *Scantinia* against the filthy sin of pederasty or sodomy. The incestuous whoredoms committed by vestal votaries, negligently passed over by his father and brother both, he punished after sundry sorts: the former delinquents in that kind, with simple death; the later sort, according to the ancient manner. For having given liberty unto the sisters Oculatae, as also to Varronilla, for to choose their own deaths, and banished those who had deflowered them, he afterwards commanded that Cornelia Maximilla, who in times past had been acquitted, and a long time after was called into question again and convicted, should be buried alive, and the parties who had committed incest with her should be beaten with rods to death in the Comitium; except one alone, a man of praetor's degree, unto whom, while the matter remained yet doubtful, and because he had confessed (after fruitless examination by torture) he granted the favor of exile. And that no religious service of the gods should be contaminated and polluted without condign punishment, the tomb which a freedman had built for a son of his with the stones appointed for the temple of Jupiter Capitolinus, he caused his soldiers to demolish, and the bones and relics therein he drowned in the sea.

9. At the first he abhorred all bloodshed and slaughter, so far forth, that (while his father was yet absent) calling to remembrance this verse of Vergil,

> *Impia quam caesis gens est epulata iuvencis.*
>
> Ere godless people made their feasts,
> With oxen slain (poor harmless beasts),

he purposed fully to publish an edict forbidding to kill and sacrifice any ox. Of covetousness also and avarice he gave scarcely the least suspicion, either at any time when he led a private life, or a good while after he was emperor: but contrariwise rather, he showed great proof oftentimes, not of abstinence only, but also of liberality. And whensoever he had bestowed gifts most bountiful upon those that were about him, he laid upon them no charge before this nor with more earnestness, than to do nothing basely and beggarly. Moreover, one legacy put down in the last will of Rustus Caepio who had provided therein that his heir should give yearly unto every one of the senators as they went into the Curia a certain sum of money, he made void. All those likewise, whose suits had hung and depended in the public treasury from before five years last past, he discharged and delivered from trouble. Neither suffered he them to be sued and molested again, but within the compass of one year and with this condition, that the accuser (unless he overthrew his adversary by that time) should be banished for his labor. The scribes and notaries belonging to the quaestors, who by an old custom (but yet against the law of Clodia), used to negotiate and trade, he pardoned only for the time past. The parcels of grounds which, after the division of lands by the veteran soldiers, remained here and there cut out, as it were, from the rest, he granted unto the old owners and landlords as in the right of prescription. The false information of matters, whereof the penalty came to the exchequer, he repressed, and sharply punished such informers. And this (by men's saying) was a speech of his, "The prince that chastens not informers, sets them on to inform."

10. But long continued he not in this train, either of clemency or of abstinence. And yet fell he somewhat sooner to cruelty than to covetousness. A scholar of the cunning player and pantomimist, Paris, being as yet of tender years and at that time very sick, he murdered for that both in skill and also in countenance and feature of body he seemed to resemble his master. Likewise dealt he with Hermogenes of Tarsus for certain figures of rhetoric interlaced in his history; and withal crucified the scriveners and writers that had copied it out. A householder, for saying these words, that the Thracian fencer was equal to the *murmillo*, but inferior to the setter forth of the game, he caused to be plucked down from the scaffold in the theater, into the plain beneath, and there to be cast before the greedy mastiffs with this label, "the Thracian-lover has blasphemed." Many senators, and some of them which had been consuls, he killed. Among whom Civica Cerealis, in the

very time when he was proconsul in Asia; Salvidienus, Orfitus, Acilius Glabrio during their exile he put to death, pretending that they had practiced innovation in the state: all the rest every one for most slight causes. As for example, Aelius Lamia, for certain suspicious jests (I must needs say), but such as were stale and harmless: namely, because unto Domitian when (after he had taken away his wife) he fell a-praising of her voice, he said, "I hold my peace." And also for that unto Titus, moving him to a second marriage, he made answer, "What! and if I should wed another, would not you also marry her?" Salvius Cocceianus, because he had celebrated the birthday of Otho the emperor, his uncle, he put to death; Mettius Pompusianus, for that it was commonly said, he had the horoscope in his nativity of an emperor, and carried about him the map of the world in certain parchments, and withal the orations of kings and brave captains written out by Titus Livius; for imposing likewise the names of Mago and Hannibal upon some of his slaves. Sallustius Lucullus, lieutenant general of Britain, for suffering certain spears of a new fashion to be called "Lucullean." Junius Rusticus, for publishing the praises of Paetus Thrasea and Helvidius Priscus, and calling them most holy and upright persons. By occasion of which criminal imputation (charged upon Rusticus), he packed away all philosophers out of the city of Rome and Italy. He slew also Helvidius, the son, for that in an interlude (as it were) and by way of a farce upon the stage he had under the persons of Paris and Oenone acted the divorce between him and his wife. Flavius Sabinus, one of his cousins german, because, upon the election day of the consuls, the crier chanced to mistake a little, and before the people to pronounce him (being consul-elect) not consul but emperor. And yet, after his victories in the civil war, he became much more cruel: for many of the adverse part, even such as lying hid a good while were found out by those that were privy unto them; he, by devising a new kind of torture, made them confess: namely by thrusting fire into the passage of their secret parts; some also he dismembered by cutting off their hands. And this is for certain known, that two only and no more of the most notorious among them, to wit, a tribune of senator's degree, and a centurion, were pardoned: who the sooner to show that they were unguilty, had proved themselves to have been effeminate catamites, and therefore could not possibly be of any reckoning, either with captains or soldiers.

11. Now, in this cruelty of his he was not only excessive, but also subtle and crafty, coming upon men when they least looked for it. A controller of his own, the very day before he crucified him, he called into his bed-chamber and made him to sit down by him upon a pallet or bed's side; he dismissed him light-hearted and merry; and he deigned him also a favor and remembrance from his own supper. Unto Arrecinius Clemens, a man of consul's degree, one of his familiar minions and bloodhounds to fetch in booties, when he purposed to condemn to death, he showed the same countenance as before time, yea and more grace than ordinary: until at last, as he went with him in the same litter, by occasion that he espied the informer against him, "How sayest thou," quoth he, "Clemens, shall we tomorrow hear this most errant knave and varlet, what he can say?" And because he would with greater contempt and disdain abuse men's patience, he never pronounced any heavy and bloody sentence without some preamble and preface of clemency, so that there was not now a surer sign of some horrible end than a mild beginning. Some that stood accused of treason he inducted into the Curia; and when he had premised a speech that he would make trial that day how dear he was unto the senate, he soon effected that the parties should have their judgement to suffer "in the ancient mode." And then, himself, affrighted as it were with the rigorous cruelty of that punishment,

would intercede in these words (for it shall not be impertinent to know the very same as he delivered them), "Permit my good lords this to be obtained of your gracious piety (which I know I shall hardly obtain), that you would do so much favor unto these persons condemned as that they may choose what death they will die: for, by this you shall spare your own eyes, and all the world shall know that I was present in the senate."

12. Having emptied his coffers with expenses of buildings and games exhibited to the people, as also with that stipend payed unto the soldiers over and above the former, he assayed verily for easement of the charges belonging to the camp by diminishing the numbers and companies of soldiers. But perceiving that hereby he was both in danger of the barbarians, and also nevertheless was at a loss to seek which way to be relieved from burdens, he made no reckoning at all but to raise booties, to rob and spoil, he cared not how. The goods of quick and dead both were everywhere seized upon; who the accusers were, or what the matter was, it skilled not. Sufficient it was if any deed or word whatsoever were objected against one, to make it high treason against the prince. Inheritances, were they never so far off and belonging to the greatest strangers, were held confiscate and adjudged to the emperor's coffers, in case but one would come forth and depose that he heard the party deceased say while he lived that Caesar was his heir. But, above all others, the Jews were most grievously plagued in the exchequer. Unto which were presented as many of them as either professed in Rome to live as Jews, or else dissimuling their nation had not payed the tributes imposed upon them. I remember that myself being a very youth was in place when an aged Jew, fourscore and ten years old, was by the procurator in a most frequent assembly searched, whether he were circumcised or no. From his very youth nothing civil and sociable he was: bold of heart, audacious withal, and

as well in words as deed beyond all measure excessive. Unto Caenis his father's concubine newly returned out of Histria, and offering to kiss his lips (as her manner was), he put forth his hand. Taking it heinously that his brother's son-in-law had attending about him his servitors also clad in fair white, he cried out these words of Homer:

> There is no good plurality
> In lordship and in sov'reignty.

13. But when he was mounted once to the imperial seat, he stuck not in the very senate to make his boast that he it was who had given unto his father and brother both the empire, and they had but delivered it up to him again. Also, when after divorcement he brought home and remarried his wife, he bashed not to give it out that she was called to his sacred bed. Moreover, upon the day when he made a great dinner unto the people, he was well content and pleased to hear their acclamation throughout the theater in these words,

> *Domino et dominae, feliciter.*
> All happiness to our lord and lady.

Likewise at the competitions in the Capitol, when all the people besought him with great consent and one accord to restore Palfurius Sura (one in times past degraded and thrust out of the senate, but at that time crowned among the orators for his eloquence), he vouchsafed them no answer, but only by voice of the public crier commanded them silence. With similar arrogance, when as in the name of his procurators he issued any formal letters, thus he began: "Our lord and god thus commands." Whereupon afterwards this order was taken up, that neither in the writing or speech of any man he should be otherwise called. No statues suffered he to be erected for him in the Capitol but of gold and silver, and the same of a certain weight. As for arches with their four steeds together with the ensigns and badges of triumph, he built them stately, and so many in every quarter of the city, that on one of the said arches there was this mot in Greek written, *arkei*, i. e., "it is enough." He took upon him seventeen consulships, more than ever any man before him. Of which, those seven in the middle, he bore continually one after another; and in manner all in name and title only, but none of them beyond the Kalends of May, and most to the Ides only of January. Now, after his two triumphs, having assumed into his style the addition of Germanicus, he changed the denomination of the months September and October, calling them after his own names Germanicus and Domitianus, for that in the one he entered upon his empire, and was born in the other.

14. In these courses that he took, being both terrible and odious unto all men, surprised he was in the end, and murdered by his friends and freedmen that were most inward with him, who together with his wife conspired his death. The last year and day of his life, the very hour also and what kind of death he would die, he had a long time before suspected. For when he was but a youth the Chaldean astrologers had foretold him all. His father also one time at supper, when he saw him forbear to eat mushrooms, laughed him to scorn as ignorant of his own destiny, for that he did not fear the sword rather. And therefore being always timorous and stricken into his pensive dumps upon the least suspicions presented, he was beyond all measure troubled and disquieted, insomuch as it is creditably reported that no other cause moved him more to dispense with that edict which he had proclaimed for the cutting down and destroying of vineyards, than certain pamphlets and libels scattered abroad with these verses (in Greek),

> Eat me to root; yet fruit will I bear still and never miss
> Enough to pour on Caesar's head while sacrificed he is.

In the same fearfulness he refused a new honor and that which never was devised before, offered by the senate unto him (though otherwise most eager and greedy of all such things), whereby they decreed that so often as he was consul, the knights of Rome, as it fell by lot to their turns, should in their rich and gay coats and with military lances march before him among the lictors and other sergeants and apparitors. When the time also of that danger drew near which he suspected, he became perplexed every day more than other: and therefore he garnished the walls of those galleries wherein he was wont to walk with the stone phengites; by the images rebounding from the brightness whereof he might see before his face whatsoever was done behind his back. The most part of prisoners and persons in duress he would not hear but being alone and in a secret place, taking hold first of their chains in his own hand. And because he would persuade his household servitors that no man would be so hardy as to lay violent hand upon his own patron to kill him, no, though much good might ensue thereof, he condemned Epaphroditus, the secretary of Nero, for that it was thought his lord and master (after he was forlorn and forsaken of all) had his helping hand to dispatch him out of the world.

15. To conclude, his uncle's son Flavius Clemens, a man for his laziness and negligence most contemptible (whose sons being yet very little ones he had openly ordained to be his successors and abolishing their former names, commanded the one to be called Vespasian and the other Domitian), he killed upon a slender and small suspicion, even when he was scarce out of his consulship. By which deed of his most of all he hastened his own end and destruction. For eight months' space together, so many lightnings were seen and reported unto him that he cried out, "Now let him strike whom he will." The Capitol was smitten and blasted therewith; the temple also of the Flavian lineage; likewise his own house in the Palatium,

and very bed-chamber. Moreover, out of the base of his triumphal statue, the title being driven by force of a storm, fell down into the sepulchre next adjoining. That tree which being overthrown had risen up again when Vespasian was yet a private person, fell suddenly then a second time. The image of fortune at Praeneste, which all the time of his empire, when he recommended unto her the new year was wont to give him a happy answer and always the same, now in this last year delivered one most woeful and not without mention of blood. He dreamed that Minerva, whom he worshipped superstitiously, departed out of her chapel and said she could not protect him any longer, for that she was by Jupiter disarmed. But with no one thing was he so much disquieted as with the answer of Ascletarion the astrologer, and the accident that chanced unto him thereupon. This Ascletarion, being informed against and not denying that he had delivered what by his art and learning he foresaw, he questioned with and asked what his own end should be; and when he made answer that his destiny was to be torn in pieces by dogs (and that shortly after), he caused him presently to be killed; but to reprove the rashness and uncertainty of his skill and profession, he commanded that he should be buried with as great care as possibly might be. In the doing whereof accordingly, it fortuned that by a sudden tempest the corpse being cast down out of the funeral fire, the dogs tore and rent piecemeal when it was but half burnt; and the same happened to be reported unto him among other tales and news of that day, as he sat at supper, by Latinus, the player and counterfeit jester, who as he passed by, chanced to see and mark so much.

16. The day before his death, when he had given commandment that certain mushrooms set before him should be kept against the morrow, he added moreover, "if I may have the use of them"; and turning to those that were next him he said

that the day following it would come to pass that the moon should embrue herself with blood in the sign Aquarius, and some act be seen whereof men should speak all the world over. But about midnight so scared he was that he started out of his bed. Hereupon in the morning betimes he gave hearing unto the soothsayer sent out of Germany, who being asked his opinion about the lightning, had foretold a change in the state: and him he condemned. And while he scratched very hard at a wart in his forehead which was festered, seing blood run out of it, "would God," quoth he, "this were all." Then asked he what was o'clock and instead of the fifth hour, which he feared, word was brought for the nonce that it was the sixth. Being joyous hereupon that the danger was now past, and hastening to cherish his body and make much of himself, Parthenius, his principal chamberlain, turned him another way, saying there was one come who brought tidings (I wot not what) of great consequence, and of a matter in no wise to be deferred. Voiding therefore all persons from him, he retired to his bed-chamber, and there was he murdered.

17. As touching the manner how he was forlaid and of his death, thus much (in manner) hath been divulged. While the conspirators were in question with themselves and doubtful when and how they should set upon him, that is to say, whether he bathed or sat at supper, Stephen the procurator of Domitilla, and at the same time in trouble for intercepting certain monies, offered his advice and helping hand, who having for certain days before bound up and enwrapped his left arm (as if it had been amiss) with wool and swaddling bands, thereby to avert from himself all suspicion, at this very hour interposed fraud and made a lie. For, professing that he would discover the conspiracy, and in that regard admitted into the chamber, as Domitian was reading of a bill which he preferred unto him, and therewith stood amazed, he stabbed

him beneath, near unto his privy parts. When he was wounded and began to struggle and resist, Clodianus, a subaltern, and Maximus, a freedman of Parthenius, and Satur, the dean or decurion of the chamberlains, with one out of his own sword-fencer's school came in upon him, gave him seven wounds and killed him outright. A page of his, who stood by (as his wonted manner was) because he had the charge of his bed-chamber's Lares, and was present at this murder committed, made this report moreover, that Domitian at the very first wound given immediately bade him reach the dagger that lay under his pillow, and to call in his ministers and servitors; but at the bed's head he found nothing at all thereof save the shaft only, and as for the doors besides, they were all fast shut; also, that Domitian in this mean space took hold of Stephen, bore him to the ground and wrestled with him for a long time, and that he one while assayed to wrest his sword out of his hands, another while (albeit his fingers were hurt and mangled) to pluck out his eyes. Well, killed he was on the fourteenth day before the Kalends of October, in the forty-fifth year of his age, and the fifteenth of his empire. His dead body was carried forth upon the common bier by the ordinary bearers, and Phyllis, his nurse, burned it in a funeral fire, within her country manor situated upon the highway Latina. But the relics thereof she bestowed in the temple of the Flavian family, and blended the same with the ashes of Julia, the daughter of Titus, whom she had reared and brought up.

18. Of stature he was tall, his countenance modest, and given much to redness; his eyes full and great, but his sight very dim. Besides, fair he was and of comely presence, especially in his youth; well shaped all his body throughout, excepting his feet, the toes whereof were of the shortest. In process of time he became disfigured and blemished with baldness, with a fat grand-paunch and slender shanks, and yet

they grew to be so lean upon occasion of a long sickness. For his modesty and shamefacedness he so well perceived himself to be commended, that one time before the senate he gave out these words, "hitherto certainly you have liked well of my mind and my countenance." With his bald head he was so much irked, that he took it as a reproach unto himself if any man else were either in jest or good earnest twitted therewith; albeit in a certain little book which he wrote unto a friend of his concerning the nourishment and preservation of the hair of the head, he by way of consolation both to that friend and also to himself, inserted thus much from Homer's Iliad,

> See'st thou not yet how big and tall,
> How fair I am and comely withal?

"And yet," quoth he, "my destiny and fortune will be to have the same defect of hair; and with a stout heart I endure that the bush of my head waxeth old in my fresh youth. And this would I have you to know, that nothing is more lovely, nothing more frail and transitory than beauty and favor."

19. Being impatient of all labor and painstaking, he was not lightly seen to walk in the city. In any expedition and march of the army seldom rode he on horseback, but was carried in a litter. No affection had he to bear arms or wield weapons, but delighted he was especially to shoot arrows. Many men have seen him oftentimes, during his retiring abode at Alba, to kill with shot a hundred wild beasts of sundry sorts at a time; and of very purpose to stick some of them in the head, so that with two shots he would set his shafts in their fronts like a pair of horns. Sometimes he would drive his arrows point blank, just so against the palm of a child's right hand, standing far off and holding it forth stretched open for a mark, as they should directly pass through the void spaces between the fingers, and do him no harm at all.

He dreamed that Minerva, whom he worshipped superstitiously, departed out of her chapel and said she could not protect him any longer, for that she was by Jupiter disarmed.

20. All liberal studies in the beginning of his empire he neglected; albeit he took order to repair the libraries consumed
with fire, to his exceeding great charges, making search from
all parts for the copies of books lost, and sending as far as to
Alexandria to write them out and correct them. But never
gave he his mind to know histories; or to have any skill in
verse, or to write ought, though necessity so required. Except
it were the commentaries and acts of Tiberius Caesar he never
used to read anything. For his epistles, orations and edicts, he
employed the wits of other men to draw and frame them.
Howbeit, his ordinary speech was not unelegant; and otherwise you should have him come forth even with notable
sentences and apophthegms. As for example: "Would God,"
quoth he, "I were as fair and well favored as Mettius thinks
himself to be"; and seeing one's head party-colored, with yel-
lowish and white silver hairs intermingled, he said it was snow
and mead mixed together. His saying it was that the condition
of princes was most miserable, since they could not be credited
with detecting a conspiracy unless they were slain first.

21. Whensoever his leisure served, he solaced himself with
dice play, even upon the very work day and in morning hours.
He bathed by daytime and made his dinner so liberal to the
full, that seldom for his supper he took anything unless it were
a Matian apple, and a small sipping out of a wine jug. He feasted
often and that very plentifully, but his feasts were short and
after a snatching manner: certes, he never sat past sunsetting, nor
admitted any drinking bout after supper. For towards bedtime
he did nothing but in a secret chamber walk by himself alone.

22. To fleshly lust he was over much given. The ordinary
use of Venus, as though it were a kind of exercise, he named
clinopale, as one would say, bed-wrestling. The report went
that himself used with pincers to depilate his concubines and
to swim among the commonest naughty packs that were. His

471

brother's daughter, offered first unto him in marriage while she was yet a maiden, when he had most resolutely refused by reason he was entangled and overcome with the marriage of Domitia, not long after, when she was bestowed upon another, of his own accord he solicited and was naughty with her, even verily while his brother Titus yet lived. Afterwards when she was bereft of father and husband both, he loved her with most ardent affection, and that openly: insomuch as that he was the cause of her death by forcing her to miscarry and cast away the untimely fruit wherewith she went.

23. That he was killed the people took indifferently; but the soldiers, to the very hearts and forthwith went about to canonize him a god, and to call him Divus; ready enough to avenge his death also, but they wanted heads to lead them. And yet within a while after they did it by calling most insistently and never giving over for the authors of this murder to be executed. Contrariwise, the senate so much rejoiced, that being assembled in great frequency within the Curia, they could not rule themselves, but strived a-vie to rend and tear him now dead with the most contumelious and bitterest kind of acclamations that they could devise: commanding ladders to be brought in, his scutcheons and images to be taken down in their sight and even there in place to be thrown and dashed against the hard floor; in the end, that all titles wheresoever bearing his name should be razed and scraped out, and his memorial abolished quite forever. Some few months before he was murdered, there was a crow in the Capitol that spake these words plainly, "All shall be well," and there wanted not one who interpreted this strange prodigy thus,

> Nuper Tarpeio quae sedit culmine cornix,
> 'Est bene' non potuit dicere, dixit 'erit.'

The crow which lately sat on top of Tarpeia news to tell,
'Tis well when as she could not say, said yet it will be well.

And reported it is that Domitian himself dreamed how he had a golden excrescence rising and bunching behind his neck, and knew for certain that thereby was portended and foresigned unto the commonwealth a happier state after him. And so it fell out, I assure you, shortly after: such was the abstinent and moderate carriage of the emperors next ensuing.

THE TWELVE CAESARS

	Birth	Reign
Julius Caesar	100 B.C.	46–44 B.C.
Augustus	63 B.C.	27 B.C. – 14 A.D.
Tiberius	42 B.C.	14–37 A.D.
Caligula	12 A.D.	37–41 A.D.
Claudius	10 B.C.	41–54 A.D.
Nero	37 A.D.	54–68 A.D.
Galba	5 B.C.	68 A.D. (19 June 68 – 15 Jan. 69)
Otho	32 A.D.	69 A.D. (15 Jan. – 15 April)
Vitellius	15 A.D.	69 A.D. (2 Jan. – 22 Dec.)
Vespasian	9 A.D.	69–79 A.D. (1 July – 23 June)
Titus	41 A.D.	79–81 A.D.
Domitian	51 A.D.	81–96 A.D.

GLOSSARY

GLOSSARY

accensus: An apparitor or orderly who attended high magistrates when they walked abroad.

aedile: A magistrate who had charge of public buildings and entertainments. Aediles frequently made lavish expenditures to court popular favor with a view to election to higher office.

ancilia: Sacred shields said to have fallen from heaven in the reign of Numa, carefully preserved and carried in solemn procession in March.

apparitor: A public servant assigned to higher magistrates as escort or secretary.

augur: a member of a priestly college whose charge was divining the future by interpreting omens, especially lightning and the flight, notes, or feeding of birds.

Augustales: A college of priests charged with the celebration of the Augustalia, in memory of Augustus.

auspices: A form of divination practiced by a commanding general before any important enterprise. The actual enterprise might be carried out by a representative, but the responsibility and the honors belonged to the man who had taken the auspices.

bonum factum: A formula sometimes used in decrees and the like to signify "May it turn out well!"

caduceus: A herald's staff, betokening a peaceful embassy; properly, the winged, serpent-twined staff carried by Mercury.

Campus Martius: Mars Field, an exercise or assembly field at Rome, frequently associated with elections.

canis: "Dog" – applied to a constellation, a bad throw at dice, a Cynic philosopher, or any shameful person.

caveat: "Let him beware" – used to introduce a warning or proviso.

censor: A magistrate, appointed every fifth year and serving for a year and a half, whose function was to review the lists of senators and knights and eliminate those who failed to meet certain moral and financial requirements. The censor also executed certain contracts for the state.

centumviri: A bench of judges mainly concerned with testamentary suits.

centuries: Unit divisions of the Roman people for electoral purposes; originally military units.

centurion: An infantry commander, originally of a unit of one hundred men.

circus: An enclosure for horse-racing, the oldest and largest of which was the Circus Maximus. A special performance held there was called Circensian Games.

Codeta: A place near the Campus Martius, originally named for plants growing there which resemble horses' tails.

cohort: A military unit, usually the tenth part of a legion.

comitium: A place of assembly in Rome, situated in the Forum.

Compitalitii: Having to do with the Compitalia, a festival in honor of the lares celebrated at crossroads.

congiary: Gift distributed to the common people by the emperor.

consul: Chief magistrate of the Roman republic; two consuls were elected each year.

Curia: The Roman senate-house.

Curule: The *sella curulis* was an ivory stool used by higher magistrates. The term curule was transferred from the seat to the magistracies.

decemvir: A member of any of several ten-man permanent commissions.

decurion, decury: A councillor of a municipality.

denarius: The standard silver coin of Rome (the penny of the New Testament); the gold denarius was worth 25 silver denarii.

ducenarii: Commanders of 200 men.

ducentesima: A tax of 0.5 %.

equestrian: A social (originally military) rank requiring possession of certain wealth.

fasces: A bundle of rods, including an axe, borne by lictors as a symbol of magisterial authority.

flamen: Priest of a specific deity.
Flamen Dialis: Priest of Jupiter.
flaviales: Priests for the cult of the Flavian house.

Gemonia: Stairs up the Capitol, upon which executed criminals were exposed.
genius: The daemon within a male.
Greek kalends: The first day of each Roman month was called the kalends. Since the Greeks did not use this calendar, "Greek kalends" means "never."

ides: The 15th day of March, May, July, and October; the 13th of other months.

Jupiter Capitolinus, Latiaris, etc.: Particular aspects or shrines of Jupiter.

kalends: See *Greek kalends*.

lares: Deities originally of farm-land and then of the domestic larder.
laticlave: A broad stripe of purple, a mark of senatorial rank.
legion: A major division of the Roman army, with a theoretical strength of 6,000 men.
Liber Pater: The Italian god of wine, usually identified with Dionysus.
lictor: Beadle who attended a Roman magistrate; the number of lictors varied according to the rank of the magistrate. Each lictor carried *fasces*.
Lupercalia: A Roman festival celebrated on February 15, originating in the early pastoral period of the city.
lustrum: The ceremony of purification conducted by the censors every five years.

Mars field: See *Campus Martius*.
mirmillo, murmillo: A type of gladiator.
modii: Dry measures; pecks.

naumachia: A sham sea-battle.
nones: The seventh day of March, May, July, and October; the fifth of the other months.
nundinae: Market-days.

Palatine, Palatium: One of the seven hills of Rome, which held the imperial residences.

Palilia: A rustic festival.

Parens Patriae, Pater Patriae: Parent, or Father, of his Country – a title of honor bestowed upon emperors.

patrician: A member of the hereditary nobility, contrasted with plebeian.

peculium: The (extra-legal) private property allowed a slave.

phengites: A kind of crystallized gypsum used for window panes.

pontifex: Priest of a public cult.

popularia: Pertaining to the people; sometimes used of the common seats in the theatre.

praefect: An officer of the army or a commissioner of a military or civilian charge.

praetexta: The outer purple-bordered garment worn by higher magistrates.

praetor: A magistrate, next to a consul in rank, who exercised judicial functions.

praetorium: General's headquarters in camp.

proconsul: A provincial governor of consular rank.

propraetor: A provincial governor of praetorian rank.

proscenium: Stage, theatre.

quaestor: An inferior curule magistrate whose duties were mainly financial.

quindecemvir: A member of a commission of 15, particularly that in charge of the Sibylline Oracles.

Quinquatria: A religious festival connected with Mars and Minerva.

Regia: Traditionally, the home of King Numa in the Forum; seat of the Pontifex Maximus under the republic.

retiarii: Gladiators who used an iron net.

rostra: The speaking platform in the Forum, so called from the ships' beaks (*rostra*) with which it was decorated.

Salii: The leaping priests of Mars.

Saturnalia: The carnival festival at the end of December.

Scala gemoniae: See *Gemoniae*.

secutores: Pursuers – a type of gladiator.

senio: Of the number six; a throw at dice.

septa: An enclosure; specifically, for voting.

septimontial: Of the Feast of the Seven Hills.

sesterces: Coins of small value.

spintriae: Male prostitutes.

sportula: Literally, "little basket"; a gift made to dependents.

stellate fields: a region in southern Campania.

Subura: A slum region in Rome.

talent: The largest monetary unit.

theatralis: Relating to the theatre; licentious.

Thraces, Threces: Thracians, a kind of gladiator.

tribune: A plebeian magistrate, with the power of veto.

Velabrum: A quarter of Rome.

Vestal virgin: A member of an exclusive patrician order of priestesses of the goddess Vesta; their house was in the Forum.

Venus Genetrix: Venus the Mother (of Aeneas), patron deity of the Julian clan.